DISCOURSE AND IDEOLOGY

Also Available from Bloomsbury

CAPITALIZING RELIGION
Craig Martin

SPIRITUALITY WITHOUT GOD
Peter Heehs

STEREOTYPING RELIGION
Edited by Brad Stoddard and Craig Martin

DISCOURSE AND IDEOLOGY

A CRITIQUE OF THE STUDY OF CULTURE

Craig Martin

BLOOMSBURY ACADEMIC
LONDON • NEW YORK • OXFORD • NEW DELHI • SYDNEY

BLOOMSBURY ACADEMIC
Bloomsbury Publishing Plc
50 Bedford Square, London, WC1B 3DP, UK
1385 Broadway, New York, NY 10018, USA
29 Earlsfort Terrace, Dublin 2, Ireland

BLOOMSBURY, BLOOMSBURY ACADEMIC and the Diana logo
are trademarks of Bloomsbury Publishing Plc

First published in Great Britain 2022

Copyright © Craig Martin, 2022

Craig Martin has asserted his right under the Copyright, Designs and Patents Act, 1988, to be identified as Author of this work.

For legal purposes the Acknowledgments on pp. xviii–xix constitute an extension of this copyright page.

Cover design by Tjaša Krivec
Cover Image: *The Symbolical Head, Illustrating All the Phrenological Developments of the Human Head* was created by the leading American phrenologists, brothers Niles Fowler (1811–1896) and Orson Squire Fowler (1809–1887).
© Everett Collection Historical / Alamy Stock Photo

All rights reserved. No part of this publication may be reproduced or transmitted in any form or by any means, electronic or mechanical, including photocopying, recording, or any information storage or retrieval system, without prior permission in writing from the publishers.

Bloomsbury Publishing Plc does not have any control over, or responsibility for, any third-party websites referred to or in this book. All internet addresses given in this book were correct at the time of going to press. The author and publisher regret any inconvenience caused if addresses have changed or sites have ceased to exist, but can accept no responsibility for any such changes.

A catalogue record for this book is available from the British Library.

Library of Congress Cataloging-in-Publication Data
Names: Martin, Craig, 1976- author.
Title: Discourse and ideology : a critique of the study of culture / Craig Martin.
Description: 1 Edition. | New York : Bloomsbury Academic, 2021. |
Includes bibliographical references and index.
Identifiers: LCCN 2021013244 (print) | LCCN 2021013245 (ebook) | ISBN 9781350246287 (paperback) |
ISBN 9781350246294 (hardback) | ISBN 9781350246300 (pdf) |
ISBN 9781350246317 (epub)
Subjects: LCSH: Ideology. | Discrimination. | Social institutions. |
Distributive justice. | Culture. | Poststructuralism.
Classification: LCC HM641 .M369 2021 (print) | LCC HM641 (ebook) | DDC 306–dc23
LC record available at https://lccn.loc.gov/2021013244
LC ebook record available at https://lccn.loc.gov/2021013245

ISBN:	HB:	978-1-3502-4629-4
	PB:	978-1-3502-4628-7
	ePDF:	978-1-3502-4630-0
	ePUB:	978-1-3502-4631-7

Typeset by Integra Software Services Pvt. Ltd.
Printed and bound in Great Britain

To find out more about our authors and books visit www.bloomsbury.com and sign up for our newsletters

*We will never be finished with the reading or rereading of Hegel, and, in a certain way,
I do nothing other than attempt to explain myself on this point.*

Jacques Derrida, Positions *(1981: 77)*

For Glenn, who tolerates my rants

CONTENTS

Preface	x
Acknowledgments	xviii
Introduction: Contingency	1
1 **Critique**	13
2 **Things**	41
3 **Discourse**	77
4 **Domination**	103
5 **Ideology**	145
6 **Recrement**	175
7 **Case Study: Racist Ideology in the United States**	205
Coda	247
Notes	256
Bibliography	260
Index	269

PREFACE

I was trained at the tail-end of poststructuralism's sweep through the humanities, which—in the United States—took place primarily during the latter third of the twentieth century. I started graduate school in the year 2000, around the time that graduate programs ceased to require students to read French philosophers like Jacques Derrida and Michel Foucault or feminist theorists such as Judith Butler or Donna Haraway (as well as their German philosophical sources). I consider myself lucky to have landed in graduate programs in which I could still take courses such as "Kant's First Critique," "Hegel," "German Idealism," "Heidegger's *Being and Time*," "Freud and Jung," "Lacan and Derrida," "Marx and Foucault," "Deleuze," or "Kristeva and Irigaray." As that is apparently no longer possible in most religion graduate programs, it is not surprising that contemporary attempts by scholars of religion to make sense of poststructuralism's influence on the academic study of religion are increasingly based on how this intellectual tradition is presented in secondary literature.

There are many books in the field of religion that engage in discourse analysis from a poststructuralist perspective, such as Catherine Bell's *Ritual Theory, Ritual Practice* (1992), Richard King's *Orientalism and Religion: Postcolonial Theory, India, and the Mystic East* (1999), Russell McCutcheon's *The Discipline of Religion: Structure, Meaning, Rhetoric* (2003), Tomoko Masuzawa's *The Invention of World Religions: Or, How European Universalism Was Preserved in the Language of Pluralism* (2005), or Tim Murphy's *Politics of Spirit: Phenomenology, Genealogy, Religion* (2010). Each of these books is brilliant, in my opinion. However, on my interpretation these works were deeply inspired by primary sources that scholars who came later weren't required to read and, as such, these scholars may lack a full understanding of the theoretical assumptions that lie behind the works. In the academic study of religion, no one has written a general theory of discourse or ideology that accounts for this set of theoretical assumptions. Although I don't directly engage with these scholars in *Discourse and Ideology*, in a sense my book is designed to reveal the theoretical assumptions I think lie behind their work, so that it is easier for other scholars to understand and utilize this approach with sophistication. (Of course, any of these authors might contest my account of poststructuralism; I don't claim to speak for them.)

This book is not a survey of theories of discourse, ideology, domination, or hegemony; as such, do not expect a systematic consideration of how prior theorists have talked about such things (there are already many books on the market that provide useful surveys). I would like to note, however, that I consider the following texts to be essential reading and foundational to the approach I take to discourse and ideology (some of which I refer to below, some of which I do not): Karl Marx and Friedrich Engels, *The Marx-Engels*

Reader (1978); Antonio Gramsci, *Selections from the Prison Notebooks* (1971); Louis Althusser, *On the Reproduction of Capitalism: Ideology and Ideological State Apparatuses* (2014); Michel Foucault, *Archaeology of Knowledge* (1972), *History of Sexuality, Volume 1* (1978), and *"Society Must Be Defended"* (2003); Raymond Williams, *Marxism and Literature* (1977); Marshall Sahlins, *Culture and Practical Reason* (1976) and *Islands of History* (1985); Göran Therborn, *The Ideology of Power and the Power of Ideology* (1980); Ernesto Laclau and Chantal Mouffe, *Hegemony and Socialist Strategy: Towards a Radical Democratic Politics* (1985); Bruce Lincoln, *Discourse and the Construction of Society* (1989); John B. Thompson, *Ideology and Modern Culture: Critical Social Theory in the Era of Mass Communication* (1990); Pierre Bourdieu, *Language and Symbolic Power* (1999); Judith Butler, *Gender Trouble* (1990) and *The Psychic Life of Power* (1997); Rudi Visker, *Michel Foucault: Genealogy as Critique* (1995); and Terry Eagleton, *Ideology: An Introduction* (2007).

To further understand my aims in this project, let me point to the scholars in the academic study of religion that serve as implicit or explicit conversation partners in the book. First, to some extent this project is designed to offer a defense of Bruce Lincoln's approach to studying discourse, ideology, and domination, but with a somewhat more sophisticated philosophical justification. My approach to discourse and domination is deeply influenced by his work, but I hope to offer a more thorough defense of how we can better warrant or justify the sorts of claims he makes, as opposed to just insisting that scholars must use "footnotes" (which is about as close to epistemic considerations as Lincoln gets when discussing what makes the claims of scholarship warranted in *Theorizing Myth: Narrative, Ideology, and Scholarship* [1999: 208–209]).

Second, although I have been deeply influenced by the work of Russ McCutcheon and of those who are members of the Culture on the Edge collective (a group I am proud to be a part of), I find that our (sometimes narrow) focus on constitutive discourse, while quite sophisticated, tends to leave a number of potentially important empirical questions unasked and unanswered. It is all well and good to point out that if we define child abuse one way, some things will be true and some things won't, that if we change the definition the things that are true will change as well, and that the choice of one definition over others likely reflects certain investments—but I think it is useful to go further and ask questions such as the following. What does the evidence show if we adopt one definition or another? How might attention to the empirical evidence we produce when adopting a particular definition practically help us understand the world better (even as we recognize that such evidence is contingent on language, power, institutions, etc.)? My theory of discourse and method of reading is deeply indebted to Russ's work, but I think we can and ought to add to it a theory of empiricism (such as the one I attempt to provide in the chapter on ideology and use to analyze the empirical claims of PragerU in Chapter 7).

Third, I continue to be appalled at the extent to which scholars of religion get their understanding of poststructuralist approaches from secondary sources that (1) tend to be unsympathetic to such approaches and (2) often misrepresent the works of Derrida, Foucault, and Butler, usually because they interpret them as Kantians who insist that

Preface

"reality" is out there somewhere, on the far side of discourse, inaccessible to subjects locked inside a prison house of language (I myself have been accused of being a neo-Kantian [see Stowers 2020]). Mark C. Taylor, the scholar of religion who most helped bring Derrida into our field's canon, explicitly acknowledges throughout his work that Derrida is deeply indebted to G. W. F. Hegel (see Taylor 1982, 1984, 1986, 1987a, b, and 1993), and there is a massive body of secondary literature outside the academic study of religion that draws attention to that fact (see Barnett 1998; Gasché 1986 and 1994; Caputo 1993 and 1997; and Braver 2007). As I will show in the chapters on "Critique" and "Things," the idea that poststructuralists are neo-Kantians who think that "language" gets between us and "things-in-themselves" or "noumena" is simply not supported by the evidence.

Astute readers will note that most of the themes covered in this book are similar to the themes covered in my previous book, *A Critical Introduction to the Study of Religion*. That book was, of course, a textbook designed for undergraduate readers, and as such could not include the level of detail of argumentation included in this volume. In addition, to some extent this book is a response to criticisms that *A Critical Introduction* was superficial in some respects—as if a textbook could be a monograph. It seems clear to me that, in a sense, Pierre Bourdieu wrote the same book four times; compare, for instance, *Outline of a Theory of Practice* (1977), *Distinction: A Social Critique of the Judgment of Taste* (1984), *The Logic of Practice* (1990), and *Pascalian Meditations* (2000). As I read these four books, they reflect Bourdieu's serial attempts to offer an increasingly systematic account of how to understand relations between culture and power, in each case adding new empirical evidence and new concepts for bringing that evidence into relief along the way. Each repeats many of the claims of the former, but each is also more sophisticated than the last. This series of books is, perhaps, best understood as the manifestation of Bourdieu's obsession with offering a systematic account of systems (while I don't speak much about Bourdieu in this book, it should be clear that much of what follows is deeply inspired by Bourdieu's work—particularly his ability to show how just about anything mundane can be charged with immense social significance). To some extent, *Discourse and Ideology* is my second such book attempting to offer a systematic account of systems, but with a much more sophisticated philosophical justification than did my undergraduate textbook. Perhaps one day I will write a third.

In a sense, this book could have been less technically titled *How Words Work*. The whole book is about the fact that, over time, words acquire positive and negative associations, associations that clever rhetoricians can exploit to influence the behavior of others. Three things worth noting about rhetoric include the following. (1) It is likely that most of my readers are daily surrounded by such clever rhetoric. (2) In addition, value-laden rhetoric is likely constitutive of the official structure of the organizations in which you live and work. For those who are reading this book in a university capacity of some sort, it's likely your institution has "foundational" documents—for instance the college's "mission statement"—that are loaded with lofty words saturated with positive associations. On the one hand, these documents are constitutive of structure of the institution. On the other hand, they are liable to be trotted out on occasion by the college administration to justify or legitimate decisions liable to be received as controversial—for it is always a little bit harder to publicly challenge such decisions if they are said to have been necessary for the student's "intellectual, moral, social and spiritual growth," or for the "development of humanity" (these particular lofty words are from my own college's mission statement). Faculty at my college were recently told by the provost that although our mission statement is "timeless"—his word—it is time to update it. It seems to me that if it were "timeless," it wouldn't need updating; perhaps "timeless" is just another lofty word useful for authorizing what we do. (3) Those readers situated in a university context likely produce such rhetoric themselves on many occasions, using lofty terms with positive associations such as "critical thinking," "justice," "sustainability," or "mental health." Some professors encourage the development of things like mental health resources and policies that take seriously the fact that many of our students suffer from mental health problems that we would like them to be helped with rather than punished for. We couldn't even bring about those things *unless* we used rhetoric filled with lofty words and positive associations. Calling our words rhetorical isn't an insult—rather, the point is just to attend to the fact that this is how persuasion works (and if we want to get those mental health resources, we'll have to be persuasive).

I beg those readers who identify as "realists" or as "liberals" not to defensively respond to the fact that I criticize realists and liberals. The labels of political or epistemological views are ultimately not particularly important to me. Rather, please consider my arguments. On the one hand, you may identify as a realist or a liberal and yet may not hold the specific views I'll be criticizing when talking about these intellectual traditions. On the other hand, you might think "poststructuralism" and "anti-realism" are idiotic views to hold, and yet nevertheless might agree with many of the arguments below. Please react to my argument, not the taxons I use to refer to a particular position.

Note: throughout this book I sometimes use an English third-person plural pronoun (they/them/their) in place of a first-person singular pronoun (one, he/him/his, she/her/her). Given that many people increasingly disidentify as either strictly male or female, a gender-neutral first-person pronoun is long overdue in my opinion (at least for those of us uncomfortable with referring to a person as an "it"). "They" is increasingly taking on this duty—so much so that "they" is now listed as a legitimate (i.e., *not slang*) third-person singular pronoun in mainstream dictionaries—and this move is one I applaud and employ here.

At times I talk of people "serving their interests" and "serving their sympathies." The latter is unusual in contemporary English, but I mean almost the same by it as by the former phrase. People act in ways that serve their interests when their behavior benefits them in some way. People act in ways that serve their sympathies when their behavior benefits those with whom they are sympathetic, which may or may not include themselves, depending on the context.

***

As Derrida notes in his brilliant essay on Hegel titled "Outwork, Prefacing" in *Dissemination* (Derrida [1972] 1981), prefaces are paradoxical genres. Typically written

Preface

when the manuscript as a whole is already complete, prefaces function as both an end and a beginning. They are a beginning in that they are, for many readers, the first thing they will read—the preface situates the following work, tells the reader the context, where the book leads, and where it hopes to end up. At the same time, insofar as it is written at the end, it is a teleological genre: the author tells the reader, "see, here is—in a nutshell—what will grow into a tree by the end of the book." As Derrida puts it, "Here is what I wrote, then read, and what I am writing that you are going to read" ([1972] 1981: 7). The preface is to an acorn as a book is to an oak. However, as Derrida notes, teleologies never unfold as planned. Perhaps readers will not end up where I want them to. As soon as the book is out of my hands—and if you are reading this, it already is—*a priori*, people can make out if it what they would like (you could use it as a doorstop, for instance). In addition, I am one such reader; what I make of this book may change upon rereading it, particularly after hearing from others.

The date signed below is July 31, 2020. What this book will have meant is contingent in part on this date: the deadline for the submission of my manuscript to the publishers for outside review. From one perspective, this date is relatively arbitrary. I've been working on this book for about four years, although it builds on knowledge formed prior to that point. It is therefore no surprise that the escalating discourses on race in the United States and the international pandemic of 2020 shape the following; we can only ever write from where we sit. Over this four year period, I've written chapters, added new chapters, *reread* and *revised* previously written chapters to make them consistent with the newer ones, and so forth—until completing this "preface" on Friday, July 31. After that date, I can no longer go back and revise the chapters to fit with new knowledge. (This last claim is, of course, not entirely true, and for two reasons. Frist, it is always possible to squeeze in a few changes between when a manuscript is submitted for review and when it is typeset—including additions like this very parenthetical remark. Second, in the future I can always *reinterpret* what I previously wrote when I arrive at what I think to be a clearer formulation: "see, this is what I really meant to say even though I didn't put it clearly back then." In these cases, what I will have meant depends as much on future interpretation as what I wrote in the past. Derrida is correct: prefaces are never capable of fully circumscribing and securing the meaning of what follows.)

The knowledge contained herein is contingent upon this specific date, which is determined by two particular institutional reasons. First, I must prepare to reorganize my courses for fall 2020 on the basis of new institutional guidelines required by the international pandemic we are presently experiencing. Given that "summer" for a tenured scholar such as me will end around the end of August 2020, I must complete the revisions I desire to make before the end of July if I am to be adequately prepared for September. Second, a publisher will not wait forever for a manuscript. Should I promise the book by summer 2020, but not deliver until 2021, it is far less likely that the book would be published. Institutional conditions limit how far knowledge reaches.

However, "what Craig Martin thinks" will likely not end on the date signed below. Who I am is likely to continue to change, perhaps for the better, perhaps for the worse (these decisions are always subjective, of course, as they are dependent upon particular readers' views of what counts as "better" or "worse"). This book, then, captures "what Craig Martin thinks," but only in a conditioned sense: at best, it only captures "what Craig held to be true" from the time I began the book until the time I completed it—from 2016 to 2020. The "subject" this book claims to reveal—and indeed it does reveal to some extent what I think, if we limit that to the window that closes on July 31—is not a fixed subject but a mobile one.

The claims that I hold to be true are also contingent, of course, on institutional conditions to which I submit myself as a "subject," conditions that make me the subject that I am, or, by the time this appears in print, who I "was." I teach at a small liberal arts college with a 4/4 teaching load and almost no funding for research. Consequently, it is not surprising that this book covers matters that can be examined without having to do, for instance, social scientific research projects—projects of the sort that are not made possible within my institutional conditions. Rather, the book tends to cover what one discovers if one reads as widely as possible and attempts to integrate what one has read. Why focus on rhetoric at the expense of other considerations? In part because I can read and write about rhetoric without much institutional funding. The institutional context is a condition of possibility of the sort of knowledge produced by subjects situated in such a context.

In addition, this research was also made possible by the fact that my partner and I have no children. Each summer, I can sit on my back porch and read and write largely without interruption; if we had children, that would not have been possible. Not bearing responsibility for children is a privilege that capacitates scholarly production; bearing responsibility for rearing children is something that, by contrast, to some extent incapacitates scholarly production. Women, it is clear, suffer the most from the lack of such privilege, as women—more than men—are expected in our society to bear the greatest responsibility for attending to or rearing children. In the spring of 2020, several academic journals publicly reported that once primary, secondary, and postsecondary schools nationwide went online in the United States—that is, when professors were teaching from home and caring for their children who were now learning at home—the journal editors continued to receive the same number of submissions from men but almost no submissions from women (see, for instance, Viglione 2020). By all accounts, male privilege demonstrably capacitates scholarly production.

I would also like to suggest that the *reception* of my claims in this book—are they persuasive or not?—is in part contingent upon the extent to which I was able to use a sufficient number of cues, signifiers, or sign-posts that readers are already familiar with. I can drop a reference to Kant and expect that many readers—for example, those academics in contemporary Euro-American humanities disciplines—will have at least a minimal understanding of my point. This is clearly not the case for figures, such as Nagarjuna, which I mention on occasion. There is a Euro-American privilege in the academic study of religion. In my opinion, there is nothing intrinsically superior about the philosophical interlocutors I cite, such as Kant, Hegel, Derrida, Foucault, Butler, etc. (they *all* say unsophisticated things at times). There are writers from other cultural centers that are as equally sophisticated as these; however, referring to classic Asian or South

Preface

Asian philosophers, for instance, will not make this project as accessible and persuasive to Euro-American readers as references to Kant will. If the intellectual referents I was surrounded with as a graduate student carry more weight with my audience, that is not as a result of my own personal choices—to my recollection, I did not choose to be born in the United States—but rather the result of the fact that I was lucky to be born in a relatively affluent and influential cultural center made possible by European and American imperialism. If Kant carries more weight than Nagarjuna, it is likely because those at the center of empire are more familiar with Kant than Nagarjuna. (If readers are not already familiar with Jan Westerhoff's brilliant work on Madhyamika philosophy and philosophical anti-realism, consider checking it out; I cannot recommend it highly enough. See Westerhoff 2009, 2010a, b, 2011, 2018, 2020.)

Here we have, then, condition after condition: this book reflects the thoughts of a person situated at the intersection of a number of institutions: publishing institutions, institutions of higher education, institutions of white and male privilege, imperialist institutions, etc. The knowledge claims that follow are therefore contingent upon these institutional conditions of possibility of the production of the knowledge claims. Take away the conditions and the knowledge produced would not be possible, or wouldn't be persuasive.

While these reflections might be seem indulgently narcissistic—these considerations are all about me—it seems clear to me that we might always want to consider taking such matters into account. Recently I was in a conversation with two senior scholars of religion (both of whom present as white and male) who insisted to me that race no longer mattered in the academy—there are minorities at every level of scientific research, they assured me. By contrast, I tried to persuade them that scientific research—the sort they themselves hail as most authoritative—shows that minorities appear to suffer from implicit bias and stereotype threat in ways that we do not, as yet, have a means of entirely preventing. Race, it appears, does matter, and ignoring that fact—namely, ignoring the conditions that make success in the academy possible—functions to allow things like implicit bias to function without consideration and without rectification. Scholars with a great deal of privilege can perhaps ignore such conditions with impunity, as such conditions do not disadvantage them. For those of us who do not want to ignore such conditions, it is clear that sometimes being white and male are two important conditions of possibility of scholarly production—and therefore we might want to operate on those conditions.

Hegel arguably hoped to close knowledge with his prefaces—to outline the beginning and the end of what we ought to know. Derrida, by contrast, suggests that knowledge is *a priori* revisable—even concluding remarks are opening remarks. This particular book attempts to systematically attend to the conditions of possibility for making empirical claims about discourse, sorting out empirically supported claims from those that are not empirically supported, and demonstrating that some unwarranted empirical claims function to reinforce social domination. However, because knowledge production is *a priori* open-ended, I reserve the right to think different thoughts in the future; indeed, who can resist indulging in thinking new thoughts, except those who refuse to think beyond where they already stand (perhaps like those two white men who refused to consider new social scientific evidence at odds with the views they already held to be authoritative)? Consequently, I look forward to hearing from subjects in different institutional contexts, particularly those with less privilege than I (although, to be clear, by no means are they responsible for educating me). What here is useful for you and what is not? Which concepts are useful and which are not? What translates well and what translates poorly for your projects? To serve the readers I hope to serve, how might I revise my thoughts? Criticism moves thinking forward, and I hope never to sit still until I lie in a coffin.

Craig Martin
Syracuse, NY
July 31, 2020

ACKNOWLEDGMENTS

Writing a single-authored book is at once a solitary and a collective affair. It is solitary in the sense that I can only write under conditions that permit me to spend a great deal of time, alone, reading, thinking, writing, and revising (conditions permitted by social and economic privilege). However, much of what I write is in part a response to a challenge, a misunderstanding, or a caricature of my view—I could not clarify the approach I take to my studies without engaging with the thoughts of others. Consequently, many thanks to all of the conversation partners I've spoken with over the years, as well as those many readers who offered comments on rough drafts of various chapters. This book took four years to write, and I've forgotten who all were generous enough to offer written comments—there were too many to recollect; however, you know who you are, and I'm in your debt.

Many thanks to my colleagues at St. Thomas Aquinas College. I could not have thought through some of the problems I was attempting to address in this book without chatting about biology with Ryan Wynne, criminology with Ellen Chayet, economics with Meghan Mihal, education with Regine Rossi, management with Pam Derfus, social psychology with Ben Wagner, etc. You all pressed me to account for how the work I do is empirically supported in the ways your own work is, and I think this book is better for it. I want to thank Ben in particular for pointing me to the social scientific studies that were foundational to my argument in the chapter on recrement. In addition, I've benefitted greatly from many conversations I've had with my closest disciplinary colleagues in religion and philosophy—Rob Trawick and David Keppler—both of whom kindly read and commented on rough drafts of chapters. Thanks to all of the above and also to Staci Shultz, Paul Dent, and Laura Dent for emotional support and commiseration about pedagogy, institutional politics, and more.

For a few years now I have been the editor of a book series with Bloomsbury Academic, titled Critiquing Religion: Discourse, Culture, Power. I would like to thank the authors and editors who have contributed to the series—I learned a great deal from each and every one of your projects. I would also like to thank Lalle Pursglove, the religion editor at Bloomsbury, with whom I've truly enjoyed working with over the last several years.

Thanks also go to two institutions that have made it possible for me to do the work I do: the North American Association for the Study of Religion (NAASR) and the scholarly collective Culture on the Edge. When I began my career, I struggled to find a place in the American Academy of Religion where the type of questions I was interested in asking were of interest to others. NAASR and Culture on the Edge, by contrast, were institutions that opened spaces for me to ask my own questions and helped me access publication routes for my findings.

Acknowledgments

As always, I would like to thank my students; they are the first on whom I try out new ideas or new ways of thinking, seeing if they are useful or not for the purposes of studying the things we study. I could not be a clear writer if you did not frown at me and contest the claims I make, thereby pressing me to further clarity (or pressing me to change my mind). Thanks in particular go to Angela Banta, Kayla Farley, Savannah Finver, Emily Hough, Kayla Hunter, Sarah Montello, and Dani Tocci: this book could not have been written without the studies we did of Hegel and Derrida. Last, I want to thank the students in the two sections of "Philosophy of Social Science" I taught during the fall of 2020, when I tried out some of the arguments of this book in class; you were generous with me when I stumbled and helped me identify a multitude of ways I could clarify my argument.

Many thanks to those members of the William James reading group I held online in the summer of 2020—in particular Andie Alexander, Matt Baldwin, Savannah Finver, Simone Fracas, and Ben Wagner. Although I don't have much to say about William James in this book, working through his claims in *A Pluralistic Universe* (1996) helped me clarify some of my arguments in this book.

I would like to thank Routledge for permitting me to use some of the material from Craig Martin, *A Critical Introduction to the Study of Religion* (© Craig Martin 2012; reproduced with permission of The Licensor through PLSclear) in Chapter 4, and some of the material from Craig Martin, *A Critical Introduction to the Study of Religion*, Second Edition (© 2017 Craig Martin; reproduced with permission of The Licensor through PLSclear) in Chapter 2. Thanks also to Equinox Publishing for permitting me to use some of the material from Craig Martin, "'The Thing Itself Always Steals Away': Scholars and the Constitution of their Objects of Study," in Leslie Dorrough Smith (ed.), *Constructing "Data" in Religious Studies: Examining the Architecture of the Academy* (© Equinox Publishing 2019) in Chapter 2. I would like to thank University of Chicago Press and Bloomsbury for permission to use a quotation from Jacques Derrida's *Positions* as the epigraph for this book (© The University of Chicago 1981; reproduced with the permission of University of Chicago Press; © Jacques Derrida 2002, *Positions*, Continuum Publishing, used by permission of Bloomsbury Publishing Plc.).

Last, I want to thank my friend Glenn, who tolerates my rants as I attempt to verbalize what I think I'm doing as a scholar. In addition, a considerably significant point I make in Chapter 6—that social functions need not be unconscious—I owe to his feedback alone.

INTRODUCTION: CONTINGENCY

What we tend to count as knowledge is contingent upon the means by which we produce knowledge.

This poststructuralist claim—the sort of claim we might see in the writings of philosophers such as Jacques Derrida, Michel Foucault, and Judith Butler, and one that is rooted in Immanuel Kant's definition of "critique" as a type of philosophical study that attends to the *conditions of possibility of knowledge*—is at once both banal and radical. It is banal in the sense that, yes, of course, few would object that what we hold to be true—about viruses, for instance—is *contingent* upon the use of language (for we cannot hold it as true that "viruses are contagious" without knowing what "virus" and "contagious" mean), *contingent* upon an educational system that requires youth to take courses on things such as "biology" or "natural science" (for we would not hold the findings of contemporary sciences as true unless we were educated to respect as authoritative the findings of professional scientists), *contingent* upon capital (for scientific research on viruses cannot be completed without funding), *contingent* upon institutions (for authoritative scientific research is typically conducted in universities that have infrastructures that make that research possible), *contingent* upon publishers and news media (for we could not hold as true scientific claims that are not circulated via media of various sorts), etc. To some extent, these examples are so obvious as to barely be worth pointing out.

Yet this claim is also radical because many people—who typically identify themselves as realists—would like to claim that what makes something true is *only the world itself,* not consciousness of the world. On this view, whether there is a tree in my front yard, for instance, doesn't depend on what anyone in particular thinks about it or whether anyone has seen a tree in my yard, but rather on the sheer fact that it is just objectively true that *there is* a tree in my front yard, *even if no one ever saw it;* things are what they are *completely independently* of the consciousness of the people who produce knowledge about those things. This is, in fact, the central claim of the type of realism to which I'm objecting in this book (there are, of course, other types of realism, but those do not concern me here). On this view, when the proverbial tree falls in the forest it *obviously makes a sound,* even if there is no one there to hear it. Truth is therefore determined *solely* by the world itself, not on our consciousness of the world. It's clear why they might say that. First, people make claims all the time that they want to be true but which aren't empirically supported, and most of us—poststructuralists included—tend to think that phrases such as "wanting something to be true" and ones like "supported by empirical evidence" don't mean the same thing. Second, we often discover things that, on the one hand, it seems reasonable to assume had been there before we discovered them, and, on the other hand, it seems unwarranted to suppose they magically came into existence at the moment of discovery and as a result of discovery—for how could we find something that didn't exist before its discovery? That seems to violate what we typically expect when it comes to cause and effect (except at the quantum level, a level at which we have a great deal of evidence that discovery appears to function as a cause). For the realist, if we define truth relative to consciousness, then "truth" could always be so subjective as to be potentially indistinguishable from wishful thinking—and therefore unworthy of being called "knowledge" or "truth" in the first place.

When poststructuralists report that Derrida, Foucault, and Butler say things like "truth and knowledge are contingent upon discourse," realists appear to interpret the claim as if it were equivalent to the following: "discourse comes between us and the world, or between subjects and objects. If discourse gets between us and reality, we cannot know whether our discourse accurately reflects the world. We must accept the limits of knowledge: ultimately, we're in a prison house of language and must therefore always be skeptical about whether the nature of the reality resembles our representation of it." For realists who interpret poststructuralist claims in that manner—usually on the basis of how popular secondary sources report on what Derrida, Foucault, and Butler wrote—this sort of skepticism seems obviously self-defeating: if the world is on the other side of discourse, *a priori* we can't compare any particular discourse on reality with reality, in which case, *how can we trust that poststructuralists' representation of reality is more accurate than anyone else's*? In many conversations I have had, the realist considers this a "mic drop" moment and, in my experience, after having said this they tend to consider the matter settled—for in their mind, they provided a logically true argument that followed directly from the given premises. And they're not wrong: that argument does logically follow from those premises. The problem is that the premises they are working from are provided by caricatures of poststructuralism in secondary texts.

I have read and reread the works of Derrida, Foucault, and Butler over the last twenty years, and I've yet to see in their writings the claim attributed to them by the realist imagined above. On the contrary, on my interpretation of their writings they instead hold the not-very-radical view that subjects and discourses aren't outside the world, but *part of the world* (and, in fact, I'd be surprised if realists thought that subjects and discourses were outside of the world either). The idea that the world is somehow out there, on the other side of discourse, is likely *nonsensical for all parties*. The mic-drop argument only works if we accept the realist's representation of secondary sources' representations of the writings of Derrida, Foucault, and Butler, and we need not do so.

I would argue that realists tend to frame poststructuralists' arguments in this way because they are insufficiently attentive (likely for institutional reasons that I'll discuss below) to the fact that poststructuralism developed out of a tradition of continental philosophy that began with Kant, but which *did not end with Kant*. The realist's interpretation of poststructuralism would make perfect sense if Derrida, Foucault, and Butler were Kantians: on many interpretations of his work, Kant dualistically divided the world into phenomena and noumena and denied that we could have any knowledge of

Introduction: Contingency

the *real world* (i.e., "things-in-themselves" or "noumena"), which lies, out there,[1] *beyond our representations of things*.

To be fair, realists trained in the Anglo-American analytical philosophical tradition of the twentieth century were likely systematically exposed to caricatures of Hegel as a spiritualistic monist guilty of committing himself to ridiculous metaphysical absurdities; as such, it's unlikely that they received any significant training in the writings of post-Kantian German Idealists. In addition, they were also likely systematically exposed to caricatures of Derrida, Foucault, and Butler as postmodern obscurantists who did little more than attack truth and make puns (see, for instance, the infamous letter written by analytic philosophers objecting to Cambridge University's announcement that they were giving Derrida an honorary degree, a letter that accuses Derrida of saying things that no one has found in Derrida's writings [Derrida 1995: 419–421]). Consequently it makes sense that when realists trained in the analytical tradition hear "discourse conditions truth," they might have interpreted it as a kind of Kantianism. And of course—to be fair once more—some people who identify as poststructuralists do interpret Derrida, Foucault, and Butler as Kantians of some sort. However, in doing so they leave out and arguably cannot make sense of many of the claims made by Derrida, Foucault, and Butler, particularly those claims that are *explicitly* derived more from the legacy of Hegel than the legacy of Kant. I will argue in this book that to comprehend the claims of Derrida, Foucault, and Butler—particularly the claims they make about Hegel—beyond a superficial level, we must be sensitive to Hegel's criticisms of Kant.

To anticipate the argument I will make in Chapter 1, Hegel argues that Kant's idea of the "things-in-themselves" or "noumena" is completely useless, and for reasons that Kant himself accepts. For Kant, *by definition we can know nothing empirical about "things-in-themselves"* that, *a priori*, do not appear to us; as a result, the concept is useless for understanding any "things" that are of interest to us who live in a phenomenal world—things like "viruses," for instance, about which we could not have knowledge *unless* they appeared to us. For Hegel and the poststructuralists, however, to make sense of things like "viruses," to "see" them or "know" anything about them, we have to use, at the very least, contemporary scientific discourses on virology. Ancient Greeks who divided the human body into the four humors had four main concepts: "blood," "yellow bile," "black bile," and "phlegm" and, consequently, could not see or have knowledge of viruses. That knowledge had to wait until we as humans developed a discourse about viruses in the nineteenth century (as well as a certain technical ability to manipulate and experiment on the material world), which allowed us to produce knowledge about viruses; the empirical evidence about viruses could only be gathered once we had different concepts than those contained in the theory of the four humors.

Thus when poststructuralist Hegelians such as Derrida, Foucault, or Butler claim that discourse conditions knowledge, this is not to say that discourse gets between us and things-in-themselves; that sounds like Kant's claim, not ours. We have no use for the idea of things-in-themselves and, arguably, neither do realists, as—by definition—a thing-in-itself is something that we cannot have any knowledge of, *a priori*. We can have knowledge only of those things that appear to us, and the appearance of things like viruses was apparently contingent upon nineteenth- and twentieth-century vocabulary and technological prowess; earlier generations could not see or develop knowledge of viruses.

Contrary to the realist's portrayal of poststructuralism, "discourse conditions reality" isn't meant to encourage a form of skepticism according to which we ought to doubt whether viruses exist because we can't be sure that our representations of them match how they are in-themselves; rather, the argument is (1) that "things-in-themselves" isn't a particularly useful concept for thinking about knowledge, particularly as "empirically warranted knowledge" is usually understood to mean "things we have evidence for *because we have seen them*," (2) that if we change our vocabulary, we will see different things in the world, and (3) that not everyone uses the same vocabulary.

In addition, it is difficult to see how realists could have knowledge of viruses that is not contingent upon those things listed in the "banal" paragraph above, *things like language, education, capital, institutions, publishers*—and, we might add, *power*. In practice, we always have to depend upon *historically specific* concepts to bring objects in the world into relief, concepts such as "novel coronavirus" or "COVID-19" (the latter concept explicitly bears the marks of its historically specific appearance, as the "19" is short for "2019," the year in which the concept was first employed); we also have to depend on an education system that trains scientists and a circulation of capital that makes possible the sorts of biomedical research centers that permit those scientists to conduct tests on such viruses and share their research. Power matters for what we can and cannot know: those findings that private drug companies discover when conducting tests in private but which they have the power to keep private cannot be knowledge for those who do not have access to their findings.

The realist seems to fear that if we make truth contingent upon something like power—if truth is relative to power—then what makes something true is a person's ability to shout the loudest, the size of their fists, or relative firepower of the weapons they carry. It's an odd concern, because challenges to dominance do not appear to be contingent upon the adoption of a realist epistemology, or any epistemology whatsoever. The realist also fears that if we make knowledge relative to power, we shift the locus of truth *away from* the world-as-it-is-in-itself—which is apparently the only thing they think we ought to appeal to in order to warrant truth claims—and thereby open Pandora's box: if power makes something true, then perhaps we will have no means of contesting claims made by those more powerful than us with whom we might disagree (again, it's an odd concern, for people without power contest claims all the time). Foucault is widely feared to have led us into a "post-truth" culture wherein everything is relative and therefore anything one wants to be true must be true; it is Foucault's fault, we are led to believe, that people don't believe in climate change (see, for instance, Roberts 2011) or that Donald Trump could become president of the United States (as if the people who voted for him did so because they had read Foucault and came to the conclusion that "might makes right"—hardly a creditable claim, but one that is often made; see, for example, Calcutt 2016 or Kakutani 2018).

The problem is that we don't have any evidence that poststructuralists such as Foucault ever said anything along the lines of "power alone makes something true"—I've read just about everything he wrote from the 1960s and the 1970s that is available in English, I've read some of it in French, and I've never come across such a claim. In the texts of his that I've read, it appears to me that he accepts that power is *only one of many* conditions of possibility of knowledge. (I suppose this point could not appear to the realists who never read what Foucault actually wrote in the first place—reading a philosopher is apparently an important condition of possibility of knowledge about what that philosopher wrote. As long as Foucault remains an imagined but unknown "thing-in-himself" that never appears to a realist because they never read what he wrote, *a priori* they cannot have knowledge of what he wrote. How can we justify our claim to have knowledge about what Foucault wrote without looking at evidence—his writings—to warrant our claims? That is possible *only if* reading secondary sources *is sufficient in a social context*—such as the present academic study of religion—*to count as "knowledge"* of an author's writings.)

Foucault does not deny that we can make true claims and false claims—his work is filled with claims he alleged were true—nor does he claim that power alone makes something true; rather, on my interpretation he only appears to deny that the claim that "we would probably find viruses *if* we deployed the concepts of virology and *if* we went to look for them using our currently available technology" is in itself sufficient to warrant the claim that "twenty-first-century biomedical knowledge of viruses is true." Usually what we call "warrant" requires actual evidence (to presume otherwise would presume we could knowledge of things prior to looking for them), and, for Foucault, evidence gathering in support of those things we call knowledge appears to be contingent upon conscious minds, concepts we use to divide up evidence, institutions with capital that make evidence gathering possible, and so forth. I would press the realist: if the only condition of possibility of true knowledge is that viruses-in-and-of-themselves exist (an odd claim of course, as, by definition, for Kant we cannot know anything about things-in-themselves), why make an effort to learn how to use concepts, why go to school, why support government funding for the sciences, and why read news reports about things like viruses? The answer should be clear: without those *other conditions of possibility* of knowledge, we couldn't "know" that, for instance, it might serve our interests to wear masks during a pandemic. What I think the realist misses is that when poststructuralists say "truth is contingent upon discourse and power," they don't mean "saying something is true makes it true" or that "power alone makes things true," they mean something closer to "developing special discursive vocabularies and material capital are important conditions of possibility of gathering into evidence those things we usually want to warrant what we call knowledge." Upon reflection, it appears that what we usually call warranted knowledge is contingent on a wide variety of conditions that are constantly variable.

This book will argue that attending to knowledge's contingencies makes knowledge stronger rather than weaker—for how can we control for contingencies that we do not take into account in the first place? In any case, any claim that one's discursively conditioned knowledge is noncontingently true is *a priori* false, at least given what we usually mean by words such as "discourse," "knowledge," and "contingency."

Discourse and Ideology

However, it is a false claim that, at times, has considerable political consequences that we can study and develop knowledge of, consequences that some readers might find objectionable.

***

This book, then, is a *poststructuralist critique* (in the sense of considering conditions of possibility) of the knowledge of *discourse* and *ideology*, both of which are elements of human culture that are of interest to me because they are often (although not always) used in the service of reproducing relationships of *domination*. To add a gloss on each of these key terms:

- I stipulatively define *poststructuralism* as the philosophical position best exemplified by the philosophical writings of Derrida, Foucault, and Butler, all of whom are situated in an intellectual tradition that starts with Kant and passes through Hegel, Husserl, and Heidegger. The details of this genealogy that runs from Kant to Butler will be outlined in the chapters on "Critique" and "Things."
- I define *discourse* as words, spoken or written, strung together to form phrases, slogans, sentences, monologues, conversations, paragraphs, missives, tracts, manifestos, speeches, books, and so forth. (To be clear, what we call "culture" includes much more than discursive forms; I do not claim to be attempting to produce knowledge about all forms of culture, but only discursive ones.) First, discourses serve a *constitutive* function in that they are conditions of possibility of individuating the objects in the world about which we make knowledge claims. Second, discourses also function as conditions of possibility of *empirical claims* about the objects individuated—without discourse, we could not make true or false claims about the world. Third, discourses also function to *distribute and modulate sympathies and antipathies*—discourses serve as one important condition of positive and negative affective responses to other persons, groups, or worldviews. Fourth, discourses may also function as *recrement*, which I define as discursive claims that are very similar to what we might refer to as "bullshit" in everyday colloquial speech—discursive claims that are reported because they accomplish something for the person who makes the claims, but which may very well not in fact be "believed" and which they may deliver in bad faith. These matters will be covered in the chapters on "Things," "Discourse," and "Recrement."
- I define *ideology* as collections of claims about the world that are empirically unwarranted or demonstrably false according to the rules of someone's discourse, yet which function to reinforce social domination. Because ideology concerns what is *false*, the chapter on "Ideology" primarily focuses on what it might mean to say that an empirical claim is *warranted*, but according to an epistemology consistent with the limits of knowledge recognized by poststructuralist philosophers.

Introduction: Contingency

- I define *domination* as relations between subject positions—positions that are themselves constituted by authoritative or powerful discourses—that *asymmetrically capacitate subjects,* in the sense that they make it easier for subjects in some social positions to serve their interests compared to subjects in other social positions. These matters are discussed in the chapter on "Domination."

Readers may have noticed that each of the previous bullet points begin with "I define"; although this qualifier makes my prose perhaps painfully repetitive, insofar as I accept that what is true or false is contingent not only on the world but also on discourse, I feel obligated to make it explicit where I am using words in ways that may be different from the way other scholars use words. There is a considerable gulf between the claim that "I use the word 'ideology' this way rather than that way" and the claim that "the word 'ideology' *really* means …" What we find in the world is often contingent upon the words we use to bring that world into relief; if we want the knowledge we produce to be useful, it is crucial that we be clear and precise about how we use those words—otherwise we risk conflating things that we might want to keep separate in our analysis, or separate out things that we might want to consider side by side in our analysis. My presentation of discourse and ideology often differs from that of other scholars; this is intentional. My goal is not to review the history of how these terms have been used but rather to point to a use of the terms that is most productive for the particular goals that I'm pursuing (the knowledge I might produce while pursuing those goals is, as should be clear, contingent upon those goals).

***

Some readers might object to the fact that I identify as a poststructuralist and yet continue to use the term "ideology." According to a common narrative—not my own, to be clear—after the "linguistic turn" we can no longer speak of ideology because doing so requires us to contrast "ideology" with "the world as it *really* is," and most forms of poststructuralism accept that there is no one way that the world "really is" apart from discourse. Foucault, for instance, systematically makes negative remarks about the concept of ideology in his writings (particularly those from the 1970s). In an interview titled "Truth and Power," he explicitly claims that the "notion of ideology appears to me to be difficult to make use of," in part because ideology always "stands in virtual opposition to something else that is supposed to count as truth" (Foucault 2000: 119). Foucault, however, is not particularly interested in "objective truth" but rather "how effects of truth are produced within discourses that, in themselves, are neither true nor false" (119).

Because of claims like this, the common narrative suggests that Foucault reduces truth to power and thus makes truth entirely relative, so that there is no position from which one could claim that a particular discourse is "ideological," because one no longer has a "truth" with which to contrast an "ideology." As Jan Rehmann puts it, from the perspective of poststructuralism, "'ideology' belongs to an outdated understanding of the sign which is supposed to conceal something real" (Rehmann 2014: 215). As Sara Mills notes, this type of interpretation "seems to suggest that, within a discourse theory view, all statements … have the same status and validity"—in which case, on what grounds could one assert that a particular statement is false or ideological (Mills 2004: 29)? Jonathan Joseph accuses his anti-realist opponents of saying "that there are no rational grounds for preferring one belief to another and that essentially all beliefs are equally valid" (Joseph 2002: 13; notably, Joseph cites no sources for this accusation). Although not writing specifically about Foucault, in *Ideology and Modern Culture* John B. Thompson puts the objection this way: "The epistemological problems raised by [this] approach are what may be described as *the epistemological problem of radical historicism*. If all knowledge … is socially and historically situated and is intelligible only in relation to this situation, then how can we avoid the conclusion that all knowledge is merely relative to the social-historical situation of the knower" (Thompson 1990: 49)? It is for this reason that Thompson recommends that we redefine "ideology" not in terms of "obscuring truth" or "false consciousness" but rather in terms of discourses that sustain domination: on his definition of the term, "*to study ideology is to study the ways in which meaning serves to establish and sustain relations of domination*" (56)—in part because domination is sustained *not only* by claims that are false but *also* by claims that are true (57).

Because I take quite seriously Foucault's critique of the concept of ideology, I would like to take a moment to address this common narrative. First, on my reading Foucault does not claim that nothing can be either true or false; on the contrary, he makes it clear that his work attends to the *historically specific conditions of possibility that make a claim count as true or false*. Second, he accepts that power is one of the conditions of possibility of knowledge, but the Marxists he criticizes appear to deny this. Foucault opposes himself specifically to those particular Marxists who present the knowledge claims of others as if they were "distorted" or "biased" because such claims function to reinforce a class hierarchy, while presenting their own knowledge claims as "objective" by contrast—as if Marxist claims were not equally invested. For Foucault, these naïve Marxists have missed a lesson they ought to have learned from Friedrich Nietzsche: "Behind knowledge, at the root of knowledge … are drives that would place us in a position of hatred, contempt, or fear before things that are threatening and presumptuous" (Foucault 2000: 12). Intersubjectively verifiable knowledge claims that demonstrate that some forms of capitalist culture function to legitimate relations of exploitation are likely only possible because someone who hates relations of exploitation felt it was worth the effort to demonstrate the point—hatred may be an important condition of possibility of knowledge. For Nietzsche (on Foucault's interpretation),

> if we truly wish to know knowledge, to know what it is, to apprehend it at its root, in its manufacture, we must look not to philosophers but to politicians—we need to understand what the relations of struggle and power are. One can understand what knowledge consists of only by examining these relations of struggle and

power, the manner in which things and men hate one another, fight one another, and try to dominate one another, to exercise power relations over one another.

(Foucault 2000: 12)

"Knowledge is always the historical and circumstantial result of conditions"—political ones, for instance—"outside the domain of knowledge" (Foucault 2000: 13). If we do not take these conditions of possibility of knowledge into account, we cannot fully account for the limits of knowledge.

For Foucault, then, the problem with Marxist criticisms of ideology is not that there is never a warrant for saying that a claim is false, but rather because—for them—the problem with ideology is that it is *invested* in ways designed to serve the interests of some over others. For Foucault, *all knowledge* is the result of investments that hope to serve the interests of some over others:

> in actual fact, political and economic conditions of existence are not a veil or an obstacle for the subject of knowledge but the means by which subjects of knowledge are formed ... There cannot be particular types of subjects of knowledge, orders of truth, or domains of knowledge *except* on the basis of political conditions that are the very ground on which the subject, the domains of knowledge, and the relations with truth are formed.
>
> (Foucault 2000: 15)

"There couldn't be any knowledge without power" (31)—not in the sense that "truth" is by definition "what we would like to be true" or "the claims of those who have the biggest guns," but rather in the sense that power is one of many conditions of possibility of knowledge. Consequently, Foucault's problem with Marxist ideology critique is that Marxists fail to recognize the conditions of possibility of their own knowledge.

In addition, Foucault quite explicitly claims that "the problem *does not consist* in drawing the line between that which, in a discourse, falls under the category of scientificity or truth, and that which comes under some other category" (Foucault 2000: 119; emphasis mine). That is, he *explicitly claims* that the problem with ideology critique is *not* that we have no means of distinguishing truth from falsehood. It is just that Foucault's interests lie not with identifying what is true or false with respect to a particular discourse, but rather in identifying the rules according to which a particular discourse makes certain true and false claims possible: the problem that interests him "consists in seeing historically how effects of truth are produced within discourses that, in themselves, are neither true nor false" (119). As I will argue in the chapters below, a definition can be neither true nor false; a definition is a condition of possibility of truth claims, which are only possible once we have definitions in place. For example, we cannot know how many murders there were in our city last year until we have established a definition of murder, and there is not only one way to use the concept—a "duel" between two "gentlemen" with pistols resulting in the death of one or more of them might once have been considered "fair and legal" but might, in many cities today, be classified as "murder." Until we establish a definition for murder—separating it from, for instance, "manslaughter" or "accidental death"—we cannot "know" how many murders there were last year in our town; the definition of murder is neither true nor false but rather a condition of possibility of true or false claims about murder. In addition, if we change our definition, what is empirically true will change as well. There are some things presently called "justifiable police homicides" that many people would like to redefine as "murder." This is why, for anti-realist poststructuralists, whether there is a tree in my front yard *can't be true independently of consciousness*—for we must formulate a definition for "tree" if there are going to be any truths about them in the first place, and definitions of words are, by most accounts, contingent upon consciousness. "Truth is a thing of this world," and

> each society has its regime of truth ... —that is, the types of discourse it accepts and makes function as true; the mechanisms and instances that enable one to distinguish true and false statements; the means by which each is sanctioned; the techniques and procedures accorded value in the acquisition of truth; the status of those who are charged with saying what counts as true.
>
> (Foucault 2000: 131)

Attention to these conditions of possibility of knowledge arguably make our knowledge more rather than less sophisticated, for if we ignore how we're using nonuniversal, historically specific words, if we ignore the nonuniversal, disciplinary specific rules by which we weigh evidence and warrant empirical claims, or if we ignore the nonuniversal disciplinary specific methods or procedures we use to investigate the world, the knowledge we produce is liable to be sloppy, more easily contested, and less persuasive. Despite the fact that poststructuralists attend to the fact that what counts as true is historically conditioned, we are not thereby prohibited from saying that some claims are false *on the rules of our own discourse or someone else's*.

Returning briefly to Thompson: he claimed that "If all knowledge ... is socially and historically situated and is intelligible only in relation to this situation, then how can we avoid the conclusion that all knowledge is merely relative to the social-historical situation of the knower?" Because there are no noncontingent forms of knowledge with which we could compare our historically conditioned forms of knowledge, he gave up on defining ideology as a discourse that is in some sense false. But I would argue that this move doesn't solve the problem so much as kick the can further down the road.

Thompson seems to intuit this point without fully realizing it, for he considers a possibly important objection to his approach. He imagines an interlocutor pressing him: "It's all very well in principle to define ideology in terms of the ways in which meaning serves to establish and sustain relations of domination, but how can you ever tell in practice whether particular symbolic forms are serving to sustain or disrupt, to establish or undermine, relations of domination" (Thompson 1990: 70)? Thompson's response? "It is difficult to provide a general response to questions such as these" (70). We might

Introduction: Contingency

never be fully warranted in presenting our interpretation of the function of a form of ideology as noncontingently true: "If the critic is looking for proof, for incontestable demonstration, then he or she will be disappointed" (71). But asking for evidence is not the same as asking for *uncontestable* evidence.

> The disappointment stems more from the critic's expectations than from the analyst's results. In analyzing ideology, in seeking to grasp the complex interplay of meaning and power, we are not dealing with a subject matter that admits of incontestable demonstration (whatever that may be). We are in the realm of shifting sense and relative inequalities, of ambiguity and word-play, of different degrees of opportunity and accessibility, of deception and self-deception, of the concealment of social relations and of the concealment of the very process of concealment.
>
> (Thompson 1990: 71)

Thompson wryly concludes, "To approach [ideology] in the expectation that one could provide incontestable analyses is like using a microscope to interpret a poem" (Thompson 1990: 71).

What I think Thompson misses is that, despite the fact that he doesn't want to define ideology in terms of falsehood because we have no noncontingent way of demonstrating what is true, saying that an ideology reinforces social domination, or that it is "deceptive," or that it "conceals" already entails making the claim that some things are true and some things are false. Of course, such claims rarely go uncontested, but that's true of just about all knowledge claims worth making. There is a reason that newspapers don't report that "the District of Columbia is the capital of the US," despite the fact that it is clearly true (at least for those of us who haven't claimed to secede and form our own United States with our own capital); the claims about Washington, DC, worth making, the ones of interest, are the ones that someone out there might contest. *Ideology critique need not commit itself to presenting its knowledge claims as noncontingent or uncontested, but that leaves ideology critique in the same boat as all other knowledge claims.*

Perhaps the greatest weakness of poststructuralist theorists has been in their reluctance to explicitly connect discourse analysis to a robust account of empirical evidence, something I wish to address in the chapter on ideology. The reluctance has likely been the result of the fear that defenses of empiricism lend themselves to naturalizing or dehistoricizing empirical evidence (overly confident philosophers who thump the table to insist that it is "real" are often the ones who ignore the fact that the concept of a "table" and philosophical concepts such as "the world-as-it-is-in-itself" are not universal but rather historically specific). However, I refuse to choose between poststructuralist critique and empirical evidence; I'm a poststructuralist *and* an empiricist. In the chapters below, I will present textual evidence showing that Derrida, Foucault, and Butler make similar claims, if only we attend more carefully to their writings, as opposed to caricaturing them on the basis of having read only secondary literature.

Discourse and Ideology

In any case, if I use the concept of ideology, it is not because I have not understood Foucault's criticism of classical Marxist forms of ideology critique that present objective knowledge as unconditioned by power. Rather, as Foucault himself notes at one point, "the definition of 'ideology' needs to be revised" (Foucault 2000: 87), and consequently I will define ideology very differently than did such classical Marxists.[2]

***

My narrow focus on approaching discourse and ideology on the basis of my reading of Derrida, Foucault, and Butler may seem monomaniacal at times. However, how better can we account for the strengths and weaknesses of an approach than to follow it all the way down, wherever it may lead? Scholar of religion Jonathan Z. Smith once wrote: "Without the experience of riding hell-bent for leather on one's presuppositions, one is allowed to feel that methods have really no consequences and no entailments" (Smith 2007: 93). When we cobble together a method or theory by picking or choosing whatever strikes our fancy at the moment, but without a systematic consideration of how those things we're choosing fit (or don't fit) together, "none of them is ever subjected to any interesting cost accounting" (93). If I'm riding hell-for-leather on a very particular poststructuralist horse, it is in part because I want to do some cost-accounting: what does this approach help us see that other approaches do not and, conversely, what does this approach leave unconsidered, or what does it ignore to focus on other things?

CHAPTER 1
CRITIQUE

The concept of "critique," as I use it, is based on a philosophical tradition that goes back to Immanuel Kant's *Critique of Pure Reason* and can be traced through G. W. F. Hegel's phenomenology; Jacques Derrida's, Michel Foucault's, and Judith Butler's poststructuralism; and—I will argue—the contemporary biological sciences, as seen in the work of Anne Fausto-Sterling and Rebecca M. Jordan-Young. In this chapter, I want to tell the story of the concept of "critique," describe how it comes to us, and to make an argument regarding which parts of this intellectual tradition are worth saving and which are not.

Before proceeding, please note: I don't claim this story is true in any objective sense, or that it reflects the "true meaning" of these author's writings (indeed, I'm not even sure what it would even mean to say that a particular reading reflects the "true meaning" of a text or body of texts). Some readers might object to my interpretation of Kant, Hegel, etc. My interpretation of these authors is—*as are all interpretations*—based on what *I* discover when I read their works. I claim to have learned valuable lessons from each of them. It is quite possible that what I discover in their works aren't in their works but are my own ravings, my own obsession.[1] Although I'm happy to field arguments claiming I've missed the lesson other readers may want me to learn from a particular author (or which readers think the author herself would have wanted me to learn), nevertheless what is most of interest to me is whether the lesson that I think I'm learning is practically worthwhile, even if it results from what others believe to be a "misinterpretation" of the author I claim to have learned it from. I'm happy to acknowledge my reading of this intellectual tradition is tendentious (although it's unclear to me that this in any way distinguishes my interpretation from any other).

In addition, my interpretation of Kant focuses narrowly on his use of the concepts *a priori*, *a posteriori*, phenomena, noumena, and things-in-themselves. If I do so, it is not because these are the most important parts of Kant's work we should attend to, but because presentations of Derrida in secondary literature often involve depicting him as a naïve Kantian. My friends who are more sympathetic to Kant have pointed out to me that this focuses on—in their opinion—Kant at his worst rather than his best. If, therefore, I belabor Kant's faults it is not because I think there is nothing else he said worth considering, but because people often take Kant's greatest faults and project them onto Derrida; to show how Derrida is in many ways not a Kantian, we must attend to the fact that by the time Kant arrived in France in the twentieth century, the most objectionable parts of Kant's philosophy had long since been abandoned.

Discourse and Ideology

Along the way, the examples of what I take to be their point are often my examples. For instance, I suggest that one argument Hume makes is perhaps best exemplified by the same argument made by contemporary physicists about the big bang. Of course that example could not have been Hume's—he died long before twentieth-century physics was developed—but I hope sympathetic readers will be open to seeing how the arguments are similar.

It is worth noting once more that I don't refer to Kant, Hegel, and others because dead white European men are superior thinkers, but rather because I want to incorporate the widest number of useful intellectual lessons in my scholarship—and I believe they still have useful things to teach us. That is also why I also read and teach, for instance, Madhyamika philosophy and the Upanishads, without which my position on the usefulness of the distinction between "empirical" and "nonempirical" would be far less sophisticated. However, I cannot ground my position in their work with equal sophistication because I'm a mere novice when it comes to understanding the details of ancient Indian philosophy.

Immanuel Kant, Phenomena, and the Critique of Knowledge

The interpretation of philosophy is a complicated affair, and one thing I have learned from Friedrich Nietzsche is that paying attention to the philosopher's apparent goals is useful for understanding the claims they make. In *Beyond Good and Evil* (1998), Nietzsche writes:

> Little by little I came to understand what every great philosophy to date has been: the personal confession of its author, a kind of unintended and unwitting memoir; and similarly, that the moral (or immoral) aims in every philosophy constituted the actual seed from which the whole plant invariably grew. Whenever explaining how a philosopher's most far-fetched metaphysical propositions have come about, in fact, one always does well (and wisely) to ask first: "What morality is it (is *he*) aiming at?"
>
> (Nietzsche 1998: 8–9)

That is to say, to understand a philosophy one must understand the end toward which the philosopher aims. To understand Kant's definition of "critique," we might do well to look not first at his "far-fetched metaphysical propositions"—of which there are many— but rather the hints he gives us about where he would like to end up. While such an approach is "suspicious," to use Paul Ricoeur's term (see Ricoeur's *Freud and Philosophy* [1970], wherein he calls Marx, Nietzsche, and Freud "masters of suspicion"), at times it also permits generous reconstructions of a philosopher's arguments—for how better can one defend a philosopher's position than to show that there are better arguments that get them to where they wanted to go?

Kant's *Critique of Pure Reason* ([1781] 1998)[2] was written in response to seventeenth- and eighteenth-century European criticisms of metaphysics and Christian theology.

Critique

Consequently, to make sense of how Kant uses the term "critique," we must first back up and consider (1) some philosophers' idiosyncratic ways of talking about God, (2) how Kant uses the words "a priori" and "a posteriori," and (3) an intellectual challenge about God that Kant felt he had to meet.

First, according to many forms of theism—including Kant's—God is by definition infinite or unconditioned. By definition "infinite" literally means "without limit," while "unconditioned" means "without any conditions"—usually causal conditions (that is, God makes causal interventions in the world but is not himself caused by anything other than himself). Most forms of commonsense theism do not imagine God in a way that would satisfy philosophers who want to insist on God's infinity, because traditional theists imagine God as another being, just a being with powers far above and beyond what powers humans have. For most commonsense theists, you and I are not God; God is another being. For philosophers who want to take God's infinity seriously, however, this claim quite literally limits God. If I am not God, then there is a dividing line between me and God, and I'm on the other side—and that line circles God like a fence, limiting God, making such a God by definition "finite" rather than "infinite." This is why some ancient Indian philosophers who wrote the Upanishads claimed that all human spirits are just a small part of Brahman (their name for their infinite spirit) rather than separate from Brahman; that was how they could reconcile the existence of an infinite spirit with human spirits (see, for instance, the Brihadaranyaka Upanishad and the Chandogya Upanishad [Goodall 1996]). In the Bhagavad-Gita, the infinite god (called Krishna rather than Brahman) extends even further and encompasses *both* spirit *and* matter: Krishna claims, "all the universe, *animate and inanimate*, and whatever else you wish to see ... all stands here as one in my body" (Stoler Miller 1986: 98, emphases mine). Similarly, early modern philosopher Baruch Spinoza insisted in his *Ethics* that "nature" was not separate from God, but in some way *identified with* God (see Spinoza 1994). The details of what exactly he meant are contested by Spinoza scholars, but in any case his identification of nature with God was designed to protect God's infinity. As I will show below, Hegel makes the same argument: all finite things must be *part of* the infinite; if they're separate—if the infinite is *outside* the finite—then the so-called "infinite" is really just another finite being alongside other finite beings. To anticipate one of Hegel's criticisms of Kant, he points out that although Kant defines God as the "infinite" or "unconditioned," Kant also separates God from the phenomenal world, in which case—at least according to Hegel—Kant's god isn't actually infinite.

In summary, some philosophers contrast finite or conditioned beings with infinite or unconditioned beings. As readers will note below, Kant explicitly refers to his god as "infinite" and "unconditioned." To understand his arguments in the *Critique of Pure Reason*—as well as Hegel's criticism of his arguments—we have to keep in mind that Kant is using this technical definition (i.e., god is infinite, unlimited, unconditioned) rather than a commonsense definition of theism.

Second, Kant was familiar with Hume's arguments in *A Treatise of Human Nature* ([1739–1740] 1985) and *An Inquiry Concerning Human Understanding* ([1748] 1993) about the lack of direct empirical evidence for causation. Indeed, Kant once wrote that

Discourse and Ideology

"I freely admit that the remembrance of *David Hume* was the very thing that many years ago interrupted my dogmatic slumber and gave a completely different direction to my researches in the field of speculative philosophy" (Kant 2004: 10). Kant acknowledges Hume's point that the causal claims we make about the world are not warranted by empirical evidence alone. We never literally "see" causes, we only infer them from the other evidence. When watching billiard balls bounce off of one another on a table, we easily note correlations: when this ball touches that ball, it stops but the other ball starts moving. Hume is right: no "cause" appears in our field of vision—only moving balls. One might argue that there's a "transfer of energy" from one ball to the next, forcing the next one to move, but such energies are inferred from the evidence, not seen. Healthy skepticism perhaps requires us to admit that correlation is all we have empirical evidence for (I will return to this point when discussing the concept of causation in the chapter on ideology). Kant acknowledges Hume's point that causation is literally not visible, but he adds that is only because causal claims depend not only on empirical evidence but *also* on human cognition that contributes elements *not contained in the phenomenal field*: "our experiential cognition is a *composite* of that which we receive through impressions *and* that which our own cognitive faculty (merely prompted by sensible impressions) provides out of itself" (Kant [1781] 1998: 136, emphases mine). That is to say, Hume was right that while we do not see a cause on the billiard table—only rolling billiard balls— that is because claims about causes in part come not only from empirical evidence but also from human thought.

Kant uses the terms "a priori" and "a posteriori" to draw attention to the distinction between what is true on the basis of evidence, and what is true on the basis of something other than evidence. For Kant, what is "a priori" concerns things provided by cognition that aren't provided by experience (that is, the collection of information using sensory perception), while "a posteriori" refers to things that we can only know after having conducted empirical investigations. The traditional example of an *a priori* claim is "all bachelors are unmarried." It is not necessary to do any empirical research to discover whether bachelors are unmarried—all bachelors are unmarried because "unmarried" is part of the definition of "bachelor." By contrast, to discern whether there are any bachelors living in one's neighborhood, someone must go and look. *A priori*, a bachelor is unmarried; *a posteriori*, perhaps upon investigation there are five bachelors in my neighborhood.

I would argue that to make the most of Kant's terminology here, we ought to accept a position he would have rejected: *whether a claim is* a priori *true depends on conventions of language*. As should already be clear, it is not a foregone conclusion that everyone uses the word "God" in the same way. For Kant, *a priori* God is infinite or unconditioned because that's how Kant has defined "God" in the first place. For commonsense theists who think of God as just a more powerful being separate from them, "God" may not be *a priori* infinite (and these theists might not even know what "infinite" technically means). If we change our conventions, which things are true *a priori* will change as well. To be clear, I do not think that Kant thought of *a priori* knowledge as based on conventions in this way; for Kant, what was *a priori* true for one human was *a priori* true for *all* humans. However, there's no reason we need to adopt his more supernatural, nonempirical way of talking about *a priori* knowledge. Thinking of *a priori* truth in terms of conventions saves what is most useful about his vocabulary and drops what is, at least for me, far less useful.

This distinction is useful for thinking carefully about why students studying symbolic logic or algebra need not perform empirical research to complete their studies. Because of how we define terms such as "two," "plus," "equals," and "four," it is *a priori* true (provided we're using a base-10 number system and not a base-2 system) that 2+2=4; while it might be useful to illustrate the point using, for instance, a collection of apples, no empirical research is actually necessary to determine the truth of the mathematical equation. By contrast, all empirical sciences require not only understanding the concepts of the discipline but also research on the world using those concepts. Math concerns *a priori* findings; chemistry concerns *a posteriori* findings.

The third thing we must keep in mind when trying to understand Kant is that by the time he wrote the *Critique of Pure Reason*, the classical arguments for the existence of God were beginning to be widely rejected (Hegel, writing just a generation later, suggests that by the beginning of the nineteenth century they were "obsolete" [Hegel [1830] 2010: 30]). In *Dialogues concerning Natural Religion,* Hume offers devastating critiques of the previously popular arguments for the existence of God. (Note: although Kant had not read Hume's *Dialogues concerning Natural Religion* [(1779) 1990] before publishing the *Critique of Pure Reason*,[3] I cite Hume because he offers what is in my opinion the clearest presentation of the criticisms that were circulating in Europe at the time.) I cannot review all of Hume's criticisms of the arguments for the existence of God; one example should suffice for my immediate purposes. Consider the cosmological argument for the existence of God. In sum, the cosmological argument makes two assumptions: (1) everything has a cause and (2) the world exists and, consequently, must have a cause. What is the cause that brought about the existence of the world? It cannot be just any cause. Consider an analogy: every child has a parent (in the biological sense), and each parent in turn must have had a parent, and so forth. We might be able to imagine an infinite chain of parents and children stretching backwards and forwards from our present moment, but looking backwards we would be stuck with an infinite regress without a starting point—that is, this infinite chain *as a whole* would not have a cause. Since all things have causes (such is the premise of the cosmological argument), this cannot be true. Consequently, the theist claims, the only way to account for the existence of the whole infinite chain of causation in the first place is by positing that there must be an unconditioned, infinite, eternal being who is his own cause—an unmoved mover, to use Aristotle's term for a being that causes other things but is not caused himself[4]—that creates the whole causal chain. (Of course, they had no empirical evidence that this being was a "he," but they never would have referred to "him" in any other way; attention to the difference between *a priori* and *a posteriori* reveals that many of the things humans hold to be true are apparently based on something other than evidence.)

> In the infinite chain or succession of causes and effects, each single effect is determined to exist by the power and efficacy of the cause, which immediately preceded; but the whole eternal chain or succession, taken together, is not

determined or caused by any thing: And yet it is evident that it requires a cause or reason, as much as any particular object, which begins to exist in time.

(Hume 1990: 99)

Thus the cosmological argument for the existence of God concludes we must "have recourse to a necessarily existent being, who carries the REASON"—that is, the cause—"of his existence in himself; and who cannot be supposed not to exist without an express contradiction" (Hume 1990: 99).

Hume is unpersuaded by the cosmological argument, because the solution—that there is an eternal being outside of or unconditioned by time and space that created time and space and the chain of cause and effect that takes place within it—violates the premises. If everything is to have a cause, and if causes and effects are in time—in the sense that causes *by definition and a priori* temporally come before effects—then a being could only cause the world to exist if that being temporally came *before* the effect. An eternal being that exists unconditioned by time and space cannot have caused the world to exist because causation always takes place within time and space, and hence such a being would have to exist *in time and before* the causal chain. How can the infinite chain or succession of cause and effect in our temporal world "have a cause; since that [causal] relation implies a priority in time and a beginning of existence" (Hume 1990: 101)? *A priori*, a being outside of time *cannot cause anything* in time, because we typically define "cause" as "what came before." It is for this reason that some physicists suggest that speaking of the causes of the big bang is nonsensical—before the big bang time did not exist (at least according to the best empirical evidence we have at present), and as such the question asks us to find what temporally came before temporality existed.

Kant was persuaded that this sort of criticism was right, although based on a technicality. He reviews these sorts of criticisms in the part of the *Critique of Pure Reason* titled the "Transcendental Dialectic." He goes through a definition of what it means to say that a being is conditioned or unconditioned (see Kant [1781] 1998: 464–466), and then goes on to point out that when we speak of the causes of the origin of the world and the relation of the world to the unconditioned, we're led into contradictions of exactly the sort Hume pointed to. Remember, for Hume a being outside of time cannot cause anything within time, because to be a cause means "to come before" (i.e., *in time*). As Kant puts it, if an unconditioned being were to cause beings in time to come into existence, "it would have to begin to act then, and its causality would belong *in time*"; "consequently, it itself, the cause, would not be outside the world, which *contradicts what was presupposed*" (491, emphases mine).

Kant's path directed him to attempt to reconcile this criticism—which he accepted as *a priori* true, based on what words such as "unconditioned," "cause," and "time" mean in the first place—with his own desire to offer reasons for which we nevertheless ought to accept that there is an infinite, unconditioned, eternal God. For Kant, the problem is that our knowledge about causes and effects only apply to things we experience, but not to those things—like God—that are unconditioned by time and space and therefore—*a priori*—lie outside of our experience. "Critique" was, for Kant, a way to limit the reach of claims about causes and effects.

Kant opposes critique to dogmatism: dogmatism makes claims for which we do not have warrant in our experiences by refusing to recognize the limits of thought. A dogmatist "pledges himself to extend human cognition beyond all bounds of possible experience" (Kant [1781] 1998: 102). By contrast, critique entails reflexively attending to the limits of reason or empirical knowledge. In particular, empirical knowledge is constrained by conditions of possibility: time and space. Without time and space, we could not experience the world. To offer my own example: in fictional worlds portrayed in movies, time can be frozen, although some subjects are capable of moving around in space despite the fact that it is frozen for everyone else. As such, time is not really frozen so much as time is frozen for some subjects but not others—time is decidedly not frozen for those subjects moving around while everyone else stands still. If time were truly frozen—for everyone—no one would experience anything. Consequently, time is one crucial condition of possibility of experience and knowledge; without time we could not have knowledge. For Kant, all empirical knowledge worth its salt requires warrant from experience—we have no business claiming to have empirical knowledge of things outside of our experiences. In general, then, *"critique" attends to the limits of knowledge by drawing attention to its conditions of possibility.*

From this perspective, *a priori* we can have no empirical evidence for God, who is unconditioned, namely, unlimited by time or space, in which case by definition God cannot appear in time or space. When speaking from experience, "the unconditioned cannot be thought at all without contradiction" (Kant [1781] 1998: 112, emphasis removed). As all objects we experience are, *a priori*, in time and space, we cannot experience God. However, if we separate our experience of things from things as they are in and of themselves, or if we separate our representations of things from things-in-themselves, "the contradiction disappears ... [O]ur representation of things as they are given to us does not conform to the these things as they are in themselves" (112, emphasis removed). Things-in-themselves are, on this view "supersensible" (112), that is, beyond the senses. The "unconditioned ... [is] beyond the boundaries of all possible experience" (112). "Souls" and "free will" are other things in themselves that we cannot experience. We can think them, but we cannot experience them and, as such, cannot have empirical knowledge of them. Perhaps the most telling statement in the *Critique of Pure Reason* is the following: *"I had to deny knowledge in order to make room for faith"* (117, emphasis mine).

Arguably, Kant's most infamous terminological invention is the distinction between phenomena and noumena. Phenomena is what appears to us (in time and space), while noumena is what does not appear to us. Things-in-themselves—like God, souls, free will—lie outside of experience and are therefore classified as noumena. For Kant, *a priori* we can have no empirical knowledge of noumena. At the end of the day, here is the lesson Kant wants readers to learn from applying "critique": *we can go on talking about God, souls, and free will, despite the fact that we have no empirical evidence for them.* The fact that this is where he wants to end up might help us explain the twists and turns he takes to get there, which are often confusing and unpersuasive to those of us who don't share his desire to keep talking about God.

So Kant considers the challenge met: of course Hume and others were technically right that the cosmological argument doesn't make sense and contradicts itself, but that's only because it attempts to make empirical claims about things that are not empirical. Our knowledge is constrained by conditions of possibility that make God literally unseen, unheard, untouchable. Those constraints limit empirical knowledge, but simultaneously make room for faith.

I will argue below that the concept of noumena—or the idea of things-in-themselves—is useless for all practical purposes, for reasons outlined by Hegel. However, the concept of "critique" remains useful; Kant was right that empirical knowledge is in fact constrained or limited by conditions of possibility, and attention to those conditions is useful for those of us who wish to avoid making knowledge claims that lack empirical warrant.

In summary, thus far I have argued:

- Kant uses the term "God" as a technical term, referring to a being that is infinite, unlimited, or unconditioned, rather than the common sense use of the term "God";
- although he does not use the terms in quite this way, in my opinion the most useful way to appropriate "a priori" and "a posteriori" is the following: "a priori" truths concern things that are logically true because of how terms are defined, whereas "a posteriori" claims concern what requires empirical investigation for their warrant;
- Kant accepted the devastating criticisms of the arguments for the existence of God—we cannot make empirical claims about an unconditioned god without contradiction; and consequently
- he claims that his god is beyond empiricism, so of course we cannot speak of his god empirically without contradiction—although we can have faith in him.

While I am by no means a Kantian, in my opinion we have Kant to thank for putting the final nail in the coffin for attempts to make empirically supported claims about infinite divine beings outside of our world.

G. W. F. Hegel, Things-for-Us, and Further Conditions of Possibility of Knowledge

On my reading, Hegel's most useful criticisms of Kant's idea of noumena are the following. First, on Hegel's view, Kant contradicts himself when it comes to talking about an unconditioned god because noumena *a priori* and by definition cannot appear in phenomena. As such, Kant's unconditioned, infinite god is *conditioned or limited* by the boundary between noumena and phenomena. Kant's god is, *a priori, outside* phenomena, in which case it is no longer infinite. Because he separates his god from the empirical world, *a priori* "the *infinite* (i.e., God) is in this way represented as *grounded and dependent*" (Hegel [1830] 2010: 98). Elsewhere he puts it this way, "Here infinity is rigidly set over against finitude, although it is easy to see that when both are opposed to each other the infinity, which is supposed to be the whole, appears as *one side* only and is bounded by the finite. A bounded infinity, however, is itself something merely finite" (69). This is why Hegel defends Spinoza, who—on Hegel's view—understands better than Kant that if his god is to be unconditioned, we must "merge[] God with nature" (98). For Hegel, this isn't some radical metaphysical claim about the nature of God (or *spirit*, Hegel's favorite term for what is unconditioned); rather, this is just an immanent critique that is *a priori* true *based on how Kant himself defines terms such as "God," "unconditioned," and "infinite."*

Second, and more importantly for my purposes, according to Hegel we should dispense with the idea of the thing-in-itself because, *a priori*, quite literally we can know nothing empirical about it. In *The Science of Logic*, Hegel points out that, on Kant's view, by definition, "things in themselves ... [do] not fall within the scope of knowledge" (Hegel [1832] 2010: 26). The *"thing-in-itself"* is for all practical purposes a "nothingness" (27). The only thing we need to know about things-in-themselves is that we can't know anything about them, so let's move on to something we can know. At one point Hegel jokes that people wrongly complain that things-in-themselves are hard to comprehend; for Hegel, since the concept identifies something that we can attach no predicates to, they are empty, practically nothing—in which case they are *easy to understand* because *a priori* there's nothing to know about them.[5] As John McCumber puts it, for Hegel "the thing in itself is not really unknowable; indeed, everything about it can be known perfectly, since there is nothing in it. The thing in itself is therefore ... the easiest of all things to know" (McCumber 2014: 54). At the end of the day, things-in-themselves "neither can nor need be spoken of" with any substance (55). Rather than focus on the thing-in-itself—or the realist's idea of "the world as it is in itself, independent of consciousness"—Hegel suggests the only empirically useful way to talk about things is to describe *how they appear to us*; we cannot say anything empirical about the thing-in-itself, but we can say lots about *things-for-us*. As Jean Hyppolite puts it in one of his essays on Hegel, on Kant's view, we are left with "ineradicable skepticism, or a critical philosophy which distinguishes on the one hand an objective truth relative to human understanding and on the other an absolute, inaccessible in-itself which can only be the object of faith, or a radical transcendentalism" (Hyppolite 1969: 170). By contrast—and this is the crucial point—Hegel "rejects any notion of transcendence ... *There is no question of another world; there is no thing-in-itself, no transcendence*" (170, emphasis mine).

Notably, Kant comes to almost the same conclusion in the *Critique of Pure Reason*. He notes that referring to "real things" independently of how they appear to us "has no meaning at all" (Kant [1781] 1998: 512). However, he immediately backs away from this point to separate "real things" from "things-in-themselves"; apparently it is nonsense to speak of "real things" outside of how they appear to us, unless those things are "things-in-themselves," for instance, God, souls, and free will. For Hegel, this is one more example of Kant not following his argument to its logical conclusion.

Hegel is quite cavalier and glib about when he discusses Kant's idea of the thing-in-itself because he's incensed that these points needed to be said. And he's not wrong: based on Kant's conventions, by definition nothing about noumena is phenomenally relevant. *A priori*, no one has ever seen a thing-in-itself, nor will they ever. For those of us who live in a phenomenal world, we lose nothing empirically of value by abandoning concepts that don't allow us to know anything. "Nothing is *known* that is not in *experience*" (Hegel [1807] 2018: 462). Things-*for-us* are the only things worth talking about—and all knowledge of those "things" is mediated by rather than independent of consciousness.

However, Hegel does not reject the value of critique: knowledge does in fact have conditions of possibility, and those conditions limit knowledge; consequently we should pay attention to those conditions lest we make claims for which we do not have empirical evidence. His first major work, *Phenomenology of Spirit*, considers how things phenomenally appear to us. Note: for Hegel, "spirit" is by definition infinite—*a priori*, there can be nothing outside of spirit (if there were, "infinity" wouldn't be truly "without limit"). Consequently, humans are part of spirit, and what appears to humans is also part of spirit. Spirit is, for all practical purposes, "what appears." *A priori*, the book you are holding in your hands is—if you can see it or touch it—a manifestation of spirit. On my interpretation, for Hegel, spirit isn't a grand metaphysical mystery—it's just his word for "all the stuff there ever was and ever will be that we can see and talk about." (During Hegel's life, public figures in Germany could lose their job and their livelihood if they were identified as atheists,[6] so I suspect that Hegel continued to use the Christian language of "spirit" not because he had great faith in a supernatural world but rather because speaking otherwise did not serve his immediate material interests.) Like Kant, Hegel accepts that knowledge of the phenomenal world is conditioned by time and space. That is why if we look at a "thing" from one perspective it might look different than if we looked at it from another perspective; similarly, if we look at a thing tomorrow it might look different than it does today. For Hegel, what we should do is incorporate as many of the following as possible: new vocabularies, phenomenally available empirical evidences that appear when we use those vocabularies, and theories that help understand, explain, and better manipulate empirical matters in ways that serve our collective interests—the more perspectives we gather, the less alien the phenomenal world will be to us. This is why Hegel insists in one of his books on the logic that philosophy must always be done alongside the empirical sciences, not in contrast with them: "It is a pernicious prejudice that philosophy finds itself in opposition to knowledge gained from sensory experience … Far from opposing [empirical matters], the thoughtful mind enters deeply into their content, and learns and strengthens itself in their midst" (Hegel [1830] 2010: 9). At one point he goes so far as to say that philosophy itself *is* an empirical science (35)—perhaps because studying *a priori* matters by definition entails empirical investigations of how people use words.

Hegel of course would not deny that at any particular point in time, there might be some things that we have not yet seen; we can always imagine that, if we used a particular category, we might find things we hadn't seen before having used the category. Hegel only denies that we learn anything empirically valuable by talking about such things prior to having seen them. Things-for-us are the only things of practical use, and the appearance of those particular things are contingent upon their phenomenal availability, our perception, *and the vocabulary we use to pick them out*.[7]

For Hegel, Kant was close to being right about these matters. Kant was right, for instance, to claim that many things we talk about never appear in the phenomenal field. As I write in my backyard, I see the trees in my backyard, my cat sitting next to me on the back porch, and the lawn that is grossly overdue for a mow. However, if we reflect on it, we'll realize that it seems like we never do have direct phenomenal evidence for time or space. I can see trees, cats, and grass, but I don't see the "space" in which they are sitting—that "space" is invisible. Similarly, I can't see "time." I can see that as the wind blows, the leaves in the trees move, and I can infer that it must be true that we live in time, because how else could we account for the leaves' movement? It seems unlikely that they could move if they were frozen in time. However, at no point does "time" enter the phenomenal field of vision—only moving leaves. Time and space are *a priori*, which, readers will recall, concern what is not provided by the phenomenological field but, instead, the mind. Hegel accepts that *of course Kant was right*: all categories are *a priori* matters—including time and space but also many others—that never appear in the phenomenological field.

A radical consequence: not only can things-in-themselves not appear in the phenomenological field, but neither can *any* "things." Categories are boundary-markers, but boundaries are provided by the mind, not by the phenomenal field. The concepts we use to think about the world simply don't appear in the phenomenal field. They are cognitive, not empirical; they are *a priori* matters, not *a posteriori* matters. Hegel explicitly writes, "To be sure, the content of the categories is indeed not perceivable through the senses, it is not spatio-temporal" ([1830] 2010: 88). If I were a biologist, I might think I'm looking at "part of an ecosystem" when gazing at the "trees" in my "backyard." I'm not sure how biologists precisely define ecosystem, but it is clear that the boundaries between "ecosystem" and "not ecosystem" aren't in my phenomenological field—if they were I wouldn't have to learn a biologists' special vocabulary. In addition, the boundary between my yard and my neighbor's yard is similarly not empirical. I might be able to see a fence that marks the boundary, but that fence is not the basis for the boundary—the basis for the boundary is a selection of records held by city officials. For a "thing" like an "ecosystem" or a "yard" to appear to us, more than phenomenal evidence is required. The appearance of the ecosystem is of course contingent upon phenomenal evidence, *but also upon the* a priori *categories* used to divide up the phenomenal field. The appearance of a yard is contingent upon phenomenal evidence, *but also on the city records that* a priori *define* where my yard ends and the neighbor's yard begins. Prior to the addition of the *a priori*, "things" cannot appear. Ecosystems and yards are, *a priori*, things-for-us. Thus when I say that no "thing" ever appears in the phenomenal field, all I mean is that—for someone like Hegel—since boundaries are not contained in the phenomenal field, thingness appears to be contingent upon the categories.

Hegel's method is called "dialectical," which is just a fancy word for what we would normally refer to as "integrating new vocabularies and new empirical evidences." Hegel read as widely as he could and attempted to incorporate all empirical knowledge available during his time period into one complete narrative. He was up to date on the latest scientific accounts of the natural sciences and read every book available to him about human culture—from ancient cultures to modern ones, and from every corner of the world. Of course, much of what was available to him at the time was, in retrospect, unreservedly racist, sexist, etc. In addition, Hegel seems to have spent little time reflecting on his own ethnocentrism. Thus while he reads and writes about things such as Hinduism or Buddhism, his incorporation of the views of his day was constrained or conditioned by his European prejudices and the fact that the available evidence was mostly written by colonialist, racist Christians hostile to Hinduism and Buddhism. This is why many of the things he says about these cultural traditions are often repugnant to contemporary readers. Hegel hoped to systematically integrate all forms of knowledge available to him, but his integration was conditioned by his chauvinism and the nature of the empirical reports to which he had access.

Regarding this last point: Hegel constantly emphasizes that knowledge is *mediated* or *conditioned*. We might hold it as true that "there is a book on my desk," but that knowledge is *mediated by* the fact that I can see or touch it. If no one could see or touch such a book, we couldn't have knowledge of it. In addition, presumably none of you readers have visual or tactile access to my desk at the moment in time or space that you are reading this. Consequently, for us to hold it as true that "there is—or was—a book on my desk," you would have to understand what "there," "book," and "desk" mean, and you would have to trust my judgment; language and trust are crucial *conditions of possibility of knowledge*. Beings that do not use language could not hold as true those claims we find in university libraries. Similarly, Hegel's knowledge of Hinduism and Buddhism was *mediated by* the fact that it was gathered by his racist contemporaries.

One further point crucial to understanding Hegel's "dialectical" approach is that the vocabularies or categories we use to talk about the world *inevitably change*. In the clearest survey of his views of modern philosophy—found in the *Encyclopedia of the Philosophical Sciences in Basic Outline, Part I: The Science of Logic* ([1830] 2010)—he reviews the claims made by Hume and Kant (among others), but throughout points to what vocabulary terms they use that are worth saving (e.g., the distinction between *a priori* and *a posteriori*), but also what terms are not worth saving (e.g., noumena). The history of the physical sciences reveals that vocabularies often change as new evidence comes to light or as scientists come up with new ways to account for anomalies that can't be explained very well using existing vocabularies. Physicists once referred to an "ether," a medium that allowed light and heat to pass through space; eventually physicists completely abandoned the term as useless for explaining how light and heat work; other categories, it turned out, were more useful. In one chapter in the *Phenomenology of Spirit* Hegel takes up and considers the vocabulary of phrenology and the empirical claims some of his contemporaries made using that vocabulary, but he comes to the conclusion that phrenology's findings are ultimately not sufficiently warranted to be of use in explaining human behavior. "The skull-bone is not an organ of [cognitive] activity ... Neither theft, nor murder, etc., is committed by the skull-bone ... Nor does [the skull-bone] even have the value of a *sign*" that reliably points to a subject's character (Hegel [1807] 2018: 194).

On the contrary, according to the available empirical evidence, the relationship between one's skull and one's character is entirely contingent (195). Dialectical thought involves attempting to incorporate new vocabularies that draw attention to particular empirical evidences, seeing how they fit with the other vocabularies and evidences with which one is already familiar, and either keeping or abandoning them on the basis of whether or not they are useful.

Notably, when we change our vocabulary, the things that appear to us change as well. Although here I am jumping ahead in my story of the concept of "critique," it is worth noting that Foucault illustrates this point quite clearly in *The Birth of the Clinic* (1994). There Foucault notes that over time the language doctors use to talk about the body has radically shifted—no contemporary scientist refers to the four humors, for instance. But what doctors in the past saw in the body was shaped by the vocabulary they used. Ancient Greeks *saw* blood, yellow bile, black bile, and phlegm when they looked at bodies; contemporary doctors are more likely to see things like atopic dermatitis, herpes zoster, urticarial, or rosacea. As Foucault writes, "How can we be sure that an eighteenth century doctor did not see what he saw" (Foucault 1994: x)? Foucault summarizes his task of *The Birth of the Clinic* as a whole: "The research that I am undertaking here therefore involves a project that is deliberately both historical and *critical*, in that it is concerned … with determining the *conditions of possibility of medical experience* in modern times" (xix; emphasis mine). That is to say, the project is explicitly one of critique, in the sense of considering conditions of possibility of biomedical knowledge, which usually involve technical vocabularies.

Returning to Hegel, he makes quite clear that for philosophy to be intelligible, one must learn a vocabulary that is largely alien to common sense. Most people, according to Hegel, lack the patience to do so (Hegel [1830] 2010: 31). When first learning a new vocabulary, "consciousness feels as if it had lost the ground in which it is otherwise so firmly rooted and at home" (31). "As a result, those writers, preachers, speakers, etc., are regarded as the most *intelligible* who tell their readers or listeners things which they knew already by heart: things which are familiar to them and *self-evident*" (31). To think new things, to think beyond what is already self-evident, we must use new words and concepts—a painstaking affair.

For Hegel, the problem with prior philosophers—like the empiricists—is that they tended to use colloquial categories or concepts and assumed that because they found what those categories bring into relief, those things they discovered must have existed noncontingently and that the colloquial categories are all we need. Hegel derides Kant for uncritically accepting twelve basic metaphysical categories without justification.[8] "The Kantian philosophy did not consider the categories in and for themselves, … [and] still less did it subject to criticism the forms of the concepts that make up the content of ordinary logic. What it did, rather, is to pick a portion of them … and simply accepted them as valid" (Hegel [1832] 2010). Hegel, by contrast, insists that we must introduce an indefinite number of categories, consider what each brings into relief, and justify the use of the ones we employ on the basis of their serviceability for accomplishing practical projects. It is unlikely, for instance, that a chemist gets very far in understanding "water" by only using colloquial categories such as "water"; nor will she get very far in using Kant's twelve basic metaphysical categories. To understand water, contemporary chemists will need further categories, for instance, "hydrogen," "oxygen," "molecule," "atom," "proton," "neutron," and "electron."[9] The difference between classical empiricism and Hegel's approach concerns "the … modification of the categories" (Hegel [1830] 2010: 37). Hegel of course accepts some of the empiricists' findings, but "develops them further and transforms them with the help of *additional categories*" (37, emphasis mine).

In fact, Hegel's *Science of Logic* starts with some basic concepts, such as "being," but he notes that saying that something "is" or that it "exists"—by itself—doesn't tell us much of interest about a "thing," particularly because what a thing "is" changes over time By contrast, he argues, a concept such as "becoming" is far more useful because it invites us to attend to the fact that all "things" are temporally contingent. "Becoming" overcomes some of the weaknesses of basic categories like "being," but Hegel goes further to argue that even "becoming" is inadequate and deserves further, more sophisticated consideration in relationship to other concepts. Similarly, as already noted, he finds the concept of the "thing-for-us" to be more useful than the concept of the "thing-in-itself" (see Hegel [1832] 2010: 93–100). He walks his readers through a consideration of the usefulness of concepts such as "existence," "being-for-itself," "being-for-others," and so forth. As George di Giovanni notes in the introduction to his translation of the *Science of Logic*, the book is not about "things" but rather on the categories we use to talk about things.

> Hegel's thesis is that, starting from the least that one can say about an object in general while still making sense, one can proceed to identify sets of predicates, namely the categories, each of which defines the limits of a type of discourse suited to the subject matter. Each set is arrived at by virtue of a reflection upon the prior [categories] … The Logic itself is a discourse about discourse which … defines the norm of intelligibility against which all other types of discourse, all of them more or less open-ended in their own spheres are to be measured.
>
> (Hegel [1832] 2010: xxxv)

That is to say: this book is about which categories are most useful for understanding the world. On Hegel's view, the categories we use are not part of the furniture of the universe but rather historically specific human inventions that help us make the universe intelligible to ourselves. One of Kant's biggest failures, for Hegel, is to not recognize that his categories are historical and social creations. Since Hegel values concepts such as "becoming" over "being," this is no surprise—we *become* knowledgeable over time as we interact with the world, and our categories become different as a result (see Hegel [1832] 2010: lxi). It is for this reason that Hegel insists that the division of his book into sections on concepts such as "being," "existence," "quantity," "quality," etc., are "only of historical value" (34). The division of the book is merely "provisional" (38) or "preliminary" (56), because it is based on the thoughts of someone historically situated at a particular place and time (38). He anticipates that the way we talk about categories might (and arguably must) change—that's why philosophy must constantly work alongside the always-changing empirical sciences.

I would add something that Hegel does not draw attention to: the use of competing vocabularies might be necessary even for understanding *the same "thing."* Consider something like what is called "holy water." We could study it from the perspective of chemistry, and in doing so we would probably break down a sample of holy water into its chemical components. Presumably a contemporary biologist would break the sample down not into its chemical components but rather attend to the microorganisms that might exist in the water. Someone using discourse analysis might point to the fact that calling some water "holy" and other water "not holy" arguably functions to reinforce the authority of the Catholic priesthood (for, according to Catholic doctrine, only priests can make regular water "holy," no matter its chemical or biological composition). Describing "holy water" in all of these ways requires the use of a wide variety of vocabularies; no one vocabulary tells the whole story. In addition, insofar as one adopts one vocabulary rather than another, one will literally "see" different things in the water. A chemist using only the vocabularies and theories of the discipline of chemistry literally cannot "see" the "Catholic priesthood"—that's not a concept we would ever find in a chemistry textbook; by contrast, those of us who use only the vocabulary and theories of the academic study of religion quite literally cannot "see" protons, neutrons, and electrons in what we study. Last, it's worth noting that which vocabulary one chooses likely depends on the particular questions or investments one has—it's not a foregone conclusion that molecules are intrinsically more interesting than bacteria, or that bacteria are intrinsically more interesting than social reproduction.

If Hegel is right that the only empirical claims worth taking seriously are ones that have warrant in phenomenal experience, "objective" truth would—theoretically—require us to integrate *all* phenomenal evidence, evidence brought into relief using the widest possible range of categories or vocabularies. A partial perspective is by definition subjective, relative—knowing what is true only from a particular perspective or within a particular vocabulary will not give us objective knowledge. "When thinking remains at a standstill," philosophers are guilty of "formalism" (Hegel [1830] 2010: 41), or what Kant might have called "dogmatism." True thinking requires *development*. The "empirical sciences do not stand still" (41), and neither should philosophy. Anything deserving of being called "knowledge" is therefore the result or "product" of "activity" (57). On the one hand, if we remove the role of thinking persons from our account of the conditions of knowledge, we can't make sense of knowledge; on the other hand, since the humans that produce knowledge are finite beings, fully integrated, objective, or unconditioned knowledge is *a priori* unobtainable.

In this section, I have argued that we can learn the following valuable lessons by attending to Hegel's writings:

- Hegel rightly suggests that insofar as nothing empirical can be known, *a priori*, about things-in-themselves, there is nothing empirically useful about speaking of them—on the contrary, the only things empirically relevant are things-for-us;

Discourse and Ideology

- which things appear to us depend in part on the categories or vocabularies one uses to bring into relief what is of interest to us in the phenomenal field;
- we should consider the widest range of vocabularies and the empirical evidences brought into relief using those vocabularies, and adopt what is most useful for our practical purposes; and, last,
- Hegel still accepts that Kant's concept of critique is useful but insists that the conditions of possibility of knowledge are more complicated than Kant allows, as Kant excludes historically or socially specific conditions as empirically relevant for understanding phenomena.

Note: I do not find all of Hegel's categories, concepts, or arguments useful for my project. Notably, given the immediate purposes of this book, I have not found it helpful to integrate, for instance, concepts such as "spirit," "religion," "absolute knowing," or "teleology," among others. Additionally, I have no use for his analysis of culture, which tends to be inflected with Euro-centric chauvinism. However, I also think that dialectically picking and choosing from the history of human thought what is most useful at present fulfills the spirit[10] of his project, if not the letter.

Poststructuralism and the Conditions of Impossibility of Knowledge

Phenomenology is the philosophical tradition that follows Kant and Hegel's lead: phenomenologists describe how things appear to us in the phenomenal world and draw attention to the conditions of possibility that make those appearances possible.[11] Like Kant, in *Ideas* ([1873] 2014) Edmund Husserl emphasized time and space as conditions of possibility for knowledge, but he completely dropped Kant's Christian agenda and talk about God, souls, and free will (Husserl's place in this intellectual tradition is particularly important for understanding poststructuralism, but a careful consideration of Husserl's work will have to wait until the next chapter). In *Phenomenology of Perception* ([1945] 2012), Maurice Merleau-Ponty emphasized material bodies as conditions of possibility for knowledge. In *Being and Time* ([1953] 1996), Martin Heidegger emphasized time above all else as a condition of possibility for the appearance of subjectivity or, to use his technical term, Da-sein. For Heidegger, time is a condition of possibility of subjectivity. Subjects unfold in time and, as such, are never "complete" or "whole." Just as truly "objective" knowledge would only come at the end of the integration of *all* phenomenal knowledge, Heidegger suggests that the subject is complete only at the end. "As long as Da-sein *is* as a being, it has never attained its 'wholeness.' But if it does, this gain becomes the absolute loss of being-in-the-world" (Heidegger [1953] 1996: 220). That is to say, living subjects are never complete; the only complete subject would be dead, in which case it would no longer be a subject. *A priori*, what it means to be a subject is to be by definition incomplete.

Poststructuralism developed out of phenomenology and builds upon its central insights. Here I stipulatively define poststructuralism as the philosophical tradition best exemplified by the writings of Jacques Derrida, Michel Foucault, and Judith Butler—all three of whom were deeply influenced by Hegel. It is often forgotten that Derrida, Foucault, and Butler studied with or were influenced by the works of the French scholar of Hegel, Jean Hyppolite. Hyppolite's major works include a commentary on *Phenomenology of Spirit*, titled *Genesis and Structure of Hegel's Phenomenology of Spirit* ([1946] 1974) and a set of essays on Hegel's *Science of Logic*, titled *Logic and Existence* ([1953] 1997).[12] Foucault, in "The Discourse on Language" (1972) claims to be "infinitely indebted" to Hyppolite. In that lecture, he notes that anti-Hegelianism always risks reconfirming Hegel's philosophy. "If, then, more than one of us is indebted to Jean Hyppolite, it is because he has tirelessly explored, for us, and ahead of us, the path along which we may escape Hegel, keep our distance, and along which we shall find ourselves *brought back to him*" (Foucault 1972: 235, emphasis mine). Hyppolite took Derrida under his wing, so to speak, when he was completing his studies; he supervised Derrida's graduate thesis, encouraged him to publish it, and opened doors to help him secure a university post (see Peeters 2013). One of Derrida's early essays on Hegel, "The Pit and the Pyramid" (Derrida 1982) was "originally presented in Hyppolite's seminar" (see Butler [1987] 1999: 177). The epigraph for this particular book comes from an interview in 1971, in which Derrida makes the rather strong claim that we "will never be finished with the reading or rereading of Hegel, and, in a certain way, I do nothing other than attempt to explain myself on this point" (Derrida 1981: 77). Derrida writes at length about Hegel or Hegelian themes in most of the books he published in the 1960s and 1970s (see Derrida [1962] 1989, [1967] 1976, [1967] 1978, [1967] 2011, [1972] 1981, [1972] 1982, and [1974] 1986). In her first book, *Subjects of Desire: Hegelian Reflections in Twentieth-Century France* ([1987] 1999), Butler includes a section on Hyppolite and in her conclusion demonstrates how both Derrida's and Foucault's works "take up Hegelian themes" inspired by Hyppolite's work (177). Butler continued to write essays on Hegel, which appear in several of her books (see Butler 1997, 2000, 2004; and Butler, Laclau, and Žižek 2000). Together, Derrida and Butler have probably published thousands of pages on Hegel. Poststructuralism, as I'm defining it, is in a way a type of Hegelianism.

Hyppolite's interpretation of Hegel focuses in particular on the fact that all knowledge is made possible because of temporality—time is a crucial condition of the possibility of knowledge development. In time, we perform research, look at the world, touch it and smell it, and gather our findings into an account of what we have experienced. As Butler puts it, in Hyppolite's reading of Hegel, "knowledge ... is only accessible to human consciousness through its own temporal life" (Butler [1987] 1999: 82). Following Hyppolite, Derrida accepts Hegel's insistence that time is a condition of possibility of knowledge, but he suggests that it is also *a condition of impossibility of knowledge*.[13] What does he mean by that? The following example is a gross oversimplification, but for someone like Derrida, *a priori* all knowledge cannot be completely integrated, in part because *in the future* we could always discover new things we had not discovered before. The American pragmatists call this "fallibility": no form of knowledge is infallible because *in the future* we might have evidence that contradicts our existing knowledge claims. For all practical purposes, "widely accepted as true" has the same meaning as

Discourse and Ideology

"not yet contested." For poststructuralists, infallible or objective knowledge—in the sense of knowledge that is unconditioned by any limits—is not achievable because of time. Knowledge is to some extent like Heidegger's Da-sein: time is a condition of the possibility of knowledge, and as long as time continues, knowledge could always change—and if time did stop, there would be no knowledge. Consequently, *a priori* objective knowledge—in the sense of unconditioned by limits that make knowledge partial, perspectival, *limited*—is impossible because time is one of the conditions of the possibility of knowledge. Time is a condition of the possibility of partial knowledge, but simultaneously a condition of *im*possibility of objective, *un*conditioned, or *un*limited knowledge. (Note, saying that "time is a condition of the impossibility of knowledge" is *most definitely not* the same as saying "time is a condition of the impossibility of *objective* knowledge"—the latter seems to be Derrida's point on my interpretation, despite the fact that he sometimes makes claims that sound more like the former.) Without the condition of time, we could not have any knowledge; consequently, no knowledge is unconditioned. "Even the grandest historical actors are not freed of the temporal exigencies that attend any human life" (Butler [1987] 1999: 79). This is true, *a priori*, because of what we mean by the conventions or definitions of concepts such as "knowledge" and "time."[14] Despite Hegel's apparent aspiration to gather together all available ideas and empirical knowledges into a complete, objective whole, he should have known better, because he understood—perhaps more than any previous philosopher (other than the Madhyamika Buddhists, for instance, Nagarjuna)—that knowledge is by definition mediated by conditions that, if only he had thought about it, make knowledge perpetually incomplete.

Deconstruction—Derrida's particular brand of poststructuralism—then, is not an approach to philosophy that attempts to dismantle all knowledge claims or argue that we can know nothing. *Deconstruction is not a form of skepticism.* In an interview that took place in 1991, Derrida claims to have spent thirty years *challenging* the presumption that his work promotes "nihilism, skepticism, or relativism"; "anyone who has read even a little of my work knows this, and it is easy to find out that far from seeking to undermine the university or research in any field, *I actively militate for them*" (Derrida 1995: 402, emphasis mine). Instead, deconstruction is a type of critique, but a form of critique that focuses on what conditions make objective, unconditioned, or unlimited knowledge *a priori* impossible. Yes, Hegel is right that all knowledge is *mediated* by conditions, but he didn't go far enough with this point. As Butler puts it, "Derrida accepts the Hegelian project ... but wants to argue that Hegel's own method for achieving that goal effectively precludes its realization" (Butler [1987] 1999: 178). Hegel accused Kant of not following his argument to its logical conclusion, and Derrida is accusing Hegel of the same. Hegel's claims about "absolute knowing" are, then, mere "pretense" (178) or a "strategy of concealment" (183) that obscures the fact that knowledge, because of the conditions of the impossibility of knowledge, will *a priori* never be "absolute."

Here I have argued the following:

- Derrida, Foucault, and Butler are in a way part of the Hegelian tradition, particularly as passed down through the work of Hyppolite, who—like both

Hegel and Heidegger—drew attention to the fact that knowledge unfolds in time, but time simultaneously places limits on the reach of knowledge;
- Derrida rightly draws attention to the fact that *a priori* conditions of possibility of subjective, conditioned, limited knowledge—like time—are also *a priori* conditions of impossibility of objective, unconditioned, or unlimited knowledge; consequently
- any claim to have achieved objective, unconditioned knowledge is *a priori* empirically unwarranted.

I would add that the very idea of unconditioned or objective knowledge is *a priori* incoherent, as it implores that ideal knowledge be obtained unconditioned by any historically specific conditions of possibility of knowledge—that is, it makes ideal knowledge by definition unobtainable.

Power and Knowledge

Contrary to accounts of knowledge that depict scientific knowledge as ideally apolitical (even as they admit that sometimes scientific knowledge doesn't achieve this ideal), poststructuralists such as Derrida, Foucault, and Butler acknowledge that the production of knowledge seems to be systematically contingent on politics, power relations, and invested researchers. At the most simple level, one cannot produce knowledge without the capital to do so, and arguments about the distribution of capital are *a priori* questions of power; consequently, any knowledge production that is made possible by the availability of capital is in part conditioned by political matters.

Derrida was born in Algeria, a French colony in northern Africa at the time, and therefore it is not surprising that in his early writings Derrida paid particularly close attention to how Eurocentrism and colonialism shaped the claims produced by modern European thinkers. In *Of Grammatology*, Derrida offers a critique of the "knowledge" of other cultures produced by famed twentieth-century anthropologist Claude Levi-Strauss (see in particular the chapter titled "The Violence of the Letter: From Levi-Strauss to Rousseau" [Derrida [1967] 1976: 101–140]). Derrida shows that Levi-Strauss used a vocabulary that in part came from colonialism and, as such, carried positive and negative valuations derived from colonialist discourses. Although Levi-Strauss attempted to invert the valuations as a part of an attempt to defend the Brazilian "primitives" he studied from negative European depictions (that is, his descriptions of their culture romanticized rather than demonized them), he was still stuck in the hierarchical vocabulary of European colonialism. Consequently, the empirical data Levi-Strauss collected using that vocabulary was *conditioned by* the legacy of colonialist ways of dividing up the appropriate control of people and resources across the globe. Despite his anti-colonialist efforts, Levi-Strauss still found that the "primitives" in Brazil lived in ways that inversely mirrored how modern Europeans imagined them. That is, despite

Discourse and Ideology

the fact that he was defending the "primitives" from negative characterizations produced by European anthropologists, he still found that "primitives" were in a way negative images of Europe. *A priori*, he would not have produced the same knowledge had he used a different vocabulary or been situated in a different social and historical context. The power relations of colonialism served as conditions of possibility of the knowledge Levi-Strauss produced.

Foucault was deeply concerned with psychiatry in many of his writings, and it's not difficult to see why: when Foucault was growing up, psychiatrists claiming to be "objective" were giving "homosexuals"—like him—lobotomies. Foucault (not unreasonably) came to the conclusion that apparently objective scientific institutions were perhaps controlled in part by politically invested researchers who used the powers available to them within those institutions to harm the interests of members of social groups they classified as "abnormal." It is not particularly surprising that Foucault ended up writing about the means by which doctors identified people as "mad" or "insane," as well as the asylums they created to physically separate the "insane" from the "sane"; nor is it surprising that he systematically criticized the claims to objectivity made by social scientists from the early modern period to the time in which he was writing.

Poststructuralist feminists such as Butler have long been interested in power and its relation to the invention of gender difference. However, notably some of the most important books written in the last twenty years on gender difference have been written not by poststructuralists in the humanities or social sciences, but by biologists—such as Anne Fausto-Sterling and Rebecca M. Jordan-Young—whose work echoes the claims made by Foucault and Butler. Neither Fausto-Sterling nor Jordan-Young are postmodern relativists who say that when it comes to gender, anything goes. On the contrary, like traditional realists, they seek out empirical evidence for the claims they make about gender difference. What makes their work compatible with the poststructuralist approach I'm defending in this book is that they're attentive to the fact that different discourses produce different realities (in the sense that what we know about the world changes when we change our vocabulary) and acknowledge that social and cultural investments shape scientific research, yet at the same time they attend to the empirical evidence produced by various discourses, showing where the empirical evidence for gender essentialism falls short of the conclusions some invested researchers would like to draw. What is particularly crucial for my purposes is that their evaluation of the evidence and the ontological commitments their work entails are conditioned by the rules of the discourse in which they swim—specifically, the evidentiary rules laid down by twentieth- and twenty-first-century biological sciences. Consequently, while they recognize that scientific research is conditioned by power and that different discourses create different realities, they are simultaneously confident that within a particular discourse, many claims are false or uncorroborated by the evidence considered relevant within the discourse.

Notably, even Judith Butler herself, in *Gender Trouble* (1990), tackles the question of biology in one chapter. Although high school biology courses teach that XX and XY genes produce female and male bodies, respectively, Butler notes that in fact genetic research demonstrates that they do not always produce female and male bodies in the way that mainstream common sense assumes. Some people with XY genes have stereotypically female bodies, whereas some people with XX genes have stereotypically male bodies. Because biologists sometimes define sex in terms of genes and sometimes in terms of external genitalia, the discourse contradicts itself by speaking of "XX-males" and "XY-females." This is incoherent because "it is precisely the designation of male and female that is under question and that is implicitly already decided by the recourse to external genitalia. Indeed, if external genitalia were sufficient as a criterion by which to determine or assign sex, then the experimental research into [genetics] would hardly be necessary at all" (108). "Clearly these are cases in which the component parts of sex do not add up to the recognizable coherence or unity that is usually designated by the category of sex" (108). However, it appears that insofar as the researchers are locked into a set of assumptions tied to a binary view of sex—according to which sex must be either male or female—they are incapable of individuating the plurality of sex phenomena into, say, a spectrum—or multiple spectrums—rather than opposites.

Butler's project is often misunderstood. For instance, according to Jan Rehmann, when it comes to thinking about sexuality, poststructuralism "tends to reduce the social to the symbolic, gendered subjectivities to a shifting play of signification, the body to conventions and norms" (2014: 218). Butler, it seems, ignores biology and turns bodies into words (218). Such claims, however, are not supported by evidence. In her writings, Butler does not reduce bodies to discourse; rather, on the very first page of *Bodies that Matter* she explicitly writes that "to claim that sexual differences are indissociable from discursive demarcation *is not the same as* claiming that discourse *causes* sexual difference" (Butler 1993: 1, emphases mine). For Butler, discourses condition the claims we make about bodies, but discourses are not efficient or material causes of bodies. To say that discourse has "the power to produce" instead means that it has the power to "demarcate ... [or] differentiate" (1).

What is crucial is that Butler's account neither invites skepticism about the existence of the world nor does it devolve into an "anything goes" relativism where, because different discourses produce different realities, we can say anything we want about sex and it will be true. On the contrary, Butler's point is that, *on the discourse's own stipulative definitions, sex is individuated, demarcated, or differentiated in two competing and contradictory ways*—sometimes what makes someone female is having a vulva, and at other times what makes someone female is having XX genes. Butler writes, "the conclusion here is not that valid and demonstrable claims cannot be made about sex-determination, but rather that cultural assumptions regarding the relative status of men and women and the binary relation of gender itself frame and focus the research into sex determination" (Butler 1990: 109). In addition, her point is not that biologists are wrong when they identify two sexes, but rather that when making such identifications biologists trade off of and reproduce commonsense views or assumptions that are not, in and of themselves, strictly scientific. To put it slightly differently: the science of sex difference relies upon a conceptual scheme that is historically contingent and could be otherwise. "Sexual difference ... is never simply a function of material differences which are not in some way both marked and formed by discursive practices" (Butler 1993: 1). All of that is to say: even a so-called "radical" poststructuralist like Butler allows that "valid and demonstrable claims" can be made about objects of scientific research, even if the discursive schemes they employ are neither universal nor uncontested, and despite the fact that a different scheme—particularly ones aligned with different interests—might produce a different reality. Such a poststructuralist approach does not avoid ontological commitments altogether, but merely notes that the ontological commitments we incur are contingent on a wide variety of social factors that may not always hold.

Explicitly drawing from both Foucault and Butler,[15] in *Sexing the Body: Gender Politics and the Construction of Sexuality* (2000) feminist biologist Anne Fausto-Sterling notes that throughout history there have been a wide variety of ways of separating "males" from "females," especially when it comes to subjects who display characteristics that are ambiguous on typical classification schemes. While modern biologists might insist that what makes a male is XY genes while what makes a female is XX genes, what are we to do with those individuals who don't exactly fit in either category, such as those who have XXX or XXY genes? In the past, before genetic testing was invented, human groups determined sex on the basis of a wide variety of criteria, including external genitalia or gonads. At one point, scientists almost defined "hermaphrodism" out of existence because they narrowly defined a hermaphrodite (or intersexual, which is the dominant term used by biologists today) as someone who had an ovary *and* a testis; on this view subjects with two ovaries and a penis were by definition "women," while subjects with two testicles but a vagina were "men." *Nothing about empirical bodies forces us to choose one criterion over others.* "Choosing which criteria to use in determining sex, and choosing to make the determination at all, are social decisions for which scientists can offer no absolute guidelines" and, as such, tend to reflect "political, social, and moral struggles" (Fausto-Sterling 2000: 3).

For instance, contemporary doctors often recommend surgery on the basis of social norms that might affect a child's self-esteem. In the United States, a baby with a large clitoris/small penis might, years later, be made fun of in a girl's locker room for having such an oddly large clitoris, while they might be made fun of in a boy's locker room for having such an oddly small penis, and, consequently, doctors might recommend undergoing surgery to reduce the clitoris and classify the baby as a "girl" (see Fausto-Sterling 2000: 56–63). By contrast, in Saudi Arabia babies with XX genes but "highly masculinized genitalia ... are initially identified as males" (58) because of a social "preference for male offspring" (59). Whether we classify these babies as male or female depends not on their bodies alone—for, as Kant and Hegel note, categories do not appear to us in the phenomenal field—but also on the social investments of those doing the classifying. There are no "males-in-themselves" because maleness is contingent upon the use of the category—with a different category a particular "male" might be reclassified as a "female." By trying to talk about the world-as-it-is-in-itself—independent of consciousness or historically specific categories—we shift our attention *away from rather than closer to* what makes a body male or female. Fausto-Sterling writes:

> we have, Butler says (and I agree), to talk about the material body. There *are* hormones, genes, prostates, uteri, and other body parts and physiologies that we use to differentiate male from female, that become part of the ground from which varieties of sexual experience and desires emerge. … But every time we try to return to the body as something that exists … prior to discourse about male and female, Butler writes, "we discover that matter is fully sedimented with discourses on sex and sexuality that prefigure and constrain the uses to which that term can be put" [Butler 1993: 29].
>
> (Fausto-Sterling 2000: 22)

Yes, male and female bodies matter—as do material hormones, genes, etc.—but without discourse we cannot differentiate such bodies.

Like Butler, Fausto-Sterling does not deny that we can make reliable empirical claims about the world. She writes, "as a biologist, I believe in the material world. As a scientist, I believe in building specific knowledge by conducting experiments. But as a … historian, I also believe that what we call 'facts' about the living world are not universal truths" but are "rooted in" historically contingent social circumstances (Fausto-Sterling 2000: 7). Of course, there are limits to what we can do to our bodies; studies show that telling homosexuals that they have or ought to have straight desires does not appear to be a reliable way of generating straight desires. However, someone with a particular set of bodily capacities might have been classified as one thing in one age and another thing in another age, and that classification may very well shape their desires. For instance, "A person of a particular genetic make-up might or might not become homosexual, depending on the culture and historical period in which he or she was raised" (17). Because ones desires are shaped not only by biology but also by culture, in another age they might have become a sodomist, a gender invert, a sapphist, or a bisexual. According to Serena Nanda in *Gender Diversity: Crosscultural Variations* (2000), in Brazil sexuality is sometimes linked—much like in ancient Greece—first to whether one is "on top" or "on bottom." In some communities, being on top makes one masculine, while being on bottom makes one feminine. Consequently, a man who penetrates another man is a masculine and straight, while the man he penetrates is feminine and homosexual. On this view, two men who penetrate one another are both "lesbians." In these cultural enclaves, "masculinity is associated with penetration and those who do not adhere to the active/passive distinction are stigmatized" (Nanda 2000: 48). It would be misleading to assume that what it means to be a "straight male" is always the same in Brazil as it is in North America or Europe. Through the process of interpellation, "sexuality is a somatic fact *created by* a cultural effect" (Fausto-Sterling 2000: 21). Quoting Elizabeth Grosz, Fausto-Sterling notes, "While acknowledging that we do not understand the range and limits of the body's pliability,

Discourse and Ideology

she insists that we cannot merely 'subtract the environment, culture, history' and end up with 'nature or biology'" (25).

In addition, like Butler, Fausto-Sterling accepts that there are often competing criteria at work within *the same* particular social or historical context. Fausto-Sterling quotes Sherry Ortner:

> no society or culture is totally consistent. Every society/culture has some axes of male prestige and some of female, some of gender equality, and some (sometimes many) exes of prestige that have nothing to do with gender ... [T]he most interesting things about any given case is precisely the multiplicity of logics operating, of discourses being spoken, of practices of prestige and power in play.
>
> (Fausto-Sterling 2000: 19)

Rebecca M. Jordan-Young, in her brilliant book *Brain Storm: The Flaws in the Science of Sex Differences* (2010), addresses exactly this problem in her review of the scientific studies that attempt to discern what makes men's and women's brains different from one another. We would like to think that studies of feminine and masculine behavior—and how those behaviors correlate with particular features of men's and women's brains—cumulatively tell us more and more about what men and women are like. However, Jordan-Young draws attention to the fact that masculinity and femininity are defined differently across different studies, so that meta-studies which pretend to accumulate and build upon existing knowledge end up comparing incomparables but elide that fact.

For example, early brain studies defined high libido as a masculine trait and low libido as a feminine trait. With this definition, scientists could identify masculinized women and feminized men. However, over time scientists' views changed, so that libido was not thought to be a sign of either masculinity or femininity—having a high libido was now thought to be consistent with both masculinity and femininity. The change in definition appears to have gone unnoticed in the literature, however, and brain studies continue to compare the results of older studies with the results of newer studies, as if they were comparable—as if masculinity meant the same thing across all of the studies. This is, as Jordan-Young clearly shows, extremely problematic, at least within scholarly discourses. I would like to quote her at length, because this is a crucial point and one Jordan-Young puts quite pointedly:

> Updating their assumptions about feminine sexuality might seem to be a fairly straightforward matter of scientific progress ... So why the critique? Aren't the changes relayed in the preceding discussion a good thing? Unfortunately ... it's not that simple. ... We might read that two different studies have shown that prenatal androgens "masculinize" women's sexuality, but we can't be confident that those two studies are talking about the same thing—in fact, there's a good chance the studies directly contradict one another. My point is not that updating the definitions is bad, but that updating the definitions has serious consequences for

how brain organization studies can be compared to see if the theory is supported, on the whole, by the evidence.

... I am convinced that [these scientists] are totally unaware of the transformation this key concept has undergone over time in their studies. As I noted early in this chapter, these scientists—like most people, probably—tend to think that masculine and feminine sexuality is a no-brainer. My sense is that over time ... scientists' definitions changed without their even realizing it. ... [O]nce we notice the change, we have to acknowledge that studies with different definitions of feminine sexuality generate irreconcilable evidence about the theory.

(Jordan-Young 2010: 141–142)

Her conclusion? "Their cavalier approach to definitions of their key variables has led them to be conceptually sloppy, and the result is devastating for the existing network of evidence about brain organization" (Jordan-Young 2010: 143). As Hegel noted in his criticism of Kant, if we naively adopt a set of categories without reflecting on why we've chosen them, what makes them useful, or how they might be conditioned by our investments, we're insufficiently paying attention to one of the very important conditions of the possibility of knowledge.

While Anne Fausto-Sterling or Rebecca M. Jordan-Young may not identify as poststructuralist Hegelians, their work fits into this tradition because they emphasize that the world as it appears to us is not dependent only on the world but also on the socially produced and politically contingent classification schemes that serve as conditions of possibility of bringing that world into relief. A neutral observer cannot tell us whether we ought to use a male-female classification scheme that focuses on genetics or one that focuses on gonads. The world itself does not tell us how to classify the world, and if we ignore the investments or relations of power that make classification schemes possible (for instance, do we want to prevent low self-esteem in the locker room, do we prefer male children for reasons related to social prestige, or do we want something else entirely?), we cannot make sense of how the world appears to us one way, while it may appear to someone else another way. Power is a condition of possibility of knowledge that might be worth attending to.

In this section I have suggested:

- social power, capital, authority, privilege, etc. are important conditions of the possibility of knowledge production;
- this is demonstrated even by apparently "realist" biologists who study sex, gender, and sexuality—for instance, the definitional lines separating males and females have changed over time in ways that reflect the investments of those drawing the lines; and
- the "scientific method" offers us no grounds for choosing one definition over others, and consequently to fully understand the conditions that make empirical claims about sex difference possible requires us to take into account the investments of those creating the definitions.

Discourse and Ideology

Conclusion

Returning to our starting point, by definition critique involves—for Kant—attending to the conditions of the possibility of knowledge. Toward this end he draws attention to a distinction between *a priori* and *a posteriori* claims. *A posteriori* knowledge claims are based on empirical evidence, while other claims are *a priori* true completely independently of the empirical evidence provided to us within the phenomenological field. For Kant, what things are *a priori* true for one person are *a priori* true for all persons. By contrast, I suggested that it would be more useful to link *a priori* truth to conventions of language; whether it is *a priori* true that all bachelors are unmarried depends on how we use the convention "bachelor"—it's always possible that the word "bachelor" could be used differently in some communities, in which case in those communities it would no longer be *a priori* true that all bachelors are unmarried. Critique requires attention to what is *a priori* and what is *a posteriori*, because whether empirical claims are warranted depends in part on how we define the terms we're using and in part on what empirical evidence for our claims we've discovered in the phenomenal field.

Hegel accepts Kant's definition of critique as concerning the conditions of possibility of knowledge but drops Kant's distinction between phenomena and noumena, because—on the basis of how Kant defines these terms—*a priori* noumena are not phenomenally relevant. We learn nothing empirically relevant by speaking of the world as it is in-itself; for those of us who live in a phenomenal world, the only empirically relevant matters are things-for-us. In addition, Hegel goes further than Kant by pointing to other conditions of possibility of knowledge; what we accept as "knowledge" changes over time as historical, social, and political conditions change or, to put it slightly differently, what counts as knowledge changes as we are exposed to new vocabularies, new empirical findings, which—*a priori*—unfold *in time*.

Derrida takes up Hegel's project but points out that although time is an important condition of the possibility of knowledge, it is also a condition of the *impossibility* of knowledge, insofar as the future always threatens to ruin what we once took to be certain knowledge. In addition, Derrida, Foucault, and Butler attend to the fact that politics or power relations are also conditions of possibility of knowledge claims—without power, knowledge would not be possible. Their form of critique therefore insists that we must attend to conditions of the possibility of knowledge beyond those emphasized by Kant and Hegel.

Contemporary biologists such as Fausto-Sterling and Jordan-Young are similarly engaged in critique: what claims about gender, sex, and sexuality are accepted as true depends in part on how one defines the relevant terms, in part on *a posteriori* empirical evidence, and in part on the values (which, like the categories, are also not derived from the empirical field) that shape the way we define the relevant and historically specific concepts we use to collect empirical evidence.

The following sorts of claims, then, are what one must accept to be identified as a poststructuralist (at least on my use of the term), most of which are likely uncontroversial:

- empirically warranted knowledge has conditions of possibility;
- "critique" is a method of analysis that draws attention to the conditions of the possibility of knowledge;
- the use of historically specific categories is one of the conditions of the possibility of the sort of knowledge we produce in universities;
- using the category of the thing-in-itself is not particularly useful, as, *a priori*, a thing-in-itself is something we cannot have knowledge of;
- passing off knowledge of things-for-us as if it were knowledge of things-in-themselves is a rhetorical slight-of-hand designed to present conditioned knowledge as if it were unconditioned, or to mask the inevitably situated or perspectival nature of one's knowledge;
- knowledge production is *a priori* open-ended, and thus any claim that one has produced unconditioned or objective knowledge is *a priori* always false;
- the categories we use constantly change, and thus attention to those changes is an important part of critique;
- knowledge is always produced by invested subjects and is made possible by power and capital; and
- the categories we choose to produce knowledge—especially ones that carry positive or negative associations and ones that structure our social formations—may serve the interests of some subjects or groups over others.

If we are going to accept Kant's insistence that empirical claims worth taking seriously require warrant in the phenomenological field, and if what appears to us in the phenomenological field is conditioned by historically specific social and political conditions that do not always hold, then critique remains a useful tool for attending to how social and political conditions limit the reach of warranted knowledge.

CHAPTER 2
THINGS

We cannot have knowledge of things prior to individuating them from the world. For instance, rates of "child abuse" can change dramatically when we change the definition of "child abuse." At one point, children were scientifically counted as abused when X-rays revealed more than a couple of healed fractures (Hacking 1991: 270); on such a definition, only those children who are submitted to the X-ray exam are counted as abused—a narrow set. However, it is "apparent that there are many other ways to harm a child than battering: ranging over topics from neglect amounting to starvation or hypothermia on one side, through prolonged, even lifetime, confinement in a cellar, to incest on the other" (270). Knowledge of a thing like "child abuse" is literally contingent upon how we individuate child abuse, or how we separate it from other things in the world—and that individuation is dependent upon the use of language and subjects or institutions that are, for the most part, deeply invested in preventing child abuse. "Child abuse" is always a thing-for-us.

Derrida has written extensively on these matters, although—to be fair—many readers may have missed this because his writings are often difficult to comprehend. In this chapter I will consider his infamous claim that "there is nothing outside of the text" and will show that it does not mean what people often take it to mean, namely, that we are locked inside a prison house of language. On the contrary, read in context we can see that he explicitly insists that the point is not about language but about ontology: even material things are like words, in the sense that they are ontologically contingent rather than unconditioned (what exactly this means should be more clear below). This point has radical consequences for how we think about where one thing ends and another thing begins, because—upon reflection—it turns out that drawing those lines between things usually involves language. Consequently, in this chapter I will first review his argument about textuality in *Of Grammatology*, and, second, I will review his critique of Husserl's phenomenological account of the appearance of "things," a critique that demonstrates the objective knowledge Husserl hopes to achieve is not possible given the very means he uses to attempt to achieve that knowledge. At the end I will turn to contemporary cognitive science research on how human and nonhuman animals individuate objects in their environment—this research shows that, in a few cases, visual object individuation isn't contingent upon the use of language, contrary to some of Derrida's claims.

Why does all of this matter? Why expend so much energy thinking about the way we divide up, demarcate, differentiate, or individuate the things of the world? Because, as should be clear in cases like "child abuse," how we define or identify objects in the world is often deeply political. What do our words individuate and draw attention to? What do our words ignore? Consideration of such matters must be front and center if we are to avoid using language that potentially reinforces social domination.

George Berkeley, Immanuel Kant, and Jacques Derrida

In his early works—from the 1960s and 1970s—Derrida extends Martin Heidegger's "destruction" of Western philosophy by offering immanent critiques of the works of Plato, Jean-Jacques Rousseau, Immanuel Kant, G. W. F. Hegel, Edmund Husserl, and Martin Heidegger, among others. Derrida draws special attention to how modern European philosophers' categories or systems of classification were part and parcel of European imperialism and colonialism—Derrida's own contribution to denaturalizing historically specific concepts. His most famous—or infamous—claim comes from *Of Grammatology*: "*there is nothing outside of the text*" (Derrida [1967] 1976: 158, emphasis in the original). In Euro-American scholarship on Derrida, this single sentence—which appears in the midst of Derrida's commentary on Rousseau's *Confessions*—has too often been read apart from the surrounding context on pages 158 and 159 of Gayatri Chakravorty Spivak's translation. Removed from its context, this sentence has inspired two broadly popular but unfortunate interpretations, both of which, at times, have served as metonyms for Derrida's work in general or, worse, for poststructuralism in general.

The first of these two interpretations reads Derrida (and sometimes Foucault and Butler as well) as a sort of linguistic Berkeleyan. Writing in the eighteenth century, George Berkeley—in *Principles of Human Knowledge* and *Three Dialogues* (1996)—advances a form of philosophical idealism that claims the material world does not exist; on the contrary, all "things" are merely "ideas" that appear to the senses of spirits, and those ideas were causally produced by God rather than a material world. Berkeley writes,

> the various sensations or ideas imprinted on the sense … cannot exist otherwise than in a mind perceiving them … The table I write on, I say, exists, that is, I see and feel it; and if I were out of my study I should say it existed, meaning thereby that if I was in my study I might perceive it, or that some other spirit actually does perceive it. … [However,] as to what is said of the absolute existence of unthinking things *without any relation to their being perceived,* that seems perfectly unintelligible. Their *esse* is *percipi,* nor is it possible they should have any existence, out of the minds or thinking things which perceive them.
>
> (Berkeley 1996: 25, emphases mine)

"Their *esse* is *percipi*"—that is, their essence is in perception alone. Following his exposition and defense of this view, Berkeley concludes: "it follows that we have no longer any reason to suppose the being of *matter*" (1996: 56).

For those who read Derrida in this manner, "there is nothing outside of the text" apparently means that all we have is discourse or language (rather than ideas, as Berkeley would have it). Perhaps we are even in a "prison house of language," with nothing on the other side of the prison walls. Butler notes the typical objection: "if everything is discourse, then is there no reality to bodies? How do we understand the material violence that women suffer" (Bulter 1995: 51). In *More Than Belief: A Materialist Theory of Religion*, Manuel A. Vásquez accuses Butler of "dissolve[ing] ... the body and matter" (Vásquez 2011: 146) and claims she and Foucault are guilty of a form of "linguistic idealism," which he claims—citing Ian Hacking—is "descended from Berkeley's ideal-ism ... [which asserts] the doctrine that all that exists is mental" (147). On Vásquez's interpretation, for Butler "whatever is, is discursive and whatever is discursive, is" (147). In his footnotes, Vásquez calls Derrida a textual monist and argues that "Derrida denies any textual exteriority" (343). In *What Is a Person?*, sociologist of religion Christian Smith explicitly cites *Of Grammatology* but actually misquotes Derrida as saying "The text is all and *nothing exists outside it*" (2010: 128, emphasis mine). Unfortunately these sorts of readings ignore the fact that in her early work Butler *explicitly* claims that "valid and demonstrable claims" can be made about objects of scientific research (Butler 1990: 109), and that *merely three sentences* after stating "there is nothing outside of the text," Derrida *explicitly* allows for "the real life ... existences of 'flesh and bone,' beyond and behind what one believes to be circumscribed as Rousseau's text" (Derrida [1967] 1976: 159). Apparently these critics couldn't be bothered to carefully read the philosophers they were criticizing.

The second unfortunate interpretation, which appears in the secondary literature far more often than the linguistic Berkeleyan interpretation, reads Derrida (and, again, sometimes Foucault and Butler) as a linguistic Kantian, which we discussed above in the chapter on critique: in lieu of Kant's opposition between phenomenological experience and the noumenal thing-in-itself, we are led to believe that the statement "there is nothing outside of the text" opposes discourse or language to noumenal things-in-themselves that lie "out there" somewhere, on the other side of language and inaccessible to subjects who have access only to discourse.[1] This reading implies that Derrida is, in some way, a dualist who separates reality from its reception in consciousness or language. For instance, in Lee Braver's otherwise sophisticated history of continental anti-realism, *A Thing of This World*, Braver claims that this passage means that "*we cannot get outside of thought, systems, ideas to reach reality itself*" (Braver 2007: 443, emphasis mine), or that, although signs refer "to an *external world ... our access to this world is always mediated by more signs*" (446, emphasis mine). Similarly, Edward Slingerland, in *What Science Offers the Humanities*, interprets "there is nothing outside of the text" in this manner:

> Of course, Derrida is not actually denying the existence of an extralinguistic reality of objects. What he *is* denying is the possibility that we can have any kind of direct access to the objects *an sich*; they are known to us only as discursive objects, strands in the woven text that makes up the humanly knowable world.
>
> (Slingerland 2008: 79, emphasis original)

Discourse and Ideology

Slingerland asserts that Derrida and other theorists in the humanities are reproducing a centuries-old distinction between mind and body, or between spirit and nature. For Slingerland, "such a rigid dualism is a serious mistake" (4). Although not talking about Derrida in particular, Titus Hjelm, in *Social Constructionisms*, mocks this sort of linguistic dualism:

> From this perspective, the "world out there" and perceptions of that world are radically separated, with no access to the former, except through discourse. It is one thing to say that the *meaning* of, say, gravity is dependent on our ways of talking about it ... It is another thing for me to jump out of a sixth story window and assume a safe landing because I'm shouting "I'm not falling!" on the way down.
>
> (Hjelm 2014: 93)

While such a view would deserve mocking, these critiques grossly misunderstand Derrida's poststructuralism, which is situated more in the Hegelian than the Kantian tradition. Like Hegel, Derrida accepts that, *a priori*, Kant's concept of the thing-in-itself is generally useless for thinking about those things we take to be "knowledge." Derrida constantly talks about "things themselves" in *Of Grammatology*, but in each instance he notes that, when pressed, the concept ceases to make sense as anything other than a rhetorical tool to warrant claims for which we do not have empirical evidence.

In her discussion of how discourses form bodies, Butler notes, "the claim that a discourse 'forms' the body is no simple one, and from the start we must distinguish how such 'forming' is not the same as 'causing' or 'determining,' still less is it a notion that bodies are somehow made of discourse pure and simple" (Butler 1997: 84). Common caricatures or crude accounts of poststructuralist philosophical positions are, in effect, "an excuse not to read, and not to read closely" (Butler 1995: 37); we must therefore revisit these not-so-simple claims with more care.

Ontology in *Of Grammatology*

To understand—in context—what Derrida means by "there is nothing outside of the text," we must take into account a set of Hegelian assumptions Derrida makes throughout *Of Grammatology*. To put this discussion in my own terms rather than Derrida's, for Derrida—as well as for Madhyamika philosophers such as Nagarjuna and the American pragmatists—all objects are both *ontologically* and *epistemically* contingent. The formation of a hurricane, for instance, is contingent upon the gathering of warm, humid air under certain air pressures. In addition, even when formed, its boundaries are porous; were its boundaries not porous, it could not form, grow, move, or dissipate. On the contrary, the fact that air and water molecules can enter and exit under constantly changing conditions makes the hurricane possible in the first place; the water molecules that are part of the hurricane one day may be part of the ocean the next. Porousness makes the object possible but also makes it impossible to be fixed. Were the matter used to make up the hurricane fixed, the hurricane would die—just as a human body without matter going in and out would also die. Ontologically, the hurricane is a "fixed" object only in relationship to a discourse that temporarily individuates the dangerous movement of matter as "hurricane." In addition, the *identification* of the hurricane as a distinct "thing" is contingent upon our discourses and our interests: we don't demarcate and create names for just any temporary wind formation—only those that are possibly tied to our interests as humans, for instance, an enjoyable "cool breeze" or "a warm front that brings rain with it."

To use Heraclitus' metaphor—and as Madhyamika Buddhists were at pains to demonstrate in their discussion of dependent origination (i.e., pratityasmutpada)—there is more than a little truth to the idea that one can never step into the same river twice: the second time one steps into a river it is a different river, with different water molecules, different debris, and different boundaries (as shores are constantly shifting). The idea that a river is a fixed river is a fiction of the discourse that individuates the river as separate from its ontological context—and it is necessarily fictional because, ontologically, the relationship between "the river" and its "context" is, empirically, ontologically unfixed. Each conditions the other: riverbanks make rivers possible, and vice versa—there could be no riverbanks without rivers. At the same time however, neither is fixed and as each changes they change the other: the river water presses up against and erodes the soil on the river's banks, while the banks press up against and change the river water (by muddying it, for instance—in addition, perhaps eroding and muddying are by definition the same thing). The existence of both the river and its banks is conditioned by the other, and—because they condition each other—as they individually change they change the other was well. On this view, only an infinite, self-sustaining object—perhaps an unmoved mover—would have fixed boundaries and, insofar as we have no empirical evidence for the existence of self-sustaining objects of any sort, object individuation, by all accounts, always presents as fixed what is not ontologically fixed. In addition, the existence of self-sustaining material objects would not be consistent with the empirical claim that "$E=MC^2$"—that is, matter can always be converted to energy and, as such, always risks becoming *not matter*—a claim for which we have a great deal of empirical evidence. The only thing that could potentially be incapable of change would be an infinite thing with no conditions of possibility other than itself—such a thing could never be affected by anything else and, as such, could remain self-identical, unlike the river or its banks. While in theory such an entity quite possibly exists, we don't—and *a priori* could not— have any empirically justified warrant for claims about such an entity: to have knowledge of such an entity we would have to interact with it, and *a priori* interaction entails the experience of change from an outside influence.

These claims are held as *a priori* true by both Hegel and Derrida, given what words like "river," "bank," "finite," "conditioned," and "time" mean. "Each conditions the other" is precisely what Hegel meant when he made confusing statements such as the following. "The object is *in one same respect the opposite of itself*; it is for itself insofar as it is for others, and *it is for others insofar as it [is] for itself*. It is *for itself*, reflected into itself, One. However, this *for itself* reflected into itself, Oneness, is posited as existing in a unity with its opposite, with *being for an other*" (Hegel [1807] 2018: 76–77). Because things are co-constitutive, they are not self-sufficient, such that when one changes the other does as well. Or, as Hegel more confusingly puts it, "the relationship [of a thing to another] is the negation of its self-sufficiency, and the thing instead perishes through its essential property" (76). Derrida himself even uses this intentionally self-contradictory style at times; in the second chapter of *Of Grammatology*, two sections are titled "The Outside and the Inside" and "The Outside Ӄ the Inside" (see Derrida [1967] 1976: 30–65). In the latter section he explicitly writes that "no structure of the entity escapes" the fact that the entity is constituted in relationship with other things, or constituted as an entity via the "penetration of the other"—clearly a Hegelian point (47).

Boundaries are, therefore, *never empirical* for finite, conditioned objects; or, as Hegel put it, categories are *a priori* matters—they're not contained in the phenomenal field. This point was humorously illustrated on a boat tour my partner and I once took on the scenic St. Lawrence River. At one point, the boat tour guide told passengers that we could look down over the side of the boat to see one of the major sights on the voyage. Like the rest of the passengers, my partner and I gawked over the side, gazing into the water, looking for—what? a sunken boat? an underwater reef of some sort? At the moment, the tour guide announced, we were right then crossing over *the international border between the United States and Canada*. The boundary was, of course, not empirical, but discursive, and thus our empirical investigation for the sight was, *a priori*, in vain. The realist's error is to think that any boundary is empirical. If all things are ontologically conditioned and thus porous, fixed boundaries are, *a priori*, not empirical. In *Of Grammatology*, Derrida explicitly repeats Kant's claim that space is *a priori* and thus nonempirical ([1967] 1976: 68); we literally never see space, we only see objects *in* a hypothesized space (which is why, when physicists talk about gravity warping space, they hypothesize about that space on the basis of how objects in space behave, not on the basis of any direction observation of space itself, which is *a priori* not visible). Because things such as categories, boundaries, and space are nonempirical, where one thing ends and another thing begins depends on the words we use to draw the lines between one thing and the next.

For both Hegel and Derrida, then, (1) objects are ontologically contingent, (2) knowledge of such objects is epistemically contingent, in the sense that we have access to objects only under epistemic conditions that do not always hold, and (3) objects are *contingent in their individuation*, in the sense that the difference between one "it" and another "it" is, for us at least, a product of two possible conditions: either a historically specific discourse that fixes an unfixed object or a nonuniversal cognitive apparatus—usually visual—that, as a result of the evolution of our species, predisposes humans to "see" never-discrete objects as discrete (I'll say more about this latter point at the end of this chapter). Poststructuralism therefore denies the existence of "natural kinds"—or, more specifically, accepts the claim that if natural kinds exist, we do not have empirical evidence for them. We have a great deal of empirical evidence that hurricanes, rivers, and nation-states exist, but their demarcation, differentiation, or individuation—their *object*-ification—is contingent.

So, in the context of *Of Grammatology*, an explicitly Hegelian book, what does it mean to say "there is nothing outside of the text"? In the book, Derrida's master metaphor is *writing*. He notes that throughout much of Western philosophy, writing has been devalued in relationship to speech. On the classic view, writing is secondary to speech; writing is the re-mark, the trace, or the reproduction of what has already been said. From the intellectual tradition starting with Plato, writing has almost always been imagined as that which is conditioned by speech, as if speech were not in itself conditioned. However, Derrida notes that all language by definition traces or reproduces what has already been said or written: words are words *only on condition* of their repetition; a "word" spoken or written only once would not be a word. His argument involves a very complex immanent critique of Ferdinand de Saussure, but his conclusion is not all that complicated: even speech involves writing *in a metaphorical sense*—every time one speaks words one is re-writing, re-tracing, or re-marking what has already been spoken, written, traced, marked. In addition, all words refer to other words, those words refer to other words, and so on *ad infinitum*. This is why, when one looks up a definition for a word in a dictionary, the definition will literally consist of *other words*. All words, written or spoken, are ontologically conditioned by other words. In *Of Grammatology*, for all practical purposes "written" means the same thing as "ontologically contingent." (Of course, words refer to other objects as well, but which objects they refer to depends on their definition; the connection of words to other words has a logical priority over their connection to things other than words.)

In addition, because words are ontologically conditioned by their relationship to other words, they always risk changing as circumstances change—much as a changing riverbank affects the river, and vice versa. Insofar as words are finite or conditioned rather than infinite or unconditioned things, their definitions and referents will—*a priori*—change over time as conditions change.

Whether we call it writing, tracing, or duplication, Derrida insists that this process is true not only of language but *even of material things*. Throughout the book Derrida makes a number of explicit claims that signal the book is *not* about writing, texts, or language *in the colloquial sense*, but about the fact that *all finite things*, insofar as they are ontologically conditioned by other things, are metaphorically *written*. All finite things are subject to "inscription in general, *whether it is literal or not* and even if what it contributes in space is alien to the order of the voice: cinematography, choreography, of course, but also pictorial, musical, sculptural 'writing'" (Derrida [1967] 1976: 9, emphasis mine). To use my own example, even an "extra-linguistic" referent such as Michelangelo's statue of David is "written" from—or ontologically conditioned by—for example, Michelangelo's consciousness, his hands, his chisels, his view of bodily ideals, his reading of biblical narratives, the block of marble from which he started, and more. "All this is to describe *not only* the system of notation secondarily connected with these activities [such as sculpture] *but the essence and the content of these activities themselves*" (9, emphasis mine). That is, the "essence" of even material referents in the world is to have been—metaphorically—written. Because all finite things are ontologically conditioned, "the thing itself is a collection of things or a chain of differences" (90). As early as the fourth page of the first chapter of *Of Grammatology*, Derrida invokes biology and the "pro-gram" in living cells as an example—perhaps his clearest—that material things are metaphorically written (9). The production of biological life entails *continually reproducing* DNA over and over. Like Heidegger's Being, this movement of things written, traced, or duplicated makes the coming-to-thingness possible, and the absence of such movement would be *death*. "Life without differance: another name for death" (71).

In *Of Grammatology*, "writing" is thus *a metaphor for ontology in general*, although an ontology in which the existence of all finite or conditioned "things" is perpetually usurped, in which case it is a non-ontology of sorts. All words are contingent upon other words, just as all finite material things are contingent upon other material things. Even if we had access to the so-called "things-in-themselves," we would be inevitably and perpetually referred further back to other things that serve as their prior condition of possibility. There are no wooden tables without trees, blueprints for tables (which could be either literally drawn or just imagined in consciousness), labor that transforms those trees into the tables outlined in the blueprints, and so forth—these are all ontological conditions of the possibility of tables. And if we went back to the trees themselves, we would find that their existence is materially conditioned on things such as tree DNA, water, soil, minerals, sunlight, and so on. If we followed sunlight to the sun, we would find that it too is not a self-sufficient thing but is in fact made up of other things. No finite thing is self-standing. As such, all things are (metaphorically) written: "no structure of the entity escapes it" (Derrida [1967] 1976: 47). "There is no chance of encountering anywhere the purity of 'reality,' 'unicity,' 'singularity'" of things (91). We never land upon a pure foundation on which we can noncontingently justify our knowledge claims, for all foundations are themselves conditioned by other "foundations." A thing is always constituted by its relationship to other things. "The presence of the thing itself is already exposed in exteriority" (203). In the last paragraph of the first chapter, Derrida notes that Hegel already made all these claims (26); there is little here in *Of Grammatology* that wasn't already said in the nineteenth century.

Thus far I have argued the following:

- some scholars interpret "there is nothing outside of the text" as encouraging a type of linguistic Berkeleyanism or a kind of linguistic Kantianism;
- by contrast, if we read *Of Grammatology* carefully, we will note that throughout the book Derrida's main point seems to be Hegelian: all things—material or linguistic—are conditioned;
- if all things are conditioned, as conditions change so do the things—sometimes even passing out of existence or becoming other things;
- if so, where we draw the line between one thing and the next isn't based on empirical boundaries between things but rather the words we use to divide things up.

"There is nothing outside of the text"

Turning to Derrida's immanent critique of Rousseau's body of writings, he claims "there is nothing outside of the text" in the midst of a discussion of Rousseau's *Confessions*. In that text, Rousseau nostalgically laments the loss of lovers, while at the same time notes that he never fully enjoyed their presence. At times his lovers were of interest seemingly only because they stood in for—or *supplemented*—absent mother-figures or previous lovers to whom Rousseau was previously attached. In addition, apparently out of fear of attachment or sexually transmitted diseases, Rousseau would turn to masturbation to satisfy his sexual desires. "Rousseau will never stop having recourse to, and accusing himself of, this onanism that permits one to be himself affected by providing himself with presences, by summoning absent beauties" (Derrida [1967] 1976: 153). In this manner, "that dangerous supplement"—namely, masturbation—"has not only the power of *procuring* an absent presence through its image: procuring it for us through the proxy of the sign, it holds it at a distance and masters it" (155). One woman supplements another—his lover "Mamma" supplements his "real" mother, and later Thérèse supplements Mamma—and Rousseau's masturbatory representations of women to himself supplemented the flesh-and-blood women themselves. Thus we have a chain of supplements, each "thing" standing in for an absent "thing" that is no longer present.

After introducing this discussion, Derrida takes a step back to consider what is taking place in his reading or interpretation of Rousseau's text. Are we learning about the "real" Rousseau? Does this reading tell us about Rousseau-in-himself? Derrida denies this is the case, because a reading

> cannot legitimately transgress the text toward something other than it, toward a referent (a reality that is metaphysical, historical, psychobiographical, etc.) or toward a signified outside the text whose content could take place, could have taken place outside of language, that is to say, in the sense that we give here to that word, outside of writing in general.
>
> (Derrida [1967] 1976: 158)

"Writing in general" is, as should be clear not "writing" or "language" in the colloquial sense—Derrida *explicitly denies this* throughout the book. Instead, by "writing in general" Derrida means something like "the ontological processes whereby things are always conditioned and thereby never self-standing or self-sufficient." Derrida insists here that there is no fixed "reality" that we could get to that would not be structured by the perpetual displacement of "things" via differance that is "writing" in the metaphorical sense. Even if we went back in time and found Rousseau, we would discover that he is not a foundation but rather a contingent, conditioned, finite being made up of DNA, the food he eats, the wine he drinks, the relationships he has with others, and so on—*ad infinitum*. He cannot serve as a "real" foundation for our knowledge about him because, as a conditioned, finite being, he is by definition changing and incomplete; as conditions

Discourse and Ideology

change—as he eats different things, develops new relationships with others—who he is changes as well. Derrida goes on:

> *There is nothing outside of the text.* And that is neither because Jean-Jacques' life, or the existence of Mamma or Thérèse *themselves*, is not of prime interest to us, nor because we have access to their so-called "real" existence only in the text and we have neither any means of altering this, nor any right to neglect this limitation ... [T]here are more radical reasons.
>
> (Derrida [1967] 1976: 158)

Note: in this passage, Derrida *explicitly denies* that "there is nothing outside of the text" means that we only have access to Rousseau, Mamma, or Thérèse through language or the text in the colloquial sense. Rather,

> in what one calls the *real life of these existences "of flesh and bone,"* beyond and behind what one believes can be circumscribed in Rousseau's text, there has never been anything but writing, there have never been anything but supplements, substitutive significations, which could only come forth in a chain of differential references, the "real" supervening, and being added only while taking on meaning from a trace and from an invocation of the supplement, etc. And thus to infinity.
>
> (Derrida [1967] 1976: 159, emphasis mine)

Derrida's argument, then, is not that Mamma or Thérèse exist only in language or in the text in the colloquial sense, but that even their flesh and bone—their DNA, their bodies digesting food, their internalized identities and social roles, etc.—are *written* in the metaphorical sense. Who they "really" are results from an idealization in fantasy or imagination, a process of identification that freezes what is, "in reality," never actually frozen. You can never step into the same river twice, and—in an important sense—who Rousseau "is" is never the same twice. Empirically, we have access only to perpetual difference; finding the "real" Rousseau, Mamma, or Thérèse depends on the *fixing* of what is, "in-itself," apparently not fixed.

In summary,

- in context, "there is nothing outside the text" does not appear to be designed to support a linguistic Berkeleyanism or Kantianism;
- rather, Derrida's claim is that all things are *written* in the metaphorical sense— that is, all things are ontologically contingent and thus perpetually change as conditions change (for instance, without cells that perpetually rewrite DNA codes, bodies could not come into being, but those codes—insofar as they are *copied*—always risk changing as they are rewritten);
- consequently, any individuation of material things requires constructing a fixed identity for something that is, in fact, not fixed—in time any "thing" one has knowledge of could change;

- even the "flesh and bone" of those people Rousseau wrote about were perpetually changing—as well as Rousseau himself—and, as such, there is no "final word" or ultimate truth to be had about them.

I hope I have put to rest the Berkeleyan and Kantian interpretations of Derrida's claim that "there is nothing outside of the text," for such interpretations fail to make sense of the other—explicitly Hegelian—claims he makes in *Of Grammatology*, which clearly concern not only epistemic but also ontological matters.

In the next section, I want to move on to a consideration of Derrida's criticisms of Husserl, particularly Husserl's description of how we individuate objects that appear to us in the phenomenal field. Derrida appears to accept much of Husserl's account of how we identify objects, but he also points out that the "objective" knowledge of such objects Husserl desires is made impossible by the very methods he uses to achieve that knowledge. *A priori*, objective knowledge is incapable of being achieved using Husserl's otherwise admirable methods of identifying and describing objects.

Husserl, Objects, and Ideality

In *Ideas*, Husserl attempts, among other things, to account for the phenomenological conditions that make cognition of objects as objects possible for human consciousness. For Husserl, because objects do not fully appear as such to phenomenological consciousness, they must be constructed or idealized for us, by us. Idealization entails picking and choosing some elements from the phenomenal field and ignoring others— just as the idealization of a lover likely involves attending to their strengths and ignoring their faults. To put it slightly differently, Husserl accepts Kant and Hegel's claim that an object's identity is never visible in the phenomenal field—when looking at a tree we don't see the definition of the word "tree"; rather, the identity of an object is instead produced for us through a cognitive process of idealization that draws lines around objects by picking some characteristics as essential to the object's identity and ignoring characteristics that one considers inessential to the thing's identity. Derrida objects to none of this. However, Husserl goes on to make a series of purportedly empirical claims about things-in-themselves that lie beyond perception, claims that Derrida demonstrates are empirically unwarranted according to the letter of Husserl's own writings. Ultimately, Derrida's critique of Husserl parallels Hegel's critique of Kant: for Derrida, Husserl unnecessarily reintroduces Kant's concept of the thing-in-itself.

All of Derrida's earliest works offered immanent critiques of Husserl's corpus, often focusing on elements related to this question of the objectivity of objects. These works include his graduate thesis, *The Problem of Genesis in Husserl's Philosophy* (2003 [originally written in 1953–1954]), his first book-length publication, a translation and introduction to Husserl's "Origins of Geometry" ([1962] 1989), and his first book, *Voice and Phenomenon: Introduction to the Problem of the Sign in Husserl's Phenomenology* ([1967] 2011; although published in the same year as *Writing and*

Difference and *Of Grammatology*, the former was merely a collection of previously published essays and the latter was written after *Voice and Phenomenon*). In what follows, I will focus on Derrida's reading of Husserl in his introduction to "Origins of Geometry" and *Voice and Phenomenon*, whose critiques of Husserl are largely parallel to one another.[2]

Husserl's phenomenological starting point for a consideration of the individuation, ideality, or idealization of objects involves a reflection on what I will call "mid-sized objects" within one's visual range. For my purposes, I'm defining a "mid-sized" object as one that an adult human could manipulate and observe all sides of without too much difficulty, barring objects whose details are too small to see without aided vision. For example, for objects one might find in a household, mid-sized objects could include anything from a bread crumb or push-pin to a desk, bed, or dresser. (As will become clear below, the size of the object *relative to human bodily capacities* is not an insignificant aspect of this definition—having bodies with which to see things in the world is apparently an important condition of possibility of having knowledge about the world, and it appears that human animals and nonhuman animals with different bodies see different things in the world.)

Husserl notes that the immediate phenomenological experience of an object is constantly changing; for instance, as one moves, as the object moves or rotates, or as the light source over the object changes, whatever appears in the visual field changes as well. In *Ideas*, Husserl's example is that of a table:

> Looking the whole time at this table, moving around it in the process, altering my position in space as always, I am continually conscious of the existence (as bodily there) of this and the same table, and, to be sure, of the same one, remaining completely unchanged in itself. The perception of the table, however, is a perception that is constantly changing; it is a continuity of changing perceptions. I close my eyes. My other senses are not in any relation to the table. Now I have no perception of it. I open my eyes and I have the perception again. *The* perception? Let us be more precise. Recurring, it is under no circumstances individually the same. Only the table is the same, and I am conscious of it as identical in the synthetic consciousness that joins the new perception with memory.
>
> (Husserl 2014: 71)

A couple of things are significant here. First, Husserl attributes unity and fixity to the table in-itself, but disunity and multiplicity to the changing phenomenological consciousness of the table. The thing-in-itself is what it is—a single, unchanging object—while consciousness of said object continually varies. Second, not only does phenomenological consciousness of the object shift, change, or flow, but it also disappears as one closes one's eyes. However, because the table has a consciousness-independent existence, it persists as a thing-in-itself even when it is not seen; "the perceived thing can be without being perceived … and it can be without changing" (Husserl 2014: 71). As Derrida will point out, Husserl's description here is a site where classic philosophical oppositions—with us since Heraclitus and Plato—between identity and difference, logic and experience, or reason and empiricism are played out.

A crucial element of Husserl's account of the experience of the "now" moment in phenomenological consciousness involves what he calls *retention* and *protention*. Retention consists of recalling what has passed out of immediate phenomenological consciousness, while protention consists of anticipating what may come next. The phenomenological experience is thus divided between a *"re-membering"* and an *"anticipation"* (Husserl 2014: 140). In the passage we are considering, Husserl draws attention only to retention and the unstable now: "the now of perception incessantly transforms itself into the following consciousness of the just-passed and at the same time lights up a new now, and so forth" (72). As such, the now moment is not only not stable but also not self-sufficient; for us, all nows refer to what is other than the now.

Consider the phenomenological experience of a spoken sentence, such as the following: "Is a bell making that sound?" Upon hearing the first four syllables, one will not as yet necessarily have heard the words "Is a bell make-," until one hears "-ing that sound," the words one might have heard could very well have been "Isabel make-," as in, "Isabel makes her own marinara sauce." The experience of the "bel" syllable is constituted on the basis of what came before and what came after. This is, of course, why the talk-to-text features on our phones often change the first words spoken as one continues one's sentence. For example, when I speak "Husserl and Derrida" into the google search feature on my phone, it first translates my speech as "Husserl and Jerry. Die"—presumably because protention anticipates that the syllables which sound like "Derr-ee" are much more often going to have referred to "Jerry" for English speakers than to an obscure French philosopher—before going on to correct to "Husserl and Derrida." The phone itself relies on protention and retention to capture the words said. Without protention and retention, phenomenological experience would consist of unrelated, punctual moments without continuity; the experience would be like that of a film in which every single frame is randomly chosen from other films. Protention and retention permit phenomenological consciousness a continuity it otherwise would not have.

Husserl also provides the example of experiencing a melody (Husserl 2014: 143): because a melody is experienced across moments of time, it can never appear in a simple, present now. "The *essence* of something of which one is in this way conscious entails the possibility of reflecting on its having-been-perceived" (143). Husserl insists that "the *entire* phenomenological time-field of the pure ego" is made up of all *"three* dimensions of the before, afterward, simultaneous" (159). Only when we have the *"entire stream* of temporal unities of experience" is that stream "strictly closed off and self-contained" (159). The logic is trinitarian: "*One* pure ego—*one* stream of experience, replete in all three dimensions, essentially hanging together in this repleteness" (159). For Derrida, this unity is, of course, belied by the very terms Husserl uses: at the very least, if retention involves "re-membering," then consciousness is dealing with "members" that must be joined, and as such do not constitute a simple, closed unity (or, as Hegel might have put it, finite things are what they are in relationship to other things, *a priori*, and as such are always marked by both difference as well as identity).

Discourse and Ideology

Returning to the previous passage under consideration, Husserl goes on to emphasize that the imagined thing-in-itself, as a whole, exceeds immediate perception: "like the perceived thing generally, so, too, anything and everything accruing to it in terms of parts, sides, inherent aspects necessarily transcends the perception" (Husserl 2014: 72). Note: the so-called thing-in-itself—at least for us—is quite literally imagined, because all sides of a mid-sized object never appear all at once. For example, because the whole table does not appear to phenomenological consciousness at once—the whole as "whole" transcends any individual perception or now moment, as I cannot see the bottom and the top at the same time—we must idealize it through protention and retention of various phenomenological moments. Its ideality—its unity and identity—is, for us, constructed out of various moments of perception. Or, as Sara Ahmed puts it in her commentary on Husserl's *Ideas*, "the object becomes an object of perception only given the work of recollection, such that the 'new' exists in relation *to what is already gathered by consciousness:* each impression is linked to the other, so that the object becomes more than the profile that is available in any moment" (Ahmed 2006: 36).

Husserl further considers the phenomenological experience of an object's color:

> The color of the seen thing is intrinsically no really obtaining inherent aspect of the consciousness of color; it appears but while it appears, the appearance can and *must* continually change in the course of ostensive experience of it. The *same* color appears "in" continuous manifolds of *shades* of color.
>
> (Husserl 2014: 72)

That is, as we walk around a table, the angles between the light source, the light reflecting off of the table, and the distance and vector of that light to our eyes is constantly changing. Arguably, in "reality" (and, as should be clear, "reality" is what is at stake here), we see shifting shades of the "same" color. As a result, the "sameness" of the color is, for us, a product of our idealization, as it is never present in our phenomenological field of vision.

This extends beyond the experience of color: "Something similar holds for sensory quality and equally for each spatial shape. One and the same shape (given in person *as* the same) appears continuously again and again 'in a different way,' in profiles of shapes that are always different" (Husserl 2014: 72). For instance, a pyramid could appear as a two-dimensional triangle from one side, or as a two-dimensional square from the bottom. Husserl insists that the shape is "given … *as* the same," but once again his phenomenological description belies that: the "same" pyramid is given through different "profiles," and its sameness—at least for us—is constructed in consciousness. This holds for an object's spatial depth as well. "A profile is an experience. But experience is only possible as experience and not as something spatial" (73). That is, for example, in a sense one's experience of a pyramid is necessarily two-dimensional rather than three-dimensional or spatial; we only ever experience *a profile* of the three-dimensional object. "What is profiled, however, is intrinsically possible only as something spatial (it just is essentially spatial) but it is not possible as experience" (73). We cannot directly experience the thing-in-itself as an object with depth; we construe its spatiality after the fact, through protention and retention of the various profiles we have experienced.

At one point Derrida uses the word "substruction" to refer to this process of idealization that Husserl describes: substruction constructs in part *by subtracting* inessential, empirical differences. This is crucial: when making a claim that something is a "thing," we separate it from what it is not, *including aspects of itself*—for to say that the table is unchanging, or that it remains the same over time, we have to ignore the fact that, quite literally, our vision of the table perpetually changes. We have to ignore those aspects of things that we take to be inessential or contingent, to arrive at what we take to be essential or noncontingent to the "thing." Derrida puts it this way: consider the imagination of geometrically perfect shapes: we start with "*more or less smooth* surfaces, sides, lines, or *more or less rough angles*, and so on ... '[P]roceeding from the factual, an essential form becomes recognizable'" (Derrida [1962] 1989: 123). From empirical "roundness" we imagine "pure" roundness, "*under* which is *constructed* the geometrical ideality of the 'circle'" (124). However, the imagined, pure roundness "is not to be confused with the multiplicity of natural shapes which more or less correspond to it in perception" (124). An object's identity or ideal shape is never present to phenomenological consciousness; only the object's various and different empirical manifestations appear. For us, the identity of the thing literally comes *at the expense* of empirical evidence.

Derrida also draws attention to the fact that the ideality or substruction of the object is necessarily contingent upon repetition of the "same" in different phenomenological experiences *across time*. Time—an essential condition of protention and retention—makes the identity of the object possible for us, since we cannot construct the object in consciousness on the basis of a single phenomenological now. However, in a way time separates the thing from itself in our immediate experience: the "it" appears now one way, and now another way, and now a third way. Phenomenological experience of a thing is a continual process of it looking like *this*, then *not* looking like this, but now *that*. Again, pure nows, without protention and retention, would be punctual moments of perpetual difference. And, crucially for Derrida, protention and retention are not in the object but in the subject. For us, the identity of the three-dimensional pyramid at any particular moment depends upon prior empirical evidence of a series of now moments that are *no longer present or which are not yet present*, except insofar as they are remembered or anticipated by a subject. The presence of the object's identity or unity is, for us, contingent upon "essential" elements that are absent in any particular perception of the object itself. Substructing an object's identity depends, essentially, on what is in part nonempirical. Hegel was right: if categories don't appear in the phenomenological field, an object's identity, its boundaries, its individuation, and so on, is contingent upon *a priori* matters provided by consciousness rather than the phenomenological field. As Derrida puts it—somewhat more confusingly—"one sees an irreducible non-presence recognized as a constituting value, and with it a non-life or a non-presence of the living present, a non-belonging of the living present to itself, a non-originarity that cannot be eradicated" (Derrida [1967] 2011: 6). What doesn't appear in the phenomenal field permits us to see "things" in the phenomenal field. As Ahmed puts it, when discussing

Discourse and Ideology

Husserl's "table," this "makes the table a rather queer object ... [T]he table is only the same given that we have conjured its missing sides" (Ahmed 2006: 36). The "sameness" of the object is shot through-and-through with irreducible difference. If we remove the differences, we cannot construct the object in consciousness in the first place. In addition, "this relation to non-presence ... radically destroys every possibility of self-identity in its simplicity" (Derrida [1967] 2011: 56). For Derrida, these conditions of possibility of the substruction of objects are *also conditions of impossibility for simple, self-identical objects*. This is, of course, a Hegelian theme: just like the river and the riverbanks, the thingness of things is constituted in and through what they are not.

For Derrida, another consequence of the fact that the ideality of the object for us is contingent upon time is that "it" is *always open to future reconstruction* (the "it" is in scare quotes because, once reconstructed, the "it" is necessarily a different "it"). What we at first take to be a two-dimensional triangle is, once turned 30 degrees to the right and 10 degrees down, reconstructed or re-idealized as a three-dimensional pyramid. However, who is to say that the pyramid could not be turned once again, at which point we might discover that there is no "back" or fourth wall to the pyramid, in which case it is more like a tent with one side open.

We might, with some level of confidence, assure ourselves that such a mid-sized object could be manipulated or turned over in our hands long enough that our idealization of it could be relatively closed; we could arrive at a point where its substruction—for all immediate practical purposes—would no longer require revision; while a little pyramid souvenir is ultimately as subject to change over time as the river is, it is liable to change more slowly since it is made out of stone rather than water. However, consider that—apart from infants or toddlers in their nurseries or play rooms—most "objects" of consciousness or discourse are not mid-sized objects. As Nelson Goodman notes in *Ways of Worldmaking*:

> Once in awhile someone asks me rather petulantly "Can't you see what's before you?" Well, yes and no. I see people, chairs, papers, and books that are before me, and also colors, shapes, and patterns that are before me. But do I see the molecule, electrons, and infrared light that are also before me? And do I see the state, or the United States, or the universe? I see only parts of the latter comprehensive entities, indeed, but then I also see only parts of the people, chairs, etc.
>
> (Goodman 1978: 71)

As a professor, I regularly make judgments about objects such as "students," the "student body," a particular student's "grade," the "faculty," the "administration," and so forth. Consider just one: the faculty. The faculty as a whole rarely appears before phenomenological consciousness all at once, and even when it does—for instance, at a commencement ceremony—one learns very little about the faculty other than their outward physical appearance (or at least those parts of physical appearance that are not covered by regalia). But when I think of my college's "faculty" as an object, the physical appearance is typically of little importance; much more important is what the faculty "thinks"—about assessment, for instance, or the college president's new agenda for the college. The view of the faculty about the president's new agenda could be constructed through retention or memories of, perhaps, phenomenological consciousness of interactions with individual faculty members, open discussions in full faculty meetings, nonverbal signals and gestures accompanying such a discussion, rumors of conversations in other departments, bitching sessions over beers at the local pub, and so on—all while necessarily ignoring other appearances of the faculty that we take to be inessential or non-represenatative. On the basis of such a substruction, one might claim: "the faculty will not like phase two of this new initiative." But with what level of certainty can we make such statements? As should be clear, temporality here provides ample opportunity for the "faculty" to be open to radically different reconstructions. *Temporality makes the substruction of the object both possible and essentially open-ended*. And, again, most of the "objects" of interest to us are not mid-sized objects—for example, our friends, our families, our health, our economy, our environment, our state, our state policies, our rights, our opportunities, our jobs, our salaries, our budgets, our debt, our future, etc., even *geometry*.

In summary,

- for Husserl, perception of an object is perpetually changing, because of the changing position of the subject, the changing position of the object, changing lighting conditions, etc.;
- to identify an object as a self-same object, subjects must collect together immediate experience of an object in a "now" moment with the recollection of prior moments of perception and anticipation of future moments;
- the construction or substruction of a self-same object in consciousness requires literally discarding some perceptions of the object or ignoring aspects that we take to be contingently related to rather than essential to the object's identity— like the changing shades of color that we take to result from our shifting angle of perception or apparent fluctuations in lighting, as opposed to the object itself; and
- such substructions of the object are inherently open-ended, as new empirical evidence may force us to revise what characteristics we attribute to the object.

Geometry, Language, and the Politics of Objectivity

Matters get further complicated when Derrida considers one of Husserl's ethnocentric philosophical goals, particularly in his essay "Origins of Geometry": to authorize as objective the truths of Euro-American math and science. In this essay, Husserl is caught in a double bind: he accepts that apparently objective truths—for instance, the Pythagorean theorem—do not descend from the heavens; however, as a type of foundationalist, he nevertheless wants to defend the objectivity of the truths of geometry. Since he does not accept that their truth is founded on a transcendent or divine origin, he must ground their truth in human history and consciousness, but the truths of geometry cannot be merely subjective or culturally relative. Husserl writes,

> geometrical existence is not psychic existence: it does not exist as something personal within the personal sphere of consciousness: it is the existence of what is objectively there for "everyone" (for actual and possible geometers, or those who understand geometry). Indeed, it has, from its primal establishment, an existence which is peculiarly *supertemporal* and which—of this we are certain—is accessible to *all men*, first of all to the actual and possible mathematicians of *all people, all ages*.
>
> (Husserl [1962] 1989: 160, emphasis mine)

As with all sciences, "tradition" is an inescapable part of this achievement of objective truth: "We know of [geometry's] handed down, earlier forms, as those from which it has arisen … [I]t is not only a mobile forward process from one set of acquisitions to another but a continuous synthesis in which all acquisitions maintain their validity" (Husserl [1962] 1989: 159). A mobile process: idealization—to objective truth—requires time and synthesis and the accumulation of tradition. However, the European Enlightenment has as one of its central principles the axiom that a claim is not true simply because it has been inherited from an authoritative tradition. How does Husserl bridge the gap between historically relative, specific human consciousnesses and objective truth?

According to Derrida, to justify the truth of claims about things such as math, Husserl for all practical purposes makes recourse to a Hegelian teleology whereby we dialectically sublate—or synthesize, to use Husserl's term—evidence until we arrive at ideal knowledge—truth itself. Husserl would of course accept that such an end is sometimes not yet reached; there are probably things we still do not know about math. However, *ideally*, phenomenal evidence will be transformed into objective truth. Husserl writes,

> The sensible utterances have spatiotemporal individuation in the world like all *corporeal* occurrences, like everything embodied in *bodies* as such; but this is not true of the *spiritual* form itself, which is called an "ideal object." In a certain way ideal objects do exist objectively in the world, but it is only in virtue of these two-leveled repetitions and ultimately in virtue of sensibly embodying repetitions.
>
> (Husserl [1962] 1989: 160–161, emphasis added)

The "spiritual" object—Husserl's word, not mine—appears at the end of a series of "corporeal" repetitions of representations of the object to ourselves; repetition and time are the levers that lift us from the subjective to the objective. Crucially, the product—geometry—is ontologically contingent upon those repetitions.

Language is clearly central to this process of the creation of geometry. When introducing language in "Origins of Geometry," Husserl makes three claims.

- The first is an off-hand comment apparently unrelated to the two points that follow: words, like "things," are themselves similarly idealized in imagination.

- Second, although words are necessary to *refer to* idealized objects—for instance, geometrical figures—those objects purportedly exist independently of the words or consciousnesses that refer to them; that is, Husserl wants to be realist about such objects.
- Third, the objectivity of the truths to which such words refer can be certain once we arrive at *invariant* constructions.

I will discuss each of these claims in turn.
First, language and words are themselves idealized. Husserl writes,

> language itself, in all its particularizations (words, sentences, speeches), is, as can easily be seen from the grammatical point of view, thoroughly made up of ideal objects; for example, the word *Löwe* occurs only once in the German language; it is identical throughout its innumerable utterances by any given persons.
>
> (Husserl [1962] 1989: 161)

As Derrida puts it in his gloss:

> A signifier (in general) must be recognizable in its form despite and across the diversity of empirical characteristics that can modify it. It must remain the *same* and be able to be repeated as such despite and across the deformations that what we call the empirical event makes it necessarily undergo.
>
> (Derrida [1967] 2011: 43)

Löwe, or "lion" in English, is substructed from all the empirical instances of the word, and—for Husserl—the empirical instances refer to the "same" idealized concept in each case. The word "lion" can appear empirically different each and every time and yet still refer to the same word. It can be spoken aloud, pronounced in a wide variety of ways, in various voices, with different accents, or even sung in different notes or keys, but the empirical instances still refer to the same word. Similarly, we could write "lion" in Times New Roman, in a sans serif font, write it in cursive, or print it, but the different marks would all refer to the "same" word. On this view, all of the empirically different marks in Figure 2.1 would refer to the "same" word, even though each mark is literally empirically different. However, as Derrida notes, the word-itself is an odd thing (which is perhaps why Husserl trots out words such as "spiritual"); the word-itself is never empirically available. We can see different, written, empirical instances of the word, but—*a priori*—we can never see the word-itself. The word-itself seems to live in consciousness. Derrida notes the irony here: despite Husserl's opposition to Platonism, which makes the *really real* exist in a nonempirical world, here Husserl similarly locates the object—namely, the ideal object—in a nonempirical space. "By determining the *ontos* as *eidos*, Plato was doing nothing else" (Derrida [1967] 2011: 45).

lion lion *lion* **LION**

Figure 2.1 "Lion" written in different ways.

Second, although words are necessary to refer to idealized objects—for instance, geometrical figures—those objects purportedly exist independently of the words or consciousnesses that refer to them. Again, Husserl wants to be realist about such objects. Derrida notes that Husserl is making claims at three different levels here. *Words* refer to *concepts*, and concepts refer to *objects*. However, in each case the object at hand (word, concept, or extra-linguistic referent) is idealized or substructed from some sort of empirical evidence that has appeared in the phenomenal field. The word "lion" is idealized from empirically different marks on the page referring to the word-itself. Concepts, for example, "infinity," are idealized from slightly different definitions written down in dictionaries or philosophy books; the definition of infinity in my copy of Hegel's *Science of Logic* is not the concept of infinity-itself, but only refers to that concept. Similarly, "extra-linguistic referents," for instance, the "truths of geometry," are idealized from different written accounts of geometry found in various books written over time; the description of geometry in any particular textbook is, however, not geometry-itself. In each of these cases, it seems the thing-itself is in consciousness rather than in the phenomenal field.

By no means does Husserl deny the nonempirical nature of the ideal to which he is referring. Indeed, as Marrati puts it, "the cost" of ideality is the reduction of the "existence of the transcendent world … [T]he site of ideality [is] the neutralization of factual existence" (Marrati 2005: 67). Or, to put it in my words, the ideal comes at the expense of the empirical—substruction literally requires ignoring differing evidence. And, in fact, that is what "reduction" is, by definition: ignoring some empirical evidence to construct an ideal version of the thing-reduced in consciousness. In *Ideas*, Husserl explicitly emphasizes the role of fantasy in constructing the objects in consciousness (given the importance of this concession, I quote at length):

> Like the geometer, the phenomenologist can only make limited use of an originary givenness as a means of assistance. To be sure, all the main types of perception and envisaging stand at his free disposal as something given in an originary way, namely, as perspective exemplifications for a phenomenology of perception, phantasy, memory, and so forth … [T]he freedom of research of essences necessarily demands operating in phantasy.
>
> … Thus, if one loves paradoxical talk, one can actually say—and if one properly understands the ambiguous sense involved, one can say in strict truth—that *"fiction" makes up the vital element of phenomenology* … that fiction is the source from which knowledge of the "eternal truths" draws its nourishment.
>
> (Husserl 2014: 127)

As Derrida puts it in his gloss on this point, fantasy "opens ideality," in the sense that such imagination (along with protention and retention) makes it possible for us to idealize these objects (Derrida [1967] 2011: 47). As with the pyramid we turned over in our hands, the object's ideality is, quite literally, *never* immediately present in the phenomenological field and—as such—is in part nonempirical. As Derrida puts it, "the thing itself always steals away" (89).

To return to Husserl's claims about language in "Origins of Geometry": despite the fact language is necessary for us to have geometry, he also wants to insist that *the objects to which words refer exist independently of language or consciousness*. The sentences in geometry textbooks are not geometry-itself, they *refer to* geometry, which *exists independently of the words in the textbook*. In his own words:

> the idealities of geometrical words, sentences, theories—considered purely as linguistic structures—are *not the idealities* that make up *what is expressed and brought to validity as truth in geometry* … Wherever something is asserted, one can distinguish what is thematic, that about which it is said (its meaning) *from* the assertion … And what is thematic here is precisely ideal objects, and quite different ones from those coming under the concept of language.
>
> (Husserl [1962] 1989: 161, emphasis mine)

This makes for an odd sort of realism: the truths of geometry are real, and real *independently* of language and any particular human consciousness—and yet everything else Husserl has already said about such objects explicitly claims that they are formed, intersubjectively, through repetition in language and consciousness and in *exactly the same way* as the words that refer to them.

Husserl explicitly notes that math and the sciences are never individual affairs: it requires a *civilization*. "Clearly it is only through language and its far reaching documentations, its possible communications, that the horizon of civilization can be an open and endless one" (Husserl [1962] 1989: 162). In addition, a civilization's written language is crucial for communication of "the objectivity of the ideal structure" of the truths of geometry across space and time (164). Third, the development of sciences is cumulative: "scientific thinking attains new results on the basis of those already obtained" (166). Fourth, scientific thinking is not passive discovery but rather a human production: "Making geometry self-evident … requires … methodical production … [c]arried out systematically" (173). Again, this is an odd sort of extra-linguistic realism: geometrical objects and truths exist independently of language, but they are *not discovered*; rather, they must be *produced* in language. (Careful readers will note that these conditions of the possibility of knowledge are very similar to the conditions of possibility of knowledge initially discussed at the beginning of the introduction to this book.)

Husserl's third claim about language and geometrical truths is that *the objectivity of the truths to which such words refer can be certain once we arrive at invariant constructions*. The sublation of the empirical and the substruction of ideality takes place *in history*, using the tools of language, but *eventually* arrives at a "*universal* a priori" (Husserl

[1962] 1989: 174, emphasis mine). When do we know we have arrived at the end, at a noncontingent, objective truth about geometrical objects? For Husserl, this takes place when we come to an unrevisable truth that can be infinitely repeated without variation: a truth is objective "only if the apodictically general content [is] invariant throughout all conceivable variation," that is, when it "can be understood for all future time and by all coming generations of men and thus capable of being handed down and reproduced with the identical intersubjective meaning" (179). Unlike "time-bound" truths, geometry "is valid with unconditioned generality *for all men, all times, all places,* and not merely for all historically factual ones but for all conceivable ones" (179, emphasis mine). For Husserl, perhaps historically specific languages are the condition of the possibility for the original substruction of such truths—they serve as the ladders that we can use to climb from history to objectivity, from the provincial to the universal—but once their invariant, universal forms are found, we can apparently kick the ladder away.

For Derrida, what is crucial is that here Husserl is writing checks that—empirically—he cannot cash. The future to which he appeals, a long future in which geometry will no longer be revisable, is *a priori not present today to any phenomenological consciousness*. The *objective* (rather than *subjective*) truth of geometry is ultimately warranted by future evidence and, as such, geometry's truth is at any particular point in time *a priori always-as-yet-unwarranted*. Despite the fact that Husserl elsewhere insists that *all truth claims must be based on empirical evidences that appear to phenomenological consciousness*—a premise that Husserl calls "the principle of principles," as Derrida reminds us (Derrida [1967] 2011: 46)—here Husserl warrants the objective truth of geometry *on the basis of a leap into the future*, and thus *beyond the empirical*. Once again, the *really real*—as something uncreated by humans, independent of consciousness, and unanchored by history—recedes further and further from the empirical. Those claims that Husserl takes to be most secure quite literally lack the warrant required by his very own "principle of all principles."

Kant, when pressed on the contradictions inherent in the arguments for the existence of God, admitted we do not and *a priori* could not have empirical evidence in time and space for a being that is unconditioned by time and space. To maintain his faith in the existence of things such as God, souls, and free will, he had to place them *outside* the phenomenal realm. Things-in-themselves are real; we just cannot see, hear, touch, smell, or taste them. For Hegel, at the end of the day Kant wanted to justify the claim that we can keep talking about his provincial, Christian god without any empirical evidence for that god, and here Derrida's claim is similar: Husserl wanted to justify the claim that we can have faith in the unrevisable, objective truths of European geometry without any empirical evidence that the claims we have at present are, in fact, unrevisable and objective (for the simple reason that, *a priori*, the future is not yet present to phenomenological consciousness and, as such, cannot be used to warrant present claims). And Derrida, like Hegel, accepts this point as *a priori* true not on the basis of some esoteric knowledge about reality, God, or geometry—rather, this is just an immanent critique based on how Husserl defines terms such as "geometry," "warrant," "phenomenal evidence," and "the future."

In "Philosophy and the Crisis of European Humanity," Husserl goes even further in his attempts to defend European philosophy and sciences from challenges to their universal, objective authority by literally appealing to a nonempirical spirit. In Europe, a "remarkable teleology," a "unity of spiritual life" (Husserl [1935] 1970: 273), or an "entelechy ... holds sway throughout all the changing shapes of Europe and accords to them the sense of a development toward an ideal shape of life and being as an eternal pole" (275). In Europe, relative "truth becomes objective truth," in the sense that it no longer "var[ies] according to nation or individual subject" (292). England and the United States belong to this spiritual unfolding, or share an "inner kinship of spirit which runs through them all, transcending national differences" (274), "whereas the Eskimos or Indians presented as curiosities at fairs, or the Gypsies, who constantly wander about Europe, do not" (273). This is why "Indian people ... experience [Europeans] as aliens ... at conferences" (275). "There is something unique here that is recognized in us by all other human groups, too, something that ... becomes a motive for them to Europeanize themselves ... whereas we, if we understand ourselves properly, would never Indianize ourselves" (275). "The spiritual *telos* of European humanity ... lies in the infinite" (275). By contrast, "Indian and Chinese philosophy" produces knowledge that remains merely "mythical" (284). I hope that it goes without saying that *teloi* are, *a priori*, nonempirical, in which case the foundation for Husserl's faith in the superiority of Europe entails reference to a thing-in-itself—a teleological spirit—that transcends the phenomenal field. Husserl's spirit of Europe is functionally identical to Kant's god, as is Husserl's foundation for the objective truth of European geometry.

Since arguments for things-in-themselves such as gods, unrevisable geometric truths, and culturally superior teleological spirits each involve an appeal to what transcends the empirical—and since, in hindsight, such arguments appear to look like unwarranted justifications for Christian and European ethnocentrisms—perhaps we should stop trying to authorize our own particular or provincial truths by appealing to things-in-themselves or what is independent of consciousness and rest content with the fact that, given the available evidence and the conditions of possibility of knowledge, the truths we hold to be certain are relative to consciousness—to say nothing of language, education, capital, power, and so on.

To summarize the points thus far,

- the identity of objects is constructed for consciousness, in time, through protention and retention of various empirical now moments in phenomenological consciousness;
- the identity substructed or produced depends on and simultaneously discards varying empirical evidences;
- this process of idealization is necessarily open-ended, as future phenomenological experiences may produce evidence that requires us to revise the objects at hand for consciousness;
- the representation of objects in and through language is a necessary condition for their individuation, ideality, or substruction, particularly objects such as geometrical figures or theorems;

Discourse and Ideology

- Husserl claims that the objective truths of, for example, geometry, have a mind-independent reality, but, as Derrida notes, he describes them as essentially dependent; and
- Husserl claims that the universal objectivity of such truths is secured by their invariant repetition throughout time, but, as Derrida notes, this claim is by definition unwarranted according to the standards of empirical evidence Husserl sets for himself.

Three Sticking Points

At this point I would like to draw attention to three sticking points against realism that follow from the previous discussion, each of which I will discuss in turn, with a special emphasis on the second:

- The only claims that are empirically warranted are claims about things-for-us.
- Object individuation is discourse-relative and variable.
- Matrices of individuation and claims about objects are essentially and indefinitely revisable.

The only claims that are empirically warranted are claims about things-for-us. Because things never appear in their entirety to phenomenological consciousness, their identity or ideality is constructed in consciousness. The identity of the object we arrive at—and "arrive" is an appropriate word, since ideality or substruction takes place *in time*—is *ours*. And we cannot say anything—true or false—about any object without engaging in the movement of ideality or substruction.

The obvious realist objection is that, of course, *for us* objects might be subject to the movement of ideality, but, arguably, the things-in-themselves—apart from any observer or speaker—exist independently of the processes of individuation. Common sense tells us that, even if we substruct the table for ourselves, what we end up calling—*at the end of the movement of ideality*—the "table" will exist even when we close our eyes; we can still stub our toe on the table while making our way to the kitchen in the dark.

First, however, we have no direct or unmediated empirical evidence from which we can speak of the table-in-itself. We only have indirect empirical evidence for the table—*because that is the only sort of evidence we can ever have for objects that do not appear in their fullness all at once* (that is, for *all* objects that exist in time). Second, the anti-realist need not deny the realist's last objection that we can stub our toes on tables we cannot presently see: of course our idealized constructions are often not only warranted on the basis of prior empirical evidence but exceedingly reliable in predicting how the stuff of the world can and will push up against our consciousness. But a subject stubbing her toe on a table entails a consciousness: toe-stubbing is, here, mind-dependent. In addition, the point that the realist seems to be pressing is tantamount to saying that the table can make impressions when no one is impressed, or that the table looks a certain way when no one is looking. Such assertions remind us of the famed one hand clapping: what kinds of contact are made when no contact is made? All knowledge of the world is conditioned by contact; we cannot have knowledge of an object without such contact.

Object individuation is discourse-relative and variable. For Derrida, (1) object individuation requires substruction, and (2) substruction is, for us, a discursively dependent process; (3) this makes "things" dependent on both consciousness and language for their existence *as* things. Note what is not asserted here: it does not follow from this that all of the stuff of the world is mind-dependent, only that the *individuation of* the stuff of the world is mind-dependent. This matters because *not all discourses individuate the stuff of the world in the same manner*, and there is insufficient warrant for the assumption that one matrix of individuation is superior to or closer to "reality" than another—although some matrices of individuation might be more *useful*, depending on a subject or a group's interests.

For an example, let me turn to *Defining Reality: Definitions and the Politics of Meaning* (2003), in which Edward Schiappa provides an account of how the definition of the word "wetlands" changed in the United States during the early 1990s.[3] At the time, conservationists who wanted to protect wetlands were in competition with developers who wanted to build houses, strip malls, etc. on existing wetlands, and each group substructed "wetlands" in a different manner.

For the conservationists, the keys to defining a "wetland" were threefold. (1) The soil had to be sufficiently saturated with water such that (2) less oxygen could get into the soil, creating conditions in which (3) only certain types of plants adapted to soil with less oxygen—called "hydrophytes"—could thrive. Their definition was not random, and nor was it based on a simple description of patches of land that were sort of wet. On the contrary, the conservationists were concerned first with protecting those species of plants and animals that could only live in these types of wetlands. Second, wetlands—at least on this construction—absorb and hold sediments that we, as humans, do not want in our drinking water, keeping the water table cleaner. Third, this sort of soil can also absorb excess water during heavy rainfall, thus protecting humans to some extent from possible floods. So the conservationists fabricated a definition of "wetland" precisely because they wanted to save certain plants and animals, improve drinking water, and protect us from floods. By contrast, developers had another sort of human interest: they wanted to make money by building on the properties designated and protected as "wetlands."

When George H. W. Bush was running for president of the United States in 1992, "wetlands" were a crucial political issue, and Bush needed to earn the votes of those citizens sympathetic to the conservationists. Consequently, one of his central campaign promises was that under his presidency he would ensure that no wetlands would be lost to development. However, at the same time he also wanted to please the developers so as to continue to get their support. When Bush finally came into office, he signed into existence legislation that protected "wetlands," but the legislation changed the substruction of "wetlands" in ways designed to serve the interests of the developers. Specifically, the legislation said that wetlands had to be *very wet*, not just below the

Discourse and Ideology

surface of the soil but also at the surface. Bush said, "I've got a radical view of wetlands. I think wetlands ought to be wet" (Schiappa 2003: 87). This benefitted the developers because this greatly reduced the number of "wetlands," as, based on the definition of the conservationists, not all of the "wetlands" were really wet or had water on the surface.

Estimates suggested that probably 30 million to 50 million acres of land that had been "wetlands" on the conservationists' definition were reclassified as "not wetlands"—reducing the number of wetlands by a third or by half—so that the developers could build houses and strip malls. A great deal of money could be made, and Bush could claim he kept his campaign promise: he *did* in fact approve legislation that protected the "wetlands," even as he redefined the term to suit his purposes. It was a successful bait and switch.

The conservationists, of course, were unhappy with these results, insofar as the "really wet" wetlands were so different from the "wetlands" they had singled out that the new legislation no longer served their interests. "Really wet" wetlands could not absorb sediments dangerous to human drinking water in the same way, could not absorb floodwaters, and did not sustain the types of endangered species that thrived in the type of "wetlands" that fit their definition. On the new definition, all of the desires of the conservationists were thwarted.

For Schiappa, what is interesting about this case is that both definitions of "wetlands" are tied to human interests, just different sets of interests. What is a wetland? The answer to that question apparently depends on whether one wants a clean water table and to avoid floods, or if one wants to build a suburb. Note: we cannot simply answer that question by going out and looking at one. The demarcation of such an object is, *a priori*, not an empirical matter. The very same patch of land might look like a wetland for the conservationists but not for Bush and the developers.

Another crucial point for Schiappa is that these definitional decisions are always related to political power, which is why they are so contested. At the end of the day, what is politically crucial is the legal definition *enforced by the state*. Conservationists can define "wetlands" differently all they want, but their definition has no real-world consequences as long as the state is endorsing and enforcing another definition.

Schiappa concludes that abstract questions like "what is a wetland?"—especially when considered outside of any social or political context—are generally useless. Rather, "the questions to ask are 'Whose interests are being served by this particular definition?' and 'Do we identify with those interests'" (Schiappa 2003: 82)? Do we want to make money or save houses from floods?

Returning to the anti-realist point, here the individuation of objects is clearly discourse-dependent. Without the discourses of conservationism, we would not have individuated "wetlands" in the first place. Their existence *as wetlands* is a product of their discursive substruction. The things of the world do not individuate themselves; had humans never evolved, no one would ever have individuated wetlands. As Hägglund puts it in his discussion of Derrida's commentary on Emmanuel Levinas's body of writings, "discrimination has to be regarded as a constitutive condition. Without divisional marks—which is to say, without segregating borders—there would be nothing at all" (Hägglund 2008: 82). I would qualify the point: it is not that there would be nothing at all, it is that there would be no "things" at all.

Here it is worth returning to the realist's primary objection, posed above: "of course, *for us* objects might be subject to the movement of ideality, but, arguably, the objects in-themselves—apart from any observer or speaker—exist independently of the processes of ideality." John R. Searle is one of the most strident advocates of this view. In *The Construction of Social Reality*, he defines realism as "the view that there is a way that things are that is logically independent of all human representations" (Searle 1995: 155, emphasis removed). Searle allows that all *descriptions* of the "brute facts" of reality—including, for instance, the "brute fact" that "Mount Everest exists independently of how or whether I or anyone else ever represented it or anything else"—are discourse-relative: "all representations of reality are made *relative to* some more or less arbitrarily selected set of concepts" (161, emphasis added). However, he insists that the "brute facts" that discourses describe *exist independently* of discourse and make discourses about them possible; for Searle, conceptual relativism "seems to presuppose realism, because it presupposes a language-independent reality that can be carved up or divided up in different ways" (165).

The problem, from the perspective of this chapter, is in the phrase "there is a way that *things* are": for Derrida, "things" *entails* individuation and individuation *entails* the intentional consciousnesses Searle wants to exclude from the "brute facts" of reality. While Searle would like to claim that "there is a way things are that is logically independent of all human representations," it appears that what we call "logic" is semantic, and semantics are, *a priori*, the result of "human representations." It is difficult for me to accept, as Searle so readily does, that it could be true that "*S* is *P*" without anyone ever having defined "S" or "P."

As should be clear from Schiappa's example, stating that "wetlands" exist *as wetlands* independently of the process of their demarcation makes little sense: of *which particular* type of wetlands are we speaking? Of course, the anti-realist could rightfully allow the following: those things that conservationists eventually individuated as wetlands existed prior to when conservationists individuated them. As Searle rightly notes,

> We arbitrarily define the word "cat" in such and such a way; and only relative to such and such definitions can we say, "That's a cat." But once we have made the definitions and once we have applied the concepts relative to the system of definitions, whether or not something satisfies our definition is no longer arbitrary or relative.
>
> (Searle 1995: 166)

However, prior to formulating a definition of "wetland," that referent to which the term *now* refers did not exist *as* wetlands then, because to exist *as* a wetland, or to be individuated *as* a wetland, is always to be *for-us*. Were we to remove the conservationists' individuation or the *for-us*, the resulting claim—"wetlands existed prior to when conservationists individuated them"—would be far more problematic. *A priori* such a claim could not be verified as true without investigation of the "extra-linguistic" referent for the word "wetland," and such an inquiry would *necessarily* require reference back to the linguistic discourses of the conservationists, or the *for-us*—in which case we're back in anti-realist territory. *The "extra-linguistic" referent is dependent for its individuation on language.*

It is for this reason that, in *Bodies that Matter*, Butler notes that referring to matter-itself or materiality to ground one's claims is problematic, because what counts as "material" is a moving target.

> What does it mean to have recourse to materiality, since it is clear from the start that matter has a history (indeed, more than one) and that the history of matter is in part determined by the negotiation of sexual difference. We may seek to return to matter as prior to discourse to ground our claims about sexual difference only to discover that matter is fully sedimented with discourses on sex and sexuality that prefigure and constrain the uses to which that term can be put.
>
> (Butler 1993: 29)

This is why, as I noted in the previous chapter, that referring to empirical bodies alone cannot ground our claims about gender difference, because the same body might be "male" on one discourse and "female" on another. The point is not that bodies do not exist and all we have is discourse; rather, the point is that we need discourses to divide up bodies, different discourses produce different bodies, and the choice of one discourse over another appears to reflect a desire to regulate the bodies individuated by discourse.

This second sticking point is perhaps the most important one because it draws attention to the social and political consequences of realism: *realism naturalizes historically specific matrices of individuation.* Realism insists that a table is just a table, as if that were the final word on the matter, as if what some might call a "table" could not be individuated differently—as a desk, as fuel for a house fire, or as garbage or debris in a landfill. While naturalizing the individuation of a table might be largely politically innocuous or irrelevant, the same is not true of objects such as "primitive savage," "woman," "madness," or "homosexual." Not all matrices of individuation substruct "woman" in the same manner, but naturalizing one individuation over others can have considerable social consequences—and *that is the risk always taken by the realist approach* to objects. As I noted above, during Foucault's life psychiatrists were literally lobotomizing the people their discourse individuated as "insane" because they were "homosexual." Or, to use another example, a realist for whom the claim that "life begins at conception" is fully naturalized is liable to have difficulty understanding or communicating with those who individuate "human life" in a different manner. Indeed, by all appearances zygotes are entities conditioned by sperm and eggs; why draw a line in this ongoing ontological process right at this point? Why say that sperm and eggs are not human life, but that a zygote is human life, particularly when the biological processes seem continuous rather than discontinuous? If we think of the relationships between these objects as the ongoing writing of DNA, a sperm, and egg, and a zygote are part of a perpetual process with no clear starting or ending point. For those who want to outlaw abortion, the line between "sperm and egg" and "zygote" is likely not founded on clear boundaries in the ongoing process of the writing of DNA, but rather on the fact that drawing the line here is legally useful for separating what they would like to extend rights to (the zygote) from what they would not (the sperm and the egg right before the one entered the other). Neither wetlands nor human life individuate themselves—humans do. For those realist evangelicals for whom "life" just is what it is, the contingency of their discursive scheme remains invisible, naturalized, and at times completely uncontested because it is viewed merely as "common sense." In such cases, *realism* is a considerable *barrier to historicization*.

One need not be a "radical" poststructuralist to come to such a conclusion about the relativity of object individuation. Euro-American analytical philosophers provide us with similar arguments. In his classic *Ways of Worldmaking*—cited briefly above—Nelson Goodman notes that "identification rests upon organization into entities and kinds. The response to the question 'Same or not the same?' must always be 'Same what?' ... Identity or constancy in a world is identity *with respect to* what is within that world *as organized*" (Goodman 1978: 8, emphasis mine). Hilary Putnam defends a similar view, calling it "conceptual pluralism." He writes,

> we might describe "the contents" of a room very differently by using first the vocabulary of fundamental physical theory [i.e., "as consisting of fields and particles"] and then again the vocabulary of tables and chairs and lamps ... [W]e can use both of these schemes without being required to reduce one or both of them to some single fundamental and universal ontology.
>
> (Putnam 2004: 48–49)

Putnam concludes by noting that "the whole idea that the *world* dictates a unique 'true' way of dividing the world into objects, situations, or properties, etc., is a piece of philosophical parochialism" (Putnam 2004: 51). From such a perspective, there is no final or unrevisable ontology or matrix of individuation.

Matrices of individuation and claims about objects are essentially and indefinitely revisable. The third sticking point is that matrices of individuation are indefinitely revisable. Time or temporality is the horizon of possibility for the substruction of objects, but openness to temporality simultaneously makes the closure of substruction theoretically impossible. Protention haunts every present now moment: it could always be the case that some future will come along that force us to revise our matrices of individuation. This could be for several reasons. First, by turning objects in our hands—in the case of mid-sized objects—or by gathering new data—for instance, by performing scientific experiments—we may see a side or profile of the objects we have individuated that have never appeared to us before. Second, "things" change and thus the objects we individuate may present new or previously unprecedented features, characteristics, or behaviors. Third, changing interests may invite us to individuate objects in a novel ways,

Discourse and Ideology

as when George H. W. Bush's political interests directed his administration to individuate "wetlands" in a different manner.

Although my defense of anti-realism ultimately might not be persuasive to many readers, I hope to have demonstrated, first, that Derrida's views are neither unargued (as Searle claims about Derrida [see Searle 1995, 159]) nor simplistically naïve—as if he could not tell the difference or recognize a distinction between a word and a referent. Second, I hope to have shown that the stakes of the discussion are not simply esoteric; insofar as realism can be used to naturalize or have the effect of naturalizing particular matrices of individuation, the question of anti-realism matters socially and politically.

The Science of Cognition

Before concluding, I wish to contrast Derrida, Foucault, and Butler's views on the necessity of language for object individuation with recent empirical research in cognitive science. In sum, the evidence demonstrates relatively conclusively that all objects are constructed for consciousness in some manner, although language is, in fact, not necessary for the substruction of some objects.

In *Visual Intelligence: How We Create What We See*, Donald D. Hoffman describes the extent to which "vision is not merely a matter of passive perception, [but rather] an intelligent process of active construction. What you see is, invariably, what your visual intelligence constructs" (Hoffman 2000: xii). Much as Husserl noted above, Hoffman notes that spatial depth is not present in phenomenological consciousness, but is provided through visual processing: "*anytime* you see depth you construct it … There are no exceptions. You construct the depth you see on the street, in your office, at a football game, or from the top of the mountain" (23). This is in part because of the nature of human eyes: the retina is made up of discrete rods and cones, so that any image on the retina is, technically speaking, like a two-dimensional pointillist painting. For instance, the image of a sphere on a retina, "has neither curves nor surfaces—only dots. But you see more than dots; you see curves and surfaces. Logic dictates, then, that you are their source. You construct each curve and surface you see" (64). As Hoffman goes on to argue, the unconscious choices our minds make when constructing what we see are not arbitrary; rather, they are shortcuts that appear to have offered *Homo sapiens* an evolutionary advantage. Most of the book goes on to demonstrate precisely what those shortcuts are—shortcuts that, in a few cases, confuse us, as is the case with what we usually refer to as "optical illusions."

Hoffman devotes a considerable time noting how visual construction can invent apparent motion. If subjects are shown two dots on a computer screen at particular intervals, first one on the left and then one on the right, human vision sees not two dots flashing in and out of existence but rather one dot moving from the left to the right. In addition, if the two dots are of different colors, human vision sees a dot moving from the left to the right and changing colors at the same time. Interestingly, our perception apparatus "sees" the dot changing color in the middle of the "movement" from left to right. "If you see the moving dot turn from green to red at the half-way point, then it turns red *before* the red dot ever comes on" (Hoffman 2000: 143–144). In phenomenological consciousness, time is out of joint.[4]

This analysis of the two-dot "illusion" is, in the way I have described it, implicitly realist. The claim seems to be that there are, *in reality*, two discrete dots, not one moving and changing color, although it might appear that way to consciousness. However, Hoffman is not contrasting human perception with the thing-in-itself, but, rather, with dots *as measured by a photometer*. A photometer attached to a clock would "see" or measure one light, then nothing, then another light of a different color. "What does this show? Simply, as we've found many times before, that you're not a photometer, nor a photometer with an attached clock. What you construct is typically more sophisticated than, and certainly different from, what a photometer and clock construct" (Hoffman 2000: 144). As such, the point is anti-realist rather than realist: we are not contrasting one construction with reality as it is in itself, but rather one construction with another construction. The phenomenal field can be individuated differently using different measuring devices. In addition, to ask what things-in-themselves look like outside measurement by a photometer, a human consciousness, or any other measuring device seems nonsensical.

In addition to the extensive literature on adult vision, there is a mountain of literature on infant cognition. The empirical evidence for infants' cognition of objects is underdetermining, however, and a number of different theories have been advanced to account for the evidence; there are several dominant views and they're greatly contested. In particular, there is a great deal of disagreement on the extent to which infant cognition is developmental—that is, the extent to which it is either "hardwired" or empirically learned through association or experimentation—or the extent to which it is fixed or variable. However, despite that, there are a number of things that are relatively certain and well established, at least at the beginning of the twenty-first century.

First, it is clear that the cognition of visual objects is far less conscious than Husserl or Derrida imply. We do not visually substruct mid-sized objects by consciously attending to the various now moments in phenomenological consciousness. Rather, there are a great number of unconscious cognitive processes operating in, for example, visual perception. To offer just one quick example, as Alison Gopnik and Andrew N. Meltzoff note in *Words, Thoughts, and Theories*, "the perceptual system already 'smooths over' our blinks" (Gopnik and Meltzoff 1997: 80). (Notably, the perceptual system also smooths over our "blind spot," which is always there and yet no one has ever seen it.) For Derrida, at least in his commentary on Husserl, it is almost as if blinks—interruptions to our visual field—are something we need to consciously subtract from our perception, insofar as they interrupt our vision of the object at hand. However, apart from when we are explicitly and consciously reflecting on how blinking interrupts our field of vision, we are unlikely to notice the way in which such interruptions are unconsciously smoothed over. Our apparatus of perception does that work in the background without our conscious help.

Second, Husserl emphasizes that the identity of an object—of a geometrical pyramid, for instance—is not ever present in direct phenomenological consciousness, but rather that we construct it for ourselves after turning over all sides of it. But we need not have language to see visual objects. The evidence demonstrates that infants—from birth—are capable of visually tracking object permanence in three-dimensional fields, in which case object construction is happening *long before* the acquisition of language and, again, *without conscious reflection*. Gopnick and Meltzoff note that the empirical evidence supports the view that "infants are born assuming a world of three-dimensional, amodal objects … For example, infants make appropriate inferences about whether their reaches will make contact with an object and about the relation between size and distance" (Gopnik and Meltzoff 1997: 83). Many of the studies done with infants focus on how their eyes track objects that pass behind opaque obstacles:

> it is clear that even these very young infants predict something about where the object will reappear after it has disappeared. Indeed, in the reaching-in-the-dark cases [in which infants reach for an object that has moved out of their visual field], the infant must continue to represent the object even when it is out of their immediate sight. If we use this minimal notion of object permanence, then even very young infants seem to have object permanence.
>
> (Gopnik and Meltzoff 1997: 83)

In addition, infants also seem to realize that "solid objects cannot pass through each other" (Gopnik and Meltzoff 1997: 85). This evidence clearly contradicts poststructuralist claims that the cognitive construction of all objects appears to be necessarily discursively dependent on language.

However, words might be necessary to see a "single" object as "the same" if there are interruptions in one's vision over time. As Susan Carey writes in *The Origin of Concepts*:

> if perceptual representations are limited to what currently experienced entities look like, feel like, taste like, and move like, objects cannot be represented as individuals that persist through time, independently of the same observer … the child could not represent a given object as the same one as one seen earlier, for sensory representations do not provide criteria for numerical identity.
>
> (Carey 2009: 34)

That is to say, we have no evidence that a toy that is "the same" for adults today as it was yesterday is viewed as "the same" for the infant. Sameness is most definitely *not* in the perception of the phenomenal field but, rather, requires cognitive work of some sort—and possibly even words.

Sometimes object individuation can be "fooled" in a sense: infants may represent two-dimensional displays to themselves in three dimensions. In such cases, our "mid-level object tracking system is *misrepresenting* these stimuli" (Carey 2009: 98). "One reason to believe that infants misrepresent 2-D pictures as real objects is that, under at least some circumstances, they attempt to pick them up" (99). It is likely for this reason that when I put YouTube videos of birds on my television, my cats swat at birds that appear to be flying out of the television screen's field, as if physical, three-dimensional birds were literally flying off of the screen. This is presumably why, for instance, they also walk behind the television to see if the birds are behind the flat screen. Infants and cats—and cats are infants in the technical sense of being *infans*, "without speech"—appear to have a cognitive capacity to construct and track three-dimensional objects that are, for adult humans, *simply not there*. In such cases, constructing three-dimensional objects from two-dimensional images doesn't appear to require language.

We have evidence that evolutionary adaptation predisposes some nonhuman animals to construct objects in ways that are to some extent conspecific (i.e., species-specific). Carey draws attention to research on indigo buntings; these songbirds, when nestlings, determine what we call "north" by individuating a pole star at the center of the night sky's rotation. Researchers can "fool" such nestlings in a planetarium by rotating the constellations around a different star, causing them to identify that alternate star as a marker for true north. This, in turn, affected the "direction the birds took off in the autumn" (Carey 2009: 15). This is conspecific because, clearly, human infants do not have the bodily or cognitive capacities to construct a pole star in such a manner. However, humans likely have alternative, conspecific cognitive capacities in the individuation of the objects in our perceptual fields, ones that operate prior to the acquisition of language. And, as is clear, the objects visually constructed in such a manner are dependent upon cognitive capacities that draw upon *nonempirical* resources rather than mere, direct perception of "reality"—for, if so, our visual field would appear like pointillist paintings, given the mechanics of our eyes. Carey also points to similar forms of research on object individuation for goslings and chicks (see Carey 2009: 16–17 and 58). In sum, different bodies see different things in the world.

Last, empirical research suggests that young infants construct object permanence on the basis of object *trajectory* rather than object *characteristics*. "Young infants do not seem to show disrupted tracking if an object disappears behind a screen and a completely different object emerges at the far edge of the screen on the same trajectory, nor are they surprised by these events" (Gopnick and Meltzoff 1997: 84). "Their predictions about the behavior of objects center on an object's movements, rather than its properties" (85). This makes sense for animals that only require crude object construction. Consider a house cat sitting in the backyard watching a bird fly in circles: the two-dimensional image of the bird that hits the cat's retina will continually change with the movement of time. Much like Husserl noted about how the perception of color changes as an object moves, the observer moves, or the light source moves, so too would the properties of the bird's image constantly change. One moment the cat might see wings spread, while the next moment the wings might be closed and the bird is more like a diving, pointed arrow. For object individuation to have an evolutionary advantage—namely, for the cat to be able to catch the bird—the changing shape of the object would need to be wholly subsidiary to its trajectory.

Discourse and Ideology

But to return to human infants: when, say, a red cube disappears behind a screen and a blue ball appears on the other side of the screen—along the same trajectory of course—a young infant's cognitive capabilities apparently construct *a single object* in the infant's conscious experience. Human adults, by contrast, would much more likely unconsciously individuate the infant's "object" as *two objects*, on the basis of its properties rather than its trajectory. Notably—*either way* the individuation of one object or two objects for consciousness is a construction performed by unconscious cognitive processes.

This research contradicts both the naïve, realist views of object perception and some of the claims about language made by poststructuralists. It contradicts the realist view because cognitive construction is a condition of possibility for there being objects in the first place. It contradicts poststructuralist claims because, at least for mid-sized objects, language is clearly not necessary for visual object individuation.

However, in defense of poststructuralists, most objects with which we—as human adults—are concerned are not mid-sized objects in our immediate field of vision. When it comes to molecules and atoms, DNA, cancer cells, the economy, limited liability corporations, the government, our daily workload, and so on, we are dealing with objects that are, in fact, dependent on language—in addition to unconscious cognitive processes—for their individuation and construction. Thus I would argue that, apart from mid-sized objects, language *is necessary* for object construction.

In this section I have argued the following:

- not all objects are individuated via language; it appears, for instance, that—as a result of evolution—neurotypical humans have been equipped with unconscious cognitive processes that permit us to construct three-dimensional objects from the two-dimensional images that strike our retinas; however,
- the unconscious construction of visual objects for consciousness may be different for children compared to adults—what babies see as one object we may see as two, and vice versa; and
- while language is not necessary to construct such mid-sized objects, most objects of knowledge that interest us are not mid-sized objects and thus must be individuated, constructed, or idealized via language.

I suspect that part of the ongoing appeal of realism is in part the result of realists' use of sight as a metaphor for knowledge. While the science of cognition reveals that no such thing as direct sight is possible for beings with our bodies (and, arguably, for beings with any kind of body), the cognitive processes that mediate sight for consciousness are largely unconscious—we literally cannot see how sight is mediated. If we used other metaphors, it might be easier to understand poststructuralism. If, like Husserl, we wished to describe how a table appears to us, we might do better to use the metaphor of touch rather than sight. If we closed our eyes and *felt* rather than looked at the table, it would be much more clear to us that knowledge of the table is mediated. We could never idealize the table in consciousness all at once via touch alone. It would take minutes of groping the table to get a sense of its contours—the table, for us, through touch, would be a more indirect and painstaking process. In addition, this indirect and painstaking process functions better as a metaphor for knowledge production than sight. If we want to produce knowledge about, for instance, trees, we won't get very far by just looking at one. Knowledge production is a time-consuming process: we would look at the tree, take pictures, compare those pictures to pictures of other trees (perhaps of the same species, perhaps of different species), take samples, look at those samples under microscopes, submit those samples to chemical analysis, submit those samples to DNA sequencing, write down our findings for people who do not have access to our trees, our labs, our DNA samples, compare our writings to what people in other labs have written about trees, and so forth—an indefinite process, and one that is conditioned by the availability of material capital. Knowledge of trees is much more like slowly feeling out the contours of the table than instantaneously "seeing" one in front of us. The metaphors we use to talk about knowledge, it seems, predispose us to think of knowledge differently and, as such, we ought to choose our metaphors carefully.

***

Despite the ontological extravagances of Berkeley's idealism, he makes a rather brilliant point about "things-in-themselves" in *Three Dialogues*. There, Philonous—the character who represents Berkeley's view—asks his rhetorical opponent: "Have [external] things a stable and permanent nature independent of our sense; or are they in a perpetual change" (Berkeley 1996: 145)? His interlocutor responds,

> Real things, it is plain, have a *fixed and real* nature, which *remains the same*, notwithstanding any change in our senses, or in the posture and motion of our bodies; which indeed may affect the ideas in our minds, but it were absurd to think they had the same effect on things existing without the mind.
>
> (Berkeley 1996: 145, emphasis added)

Philonous responds by asking,

> How then is it possible, that things *perpetually fleeting and variable* as our ideas, should be copies or images of anything *fixed and constant*? Or in other words, since all sensible qualities, as size, figure, colour, &c. that is, our ideas are *continually changing* upon every alteration in the distance, medium, or instruments of sensation; how can any determinate material objects be properly represented or painted forth by several distinct things, each of which is so different from and unlike the rest?
>
> (Berkeley 1996: 145–146, emphasis added)

That is, if things-in-themselves are fixed, how could difference appear? Perhaps, as Hegel and Derrida have argued, the "fixed and real nature" of things-in-themselves is little more than a useful fiction of consciousness, which substructs identity from difference, unity from diversity, or ideality from empiricism. Indeed, perhaps even "there is no thing itself" (Derrida [1967] 1976: 292).

CHAPTER 3
DISCOURSE

Discourse consists of vocabularies or collections of words, spoken or written, strung together to form phrases, slogans, sentences, monologues, conversations, paragraphs, missives, tracts, manifestos, speeches, books, and so forth. The contexts in which discourses appear are indefinite; discourses can be found in "high" contexts such as academic monographs or official state or corporate propaganda, but also in "low" contexts such as fortune cookies, flyers for goods and services, or arguments among family members. However, for discourse analysis—as I'm defining it—the *sina qua non* of discourse is not its content or its discursive site but its *functions*. In my opinion, the function too often ignored is *discourse's ability to encourage affective sympathies and antipathies in persuaded audiences*.

In this chapter I will describe several functions that discourse can serve and demonstrate how discourse analysis—as a mode of cultural critique—can bring such functions into relief. The primary discursive site I will use to illustrate these matters is Bouck White's early nineteenth-century "biography" of Jesus, titled *The Call of the Carpenter* (White 1913). White's book, although purportedly nonfictional, is a wildly anachronistic account of the life of Jesus that depicts him as a working-class communist agitator. I have chosen this discursive site insofar as we can find in it all of the functions of discourse that interest me.

Before beginning, I would like to note that by no means am I suggesting that discourse serves *only* the particular functions I draw attention to, or that discourse analysis must take the shape I am giving it here. Rather, what I have attempted to do is look back over my work from the last decade and a half and formalize just what it is I have been doing when I have claimed to be doing discourse analysis. Other forms of discourse analysis focus more narrowly on, for instance, turn-taking in conversations or how passive voice is used to mystify agency—for example, as when politicians say "mistakes were made" but do not identify *by whom* those mistakes were made (see Fairclough 1992: esp. ch. 1, for a useful survey of different types of cultural critique that fall under the name "discourse analysis"). However, those forms of discourse analysis are too myopic to address the questions I am concerned with, such as "how is discourse constitutive of something like a nation-state?" or "what is the relation between constitutive discourses and legitimating ideologies?"

Although I am indebted to Michel Foucault's model of discourse analysis, in what follows I do not pretend to be an orthodox Foucauldian, and in several respects my definition of discourse or discourse analysis diverges significantly from the outline he

Discourse and Ideology

provides in *Archaeology of Knowledge*; to a large extent my discourse on discourses produces a different object than that of which Foucault wrote. My account of discourse analysis is in many ways closer to Bruce Lincoln's method of studying discourse, as elaborated in *Discourse and the Construction of Society* (Lincoln 1989) and "How to Read a Religious Text" (Lincoln 2006: esp. 131–133).[1] There Lincoln emphasizes how discourses constitute and rank the imagined objects of which they speak, how discourses legitimate such rankings, and the relation between such rankings and the social position of the various groups to which the discourses refer.

In what follows, I will begin by focusing on the constitutive functions of discourse—namely, how discourse constitutes its own referents. Second, I will turn to descriptive discourse, which makes empirical claims about already constituted referents. Last, I will move on to how discourse functions directly in relation to social power, particularly insofar as it can assign and naturalize social roles, sympathies and antipathies, and so on.

Constitutive Discourse

In *The Archaeology of Knowledge*, Foucault emphasizes the constitutive role of discourse in the creation of objects: discourses are "practices that systematically form the objects of which they speak" (Foucault 1972: 49). At the very least, this production of the objects of discourse includes the processes of substruction or idealization described in Chapter 2 of this book. Objects do not individuate themselves; mid-sized objects require at the very least perceptual and cognitive processes for their idealization, and other objects—for instance, wetlands, geometry, industries, economies, or nations—have spoken or written discourse as their condition of possibility. In addition, as Butler notes, to say that discourse "produces" or "forms" objects is not to say that discourse is a material or efficient cause of objects; rather, "produce" means "demarcate" or "differentiate" (Butler 1993: 1). Since "wetlands" do not individuate themselves, we must produce discourses and deploy matrices of individuation to create them; discourse is then both a constitutive and a necessary (but not sufficient) condition of possibility of such objects. As such, one of the chief goals of discourse analysis is to describe *how* discourses constitute their objects, so that we may recognize their contingency. In this way discourse analysis is necessarily *meta*: discourse analysis is a discourse on discourses; it makes an object of the making of objects.

Discourse analysis, when focusing on discourse's constitutive function, often has a semantic focus; to understand how wetlands are individuated or idealized, we must pay careful attention to key words in discourses on wetlands, how the terms are defined or systematically used, as well as their extension (i.e., tracking reference, or which things in the world are "picked up" by the word or concept at hand). Such research can be either synchronic—focusing on how terms function at a particular historical moment—or diachronic—focusing on how the uses of terms change over time. Philology, the historical study of words and language, may be particularly useful for reconstructing the drift of individuation and extension across historical time periods.

In addition, when forming objects discourses also sort and distribute objects as *same* or *equivalent, different*, and sometimes as *ranked*. In a fisherman's discourse, a shark and a dolphin might be equivalent insofar as they are distributed as "unwanted things that end up in my nets." By contrast, in a biology teacher's discourse, a shark and a dolphin might be distributed as different—one being a fish and one being a mammal. Whether things are equivalent or not *depends on the discourses that distribute them as such*. Similarly, discourses often rank what is distributed, although this is a contingent rather than necessary feature of discourse. For instance, the Carnegie classification system for colleges and universities creates groups such as "R1," "R2," "M1," and "M2"; however, in addition to creating these groups, the classification has a distributive ranking built into the terms used. "R1" has a normative valuation embedded in it that ranks it "above" "R2." Such a distributive ranking also appears in the evolutionary classification of "primitive savages" and "civilized nations" or "third world" and "first world" nations. As such, ranking discourses can function to *normalize* whichever objects sit at the top of ranked hierarchies, as well as derogate remainders.

As noted in Chapter 2 in this book, objects are discursively dependent for their individuation, but the objects individuated may not be existentially dependent upon discourse. Consider the term "planet": this term has been used in various—and competing—ways, such that the object individuated as "Pluto" was at one time also identified as a "planet" but is, in fact, no longer identified as such. Whether or not Pluto is a planet is a historically specific and discursively dependent fact. However, few would go so far as to say that Pluto is existentially dependent on discourse. As Foucault notes in *Security, Territory, Population*—a posthumously published series of lectures from 1977 to 1978—there is a difference between "the cosmos itself" and the discourses we use to individuate objects from it. By contrast, however, something like a state is existentially dependent upon discourse: without subjects who imagine it into existence with discourse it would not have a material existence. Foucault claims (and due to the importance of this point, I quote at length),

> My aim has not been to give you the history of the planet Earth in terms of astrophysics but to give you the history of the reflexive prism that, at a certain moment, allowed one to think that the Earth was a planet. It is the same kind of thing, but with a difference however. The difference is that when one simply does the history of the sciences, of the way in which we learned, the way in which we constituted a knowledge in which the Earth appears as a planet in relation to the sun, then it is quite clear that in doing a history like that one is doing the history of a completely autonomous and independent series that has nothing to do with the evolution of the cosmos itself. *It goes without saying that the fact that since a certain point in time we have known that the Earth is a planet has had no influence on the Earth's position in the cosmos.* However, the appearance of the state on the

horizon of a reflected practice at the end of the sixteenth and the beginning of the seventeenth century has been of absolutely capital importance in the history of the state and in the way in which the institutions of the state actually crystalized.

(Foucault 2007: 276, emphasis mine)

Despite the fact that Foucault is an anti-realist, he still freely admits that "it goes without saying that the fact that since a certain point in time we have known that the earth is a planet has had no influence on the Earth's position in the cosmos." Knowledge that the earth is a planet apparently had to wait until humans developed special vocabularies that defined "planets" and set them apart from other things in what we colloquially call "outer space," but it does not follow that the word "planet" was a material cause or efficient cause of the earth. By contrast, Foucault calls the creation of something like a state a "reflexive event," in the sense that its creation requires a reflexive relationship between subjects who speak a state into existence, the state thus created, and then other subjects who internalize a state that appears to them as an objective institution. Social formations do require words as efficient causes.

The process by which this comes about is described by Peter L. Berger and Thomas Luckmann in *The Social Construction of Reality: A Treatise in the Sociology of Knowledge* (1967). Despite the fact that humans "manifest[] immense placticity" (Berger and Luckmann 1967: 48) and, as a result, could produce an indefinite number of behaviors, in practice humans tend to produce a (relatively) small number of habitualized behaviors. With habitualization, "the action in question may be performed again in the future in the same manner and with the same economical effort" (53). Once ritualized behaviors and social interactions are crystalized and reified, future generations are socialized into them, and "the institutions are experienced as possessing a reality of their own, a reality that confronts the individual as an external and coercive fact" (58). That is, despite the fact that our invented institutions were created by us, and, as such, are capable of revision or replacement, for future generations "an institutional world … is experienced as an objective reality" (60).

Ian Hacking draws attention to the role of the classification of humans in this process. Hacking distinguishes between "indifferent kinds" and "interactive kinds," which demonstrate a "looping effect." Concerning indifferent kinds, Hacking notes that "qarks are not aware"[2] and "plutonium does not interact with the idea of plutonium" (Hacking 1999: 105). By contrast, humans are often conscious of and respond to the categories by which they are identified and, as such, experience "classificatory looping" (109–110). The example he provides is of children who were identified in the past as being "retarded" or "mentally handicapped"; not only does the classification "become embedded in a complex matrix of institutions and practices" (112), but children thus identified are conscious of the classification, and it shapes not only how they self-identify but also how they behave. The point is that ascripted identities not only shape how people act toward subjects so labeled, but also that insofar as the ascripted identity is internalized it literally creates a different subject, with new and different behaviors. Hacking writes that once new distinctions, labels, or classifications are made, "new realities effectively come into being" (Hacking 2002: 103). Indeed, social realities are "conditioned, stabilized, or even created by the labels we apply to people, actions, and communities" (103). Thus can discourses—as practices—form subjects in addition to objects.[3]

This is, of course, the same process that Louis Althusser describes as "interpellation." Although using the term "ideology" rather than "discourse," Althusser writes that "ideology 'acts' or 'functions' in such a way as to 'recruit' subjects among individuals (it recruits them all) through the very precise operation that we call *interpellation* or *hailing*" (Althusser 2014: 190). His classic example is of a man responding to a police officer yelling, "Hey, you there" (190)! Insofar as the man so hailed turns and responds, "he becomes a *subject*. Why? Because he has recognized that the hail 'really' was addressed to him and that 'it really was he who was hailed' (not someone else)" (190–191). Althusser notes that this happens even before subjects are born—as when, for example, parents buy all pink clothes for a soon-to-be-born daughter. However, the process of interpellation is never simple:

> ideologies never stop interpellating subjects as subjects, never stop "recruiting" individuals who are always-already subjects. *The play of ideologies is superposed, criss-crossed, contradicts itself on the same subject*: the same individual always-already (several times) subject. Let him figure things out, if he can.
>
> (Althusser 2014: 193–194, emphasis added)

Although discourse brings subjects into being by giving them an ascribed identity, subjects—and objects—are almost always classified through multiple and often *competing* matrices of individuation.

When discourse is constitutive rather than descriptive of subjects and objects, discourse more resembles a blueprint than a map. Maps, we tend to assume, trace or track the boundaries of *already delimited* distributions in the world; by contrast, blueprints are models on the basis of which we create the delimited distributions of our world in the first place. For example, in 1606, the British colonists who first came to North America used the words "charter," "colony," "sea coasts," "America," "Virginia," and "Christian people"—among others—as blueprints for the formation of the colony of Virginia and the town of Jamestown. Or, to put it differently, *discourse gerrymanders* such spaces into existence. In addition, insofar as discourses gerrymander objects into existence, they simultaneously establish or imagine idealized or desired relations between the objects individuated. For instance, legal discourses on lawyers, law firms, clients, judges, and so on, establish not only what these objects are but also permitted and disallowed relations between them—attorney-client privilege is contingent upon a discourse that mandates that some potentially relevant legal evidence may rightly be kept private.

However, this is not to say that discourse cannot map. In the twenty-first century, when creating a Google map of Jamestown's tourist destinations, the internet service marked or mapped sites that were long since individuated by previously operating

Discourse and Ideology

discourses. Of course, there is no doubt that maps likely always introduce new discursive elements that can serve a future constitutive function in ways that depart from prior discursive blueprints. We are describing here a perpetual cycle in which any particular element is either constitutive or mapping relative to the subjects that use it and their prior exposure to other, related elements.

In summary,

- constitutive discourse individuates objects through the application of a matrix of individuation, a matrix that distributes objects as same, different, and sometimes ranked;
- this does not necessarily mean that discourses are material or efficient causes—it means that where one thing ends and another begins depends on the lines discourse draws;
- insofar as humans respond to how they are classified, the matrices of individuation that interpellate them literally make them what they are; human identities and practices are discursively dependent, and human groups are therefore existentially dependent on discourses that serve as blueprints for social life and establish desired relations between the subjects interpellated—that is, when it comes to human classification, it appears that discourse does function as a material and efficient cause; and
- discourse is not always constitutive—at times it maps what has already been constituted.

Constitutive Discourse in *The Call of the Carpenter*

In *The Call of the Carpenter* (1913), Bouck White offers readers an account of the life of Jesus, focusing on his class status as a member of the proletariat. The account is of course fundamentally anachronistic, as the class division between proletariat and bourgeoisie is a product of a distinctly industrial capitalist mode of production invented centuries after the historical Jesus was long since dead. However, the fact that historical claims may be empirically false in no way prevents historical discourses from having constitutive roles in present or future circumstances.

White signals to readers that the book concerns twentieth-century social issues in the opening pages of the preface, titled "The Posture of Affairs," in which he contrasts the rise of "democracy" with the decline of "the Church." Democracy, he claims, is overtaking the world like a tidal wave. "Quietly as the march of the stars, and as irresistible, the coronation of the common people is drawing night" (White 1913: vii). What accounts for the march of democracy? "The disinherited classes are refusing to remain disinherited" (viii). By contrast, the Church—by which White appears to include both the Catholic Church and Protestant denominations—is exhibiting a "rapidly increasing departure," a desertion or secession that "cannot be extinguished by derision, vituperation, or force" (ix).

According to White, the rise of democracy and fall of the Church are directly related events: the health of one is inversely correlated with the health of the other. Why? Because the Church and its clergy have always sided with the ruling classes against the working classes: "the divine right of property is remembered—that the mass of people are born with saddles on their backs, and a favoured few booted and spurred to ride them legitimately by the grace of God. The priest and the exploiter—natural born twins" (White 1913: xi). For White, "the Church has allied itself with land and capital, and generally with the master against his workmen" (xi–xii). He goes on to quote— as exemplary—a minister who discourages the education of the working classes, for fear that knowledge would produce dissatisfaction: "there is a risk of elevating, by an indiscriminating education, the minds of those doomed to the drudgery of daily labor above their condition, and thereby rendering them discontented and unhappy in their lot" (xvii). Instead, the minister recommends an "economical" education for the masses, focusing on key doctrines from the Bible but little else, so they learn nothing that might encourage them to rise above their station (xvii). Insofar as the Church has aligned itself with the ruling classes, the "bitterness" of the proletariat toward the Church is understandable (xvii). Indeed, a "consciousness of power is maturing in the breast of the proletariat" (xvii). They are learning that the "social well-being of the people … is continually being obstructed by conceptions of political subserviency and passive obedience to despotic authority, which is directly traceable to Christian doctrine" (xvii).

However, White goes on to argue that the working class' disgust with the Church extends only to "organized religion" (White 1913: xii), not to Jesus himself: "on the contrary, the Workingman of Nazareth probably never stood higher in their esteem or more ardent in their affections" (xxi). The remainder of the book attempts, therefore, to recover the authentic message of Jesus the Galilean that has been lost, eroded, or corrupted by the Church.

In the narrative that unfolds, White equates the citizens of first-century Galilee with the modern proletariat and equates the first-century Roman Empire with the capitalist mode of production. According to White, the Romans exploited those under the empire's thumb via excessive taxation, taxation that amounted to theft: there was "no pretense that she was levying it on the peoples with their consent, or was to expend it for their benefit. It was the spoils of conquest, and was extracted at the point of the sword" (White 1913: 3). Although exploitation via taxation is not in all ways identical to the exploitation of wage labor, White depicts them as equivalently exploitative.

It was in this ancient, exploitative context that Jesus was born, "a leader who was to call back to self-respect the peoples thus subjugated, raising up in them once more a free spirit" (White 1913: 4). Insofar as his "gestation" took place in these terrible conditions, Jesus became a man with a "vision [of] a world-wide union of the toiling masses against the legalized brigandage" of Rome (4). White suggests Jesus' fate as a revolutionary was inescapable, given the fact that he nursed at the breast of an oppressed mother:

> [Mary's] starvation diet is thinning the milk in her breasts. A woman never so revolts against an unjust economic system with its skimpy nourishment, as when

she becomes a mother, and the asking eyes of a babe look into hers, a babe asking nutriment which it gets not ... [T]hat babe is drawing a spirit of insurrection in with the milk from his mother's teats. For that milk had been curdled by the thought of injustice.

(White 1913: 31–32)

For White, *Jesus was breast-fed revolution*. The biography proceeds to narrate Jesus' childhood among the proletariat, his mission as an adult to lead a revolt against the capitalist class, and the eventual betrayal and execution that resulted from his revolutionary aspirations.

What objects are individuated by White's discourse? Arguably, the book's point of emphasis is on the following objects: the first-century Roman Empire, the authentic teachings or message of Jesus, the contemporary capitalist mode of production, the contemporary working class, and the contemporary Christian Church. None of these objects are created from scratch; White's narrative is articulated upon already existing discourses on such objects. In particular, he appears to individuate the working class and the capitalist mode of production in the same way as popular communist writings of his day.

However, when it comes to the other three objects—Jesus, Rome, and the corrupt Church—White is doing something relatively novel. White's "Jesus," White's "Rome," and White's "the Church" draw upon existing discursive individuations falling under these names, but he creates objects that are new insofar as *he reorganizes those characteristics he defines as essentially and contingently related to their identities*. For instance, White's "Rome" is paradigmatically exploitative, and, as such, perhaps those parts of "Rome" that were not exploitative do not represent its true identity. Similarly, White's Jesus essentially defends the interests of the working classes, and, as such, perhaps those sayings or actions of Jesus that contradict this account are therefore inessential to understanding his character. In White's discourse, a new Jesus, a new Rome, and a new Church are imagined into existence.

It might be tempting to judge White's "authentic Jesus" as a mystification of reality or the past—as if *his* Jesus were not the *real* Jesus. Of course it is true that some of the historical claims White makes are false—not only by our standards of history but even by the standards of his day—but when it comes to individuating (as opposed to describing) an object, there is no final ontology. Whichever characteristics of a "thing" that we take to be primary or secondary, essential or contingent, are always and *a priori* observer relative. Even if we had direct access to first-century Palestine and were able to interview the man named "Jesus" and his family and friends, we would likely get different accounts of who he *really is*—just as we would get different accounts of which traits are essential to who "Craig Martin" *really is* depending on whether we asked him, his wife, his mother, his coworkers, or his students (or, as we noted in the last chapter, Rousseau and his lovers are never fixed objects). Objects do not individuate themselves, and—to put the same point differently—neither do the nominal essences of our definitions appear within the empirical fields available to us. Jesus' identity is no more empirically available than is the definition of a wetland.

White is actually quite explicit about how he idealizes, substructs, or individuates his Jesus from the empirical evidence available to him. On the one hand, he notes that there are contradictions between the Gospels, such that "no entirely coherent narrative can be extracted from the records as they stand" (White 1913: 21). In these cases, White claims that we must accept "that interpretation which harmonizes the greatest number of statements and has the fewest contradictions" (22). On the other hand, White insists that history has traditionally been written from the perspective of "kings and conquerors"; by contrast, we need a history from the perspective of "the people" (5). In addition, he suggests that the rich of the ancient world suppressed histories from the perspective of the people (6). Democratic historians, by contrast, must focus on how the "spiritual" teachings of Jesus were rooted "in the industrial condition of the masses" (7).

> The reader has caught the drift. We here address ourselves to view Jesus, the Carpenter of Nazareth, from the viewpoint of economics ... But we shall be rigorously historical. The present is not a work of the imagination. It affirms to be a piece of cool, scientific history. If the portrait of The Carpenter here unearthed differs from the one commonly viewed, may it not be because accretions of time have defaced the picture, blurring its aforetime sharpness?—incrustations which are now peeling off, by grace of the critical scholarship of our day, revealing some vivid tints in the portrait. The attempt in these pages is that of a restoration. It slavishly follows the ancient records, and is ambitious of nothing more than to retrace the picture as it was at the first. No originality is claimed.
>
> (White 1913: 5)

For White, in practice this means that the democratic historian must pick and choose elements from the narratives in the Gospels that most honestly reflect Jesus' economic conditions (i.e., industrial capitalism), and discard the "accretions" most likely added by the Church (which is on the side of capital).

To consider just one example, White insists that when Jesus said his followers were to "turn the other cheek," this was by no means in the spirit of pacifism. On the contrary, White claims that Jesus intended to upend "the intrenched ruling class" (White 1913: 100) in Jerusalem by seizing the temple, particularly insofar as the temple is the center of the Jews' relationship to their own history: "once in possession [of Jerusalem], he would have behind his propaganda the momentum of two thousand years of Jewish history. ... The propagandist who obtains history for his ally has half won the battle" (99). However, the seizure of Jerusalem would require all of his followers to work together seamlessly. For this reason it is clear to White that the interpretation of "turn the other cheek" as promoting nonviolence is "a misreading of the text that has been of immense perversity" (104). This interpretation forgets that Jesus' immediate audience was "the wage-earner class." Citing Josephus, White claims that "the tragedy of the toiling masses has been their incapacity to unite ... The kingdom of labour, divided against itself, is brought to desolation ... The Jewish proletarian was notoriously a sinner in this matter of incohesion and bickerings ... The tendency was never more marked than at the time of Jesus" (104–105). As a result of these failures, "the Carpenter sought to foster in the Jewish masses ... a class solidarity" (105). On this view, "'Blessed are the peace-makers' ... was the counsel of a general who, discovering his soldiers fighting amongst themselves, commands among them an attitude of forbearance toward one another—not in order to lessen their militancy but precisely in order to increase their militancy" (106). Thus, for White, this passage means exactly the opposite of what it is typically interpreted to mean. At another point White deliberately takes a quotation from the Gospels out of context, but justifies it to readers, saying

> it is true that this is to splinter off the passage from its context. But there is justification for this use of the Gospel records. Those records lay no claim to continuity ... [T]hey are memorabilia, a collection of sayings gathered up from the original auditors years after his death. In many cases the connection has been hopelessly lost, and can be restored only by a free process of selection, piercing the broken torso out of fragments.
>
> (White 1913: 37)

In any case, he adds, Jesus' sayings are like "the ejecta of a volcanic nature ... too explosive to pause for unity" (White 1913: 37). In general, White's *modus operandi* is therefore to pick and choose the material from the Gospels that supports his general thesis and then to reinterpret the remaining or conflicting material in light of that thesis—and his selective privileging is justified by his interpretation of the nature of the materials as being discontinuous in the first place. As should be clear, whether something in the Gospels is "authentic" or an "accretion" added by the Church is largely based on what White wants the text to say.

How does White distribute sameness and difference, and how does he rank the objects of his discourse? As is clear, White connects and positively values the objects on the left and devalues the objects on the right.

(+) / (-)
Jesus/the Church
Democracy/Organized Religion
Galileans/Romans
Working class/Ruling class
Slave class/Ruling class
Socialism/Capitalism

One equivalence worth noting here is the rhetorical homological equivalence between slaves and the working class. In his chapter on "Empire," White passes back and forth between claims about the working class and Roman slaves as if they were the identical objects. Part of the reason for this is likely the fact that insofar as the Roman Empire existed long before industrial capitalism and the creation of the proletariat, to make connections or comparisons between the past and the present White must find an ancient equivalent of his contemporary working class. Of course other authors might distribute slaves and the working classes as different rather than the same, but White elides all such possible differences that might serve as the basis for such a determination. On his discourse, they are apparently the same.

What function did this discourse potentially serve in White's contemporary context? I would argue that, above all else, his discourse functions to distribute sympathies and antipathies. White's discourse seems to reflect a desire to bring into existence readers who will imagine themselves as authentic followers of Jesus' message—a new church to displace the existing, corrupt one—followers whose sympathies lie with the items on the left and whose antipathies lie with the items on the right. Had White's discourse been received by his contemporaries as authoritative, it could have served as a blueprint for a new type of Christian subject and a new type of church. I would go so far as to say that perhaps the most important function of discourse—a function that is completely ignored by modes of analysis that narrowly focus on whether discursive claims are empirically supported or not—is that it *encourages sympathies and antipathies* in persuaded audiences.

Empirical Discourse

As Foucault notes, constitutive discourses serve as conditions of possibility for truth claims. No claim about a wetland will be true or false independently of the concept's delimitation and extension. Constitutive discourse, in itself, can no more be true or false than definitions can be true or false—truth and falsehood depend, *a priori*, on already established definitions. This makes all truth claims discourse-relative, although not arbitrary. Despite his anti-realism, even Foucault notes that, given the rules of discourse, many empirical claims are demonstrably false. In *"Society Must Be Defended,"* he writes—in his discussion of modern French historian Boulainvilliers—that the "grid of intelligibility established by Boulainvilliers ... does, I think, establish a certain regime, a certain division between truth and error, that can be applied to Boulainvilliers's own discourse and that can say that *his discourse is wrong—wrong as a whole and wrong about the details*" (Foucault 2003: 164, emphasis mine). For instance, a tally of the population of the Roman Empire in the first century CE—an empirical claim—will be *a priori* dependent upon the construction of *who* will be counted as a part of the empire. No empirical claim about Rome can be true or false prior to having settled that question, and thus the discourse that constitutes Rome serves as a condition of any truth claim about Rome. However, once we have defined "Rome," many claims about the population of Rome will be demonstrably false.

The evaluation of empirical discourse is also complicated by the fact that constitutive discourse does not always define or individuate objects with precision. Theoretically, for so-called "scientific" discourses, definitions include all necessary and sufficient characteristics for the identification of an object under the extension of the concept defined (i.e., x is defined as any object with characteristics y and z). This is, however, only true for monothetic definitions. Polythetic definitions, by contrast, circumscribe the use of words or concepts by pointing to characteristics or features *typical* but *not necessary* to all objects that fall under the definition (i.e., x is defined as any object with several but not necessarily all of the characteristics y, z, a, b, and c). Further, the extension of a concept may depend upon an ideal type rather than a set of characteristics. For instance, "religion" is a modern concept whose extension—at least in colloquial discourse—often covers "Christianity" and "cultural traditions that are arguably in some way *similar to* Christianity." To put it slightly differently, often discourses substitute the presentation of paradigmatic exemplars in place of a precise definition. The use of exemplars is often emotionally charged—people may present a horrific case as representative of all cases that are members of a class or set. Last, the extension of a word or concept may be *ostensive*; people may learn the application of the term by noting the objects—perhaps an arbitrary set—to which people apply the term.

Ideally, "scientific" discourses make non-tautological claims about objects with monothetic definitions; for example, all members of *Homo sapiens*, defined as x, demonstrate characteristics y and z (i.e., characteristics not included in x). However, the more loosely an object is defined, the more problematic empirical generalizations about such objects become, for reasons that should be self-evident. Referents of polythetic definitions and ideal types are more than a little ambiguous, and thus precise claims about them are likely impossible. What true generalizations can be made about vaguely defined objects, for instance, "rock music"? Any claim that begins with "all rock music" is likely to run aground on counterevidence rather quickly, given the wide variety and sometimes mutually exclusive ways in which the term "rock music" is ostensively applied. In summary, the truth of empirical discourse depends on how the objects to which they refer are individuated by constitutive discourse. However, the truth or falsehood of empirical discourse is difficult to discern for those objects that are individuated ambiguously.

In this section, I have claimed the following:

- whether an empirical claim is warranted depends in part on how one defines the terms used in the empirical claim;
- discourses do not always define terms with precision;
- at the very least, discourses can define terms in all of the following ways:
    - monothetically (i.e., x is defined as something with characteristics y and z),
    - polythetically (i.e., x is defined as including some but not necessarily all of the following: y, z, a, and b),

- ostensively (i.e., what I am pointing to is an *x*), or
- according to an ideal type (i.e., *y* reflects the paradigmatic features of *x*); and
• consequently, whether an empirical claim about an object is warranted is increasingly complicated in proportion to the ambiguity of the object's definition.

Empirical Discourse in *The Call of the Carpenter*

Although White is to some extent constituting new objects of discourse with his talk about the authentic Rome and the authentic Jesus—namely, insofar as he reorganizes in novel ways what characteristics he takes as essential and which are contingent—he nevertheless wants to make empirical claims about a Jesus and a Rome *already individuated* by existing historical discourses.

Part of the problem here is that White does not provide an explicit definition of Rome, either monothetic or polythetic. I would argue that he tends to define Rome according to an ideal type, wherein his idealized Rome is essentially cruel and exploitative: "the Roman Empire was a world-wide confederation of aristocracies for the perpetuation of human servitude. ... Economic exploitation was the end in view, the organizing principle throughout" (White 1913: 7). This claim could be taken as either constitutive or empirical. If constitutive, he is defining who the Romans really were on his definition. If empirical, he is claiming that an already individuated Roman Empire clearly had exploitation as its central purpose. In support of this view, White can cite a great deal of empirical evidence that those who identified as members of the Roman Empire committed atrocities that White's contemporaries would have received as cruel and exploitative. For instance, he notes that gladiators were forced to fight to the death (28–29) and that while the poor in Galilee starved the Roman elites *vomunt ut edunt, edunt ut vomunt* (31). By contrast, if we are to take White's claim about the centrality of exploitation to the empire as a strictly empirical claim, it is more than a little dubious, insofar as it is unlikely that something as broad as "the Roman Empire"—spanning much of the globe and across centuries of time—had a single, simple organizing principle.

However, even if we accept that this claim is constitutive—if we accept he is defining exploitative Rome as the true Rome—he goes on to make empirical claims that are clearly false. For instance, at one point White writes that "Rome appeared with her proposal of a world-wide federation of *capitalist classes* against this restive *proletariat*, whereby they could pool their separate armies into a military unit, and hurl its entire weight against a popular uprising in any one of the countries" (White 1913: 8–9, emphasis added). At another point, White writes that the Roman Empire was founded on "the *solidarity of capital*, the oneness of the interests of property irrespective of national boundaries" (12, emphasis added). In addition, Jesus' birth in a "manger" means that "Jesus belongs to the proletariat by birthright" (24). In one chapter White describes Galilee as being subjected to the "creeping paralysis" of "industrial despotism"—an "economic tragedy" (41). What is clearly dubious about these empirical claims is that industrial capitalism—on pretty much *any* definition—did not exist in ancient Rome. As such, all of White's claims about the "capitalist ruling classes" among the Romans—as well as the "proletariat" or "working classes" among the Galileans—are blatantly false and anachronistic. Had he contained himself to more generic and less historically specific terms to talk about the Romans—elsewhere he uses terms such as "tyranny," "despot," "oppressive," "oligarchy," etc.—his claims would have been less empirically problematic.

In addition, although White assumes that the authentic message of Jesus in the Gospels has "accretions" added to them by the Church—accretions that obscure the historical facts—he nevertheless seems to take the Gospels to be relatively reliable accounts of what the historical Jesus said or did. Given the historical-critical scholarship on the New Testament from the last couple of centuries—which demonstrates that the Gospels are more hagiographical than historical—his faith in the empirical reliability of the Gospels is more than a little credulous. Thus the empirical claims White makes about, for example, the lives and personalities of Jesus, Joseph, and Mary, lack—for us—the sort of warrant modern historiography requires.

Establishing and Contesting Normative Associations in Discourse

In addition to the fact that a particular discourse may contradict itself, another crucial problem is that the "we" in "we define *x* in such and such a way" is necessarily a moving target, in part because it is *a product* of such claims in the first place. Statements such as "we agree that wetlands must be really wet" are often necessitated by the fact that *there is no such agreement*, because there are other we's out there who define wetlands differently. Definitions are contested, and a clever way to contest a definition is to assert one's own and imply that it is uncontested. In such cases, "we agree" constitutes a "we" by excluding and making invisible a disagreeing "them." Accepted definitions, then, are products of a will to hegemony. As philosopher Chiara Bottici notes, "in the case of social entities such as nations, classes and states, we are not dealing simply with abstract notions, but with socially constructed beings: it is because there are narrating bodies that behave *as if* such beings existed, that they do *actually* exist" (Bottici 2007: 241). However, "the problem is that there is not a single 'self' that can tell the whole story … [I]n the case of groups, we do not have just one, but many living bodies with many different stories of recognitions to tell" (241). As a result, "it can always be the case that *there is no common story at all*" (244, emphasis added). The "we" in "we agree" is supposed to serve as the origin point or foundation of definitions for Searle, but the "we" often comes at the end, not the beginning.

Despite disagreements, hegemonic or authoritative institutions may have the power to impose a contested definition. For instance, the US state under George H. W. Bush's presidency clearly had the power to implement a particular definition of "wetland." The legal protections Bush signed into law further required, for their enforcement, the administrative operations of the Environmental Protection Agency and the Army

Corps of Engineers (among other institutions). These institutions provided the means or measures by which any particular acreage of land is identified as "wetland," as well as the official paperwork and bureaucratic administration necessary for public and legal recognition. Without such institutions, there would be no "protected wetlands" under any definition.

Above we noted that discourses distribute and sometimes rank objects. Once such a ranking is in place, such discourses may also distribute a wide variety of positive and negative associations or valuations onto the objects individuated. For instance, the discourse on "primitive savages" obviously associates savages with negative valuations, and distributes positive valuations onto those individuated as "civilized." Last, insofar as discourses can value, rank, and normalize objects constructed as the same or different, they can generate—in subjects and in part through the process of socialization—sympathies and antipathies toward such objects.

To offer just one example of the distribution of normative associations or valuations, consider John Powers's *History as Propaganda: Tibetan Exile versus the People's Republic of China* (2004). Powers surveys a wide variety of histories of Tibet, written by Tibetan, Chinese, and Western (i.e., American or European) authors. The story of the relations between China and Tibet—is Tibet an independent state or merely a small part of China's empire?—can be told in many different ways, depending on the interests or agenda of the author spinning the narrative. Of particular interest is how Powers notes the use of normative vocabulary in the works he surveys. The authors tend to use normative nouns and adjectives—with positive and negative valuations attached to them—in a *systematic* way in their narratives (see Tables 3.1 and 3.2).

In Table 3.1, Chinese authors describe Tibet using negative terms, while Tibetan authors use positive terms. Such vocabulary can go a long way toward bending the reader's sympathies toward one view or another. If the reader can be persuaded that Tibet was a nightmarish hell and a theocratic feudal state prior to the Chinese's seizure, then perhaps sympathies will fall with the Chinese state that wants to save Tibet from itself. If the reader can be persuaded that Tibet was a peaceful, tranquil, and deeply religious state before the Chinese military arrived, then perhaps the Chinese should withdraw. What is useful about this use of discourse is that in any complex or long-lived society one can find all of these things; what sizable society doesn't have both peaceful and painful moments in its history? Finding what one wants to pick and choose from the remains of the past is not particularly difficult unless there is too little material to work from, and that is almost never the case. Another rhetorical benefit to this manner of spinning narratives is that one's agenda can remain implicit or latent; one need not explicitly state that either China or Tibet are right or wrong—the normative vocabulary does the work automatically. Unstated agendas are less likely to be challenged, as there is nothing explicit to challenge. Pejoratives are wonderful for attacking without incurring the opportunity costs of appearing to be attacking.

As should be clear, whether the systematic use of normative terms will be successful in producing sympathies and antipathies is likely dependent upon repetition and vividness: the more vivid and memorable one's narrative is, the more emotionally charged it is, the

Discourse and Ideology

Table 3.1 Tibet Prior to the Chinese Takeover.

Chinese Sources	Tibetan Sources
torture	content
persecuted	happy
bitter life	poor
miserable lot	peace
incredibly barbaric	pleasant
cruel	good
savage	warmth
nightmare	satisfied
hell on earth	beautiful country
enslavement	free
Darkest, most reactionary	enlightened
Dark, cruel, and barbarous	immutable tranquility
inhuman political oppression	benevolent
lived worse than animals	lived without haste
worked like beasts	worked leisurely
feudal serfdom	no class system
theocracy	deeply religious
dictatorship	Dalai Lama's government
serf owners	no superiority or inferiority complex
blood-sucking exploitation	left us alone
rampant disease, premature death	starvation was nonexistent
backward economically	poor
Chinese overlordship	independent
Tibetan local government	central government
central government	Chinese government

more likely the readers will recall the normative relations established in the discourse. In addition, repetition is key: saying things once is unlikely have much of an effect on producing sympathies and antipathies in readers.

Once a normative dichotomy is in place, it can be turned into a series of recursive homologies (i.e., serial or nested binary oppositions that are discursively linked), wherein the same normative associations saturate each iteration of the homology. For instance, in modern Christian thought the valuations attached to the discursive dichotomy between spirit and body are reproduced on a whole series of homologous dichotomies:

Table 3.2 Western Writers on Tibet Prior to the Chinese Takeover.

Epstein, Grunfeld, Goldstein	Richardson, Smith, Thurman
powerless	Easy-going
slavery	social inequalities
bitterness	Kindly, cheerful, and contented
resigned	active contentment
primitive land	minimalist
Very little class mobility	simple and somewhat spartan
rigid and ossified feudal society	inner modernity
feudal theocracy	Religious State
theocratic state	sacred society
highly stratified society	relaxed and flexible
feudal economy	economy well organized
serflike peasants	nobility virtually expropriated
Serfs, slaves, outcastes	relatively happy land
low productivity	"small is beautiful" economy
filthiness … garbage	arts flourished explosively
Brigands, thieves, burglars	peaceful and secure
Open corruption	tolerant of diversity
torture and mutilation	cheerful
brutal forms of punishment	unilaterally disarmed society
human sacrifice	Fun-loving and playful cheerfulness
Cannibal system	nonviolence
internally disunified	nationalist consciousness
local autonomy in domestic matters	de facto independence
distinct and independent	deeply conscious of separateness
Tibetan oligarchy	Tibetan government
Population decline	balanced population

Discourse and Ideology

(+) / (−)

Spirit/Body

Inward Religion/Outward Religion

Invisible Church/Visible Church

Faith/Works

Religious Experience/Organized Religion

Although the series of terms on the left do not share identical semantic content, each holds the same *normative relation* to its partner on the right; in each case the term on the left purportedly refers to something that is to some extent nonempirical, but something nonempirical that is valued positively compared to the negatively valued empirical referent on the right.

One of the most fascinating instances of the use of normative, recursive homologies I have found is in the director's introduction to Cecil B. DeMille's 1956 film, *The Ten Commandments*, starring Charlton Heston and Yul Brynner. In the theatrical release, the film opens with DeMille stepping out from behind a curtain and addressing the theater's audience.

> Ladies and gentlemen, young and old, this may seem an unusual procedure, speaking to you before the picture begins. But we have an unusual subject: the story of the birth of freedom, the story of Moses … The theme of this picture is whether man ought to be ruled by God's law, or whether they ought to be ruled by the whims of a dictator like Rameses. Are men the property of the state, or are they free souls under God? *This same battle continues throughout the world today.*
>
> (*The Ten Commandments* 1956, emphasis mine)

For DeMille's American audience in 1956, it was clear that "the same battle" is that of the Cold War. In these brief, momentary remarks, DeMille's discourse sets up this recursive homology:

(+) / (−)

Israel/Egypt

Freedom/Slavery to the state

God's rule/Dictator's rule

Moses/Rameses

US/USSR

Discourse

On this view, Israel : US :: Egypt : USSR. These equivalences permit him to distribute a set of normative associations: freedom and God's rule are associated with Israel and the United States, while controlling dictators who see people as property are associated with Egypt and the USSR. For viewers attuned and open to DeMille's framing of the narrative, the actions of Moses and Israel can be read as flags for American freedom, and the negative associations attached to the character of Rameses can perhaps be transferred onto the memory of Joseph Stalin or the actions of Nikita Khrushchev. "Israel" and "Egypt" as portrayed in the Exodus narrative are flexible signifiers, and clever interpreters can always articulate the positive and negative associations contained in the narrative onto other narratives. Last, as is clear, this discourse would function to encourage—at least for persuaded viewers—sympathies toward the United States and antipathies toward the USSR.

Discourse analysis can also track semantic drift and the oscillating extension of categories. At the most simple level, tracking semantic drift could amount to little more than attending to how official definitions of words change over time or differ according to who is doing the defining. Tracking semantic drift is much more complicated when there are no official definitions of the relevant terms. The more contested a normative word or category is, the more it can be used as an empty floating signifier that can be articulated onto a wide variety of possible objects. The more vacuous or ill-defined terms such as "barbarian" or "cult" are—specifically, when their definitions have no certain or accepted content apart from their negative associations—the more they can be slotted onto whichever objects one chooses. In such cases, the label at hand becomes divorced from the individuating function of discourse, permitting a variety of rhetorical shell games or discursive slippages whereby the extension of the label thins or stretches, or jumps from object to object.

Just as ranking discourses can distribute positive and negative valuations onto the objects they individuate, so they may—in human social groups—similarly distribute rights and privileges or duties and responsibilities. Insofar as a state has a monopoly on legitimate violence, discourses that individuate some subjects as "officers of the state" may simultaneously award them the right to physically restrain citizens, a right denied to those not so identified as officers of the state.

In addition, subjects may in some way reject or refuse the matrix of individuation applied to them. Those subjects identified by states as "terrorists" may identify themselves as "freedom fighters." The extent to which such subjects can impose their self-definition on others depends, of course, on their ability to mobilize institutional authority. Even when rejected or refused by the subjects to which they are applied, ascripted identities—such as "illegal alien"—may continue to be enforced by authoritative institutions.

To offer just one example of how competing discourses or ascripted identities can operate on the same site, consider this story about a man from Ohio who was both alive and dead at the same time:

> A US man declared dead after he disappeared nearly three decades ago cannot now be declared officially alive, though he has returned home and is in good health, a judge has ruled.

Discourse and Ideology

> Donald Miller of Ohio left behind a wife, two children and significant debt when he fled his home in 1986.
>
> He was declared legally dead in 1994, then re-emerged in 2005 and attempted to apply for a driving license.
>
> A judge this week found death rulings cannot be overturned after three years.
>
> Judge Allan Davis handed down the ruling in Hancock County, Ohio, probate court on Monday, calling it a "strange, strange situation", according to media reports.
>
> "We've got the obvious here. A man sitting in the courtroom, he appears to be in good health," he said, finding that he was prevented by state law from declaring Mr Miller legally alive.
>
> "I don't know where that leaves you, but you're still deceased as far as the law is concerned."
>
> ("Living Ohio Man Donald Miller Ruled 'legally dead'" 2013)

What we have is a clear case of competing discourses. If this man went to the hospital, it is highly unlikely that the doctors would direct him to the morgue; according to medical discourses, he is alive. On the other hand, given the court's discourse he is dead and thus not eligible to get a driver's license. Given that he is medically alive, on what grounds, then, did the court identify him as dead? When we include the concerns of the IRS, Child Services, and the Social Security Administration, the plot thickens:

> By 1994, Mr Miller's back child support payments amounted to more than $25,000 ... and the family had heard no word from him.
>
> With Mr Miller declared dead, his "widow" was entitled to Social Security death benefits to support their children.
>
> As Mr Miller remains legally deceased, Ms Miller does not have to return those funds to the government.
>
> It remains unclear if she would have been able to collect back child support had he been declared living.
>
> ("Living Ohio Man Donald Miller Ruled 'legally dead'" 2013)

Rather than ask whether this man is really alive or really dead—as if "life" and "death" were individuated independently of discourse—we should instead ask whether he is alive or dead for any particular discourse. Here it is quite clear: this man identifies himself as medically alive, with the hope that he can get a driver's license. By contrast, this man's former wife's lawyers identify him as legally dead, with the hope that she does not have to repay his social security benefits paid out to her by the state.

However, we can ask the further question: whose discourse is authoritative? Here it appears that his ex-wife's lawyers were successful in persuading the state to authorize her claim rather than his claim. The ascripted "death" legally won out over his self-definition. Not surprisingly, authoritative institutions can always trump common sense; even though the judge said the man appears "in good health," the institution of the law—or at least those parts of it that assign the determination of "death" for legal purposes—is authoritatively binding. But, once again, there is little doubt that medical doctors would identify him as not dead. Competing discourses can function in contradictory ways on the same discursive site—such as this man's body—and a wide variety of social and political consequences can be effected by the application of such discourses. Thus the distribution of rights, privileges, duties, and responsibilities in discourse is much more politically potent when it comes to official or authoritative discourses.

It is for these reasons that Norman Fairclough claims that discourse is "a political practice [that] establishes, sustains and changes power relations, and the collective entities … between which power relations obtain" (Fairclough 1992: 67). Discourse brings such entities into existence, and, as a result, it "is not only a site of power struggle, but also a stake in power struggle" (67). That is, discourses are, on the one hand, among the means by which groups wage war; on the other hand, control of authoritative public discourse is a prize awarded to hegemonic groups or institutions. The reproduction of a hegemonic regime requires the reproduction of a discursive apparatus that constructs and naturalizes that very regime. For those who wish to contest such regimes without the use of physical force, alternative discourses must be produced, or the regnant discourse must be appropriated, twisted, and reworked in ways that produce new social objects or entail new relations between existing objects. As Foucault writes, in a sense "knowledge is never anything more than a weapon in a war" (Foucault 2003: 173). Discourses are perhaps best understood as bloodless battlegrounds for social power.

In summary,

- discourses can systematically distribute normative associations onto the objects they create, and may build iterative homologies on the basis of those normative associations;
- the normative associations function to encourage sympathies and antipathies in persuaded audiences;
- the less semantic content a term has, the more easily it lends itself to semantic drift—relatively empty terms or floating signifiers can be distributed across a wide variety of otherwise unrelated objects, carrying over positive and negative normative associations but perhaps little else;
- insofar as discourses are produced *in competition with* other discourses, they serve as a site of contestations between social groups; and
- control of official or public discourse is awarded to those groups capable of achieving hegemonic control of public institutions.

Discourse and Ideology

Establishing Normative Relations in *The Call of the Carpenter*

White's account of Galilee and Rome in *The Call of the Carpenter* distributes a great number of normative valuations onto each and organizes them into a chain of homologies related to contemporary relations between the bourgeoisie and the proletariat. Consider the normative terms he uses to talk about Galilee and Rome, in just the first two chapters alone. From these associations we learn that Galilee is full of proud citizens chafing under the rule of the Romans, which is brutal and unjust.

Galilee (+)	Rome (-)
"sturdy mountaineer folk" (White 1913: 17)	"brigands" (White 1913: 3)
"intense spirit" (17)	"conquest" (3)
"popular cause" (17)	"hold-up game" (3)
"uncommon force of character" (19)	"wolf … against … sheep" (4)
"independency" (19)	"subjugated" other peoples (4)
"humiliated by subjection" (19)	"brutality" (4)
"heartened" (19)	"overlords" (6)
"a set of the will" (20)	"master class" (6)
"resolve" (20)	"human servitude" (7)
"patriot souls" (20)	"economic exploitation" (7)
"just" (20)	"aggression" (7)
"Heaven is on the side of … the trodden" (22)	"despoiler of peoples" (7)
	"capitalist class" (8)
"hungry" (22)	"repression … [of] servile class" (8)
"oppressed classes" (22)	"cruel" (8)
"intense heart of the most intense race" (23)	"vicious" (8)
	"exploiter class" (10)
"martyrdom" (23)	"machinery of intimidation" (16)
"golden moment in history" (23)	"plunder" (16)
"the highest peak … [of] the human spirit" (23)	"invader" (17)
	"tyranny" (18)
"life that was lived democratically" (24)	"despotism" (18)
"demand for human rights" (24)	"imperious" (18)
"defenceless peasantry" (24)	"race of conquerors" (18)

"near to the starvation line" (24)
"bled to the verge" of death (24)
"lamentation and weeping and great mourning" (27)
"destitution" in the "extreme" (30–31)
"hardship and exhausting toil" (31)
"humiliating" (31)

"self-indulging" (18)
"heavy-fisted, cynical" (18)
treated the masses "as cattle" (24)
"crushing weight" (25)
"impoverishment of those already poor" (25)
"burning of villages" ((25)
"slaughter of hundreds" (25)
"pillaged" (27)
"blood lust" (28)
"animals" (29)
"luxury" (29)
"extravagance" (30)
"plutocracy" (30)
"rapacity" (30)
"unjust economic system" (31)

As noted above, the ranking of objects in discourse functions to distribute sympathies and antipathies among those to whom the discourse is persuasive. White's discourse clearly encourages readers to develop sympathies toward the Galileans and antipathies toward the Romans.

This distribution of normative associations further functions in relation to the series of homologies White sets up for his readers. His discourse encourages readers to transfer the positive associations attributed to the Galileans to the contemporary working classes, as well as to transfer negative associations attributed to Rome to the modern bourgeoisie or the capitalist mode of production itself.

(+) / (-)
Galileans/Romans
Slave class/Ruling class
Working class/Ruling class
Democracy/Capitalism

Discourse and Ideology

In this way "Galilee" and "Rome" become metonyms that can—through semantic drift—stand in for any groups in White's contemporary context. In his concluding chapter he turns away from the past to his present, and introduces discussions of America, England, France, Germany, and Italy. He claims that "Jesus seems to have foreseen" the sufferings of the "compact mass" of New York City (White 1913: 353). In fact, he even says that the "modern world, pregnant and swelling with democracy as by fecundation of the holy ghost, is approaching the birth hour" and that this is precisely of what Jesus was speaking when he claimed that "when these things begin to come to pass, then look up and lift your heads; for your redemption draweth nigh" (354). Semantic drift permits White to almost seamlessly jump from his imagined past to his imagined present, transferring positive and negative associations from one context onto the other.

Last, it is worth noting that discourses can distribute rights and responsibilities or privileges and duties. Were White's readers broadly persuaded that the working classes should overthrow the ruling classes—as Jesus himself encouraged: "Jesus planned to make the Jews the nucleus of a federation of the world's proletariat against the world's oppressor" (White 1913: 73)—then his narrative prescribes a duty to revolt, at least among those readers who accept Jesus as an authoritative figure. Insofar as White's discourse is neither official nor particularly authoritative for any community, the political effects are primarily restricted to the distribution of sympathies and antipathies, as opposed to the distribution of legal rights or duties.

Conclusion

According to this chapter, discourses can function to:

- create objects;
- distribute sameness and difference;
- rank and normalize objects;
- distribute sympathies and antipathies;
- interpellate subjects and constitute social groups;
- provide blueprints that establish desired relations between objects or subjects individuated;
- make empirical claims (which are warranted or not depending on how the objects of empirical discourse are individuated in the first place);
- establish emotionally charged paradigmatic exemplars;
- distribute normative associations;
- distribute normative homologies;
- permit semantic drift across homologies; and
- distribute rights, privileges, responsibilities, and duties.

As such, discourse analysis involves asking the following questions. In any particular discursive site, what sorts of objects are being constructed? Does the discourse rank objects individuated or assign normative valuations that produce sympathies and antipathies in subjects of the discourse? Do those normative valuations recur across a series of normative homologies? Does semantic drift capacitate the transference of normative associations across domains or the imagination of new relations between objects? Does the discourse assign rights and privileges or duties and obligations to subjects individuated by the discourse? Provided the discourse is received as authoritative, whose interests—whether we are talking about already existing groups or new assemblages brought into existence—are served or thwarted by the discourse or semantic drift at hand?

Thus far my focus in this book has been on the individuation or substruction of objects from empirical domains and the role of discourse in assigning normative relations between such objects. All along we have assumed that matrices of individuation and discursive assignments are *invested* or *interested*, or that they reflect the interests of social groups agonistically competing for social power. In the next chapter I will turn to a consideration of what "interests" are and their circular relation to discourse, as discourse is a condition of possibility of interests and interests are a condition of possibility of discourse.

CHAPTER 4
DOMINATION

Accounts of domination sometimes fail to provide a sophisticated account of the conditions of possibility of claiming that a subject or group of subjects is dominated. Throughout history, some cases of domination are relatively easy to identify and agree on: slaves who wish to be free but are held captive are clearly in a relationship of domination with those who enslave them. Such accounts are relatively easy to identify and agree on because there is an obvious class of persons who have desires that are systematically repressed or thwarted for the benefit of another class of persons (although, to be clear, there is not universal agreement on this: throughout history many have claimed that slavery serves the interests of those enslaved). Liberal theories of politics and power, which seek to protect the autonomy of individuals, typically imagine that domination can be reversed merely by lifting the constraints on individual autonomy—we are encouraged to let people be free to pursue their own life, liberty, and happiness in whatever way they wish, provided they are not harming or overriding the same rights for others. Liberty, on the liberal approach, predominantly entails the removal of social constraints—constraints like the ownership of humans. In cases like slavery, such an approach usually suffices to satisfy the consciences of social critics, but not all cases are so simple.

From a poststructuralist (rather than liberal) perspective things are much more complicated: on this view, a subject's desires and interests are *products of* rather than simply *constrained by* social forces. In addition, insofar as social forces are different from one social location to the next, subjects are socialized to have different and even competing desires and interests. A social structure experienced as liberating for one subject could be experienced as oppressive for another. Further, the more heterogeneous a body of subjects, the more difficult it will be to put in place a set of social conditions that will simultaneously serve competing desires and interests equally. The act of removing barriers that some subjects find repressive could, in itself, be felt as oppressive by subjects who have undergone different processes of socialization.

Last, and most importantly for this chapter, some subordinated subjects are socialized to accept or even celebrate the subordinate position they occupy, a position that other subjects might experience as oppressive. Critical theorists are divided on the extent to which it is desirable, useful, or analytically defensible to employ a concept such as "internalized oppression" to describe such a state, particularly as the charge of internalized oppression necessarily entails the use of a paternalistic measure of what counts as liberation. Who are we, as critics, to decide what is in the best interests of others,

Discourse and Ideology

particularly when our assertions override the claims of those we imagine we are helping? Attempts to "liberate" people subjected to "internalized domination" might produce good consciences in the mind of the "liberators," but, from another perspective, could be experienced as imperialistic. What sorts of questions can we ask about domination, but without reifying our own historically produced interests as if they were, objectively, the interests of everyone, and without potentially justifying imperial projects that risk compounding rather than relieving dominated subjects?

To anticipate my conclusions, we will have to ask reflexive questions that point not only to the social structures around us but also to the methods and criteria we use to interpret, challenge, or sustain those structures. What particular relations of domination are we talking about, with respect to what axis of subjection and privilege, and in comparison to which other axes of subjection and privilege? For which types of historically constituted subjects with which assembly of sympathies are these relations of domination of interest? With what other social conditions being equal or stable? The reflexive elements built into these questions all too often go without saying, but they need to be thought if we wish to do something other than naturalize our own particular criterion for domination, or normalize our favorite sympathies and antipathies.

I wish to set the stage for this chapter with a discussion of Mark Twain's *A Connecticut Yankee in King Arthur's Court* ([1889] 1981), as this novel offers a particularly vivid portrayal of how attempts to rescue the oppressed can arguably result in further oppression. Twain's story draws our attention to the most difficult theoretical problems with analyzing domination or oppression: if standards of liberation are variable depending on one's culture, social norms, or socialization, liberation may well be received as its opposite. From there, we will move to consider how a number of critical theorists address these difficulties, starting with religious studies scholars Bruce Lincoln and Saba Mahmood, before turning to the work of Michel Foucault and Judith Butler. Ultimately I will propose a solution to my central question that draws upon the work of the feminist philosopher and ethicist Anita Superson and political theorist Torben Bech Dyrberg, both of whom provide theoretical resources for analyzing domination without falling into either complete relativism on the one hand or imperialist paternalism on the other. In the end, I will recommend changing the question: we should not ask the abstract, free-from-any-context question "are they dominated?" but rather "on what or whose particular criteria are they dominated?"

Liberating the Oppressed to Death

Mark Twain's 1889 novel, *A Connecticut Yankee in King Arthur's Court* ([1889] 1981), is a brilliantly drawn cautionary tale suggesting that paternalistic attempts to liberate a people from internalized oppression are fraught with potentially perilous consequences. The book centers on the first person narrative of a man named Henry (Hank) Morgan, an engineer from the late nineteenth century who, once knocked out by a hit on his head during a fight, woke up in Camelot under King Arthur's court in the sixth century.[1]

Hank, whose "father was a blacksmith" and whose "uncle was a horse doctor," first trained under them but furthered his education by working at an arms factory, where he "learned to make everything; guns, revolvers, cannon, boilers, engines, all sorts of labor-saving machinery" (Twain [1889] 1981: 4). Upon arrival in the sixth century he uses these skills to establish himself as "the Boss" in the kingdom, second only to King Arthur himself, by bringing the best of "civilization" to the "infantile barbarians" of the early Middle Ages.

By the end of the book, Hank has brought about the death of many of those "barbarians." Rather than "civilizing" them, he ends up murdering them. As such, I think Hank's rhetoric does not reflect Twain's personal sympathies, so much as Hank's vocabulary stands in for or as an example of the worst sort of "white man's burden" language leading to domination rather than liberty. Consequently, to some extent I think Twain is indirectly performing discourse analysis of colonialist rhetoric. In effect, I think Twain's message is something like this: "if you belittle or demonize as 'barbarians' those you claim to want to rescue, you are contributing to the problem rather than helping—one's vocabulary goes a long way toward shaping how one sees other groups with whom you interact."

Who does Hank hope to save with the advent of "civilization"? Throughout the book, Hank uses strongly pejorative rhetoric to describe the backwardness of the sixth-century inhabitants. At times he describes them as mentally insane or barbaric. He first identifies them as members of a "circus" (Twain [1889] 1981: 6), and second as escaped "patients" from an "asylum"—and, as such, perhaps in need of a "keeper" (9). He also considers them "lunatics" (107), and at a few points he refers to them as "savages" (47, 61). To emphasize their passivity, he once describes them as "automata" (89).

Hank additionally refers to the population as nonhuman animals. "I saw that I was just another Robinson Crusoe cast away on an uninhabited island with not society but some more or less tame animals" (Twain [1889] 1981: 32). "They were the quaintest and simplest and trustingest race; why, they were nothing but rabbits" (38). At various points they are also referred to as dogs, bugs, insects (38), and worms (39).

At other times Hank's rhetoric positions the inhabitants of the sixth century as children (Twain [1889] 1981: 68). "They were a childlike and innocent lot" (13). The squabbling between the knights reminds Hank of the bickering and bullying between children; "I had always imagined until now that that sort of thing belonged to children only, and a sign and mark of childhood; but here were these big boobies sticking to it and taking pride in it clear up into full age and beyond" (14). They display the ignorance of infants; "there did not seem to be brains enough in the entire nursery, so to speak to bait a fishhook with" (14). "Here I was, a giant among pigmies, a man among children, a master intelligence among intellectual moles" (40). Because of their childish intelligence, throughout the book they are described as credulous, easily believing lies, as well as "superstitious" (85). A few notable exceptions stand out, as Hank finds a few "men" in the sixth century. One subject is identified as a "man" merely for agreeing with Hank that a democratically ruled people would not stand for the sort of treatment they received from the aristocracy. "I said to myself: 'This one's a man. If I were backed by enough of this sort … [I could make] a wholesome change in [the] system of government'" (64).

Discourse and Ideology

Last, Hank refers to the population as slaves. "It was pitiful ... to listen to their humble and hearty outpourings of loyalty toward their king and Church and nobility; as if they had any more occasion to love and honor king and Church and noble than a slave to love and honor the lash" (Twain [1889] 1981: 38). "The most of King Arthur's British nation were slaves, pure and simple" (38). Or,

> the nation as a body was in the world for one object, and one only: to grovel before king and Church and noble; to slave for them, sweat blood for them, starve that they might be fed, work that they might play, drink misery to the dregs that they might be happy, go naked that they might wear silks and jewels, pay taxes that they might be spared from paying them ... And for all this, the thanks they got were cuffs and contempt; and so poor-spirited were they that they took even this sort of attention as an honor.
>
> (Twain [1889] 1981: 38)

In sum, the sixth century is made up of sad, pitiable lot: the mentally insane, savages, animals, children, or slaves.

Throughout the narrative, Hank constantly reflects on the physical and mental suffering of these poor, uncivilized creatures. For instance, at one point, when Hank is taken as one prisoner among many before Arthur's court, he notes of the other prisoners:

> Poor devils, many of them were maimed, hacked, carved, in a frightful way; and their hair, their faces, their clothing, were caked in black and stiffened drenchings of blood. They were suffering sharp physical pain, of course; and weariness, and hunger and thirst, no doubt; and at least none had given them the comfort of a wash or even the poor charity of a lotion for their wounds; yet you never heard them utter a moan or a groan, or saw them show any sign of restlessness, or any disposition to complain.
>
> (Twain [1889] 1981: 13)

Hank concludes that "they are white Indians," by which he apparently means that like the American Indians (i.e., Native Americans), they are like domesticated animals resigned to expecting nothing other than harsh treatment by their masters.[2] At another point, Hank finds it curious that the abuse of commoners

> brought from these downtrodden people no outbursts of rage against their oppressors. They had been heritors and subjects of cruelty and outrage for so long that nothing could have startled them but a kindness. Yes, here was a curious revelation indeed, of the depth to which this people had been sunk in slavery. Their entire being was reduced to a monotonous dead level of patience, resignation, dumb uncomplaining acceptance of whatever might befall them in life. Their very imagination was dead.
>
> (Twain [1889] 1981: 103)

These poor, suffering animals deserved better; given Hank's implicitly meritocratic ideology, the fact that they were not born with nobility in their blood was surely through no fault of their own, and yet they are punished throughout their lives as a result. Hank's rhetoric presents to readers a dominated populace to whom we are initially invited to extend our sympathies: they are oppressed, although they do not know they are oppressed—all the reason more why they need saving.

Faced with these ignorant, uncivilized infants, Hank uses knowledge of modern machinery to build social capital, prestige, and eventually earn a nonaristocratic but important social rank: "the Boss." In addition, because he sympathizes with those persons without royal or noble blood, he makes efforts to save them from themselves. Hank's efforts to ease their suffering in part entail bringing the accoutrements of nineteenth-century America to this backward British nation. Upon his arrival, "as for conveniences, properly speaking, there weren't any ... There was no soap, no matches, no looking glass" (Twain [1889] 1981: 31). "There was no gas, there were no candles ... There were no books, pens, paper, or ink, and no glass in the openings they believed to be windows. ... But perhaps worst of all was, that there wasn't any sugar, coffee, tea, or tobacco" (32). Consequently, he had a great deal of work to accomplish; "the first thing you want in a new country, is a patent office; then work up your school system; and after that, out with your paper" (42). Apart from transforming the culture to be capable of providing the niceties of nineteenth-century life, Hank also hopes to transform the nation into a self-governing meritocratic democracy. The plan, of course, cannot be implemented all at once but rather in steps. "First, a modified monarchy ... then the destruction of the throne, the nobility abolished ... universal suffrage instituted, and the whole government placed in the hands of men and women of the nation there to remain" (183).

Hank's efforts at civilizing the populace are constantly thwarted by two institutions: the aristocracy and the Catholic Church. More specifically, his work is stymied by the socialization of the population as a whole with particular ideologies derived from these two institutions. These ideologies provide people with sympathies and antipathies completely at odds with Hank's meritocratic vision. The aristocracy of course has an interest in protecting existing privilege, and, Hank suggests, they could not do otherwise than defend their privilege because of their rearing. At one point Hank reflects on King Arthur's complete inability to sympathize with victims of injustice when those victims are without noble blood:

> He was a wise and humane judge, and he clearly did his honest best and fairest—*according to his lights*. That is a large reservation. His lights—I mean his *rearing*—often colored his decisions. Whenever there was a dispute between a noble or gentleman and a person of lower degree, the king's *leanings* and *sympathies* were for the former class always, whether he suspected it or not. It was impossible that this should be otherwise. The blunting effects of slavery upon the slaveholder's moral perceptions are known and conceded, the world over, and a privileged class, an aristocracy, is but a band of slaveholders under another name.
>
> (Twain [1889] 1981: 141, emphasis added)

Discourse and Ideology

Consequently, although the king's rulings sometimes seemed unjust to someone like Hank raised on the myth of meritocracy in the nineteenth century, he could not hold it against the king. Injustice in these cases, Hank claims, "was merely the fault of his training, his natural [in the sense of a 'second nature' produced by socialization] and unalterable sympathies" (Twain [1889] 1981: 142). Here Twain establishes that sympathies are not inborn or innate, but learned; change our training and we change our nature and those toward whom we will be sympathetic.

Those of non-noble birth, Hank notes, accept their subservient status because of their rearing or training as well. "Training" recurs as a constant theme throughout the novel, and is frequently invoked to excuse oppressors from oppressing and to excuse the oppressed from failing to resist their oppression. Most pointedly, at one point Hank claims,

> Training—training is everything; training is all there is *to* a person. We speak of nature; it is folly; there is no such thing as nature; what we call by that misleading name is merely heredity and training. We have no thoughts of our own, no opinions of our own; they are transmitted to us, trained into us. All that is original in us, and therefore fairly creditable or discreditable to us, can be covered up and hidden by the point of a cambric needle, all the rest being atoms contributed by, and inherited from, a procession of ancestors that stretches back a billion years to the Adam-clam or grasshopper or monkey from which our race has so tediously and ostentatiously and unprofitably developed.
>
> (Twain [1889] 1981: 91)

In a sense, Twain is working here with a theory of ideology not far from Althusser's in "Ideology and Ideological State Apparatuses" (2008), according to which we are all socialized—at the top and at the bottom of the social hierarchy—to accept the status quo, even when it disadvantages us. Not only does training determine our sympathies for others but also it determines—or perhaps even eliminates—our sympathies for ourselves.

The other institution that thwarts Hank's efforts at civilizing the masses is the church, which, he claims, divinely legitimated aristocratic rule: "the priests had told their fathers and themselves that this ... state of things was ordained by God" (Twain [1889] 1981: 62). Before "the king's and the nobles' eyes [the masses] were mere dirt" (39). Why? "Through the force of inherited ideas ... the Roman Catholic Church ... [i]n two or three little centuries ... had converted a nation of men to a nation of worms" (39). Previously, members of the masses had "pride and spirit and independence" (39), but the church beat it out of them:

> she preached (to the commoner) humility, obedience to superiors, the beauty of self-sacrifice; preached (to the commoner) meekness under insult; preached (still to the commoner, always to the commoner) patience, meanness of spirit, nonresistance under oppression; and she introduced heritable ranks and

aristocracies, and taught all the Christian populations of the earth to bow down to them and worship them.

(Twain [1889] 1981: 39)

Insofar as the church is "an enemy to human liberty" (Twain [1889] 1981: 90), were these people to suffer to the point of responding with unrest and resistance, "the gentle Church condemned him to eternal fire" (63). Hank's view of the role of the church in the subordination of the population is so strong that he considers the church more powerful than even the king (37).

Because of the intransigence of the population resulting from their training—"arguments have no chance against petrified training" (Twain [1889] 1981: 86)—they could only be fully lifted up through alternative education. In the chapter titled the "Beginnings of Civilization," a special emphasis is placed on the creation of factories and educational centers designed to train youth differently, which he calls "civilization-nurseries" (48) or "man-factories" (66).

In these were gathered together the brightest young minds I could find, and I kept agents out raking the country for more, all the time. I was training a crowd of ignorant folk into experts—experts in every sort of handiwork and scientific calling. These nurseries of mine went smoothly and privately ... for nobody was allowed to come into their precincts without a special permit.

(Twain [1889] 1981: 46–47)

It is in such factories that Hank is "going to turn groping and grubbing automata into *men*" (Twain [1889] 1981: 89).

Throughout the book, Hank notes that his view is of course considerably different from those of the sixth century as a result of his own rearing, training, or socialization in another context.

Inherited ideas are a curious thing ... I had mine, the king and his people had theirs. In both cases they flowed in ruts worn deep by time and habit ... These people had inherited the idea that all men without title and a long pedigree ... were creatures of no more consideration than so many animals, bugs, insects; whereas I had inherited the idea that humans who can consent to masquerade in the peacock-shams of inherited dignities and unearned titles, are of no good but to be laughed at.

(Twain [1889] 1981: 38–39)

At one point Hank explicitly distinguishes between "modern standards" and "the standards of their own time" (Twain [1889] 1981: 77), and he forgives people for being a product of their time. One particularly unjust and cruel queen is described as having enough "brains ... but her training made her an ass—that is, *from a many-centuries-later point of view.*

Discourse and Ideology

... She was a result of generations of training" (91). Similarly, Hank describes a woman named Sandy—who he later marries—as crazy, but only from his own perspective:

> here she was, as sane a person as the kingdom could produce, and yet, from my point of view, she was acting like a crazy woman. My land, the power of training! Of influence! Of education! It can bring a body up to believe anything. I had to put myself in Sandy's place to realize she was not a lunatic. Yes, and to put her in mine, to demonstrate how easy it is to seem a lunatic to a person who has not been taught as you have been taught.
>
> (Twain [1889] 1981: 107)

Much like sympathies, it seems that evaluations of sanity are neither natural nor innate, but learned; change the training and we change those whom we find to be sane.

At some point, Hank comes to the realization that a transformation of society will not be successful through education alone, as far too many are under the sway of the old forms of socialization. Instead, "all revolutions that will succeed, must *begin* in blood, whatever may answer afterward. If history teaches anything, it teaches that. What this folk needed, then, was a Reign of Terror and a guillotine" (Twain [1889] 1981: 103).

After years of small transformations of society here and there, and after delivering a crushing blow to the institution of knighthood (Hank defeated a number of knights in a duel in which he was armed with guns while the knights held lances on horseback), Hank allows the man factories fully to come out of hiding. "I no longer felt obliged to work in secret. So, the very next day I exposed my hidden schools, my mines, and my vast system of clandestine factories and workshops to an astonished world. That is to say, I exposed the nineteenth century to the inspection of the sixth" (Twain [1889] 1981: 240). Before long, all was different. "Slavery was dead and gone; all men were equal before the law; taxation had been equalized. The telegraph, the telephone, the phonograph, the typewriter, the sewing machine, and all the thousand willing and handy servants of steam and electricity were working their way into favor" (241). However, despite all of this "progress," everything goes wrong at this point.

Hank spends some time away from his burgeoning empire while nursing his wife and child, as the latter took sick and needed convalescing. When he returns from his time away, Hank surprisingly finds that his institutions have been shut down. During his absence, it seems, a conflict amongst the knights had brought the nation into a civil war, with Hank's noble allies ending up on the losing end. After that, the church and the remaining nobility united together against Hank's new civilization. Upon closing the churches (so as to make the church's salvific rituals out of reach) and calling for Hank's death, the populace—apparently fearing hell—turned away from the new practices. "The Church was going to *keep* the upper hand, now, and snuff out all my beautiful civilization just like that" (Twain [1889] 1981: 249).

Fewer than sixty allies out of the entire nation remain with Hank and his leaders, and almost entirely young ones at that. As Hank's right-hand man explains,

> all the others were born in an atmosphere of superstition and reared in it. It is in their blood and bones. We imagined we educated it out of them; they thought so too; the [Church's] Interdict woke them up like a thunderclap! ... With boys it was different. Such as have been under our training from seven to ten years have no acquaintance with the Church's terrors, and it was among these that I found my fifty-two [loyal boys].
>
> (Twain [1889] 1981: 256)

Because "training is everything; training is all there is *to* a person," only the cohort who grew up in Hank's civilization remained sympathetic to his cause.

Hank's right-hand man has prepared for an all-out war against the church and the remaining nobility. A fortified position in a cave had been prepared for the civilized boys and their leaders to gather in preparation for an attack, surrounded by a perimeter with an electric fence with enough current to kill instantly. In addition, all of the man factories had been rigged with dynamite, so that they could be destroyed at a moment's notice should the nobility win the day. The cables to the dynamite lead all the way back to the cave; "we shan't have to leave our fortress, now, when we want to blow up our civilization" (Twain [1889] 1981: 256).

As they prepare to be stormed by the knights, the loyal boys become restless and worry they are turning against their own people. "We have tried to forget what we are—English boys! We have tried to put reason before sentiment, duty before love" (Twain [1889] 1981: 262). However, they cannot forget that they are of the same nation as those preparing to advance on their position. "Oh, sir, consider! Reflect! These people are our people, they are bone of our bone, flesh of our flesh, we love them—do not ask us to destroy our nation" (262)! Hank persuades them, nevertheless, that the knights must be destroyed. No half-measures will suffice—they must be obliterated: "English knights can be killed but they cannot be conquered ... We must kill them all" (265).

The knights come at night, silently sneaking up to the perimeter fence. Because the electric fence kills instantly and silently, and because it is a dark night, the knights do not realize and bodies pile up one on top of another as they are electrocuted. "One could make out but little of detail; but he could note that a black mass was piling itself up beyond the second fence. That swelling bulk was dead men! Our camp was enclosed with a solid wall of the dead—a bulwark, a breastwork, of corpses, you may say" (Twain [1889] 1981: 269).

Once the army of knights became trapped between different sets of fences, Hank orders his civilized boys to open fire with a set of Gatling guns. "The thirteen gatlings began to vomit death into the fated ten thousand [soldiers] ... Within ten short minutes after we had opened fire, armed resistance was totally annihilated, the campaign was ended, we fifty-four were masters of England. Twenty-five thousand men lay dead around

Discourse and Ideology

us" (Twain [1889] 1981: 270). Immediately after celebrating their victory, however, they realize that one woman they brought inside their compound to help was actually the magician Merlin in disguise, and by bringing water to the boys as they worked, he had poisoned them all. Fifty-three die, while Hank is punished with a poisoned cocktail that put him to sleep for fifteen hundred years. "We had conquered; in turn we were conquered" (271–272).

Many readers of *A Connecticut Yankee in King Arthur's Court* interpret it as Twain's satire of what came to be called the "white man's burden": perhaps attempts to "civilize" the "uncivilized" are in some cases doomed to failure, insofar as attempts to save the uncivilized sometimes turn into attempts to conquer them. Benevolent paternalism may turn into malevolent paternalism. Two other themes stand out as equally important on my reading of the novel. First, as I have noted, Twain attributes a priority to "training" in making people who or what they are, and, second, Twain notes that different trainings will produce competing evaluations of who is sane and who is not, or who is civilized and who is not. *This ultimately makes oppression and liberation relative matters, which is why the concepts of domination or internalized oppression so fundamentally problematic.* While Hank understood himself to be a liberator helping the oppressed British nation, by using an alien standard of what counts as civilized his efforts resulted in him killing and conquering. The liberator turns into the ultimate oppressor. Judging them by his standards rather than their own Hank has made their world worse rather than better. Perhaps he could not have done otherwise, given *his* particular training. As one commentator put it: "Hank, while having generally good intentions, is blinded by his confidence in his own values. He sees Camelot as lacking all civilization, an assessment that brings out the tyrant in himself (for in his mind, such an extreme case of barbarity justifies the use of absolute power)" (Johnson 2007: 54). In the end, Hank brought the guillotine and Reign of Terror he at one point suggested that the Middle Ages needed.

In summary, Twain's novel points to the fact that, as a result of differences in socialization or training, what counts as civilized, sane, or liberating is relative; consequently, attempts to liberate others according to an alien criterion of domination may result in further oppressing those identified as oppressed. What Twain brilliantly shows is how the plasticity of reason and desire make attempts at liberation fraught with innumerable pitfalls.

Liberating the Philippines to Death

About a decade after the publication of *A Connecticut Yankee*, Twain became a public commentator on the United States' invasion of the Philippines, and a number of remarkable parallels appear.[3] In 1901 he published a sarcastic essay in the *North American Review* titled "To the Person Sitting in Darkness"—namely, to the "savages" living in the dark ages at the frontier of the United States' imperial efforts (including US missionary efforts in China, Japan, and the Philippines; Twain [1901] 1963). Twain asks, "shall we go on conferring our Civilization upon the peoples that sit in darkness, or shall we give those poor things a rest" (285)? He notes that there is material profit in it: when it comes to bringing civilization to the uncivilized, "there is more money in it, more territory, more sovereignty, and other kinds of emolument, than there is in any other game that is played" (286). However, he argues, "Christendom" has been "playing it badly of late," because the United States has done a poor job of masking the profit motive behind the veneer of salvific efforts—so much so that the "the person sitting in darkness" is starting to take notice.

Twain sarcastically suggests that there is, of course, a great deal the men in darkness can gain from being "civilized"; civilization can bring love, justice, gentleness, Christianity, protection to the weak, temperance, law and order, liberty, equality, honorable dealing, mercy, and education (Twain [1901] 1963: 286). However, the invitation to civilization will be answered only if the United States does not compromise, abridge, or "adulterate" these benefits (286). Twain insists, however, that the United States' gift of civilization *has* been adulterated of late, and that the man sitting in darkness has been the victim of a bait and switch; sadly, he has bought this product "with his blood and tears and land and liberty" (287). For Twain, the United States was increasingly failing to mask its intentions; President McKinley has been hawking his wares "*with the outside cover left off*" (287); "our Master of the Game plays it badly" (290). When it came to occupying the Philippine islands after liberating them from the Spanish, "the Person Sitting in Darkness is almost sure to say: 'There is something curious about this—curious and unaccountable. There must be two Americas; one that sets the captive free, and one that takes a once-captive's new freedom away from him, and picks a quarrel with him with nothing to found on it; then kills him to get his land'" (291). Once the Spanish were gone, the United States' alliance with the Filipinos came to an end; at that point they provoked a war with the Filipinos and subsequently seized the territory. Of course, the conflict that followed resulted in asymmetrical casualties; Twain cites a report according to which only 268 US soldiers but 3,227 Filipinos were killed over a ten month period (294). He additionally cites a report from a US soldier who admitted that they would kill wounded Filipinos rather than capturing them and providing medical assistance; "We never left one alive. If one was wounded, we would run our bayonets through him" (194). For Twain, it seems, perhaps the US soldiers are the ones in need of civilizing.

How can all of this be explained or justified to the man sitting in darkness? Twain suggests admitting that perhaps "we have been treacherous, but that was only in order that real good might come out of apparent evil" (Twain [1901] 1963: 295). Unfortunately, along the way "we have stamped out a just and intelligent and well-ordered republic … we have robbed a trusting friend of his land and his liberty" (295). Twain sarcastically adds that since "we" are civilized Christians, "this world-girdling accumulation of trained morals, high principles, and justice cannot do an unright thing, and unfair thing, an ungenerous thing, an unclean thing" (295). In any case, "we have got the Archipelago, and we shall never give it up" (295).

Of course, tensions and hostilities did not immediately cease; five years later Twain found himself once again publicly commenting on the United States' military presence

Discourse and Ideology

in the Philippines following a massacre of Moro rebels by US troops. In "Comments on the Moro Massacre" (1906), Twain writes,

> a tribe of Moros, dark-skinned savages, had fortified themselves in the bowl of an extinct [volcano] crater ... and as they were hostiles, and bitter against us because we have been trying for eight years to take their liberties away from them, their presence in that position was a menace ... It was found that the Moros numbered six hundred, counting women and children ... [When US soldiers a]rrived at the rim of the crater, the battle began. Our soldiers numbered five hundred and forty. They were assisted by auxiliaries consisting of a detachment of native constabulary in our pay—their numbers not given—and by a naval detachment, whose numbers are not stated. But apparently the contending parties were about equal as to number—six hundred men on our side, on the edge of the bowl; six hundred men, women and children in the bottom of the bowl.
> Gen. Wood's order was, "Kill or capture the six hundred."
>
> (Twain 1925: 187–188)

Once again, Twain draws attention to the asymmetrical casualties: "The completeness of the victory is established by this fact: that of the six hundred Moros not one was left alive. The brilliancy of the victory is established by this other fact, to wit: that of our six hundred heroes only fifteen lost their lives" (Twain 1925: 188–189). Further, "we abolished them utterly, leaving not even a baby alive to cry for its dead mother. *This is incomparably the greatest victory that was ever achieved by the Christian soldiers of the United States*" (190, emphasis in the original). The Filipinos were, it seems, liberated to death.[4]

The similarities between Hank's efforts in *A Connecticut Yankee* and the United States' invasion of the Philippines are clear: purported attempts to bring "civilization" to the "savages" result in those being "saved" rounded up and massacred by gunfire. Just as Hank's men surrounded and destroyed Arthur's knights to a man—those very men he hoped to civilize—so did the US military surround Filipino men, women, and children and destroyed them to a man (and woman and child). Unlike Hank, however, Twain appears to abhor rather than celebrate the "victory," and takes great pains to draw attention to the irony of it all. Although then-president Roosevelt praised his military leaders for their brilliant success in the massacre, Twain notes that Roosevelt could not have meant his praise, for the victory "would not have been a brilliant feat of arms even if Christian America, represented by its salaried soldiers, had shot them down with Bibles and the Golden Rule instead of bullets" (192).

What might make the cases different is that while Hank appears to be genuine in his sympathy with those he hopes to civilize, Twain suggests that the United States is less than completely genuine—for Twain, the project of civilizing the person sitting in darkness is nothing more than a mask for imperial theft. However, despite this difference, it is clear that the rhetoric of benevolent imperialism can be used to justify or legitimate such actions. The discourse is, for Twain, risky either way: perhaps at best it can lead to dangerous paternalistic measures, at worst it can legitimate theft and murder.

Thus far, I have argued the following:

- subjects' views of liberation and domination, as well as their sympathies and antipathies, are products of socialization and therefore variable;
- the use of an alien criterion determining whether a set of social relations is dominating or oppressive may result in efforts at liberation that so-called "oppressed" subjects—particularly ones subjected to different processes of socialization—might experience as further oppression; and
- this leaves critics concerned about social domination in a precarious situation, as their modes of critique may further contribute to the "problems" they hope to identify and relieve.

If I have focused on Twain's body of writing here, it is only because I believe he offers particularly vivid examples of the risks of critique.

Ultimately—given Twain's emphasis on how training alters both one's desires and one's sympathies, making liberation and oppression relative—I think the central lesson Twain hopes his readers will arrive at is the following: *judging whether a group is oppressed by imposing one's own particular standards of what is "liberating" may itself be a means of domination*, intentionally or unintentionally. And, as is clear, this is not a matter merely for satirical novels—*attempts at liberation can literally lead to the death of those one claims to be liberating*. Is it possible to criticize social domination without falling prey to the trap of reinforcing domination in an alternative manner? In the next section, I will turn to how these problems are addressed by a number of contemporary critical theorists.

Internalized Oppression and the Problem of Paternalism

In *Emerging from the Chrysalis: Rituals of Women's Initiation* (1991b), Bruce Lincoln considers a number of rituals across a wide range of cultural traditions that, he argues, are designed to persuade women to submit to their own dominated status. Some of the rituals require bodily modifications—ritual scarring, in some cases, or female genital mutilation—designed to make women more attractive to or easier to control by their potential mates. What interests Lincoln most about these rituals is the extent to which they interpellate women in ways designed to persuade them to voluntarily serve the needs or desires of the communities in which they reside. He writes,

> even the most pacific and seemingly benevolent of these rituals still serve to produce subjects who will thereafter accept the positions, statuses, and modes of being that society desires for and demands of them: persons whom it can use for its own purposes, as productive workers, for example, docile spouses, nurturant mothers, or anaesthetized lovers (in the last case, I think particularly of the many

initiatory rituals that feature clitoridectomy). In truth, persuasion can be more insidious, than coercion, for while the latter generally provokes some measure of resentment and resistance, skillful persuasion can avoid sowing these seeds of future struggle, insofar as *it leads its subjects to desire (or think they desire) for themselves precisely what society desires of them.*

(Lincoln 1991b: 112, emphasis mine)

What is most provocative here is the parenthetical remark in the last sentence: "or think they desire." This simple clause marks Lincoln's position in a long and theoretically complicated debate in critical theory about how group interests and social domination ought to be identified, one which arguably deserves more treatment than four words. (Note: to some extent in what follows I caricature Lincoln on the basis of this point for the purposes of illustrating various scholarly positions.)

"Internalized oppression" (or, sometimes, "false consciousness") is the concept often invoked to account for the phenomenon Lincoln identifies here.[5] Either through the mystification or naturalization of oppression—or some other distortion of reality—oppressed subjects are socialized or habituated to internalize their own oppression and, eventually, come to oppress themselves in some way. For Lincoln, these women "think they desire" what their community demands of them, and the word "think" invites us to interpret Lincoln as implying that, in reality, they have other desires they are repressing. The opposition, then, is between their real desires and the desires they only "think" they have, as a result of mystification or ideology of some sort.

There are many historical cases where we look back and see subjects desiring what we would consider it absurd to desire (as should be clear from our discussion of Twain's novel, the perspectival nature of this "we" is crucial here). Why did some nineteenth-century American women campaign against their own right to vote? Why do some women in Africa or the Middle East support and willingly volunteer for female genital mutilation? From Lincoln's perspective, perhaps they have been led to misrecognize their "real" interests, so much so that they actively work against those interests. The concept of "internalized oppression" is appealing to scholars concerned with domination who want to draw attention to asymmetrical power relations; the concern with so-called internalized oppression appears to come from a desire to liberate those who have internalized their own oppression.

For other theorists, the appeal to internalized oppression is problematic insofar as it entails a paternalist account of subjects' desires or interests. Those who point to internalized oppression claim to know what is "really" in a subject's or a group's best interests, despite their behavior, choices, reported desires, or stated interests. The problem, as Twain makes clear, is that this sort of paternalism—the sort once positively referred to as the "white man's burden," by Rudyard Kipling in his famous poem of the same name, for instance—has been used to justify colonialist endeavors. On this view, it appears that "we" know better than "they" what they desire or what is in their best interests, so we are going to help them. In Kipling's poem, encouraging the United

States to invade the Philippines, those "captives" on the frontier of colonial empires need to be saved because they are "wild" and "half devil and half child." Concern for the oppressed often—and condescendingly—entails depicting the "oppressed" as youth in need of adult guidance. From such a perspective, "helping them" might involve "conquering them"; Kipling literally refers to those intended to be saved as the white men's "captives." Arguably, in such cases judging whether a group is oppressed by imposing our own particular standards of what is "liberating" may itself be a means of domination.

In *Politics of Piety: The Islamic Revival and the Feminist Subject*, Saba Mahmood draws attention to the various ways that some Western, liberal feminists have responded to Arab Islamic women's participation in forms of Muslim culture that, to Western feminists, are "associated with ... the subjection of women, social conservatism, reactionary atavism, cultural backwardness, and so on" (Mahmood 2005: 5). For Western feminists, perhaps "women Islamist supporters are pawns in a grand patriarchal plan, who, if freed from their bondage, would naturally express their instinctual abhorrence for the traditional Islamic mores used to enchain them" (1–2). Mahmood is quite right, in my view, to identify the source of such criticisms in those parts of the liberal political tradition that teach that "all human beings have an innate desire for freedom, that we all somehow seek to assert our autonomy when allowed to do so, that human agency primarily consists of acts that challenge social norms ... and so on" (5). These political projects are propped up by a bundle of liberal assumptions shared by both anarchists and libertarians (two intellectual traditions that lie at the extreme ends of the spectrum of liberal politics)—most importantly, they assume that power can have only a negative effect on a subject's autonomy, and that resistance to the effects of power is how autonomy expresses itself. On this view—which, arguably, underlies Lincoln's statement discussed above—autonomous subjects would never willingly comply with the operation of power on their subjectivity. In addition, from this perspective "agency" amounts to the *resistance* of the operation of power. As such, if subjects are not resisting the application of power on them, they must be oppressed or dominated. "Those who are compliant with the operation of power over them are dominated": for anarchists and libertarians this is a tautology. Mahmood rightly notes that if scholars adopt these liberal assumptions, they will be stuck with a "binary model of subordination or subversion," or "repression and resistance" (14)—not particularly subtle tools for thinking about something as complex as social domination.

An additional problem, for Mahmood, is that too often Western feminists wrongly assume that their desires must be everyone's desires. However, as Mahmood notes, "we cannot treat as natural and imitable only those desires that ensure the emergence of [Western] feminist politics" (Mahmood 2005: 15). Why do they get to be the arbiters of what Egyptian Muslim women ought to want? Once again, we are back to the fact that desires vary. I can imagine Mahmood pressing Lincoln: when he claims that women submit because they "think they desire" rather than actually desire, he presumes a counterfactual—were they not fooled by ideology their *actual* desires would be directed elsewhere. As such, there exists a burden of proof that must fall somewhere: from whence do we derive evidence of these counterfactual desires, if they are not exhibited in a subject's or group's behaviors or stated interests? If we want to criticize domination on the basis of an appeal to unexpressed desires, what epistemology allows us access to them?

Rather than project our own desires onto others, Mahmood encourages us instead to return to the resources of the Foucualdian tradition, according to which subjectivity does not precede the operation of power but is constituted by the operation of power. Foucault's most explicit statement against the liberal paradigm is found in *The History of Sexuality, Volume 1* (Foucault 1978). There Foucault offers a criticism of what he calls "the repressive hypothesis"—the hypothesis that sexuality was repressed in the Victorian age. His target of course includes Freud's theories, which alleged that repression of desire was at the root of psychological and social problems. However, it is clear that his target is more so (what I am calling) the liberal tradition in general, which assumes that social power is intrinsically at odds with a subject's autonomy, rather than constitutive of it. Throughout the book, Foucault considers how power is imagined in liberal discourses, even those that have nothing to do with sexuality. On the liberal view, "confronted by a power that is law, the subject who is constituted as subject—who is 'subjected'—is he who obeys ... [,] whether the individual in question is the subject opposite the monarch, the citizen opposite the state, the child opposite the parent, or the disciple opposite the master" (Foucault 1978: 85). On such a view, power "only has the force of the negative on its side, a power to say no" (85). By contrast, Foucault wants to theorize power as positive or productive, and focuses on the production of sexuality as his starting point.

In summary,

- people subjected to different processes of socialization may desire very different things;
- social conditions one subject may experience as liberating another may experience as oppressive; consequently,
- using a concept like "internalized oppression" to critique domination may entail attributing repressed desires to subjects, desires for which we have no empirical evidence.

It appears that, in a sense, Mahmood and Foucault are covering the same ground Twain did a century ago: if desires are relative to the production of subjectivity, what counts as liberating is also relative—and consequently there is something grossly paternalistic about judging subjects according to a foreign criterion of domination.

The Production of Subjectivity and the Dissolution of Grounds for Critique

According to Foucault, during the nineteenth century there was an explosion of discourses on sexuality; despite its so-called repression, people were speaking more and more about sex. "They devoted themselves to speaking of it *ad infinitum*" (Foucault

1978: 35). These discourses functioned in a variety of ways; Foucault suggests a number of ways in particular that discourses functioned other than to repress (41–48). In part, discourses on sexuality solicited authorities to surveil subjects under their gaze, inviting them (often children) to speak of their desires; authorities would then classify the desires reported as normal or perverted. This could take place through the institution of medical authorities or the family, and techniques of surveilling sexuality through these institutions were expanded greatly during this time. In addition, permanent identities were invented and attributed to subjects on the basis of their sexual desires or actions.

> The nineteenth-century homosexual became a personage, a past, a case history, and a childhood, in addition to being a type of life, a life form, and a morphology, with an indiscreet anatomy and possibly a mysterious physiology … It was everywhere present in him: at the root of all his actions because it was their insidious and indefinitely active principle … It as consubstantial with him … as a singular nature.
>
> (Foucault 1978: 43)

The difference here is the difference between someone who commits a crime and a *criminal* or between someone who drinks and an *alcoholic*; in the latter cases the identity is characterized as something that pervades the subject's entire being, motivating it from within on a permanent basis.

For Foucault, these operations on sexuality were not only repressive in nature. They acted on bodies, touching them, inviting them to speak or confess, classifying them, naming them, and so on.[6] Rather than simply repressing sexuality, they incited it to express itself, albeit in channeled or prescribed ways. According to Foucault, these discourses would have had a feedback or spiral effect on the subjects operated on in these manners, increasing or inflating desire and pleasure (Foucault 1978: 44–45). Even outright prohibition or repression itself can have the effect of increasing desire, as prohibition is a condition of possibility of enjoyable perversions—the performance of forbidden actions is often the most titillating. As Butler puts it, for Foucault to some extent "repression generates the very pleasures or desires it seeks to regulate" (Butler 1997: 58). Pleasure is kindled "at having to evade this power, flee from it, fool it, or travesty it" (Foucault 1978: 45). Through all of these operations of power, desire and sexuality were multiplied and intensified (71).

Of course, for Foucault these effects were not limited to the production of sexuality; most of his work in the 1970s provided historically specific accounts of what Althusser called interpellation, whether the interpellation of sexuality, military discipline, or the self-surveillance of inmates in prisons. As Butler notes, "Althusser's doctrine of interpellation clearly sets the stage for Foucault's later views on the 'discursive production of the subject'" (Butler 1997: 5). On Althusser's account, everyone is a product of such subjection; no one escapes the operation of power. The study of subjectivity would then no longer focus on the extent to which subjects are prohibited from doing what they desire, but rather on how desires are in part produced by forms of power that are immanent throughout the social fields in which we reside.

> In short, it is a question of orienting ourselves to a conception of power which replaces the privilege of the law ... [and] the privilege of prohibition ... with the analysis of a multiple and mobile field of force relations, wherein far-reaching, but never completely stable, effects of domination are produced.
>
> (Foucault 1978: 102)

To return to a key point, if we accept Foucault's account of power as constitutive rather than repressive of subjectivity and desire—much as Twain saw people and their aspirations (or lack thereof) as constituted by their training—what are we to make of Lincoln's claim that some subjects are taught to "think they desire" what they, in fact, do not really desire? If we accept that power is productive, perhaps socialization produces subjects who do, in fact, desire what they think they desire, even when what they desire seems abhorrent from the perspective of a subject produced with a different training. On such a view, internalized oppression would be an oxymoron, for if oppression operated to produce or change one's desires, such that one desired one's "oppressed" position or status, then the satisfaction of one's desire would no longer be "oppressive" but instead satisfactory or liberating. The satisfaction of the desires produced by subjection would be indistinguishable from autonomy. On what grounds, then, could we allege that subjection entails "effects of domination," as Foucault puts it?

In *Michel Foucault: Genealogy as Critique*, Rudi Visker offers what is perhaps the most extensive commentary on this problem. As Visker notes, Foucault historicizes the creation of disciplined subjects, but provides us with no reason to question the forms of subjection he identifies. At times Foucault calls for us "to refuse what we are" and to create "new forms of subjectivity" (Visker 1995: 101), but on what grounds?

> If Foucault's genealogy had merely been confined [to historicizing the production of subjectivity], not only would it have been unable to lead to the political consequences he sought to attach *directly* to it, it would also have given those who do not share its political commitment an argument by which to evade Foucault's critical intentions without becoming politically suspect. For why should we refuse what we are? Why not simply acknowledge it? Why should we not accept [Richard] Rorty's call for a frank ethnocentrism or merely admit, with Charles Taylor, that "what we have become" here in the West "counts for us" and determines what we understand by "humanity" and "politics"?
>
> (Visker 1995: 101)

The contingency of an order of subjection "can in no sense be adduced as an argument against [it]" (Visker 1995: 117).

> Foucault's concept of order *appears* to render a possible attempt to criticize a particular order impossible by no longer allowing any room for a standpoint

outside that order, from which it might be criticized. The fact that the order has, so to speak, "internalized" its own conditions of validity seems to condemn any attempt at criticism from the outset to be merely a deep, but empty sigh that "what is might also be otherwise."

(Visker 1995: 118)

Lincoln's stance seems to be the following: what might have been otherwise would have been preferable because those oppressed subjects *would have* desired otherwise had not power operated on them. However, if we refuse to appeal to desires for which we do not have empirical evidence, how might we ground critique?

According to Visker, Foucault ends up implicitly condemning systematic asymmetrical power relations and hoping for a "minimum of domination" (Visker 1995: 102). However, I would suggest, Foucault provides us with no resources to define "minimum of domination," and given the way in which his work relativizes subjectivity and desire, it is difficult to see how he could justify such a definition. Additionally, Visker notes that Foucault's implicit critique of domination depends upon a disavowed normative foundation; "for all his arguing against the repression hypothesis, this does not, in the end, prevent him from merely displacing that hypothesis" onto his accounts of the *subjection* of "bodies" and "pleasures" (86). Perhaps, as Butler suggests in *Gender Trouble*, a liberal theory of subjectivity is hidden beneath the surface of Foucault's analytic at a few points in his work. In his reading of the life of Herculine Barbin— *Herculine Barbin: Being the Recently Discovered Memoirs of a Nineteenth-Century French Hermaphrodite* (Foucault 1980a)—Foucault arguably appeals to "pleasures that clearly transcend the regulation imposed upon them, and here we see Foucault's sentimental indulgence in the very emancipatory discourse his analysis in *The History of Sexuality* was meant to displace" (Butler 1990: 96). At this point, implicitly Foucault appears to accept—naively—that liberation would entail little more than the lifting of social regulation; here, "Foucault invokes a trope of prediscursive libidinal multiplicity that effectively presupposes a sexuality 'before the law,' indeed, a sexuality waiting for emancipation from the shackles of 'sex'" (97). By contrast, in general Foucault accepts that power is constitutive rather than (merely) restrictive on desire: "Foucault officially insists that sexuality and power are coextensive and that we must not think that by saying yes to sex we say no to power" (97). For Butler, the "heterogeneity" of desires—which, insofar as Barbin's sex is ambiguous, are neither strictly hetero nor homosexual—that Foucault finds in Barbin's narrative are not innate or prediscursive; on the contrary, "the heterogeneity to which Foucault appeals *is itself constituted by* the very medical discourses that he positions as the repressive juridical law" (101, emphasis mine). In part this takes place via the strict prohibition of homosexuality in the Christian community in which Barbin resided; this prohibition was an essential condition of her sexuality (105). Butler therefore insists, "the temptation to romanticize Herculine's sexuality as the utopian play of pleasures prior to the imposition and restrictions of 'sex' surely ought to be refused" (98). If we are to think "liberation," it will involve more than merely "saying no" to power.

Discourse and Ideology

Mahmood accepts this point: we cannot think of Egyptian Muslim women as "oppressed" merely because they are subject to power. Drawing upon Foucault's later works on ethics and selfhood, she notes how subjects internalize social norms in ways that capacitate "ethical" behaviors. On this view, ethics is defined as "those practices, techniques, and discourses through which a subject transforms herself in order to achieve a particular state of being, happiness, or truth" (Mahmood 2005: 28). As such, ethical subjectivity is "an effect of a modality of power operationalized through a set of moral codes that summon a subject to constitute herself in accord with its precepts" (28). Mahmood writes, "we might consider the example of a virtuoso pianist who submits herself to the often painful regime of disciplinary practice, as well as to the hierarchical structures of apprenticeship, in order to acquire the ability—the requisite agency—to play the instrument with mastery" (29). On this view, ethical agents are capacitated through subjection to external norms and social hierarchies, rather than resisting or subverting the operation of social power on them. The pianist's subjection would, in this way, be liberating despite the outward appearance of her submission to relations of power that appear—to others—to be dominating.

If we don't automatically assume there is a difference "between the subject's own desires and socially prescribed performances" (Mahmood 2005: 31), we can perhaps see that Egyptian Muslim women who submit to disciplinary practices requiring them to don gender-marked clothing and participate in daily prayer rituals may in fact be "honing particular moral capacities" (126). "The desire to pray is [not] natural, but … *must be created* through a set of disciplinary acts. That is to say, desire in this model is not the *antecedent* to, or cause of, moral action, but *its product*" (126). For Mahmood, disciplinary practices lead to the creation of habits and desires that are moral or ethical, which lead to political efforts as well—all without opposing existing social norms but rather flowing with them.

From my perspective, the problem with such an approach is that Mahmood does not appear to stop and ask *for whom* such disciplines, habits, and desires are "moral" or "ethical." Rather, in the way she uses the terms moral and ethical, it appears that *any* "set of practical activities that are germane to a certain way of life" are, by definition, moral or ethical. On her definition, "ethics" is reduced to little more than "habitual social practices," which theoretically could include any type of activity whatsoever—pillaging was once a way of life for some peoples. Yes, on her definition of the terms, these women's practices are "moral," and Mahmood gets to use the positive valences on the words "moral" and "ethical" throughout her book and to assist her in positively portraying the practices of the women she studies. However, the use of this taxon to describe these activities is, at bottom, revealing of little more than Mahmood's anthropological agenda to save the subjects she studies from criticism.

Some of Mahmood's critics—in particular, Afiya S. Zia, who writes on Muslim women in Pakistan—have argued that she romanticizes the practices of these women as exercises of their agency but without any consideration of the material, social, or political effects of their practices; "there is no discussion of the implications, outcomes, or effects of such agency which has been, in the experience of Pakistan, both vociferously anti-women at worst or silent and hence complicit at best" (Zia 2009: 238). That is, on Zia's interpretation these women's practices and communities are complicit with violence against women, and that fact is completely left out of Mahmood's analysis. While their behavior might be "ethical" or "moral" in some sense, Mahmood ignores the ways in which it might lead to unethical or immoral consequences from the perspective of the feminist analytic Zia employs. Consequently, for Zia "it is difficult to understand how these religious political parties can be understood to be potential reformists and ideologically liberating spaces, rather than politically ... conservative to the point of being fascistic" (238).

Mahmood does consider potential objections to her analytic: "a feminist concerned with relations of gender inequality might ask: ... By untethering the concept of agency from that of progressive politics for the purposes of analytical clarity, have we abandoned any means of judging and critiquing which practices subordinate women and which ones allocate them some form of gender parity" (Mahmood 2005: 37)? Her answer is that no, she does not discourage scholars from noting the patriarchal aspects of the traditions she studies. Rather, she hopes that "critique" will avoid simplistic denunciations of patriarchy and that we as scholars will leave ourselves "open to the possibility that we might also be remade in the process of engaging another's worldview" (36). In addition, she assures readers, "the [Egyptian] mosque movement ... is neither a fascist nor a militant movement, nor does it seek to gain control of the state and make Egypt a theocracy" (37). However, insofar as she has defined "ethics" so broadly, fascist or militant "ways of life" would likely count as moral according to the letter of her definition. So while Mahmood wants to insist that she is not cutting the heart out of critique or discouraging us from drawing attention to patriarchy, I would argue that is precisely what she is doing. The mode of analysis her book proposes literally encourages us to see all habitual ways of life as, by definition, "moral."

The unintended but logical conclusion of the feminist analytic she advances is parodied by *The Onion*, a popular online satirical "news" source, in a story titled "Women Now Empowered by Everything a Woman Does":

> According to a study released Monday, women—once empowered primarily via the assertion of reproductive rights or workplace equality with men—are now empowered by virtually everything the typical woman does.
>
> ... "From what she eats for breakfast to the way she cleans her home, today's woman lives in a state of near-constant empowerment," said Barbara Klein, professor of women's studies at Oberlin College and director of the study. "As recently as 15 years ago, a woman could only feel empowered by advancing in a male-dominated work world, asserting her own sexual wants and needs, or pushing for a stronger voice in politics. Today, a woman can empower herself through actions as seemingly inconsequential as driving her children to soccer practice or watching the Oxygen network."
>
> Klein said that clothes-shopping, once considered a mundane act with few sociopolitical implications, is now a bold feminist statement.

Discourse and Ideology

> ... "Not every woman can become a physicist or lobby to stop a foundry from dumping dangerous metals into the creek her children swim in," Klein said. "Although these actions are incredible, they marginalize the majority of women who are unable to, or just don't particularly care to, achieve such things. Fortunately for the less impressive among us, a new strain of feminism has emerged in which mundane activities are championed as proud, bold assertions of independence from oppressive patriarchal hegemony."
>
> ("Women Now Empowered by Everything a Woman Does" 2003)

What this parody rightly draws attention to is that if we make liberation completely relative to subjects achieving what they are socialized to want, then practically all disciplined behaviors will have to be classified as liberatory. It is for this reason that Zia has pointed out that, for all practical purposes, Mahmood argues that women's or feminist "agency can be attributed even to passive, docile, non-action and preservation of the status quo" (Zia 2009: 234). It is unlikely that Mahmood would accept such a conclusion, but it is difficult to see how it does not follow from the feminist analytic she proposes.

Subjective vs Objective Definitions of Domination

If we assume, from a poststructuralist perspective, that desires really are produced through the processes of interpellation and socialization, we cannot make Lincoln's appeal to people's *real* desires, as opposed to the ones they merely *think* they have. On the other hand, critical theorists interested in asymmetrical power relations likely wish to avoid the flattened analytic Mahmood proposes. To find a way between these two perspectives, we might adopt in modified form the distinction some feminist theorists make between subjective and objective definitions of sexual harassment.

In "A Feminist Definition of Sexual Harassment" (1993), Anita Superson makes an opposition between subjective definitions of sexual harassment, which focus on whether a minority *feels* harmed, and objective definitions, which define a behavior or practice as harassment *independently* of whether a minority feels harmed in any particular case or incident. Given a subjective definition, a misogynist joke received as unwelcome, annoying, or offensive by a woman would be classified as sexual harassment, but the same joke would not be classified as harassment *if* there were no one present offended by the joke. On an objective definition, telling a misogynist joke would be counted as harassment, even in those cases in which no one present actually feels offended.

According to Superson, one problem with subjective definitions of harassment is that "the burden of proof is wrongly shifted to the victim and off of the perpetrator with the result that many victims are not legally protected" (Superson 1993: 49). Such a policy of course discourages women from wanting to report (50). In addition, when assessing *quid pro quo* cases, a woman might be required to demonstrate that she, in particular, was materially or economically harmed by the instance of harassment for which she was on the receiving end—a particularly high bar and thus another barrier that discourages reporting (50). For Superson, making women responsible for the burden of proof adds to rather than reduces the constraints women are under.

For Superson, the primary problem with subjective definitions is that they fail to note that sexual harassment "is an attack on the group of *all* women, not just the immediate victim" (Superson 1993: 49). Whether or not any particular case involves personal animosity, outright hatred, or direct harm to an individual woman, given patriarchy's ongoing legacy sexual harassment functions to reinforce the domination of men as a group over women. According to Superson, "sexual harassment, a form of sexism, is about domination, in particular, the domination of the group of men over the group of women. Domination involves control or power which can be seen in the economic, political, and social spheres of society" (51). More specifically, "sexual harassment is integrally related to sex roles. It reveals the belief that a person is to be relegated to certain roles on the basis of her sex, including not only women's being sex objects, but also their being caretakers, motherers, nurturers, sympathizers, etc." (51). From this perspective, even if a woman is not directly materially harmed in a particular case of harassment, the harassment "reflects and reinforces sexist attitudes" (52), normalizes predatory behavior in men (53–54), and thus indirectly reinforces domination, leading to the ongoing privileging of men or masculinity in those social spheres she names, and stigmatizing women as belonging in other social spheres. As such, "when A sexually harasses B, the comment or behavior is really directed at the group of all women, not just a particular woman" (51). Superson additionally notes that this is true even when a woman does not recognize that fact—namely, she may not be cognizant of how sexism can reinforce systematic, asymmetrical power relations—or even when a woman herself holds sexist views or enjoyed, for example, the misogynist joke or catcalls at hand (57).

According to Superson,

> An objective view of [sexual harassment] avoids the problems inherent in a subjective view. According to the objective view defended here, what is decisive in determining whether behavior constitutes [sexual harassment] is not whether the victim is bothered, but whether the behavior is an instance of a practice that expresses and perpetuates the attitude that the victim and members of her sex are inferior because of their sex.
>
> (Superson 1993: 58)

In particular, she recommends that, for the purposes of law, we define sexual harassment in the following manner:

> any behavior (verbal or physical) caused by a person, A, in the dominant class directed at another, B, in the subjugated class, that expresses and perpetuates the attitude that B or members of Bs sex is/are inferior because of their sex, thereby causing harm to either B and/or members of B's sex.
>
> (Superson 1993: 46)

Discourse and Ideology

Such a definition is objective insofar as it focuses on particular behaviors that produce the effects that Superson and other feminists find undesirable—for example, behaviors and discourses that reinforce asymmetrical power relations between the men and women they imagine into existence—rather than how those possible behaviors and discourses are received by the recipients of sexual harassment. It has long been held that, when it comes to harassment, individual men's intentions are beside the point—whether or not a man intended to harass, the effects are what matter. Similarly, Superson would prefer that individual women's feelings about the reception of harassment be considered equally beside the point. Even if an individual woman enjoys catcalls, its systematic effect on women in general are what matters more. Consequently, she favors a discourse on sexual harassment that brings into relief power relations, not an individual's affect or emotional states.

Both Lincoln and Mahmood focus on the subjective aspects of social domination. For Mahmood, the women she studies must not be dominated or oppressed because they do not experience themselves as oppressed and therefore do not resist the operation of power on them (indeed: on her view the operation of power on them does not oppress but produces moral behavior). Lincoln, by contrast, identifies women who voluntarily subject themselves to relations of domination as dominated because they *would feel* dominated were their desires not mystified by ideology. For Mahmood the actual, socialized desires and feelings of women are what matter for gauging domination; for Lincoln the counterfactually imagined desires that preexist socialization are what matter for gauging domination. Both think of domination in terms of women's reception to domination, either real or imagined. They are therefore arguably working from subjective definitions of domination.

However, nothing about the concept of domination requires us *a priori* to define it in terms of how dominated subjects receive their own subjection. We could stipulate, by contrast, an objective definition of domination, focusing—much like Superson does—on asymmetrical distributions of responsibilities, privileges, and capital, as well as the capacity to effect or alter such distributions. Lincoln argued that women's initiation rituals "serve to produce subjects who will thereafter accept the positions, statuses, and modes of being that society desires for and demands of them: persons whom it can use for its own purposes, as productive workers, for example, docile spouses, nurturant mothers, or anaesthetized lovers" (Lincoln 1991b: 112). If we utilize an objective definition of domination, *it is these distributions of social responsibilities that matter*, rather than whether the women thus subjected experience (or might have experienced) their social assignments in positive or negative ways.

For those critical theorists interested in asymmetrical power relations, an objective definition of domination would additionally be useful to reorient our attention in cases in which dominant groups—"dominant," that is, on an objective definition—claim to be dominated—"dominated," that is, on a subjective definition. For instance, to offer just one brief example, in *Building God's Kingdom: Inside the World of Christian Reconstructionism* (2015), Julie J. Ingersoll considers how evangelical Christians in the United States sometimes characterize themselves as persecuted or oppressed. The particular context in her discussion concerns the evangelical creationist movement. Attending a creationist conference as a part of her fieldwork, Ingersoll notes that the participants consistently repeated the claim that the defenders of creationism—and Christians in general—are persecuted by atheists who advance evolutionary theory for the express purpose of denying the existence of a god. "Creationists charge evolutionists with the intentional misrepresentation of evidence, hiding evidence contrary to their theory, and perpetuating a conspiracy to shut creationists out of academia" (132). They claim that evolutionists force creationists to stay "in the closet," keeping their views secret, and that they are systematically "locked out of science" (133). However, Ingersoll notes that none of the creationists she studied who made such claims had credentials that would be recognized as legitimate in mainstream universities, as their doctorate degrees were from non-accredited universities, or were in subjects such as, for example, education rather than biology. What counts as "knowledge" in the biological sciences in modern universities is different to what counts as "knowledge" for creationist groups.

While I have little doubt that creationists are ingenuous or sincere in their claim that they *feel* oppressed by evolutionary biologists or atheists in general, there is little objective evidence that they are discriminated against in academia, any more so than other subjects who do not hold the relevant degrees or who do not produce the sort of evidence required by others in their field or discipline. In addition, Ingersoll notes what she saw on her way to the conference site:

> as I drove to the campus and parked in one of the church garages, I did not have the sense that I was about to enter a world of marginalized people; quite the opposite really. The garage was filled with SUVs and relatively new cars, pointing to the middle-class status of those in attendance. The conference attendees were almost uniformly white.
>
> (Ingersoll 2015: 126)

Again, I do not doubt the sincerity of those creationists who *feel* oppressed, but Ingersoll's anecdotal evidence suggests that they enjoy all the material privileges that middle-class whites in general tend to experience in the United States. If we use a subjective definition of domination, they may be dominated because they feel oppressed. If we use an objective definition of domination, there seems to be little evidence that they are subject to asymmetrical distributions of privilege, material capital, or the capacity to effect changes in such distributions. On the contrary, as Ingersoll notes, these creationists have been extremely successful in using a particular interpretation of the first amendment to litigate their way to exempting their children from educational requirements placed on almost everyone else in society, insofar as they are allowed to homeschool with almost zero government oversight. In addition, through lobbying efforts on state governors and legislatures they have gained material capital to send their children to private schools by getting the state to adopt school voucher programs. If we use an objective definition of domination, it appears that these white, petty bourgeois creationists who claim to

Discourse and Ideology

be oppressed perhaps benefit from an asymmetrical *surplus* of capital and privilege in comparison to other groups.

In summary,

- subjective definitions of sexual harassment tend to focus on individual victims' feelings, or how they receive the form of harassment to which they were subjected;
- by contrast, objective definitions of harassment focus instead not on feelings but on social structures: by this action, what asymmetrical power relations are potentially being reinforced?; and
- moving from a subjective to an objective definition of domination might save us from the difficulties inherent in attributing repressed desires to subjects in relations of domination—perhaps some subject positions are dominated, not because of how they feel or their experiences, but because they are objectively disadvantaged in relationship to other subject positions within the same social structure.

If we use an objective definition of domination, we would not need a special epistemology to give us access to people's unmanifested desires to escape the status quo.

Desires and Interests

An objective definition of domination would require us to use an objective rather than subjective construction of a subject's interests. As Steven Lukes notes in *Power: A Radical View*,

> [interests] can be interpreted purely "subjectively," so that what is in my interests is decided by what is important to me; or else it can be interpreted in a way that incorporates "objective" judgments, concerning what benefits and harms me, where what counts as benefit and harm is not decided by my preferences or judgments.
>
> (Lukes 2005: 80)

The problem, of course, is this: how do we construct objective interests in a way that is analytically useful, especially if we imagine them as divorced from a subject's preferences? The latter seems to suggest that subjects' interests are in some cases potentially served when they do not get what they want—which, on the surface, seems to be an extremely counterintuitive way to define "interests."

Lukes notes that political philosophers such as John Rawls or Ronald Dworkin appeal to things such as "primary goods" or "basic needs" when attempting to account for human welfare (Lukes 2005: 81); perhaps, as Maslow suggests, there is an objective "hierarchy of needs" according to which "basic" things such as food, shelter, clothing, and a sense of safety are universally necessary for a subject to "flourish." Many liberal theorists would include education among such "basic needs," insofar as education seems necessary for anyone hoping to "flourish." Despite the attractiveness of such an option, I would argue that it passes off historically specific "needs" as universal, and that we need a more general definition of interests, insofar as human desires are far more relative than Maslow imagines. For instance, consider the Amish who have legally won the right to exempt their children from public school in the United States after 8th grade; for them, further education is a threat to their way of life or their vision of "flourishing." We could of course claim that these subjects are irrational—liberal theorists always reserve the right to declare some subjects, for example, children or the mentally ill, as insufficiently rational to deserve protections against paternalism. However, if human desires are truly plastic, then appeals to "primary goods" or "basic needs" likely amount to the projection—and mystification—of some groups' interests as if they were universal interests; presenting one's own "basic needs" as universal possibly masks one's will-to-power. Consequently, I will avoid proposing a definition of domination and interests that focus on historically specific forms of goods or human flourishing; our definition will have to be more abstract and must refer more to the nature of social relations, as opposed to the specific goods those social relations can help subjects get.

In *The Circular Structure of Power: Politics, Identity, Community* (1997), Torben Bech Dyrberg draws our attention to the myriad complications that follow from attempts to identify what might be in the interests of a particular subject or subject position. He offers us a useful starting point for considering how we might produce a definition of interests that can serve as a fundamental part of an objective definition of domination.

Just as Heidegger suggested that subjects are *a priori* incomplete, Dyrberg accepts that subjects are not fixed, unfolding essences; they are proleptic projects that are never fully themselves but, on the contrary, moving targets. "The subject exists … as a being who is concerned with its own being, which is not a substance but rather a projection in time and space" (156). Such a subject has "interests" insofar as "the subject strives to satisfy its needs, aspirations, and the like" (Dyrberg 1997: 156); what is in a subject's interests is *whatever helps to satisfy those needs and desires.* Subjects are socialized with both short-term and long-term desires. Long-term projects may, of course, require subjects to repress short-term desires in pursuit of their long-term projects. The process of pursuing those long-term projects is proleptic insofar as it involves reflecting on past desires, choices, and trajectories, evaluations of what "worked" and what did not, anticipating possible futures, and executing choices, forming disciplines, or developing and practicing habits that are designed to work toward one possible future and avoid others. In general, I shall reserve the term "desires" for short-term desires and "interests" for long-term desires and projects; in addition, to say something is "*in* a subject's interests" is to say that it—whatever "it" is, whether resource, institution, social relation, event, etc.—assists a subject in satisfying her interests (at this point our discussion of interests is still "subjective" in Superson's sense).

So a subject is not a fixed thing but rather an unfolding, quasi-teleological, proleptic project that becomes what it is through its unfolding. In addition, subjects are always socialized with competing desires and interests. We always want more than one thing at

Discourse and Ideology

a time, and therefore our interests are not only in competition with other subjects but with themselves. The identification of what is "in our interests" is further complicated by the fact that the future is always uncertain; otherwise successful efforts expended toward the satisfaction of one set of desires may come to naught when tragic, life-altering events take place. Investing one's retirement account in the stock market might serve one's long-term interests, provided that the stock market does not crash; were it to crash, one's investment, in retrospect, likely did not in fact serve one's interests.

Dyrberg makes a distinction between "subjective interests" and "real interests." Subjective interests are those *perceived by* the subject; real interests entail what is *really* in a subject's interests. Publishing an article in a journal might subjectively seem like it serves one's interest in achieving tenure, but if it turns out that the journal is a predatory journal, then publishing there will not have served one's real interests.

> The decisions and the courses of action we pursue will always be surrounded by a greater or lesser degree of uncertainty: whether what we do is the right thing to do, whether we could do better or have done better, whether we could have predicted the outcome of events better than we actually did, whether what we did or are going to do actually prevented/will prevent what we really wanted/want. It is this unavoidable uncertainty which gives the notion of real interests its force.
>
> (Dyrberg 1997: 156–157)

(Note: "subjective interests" in Dyrberg's sense are not "subjective" in Superson's sense. For Superson, a definition of harassment is subjective when defined *relative to the desires* an individual woman has. By contrast, for Dyrberg "subjective interests" are subjective insofar as a subject has *subjective knowledge* about what may fulfill her desires—it is an epistemic subjectivity.)

For Dyrberg, the calculation of what is in an individual subject's real interests entails imagining counterfactuals. "My real interest would be the option I would go for if we imagine that, in the moment of choosing, I had already experienced all the available options and then decided this particular one" (Dyrberg 1997: 158). Such a definition of interests entails "a hypothetically assumed omniscient knowledge, which guarantees the rationality of the decision maker" (158). Of course, we do not have access to omniscient knowledge, and as a result *any* calculation of interests will necessarily and *a priori* be epistemically subjective.

The distance between what a subject currently *thinks* will fulfill her desires and what would *actually* fulfill her desires if she were to have access to such omniscient knowledge is what opens the distinction between subjective and real interests in Dyrberg's account. In addition, it is what opens the possibility for one subject to criticize another subject's subjective interests: "yes, Thai sounds good now, but you always complain of indigestion afterwards." As Dyrberg puts it, "both anticipation and evaluation employ a counterfactual kind of reasoning: what would have happened if what actually did happen had not happened, and would the alternative be preferable" (Dyrberg 1997: 159)? Dyrberg concludes from this that claims about what is in someone's or some group's interests "cannot have a solid foundation" (159). Because what is in our "real interests" on this definition is relative to our ability to predict the future and imagine future selves retrospectively evaluating possible pasts, real interests are essentially fantasies.

To illustrate the importance of fantasizing counterfactuals for thinking about real interests, Dyrberg points to the well-known film, *It's a Wonderful Life* (1946), in which the suicidal character George Bailey (played by James Stewart) is persuaded by an angel not to commit suicide by imaginatively showing him a vision of what life would be like had George never been born. This imagined world without him is, on George's evaluation, much worse, and George decides that committing suicide would neither be in his own best interests nor in the interests of his loved ones. Through this fantasy of what another life would be like, George is provided with omniscient knowledge of counterfactual possibilities, and he decides on the basis of that knowledge that *avoiding* suicide would benefit him and those around him. To repeat: the distance between what a subject thinks would fulfill her desires—on the basis of limited knowledge at any point in the present—and what would actually fulfill her desires were she to have knowledge of all counterfactual possibilities is what permits a distinction between subjective and real interests for Dyrberg, and opens the possibility for subjects with *more evidence* to criticize others' subjective interests.

While this might sound paternalistic, in point of fact this type of criticism of subjective interests is an essential component of how we structure our world and assign responsibilities. Parents, we allow, are for the most part better judges of what is in their children's real interests than those children themselves. "Eat your vegetables; they're good for you" or "I know this medicine tastes bad, but it will make you feel better" are perhaps the most obvious examples of the importance of appeals to "real interests" over "subjective interests" in our everyday lives. In the United States, the government may mandate that children receive vaccinations for certain illnesses, or may prohibit citizens from buying cars without brake lights, seat belts, or airbags—all presumably out of a concern for their citizens' real interests. As Dyrberg puts it, "there is nothing inherently totalitarian about real interests, which are, rather, an inherent feature of politics" (Dyrberg 1997: 162). While some theorists might insist that subjects are themselves always the best judges of what is in their best interests, everyday life in a society with a high division of labor proves otherwise. No individual subject could, in a society as complex as ours, be sufficiently expert to know what is always in their real interests in every aspect of her life. Consequently, for better or for worse, we often trust trained, specialized experts to decide for us what is in our real interests. Of course, trained experts are not omniscient and could be wrong about what is in our real interests; on the other hand, neither are we, as individuals, omniscient.

Thus far I am largely in agreement with Dyrberg, insofar as these definitions and distinctions seem useful for drawing attention to the complicated calculations involved in determining whether or not something serves our interests. In addition, like Dyrberg, it seems clear that "real interests" are, in a very real sense, imaginary—none of us have access to George Bailey's angel.

Discourse and Ideology

Dyrberg's account must be additionally complicated, however, by drawing attention to the fact that—in addition to being epistemically subjective—real interests are further relativized by the fact that subjects and subjects' desires *change over time*. *It's a Wonderful Life* assumes that the George at the beginning of the film is the same George—with the same real interests—at the end of the film; the only difference is the level of knowledge he has about what will serve his real interests. On this view of real interests, "the subject has to be conceived as possessing an essential identity" (Dyrberg 1997: 167), one whose desires and interests do not change after the vision of counterfactual worlds. However, that is often not the case (as Dyrberg hints but doesn't pursue).

Turning to an equally fantastical film, I would like to consider the comedy *Bedazzled* (2000). *Bedazzled* follows the genre of films based on the famous "The Monkey's Paw" story, wherein people make wishes granted by a magical totem, a genie, or the devil, only later to regret having had them fulfilled. What is crucial for my purposes here is the fact that in the film, after seeing a number of counterfactual possibilities, the main character's desires *change*. In *Bedazzled*, the socially awkward "loser" and cubicle-slave Elliot Richards (played by Brendan Fraser) sells his soul to the devil (played by Elizabeth Hurley) in trade for seven wishes; he uses most of them to attempt to get his crush, a coworker named Allison (played by Francis O'Connor), to fall in love with him. It all starts when, in a bar, Elliot whispers to himself, "Dear God, I would do anything to have that girl in my life."

At that moment, the devil suddenly appears, and, in order to persuade Elliot to sell his soul in exchange for wishes, the devil presents him with a brief vision of him and Allison taking a romantic walk on a beach, ending with passionate kisses. After seeing this possible future, Elliot signs on the dotted line (the devil literally presents a written contract to him), and immediately makes a wish to be married to Allison, as well as to be very rich and powerful. The devil snaps her fingers, and he wakes up next to Allison in a canopy bed, in a beautifully decorated bedroom, all inside a massive mansion in an equatorial climate—perhaps Columbia. Elliot is of course immediately pleased, until—minutes later—he is horrified to learn that his wealth is the result of his position as a leader of a drug cartel. At the end of this wish vignette, guerillas from a rival cartel invade his compound with machine guns, and Elliot barely escapes death. Just before dying, Elliot calls for a time-out and asks the devil for his second wish, which he hopes will avoid the pitfalls of his first.

Later in the film, after a few other failed wishes—namely, after seeing some counterfactual universes he could live in—he asks to be made witty, sophisticated, articulate, good looking, etc. He immediately appears at a lavish, black-tie party in an amazing and huge New York penthouse apartment; he appears to be a famous author and the party appears to be in his honor. Allison is, of course, present at the party, and tells a friend that she has read all of his books. She crosses the room to make small talk with him, and they pair off for a private conversation. They have a brief discussion about Sartre and Camus, and she asks him, "Don't you think secular humanism is yummy?" The narrative jumps forward to the end of the party, and the two of them wrap up their conversation in order to head back to his apartment. Upon entering Elliot's bedroom, a man in a bathrobe jumps out of his bed, asking, "What the hell is going on?! ... I've been out of my mind all night!" Elliot and Allison suddenly realize that this is Elliot's partner, and that the version of Elliot in this wish-world must be gay. Elliot assures Allison, "I'm not gay! ... Wait, I can prove to you I am not gay. Kiss me." They embrace in a passionate kiss for a long moment, and then he lets her go. With a pained look on his face, and suffering from utter disappointment, he whines, "I'm gay ... Um, well, thanks for dropping by."

One crucial issue of note here is the fact that in these two wish-worlds, he is disappointed in his circumstances *on the basis of the point of view of who he was at the beginning of the film*. That is, if he had worked for years and years to build a drug cartel, he likely would not have been disappointed in that life. If he were a gay man, he likely would not have been disappointed by his lackluster kiss with Allison. Those other Elliots might have been quite happy with the lives that cubicle-slave Elliot found unsatisfactory. Had his life taken those alternate paths, he would have been a different Elliot, and would have developed different desires and interests. So his negative evaluation of these alternate lives is fundamentally based on the introduction of alien criteria of evaluation.

By the end of the film, after six of his seven wishes end in disaster, Elliot winds up in jail and has a heart-to-heart with a strange inmate who, the movie hints, just might be God in disguise. Elliot is told, "the devil gonna to try to confuse you; that's her game. But in the end, you're gonna see clear to who and what you are and what you're here to do. Now, you're gonna make some mistakes along the way; everybody does. But if you just open up your heart and open up your mind, you'll get it." God, it seems, is encouraging Elliot to find out his *real interests*—who you really are and what you really want—as opposed to his subjective interests.

Elliot then returns to confront the devil and refuses to make his last wish. When the devil asks him why not, he says: "There's nothing I want. Well, there are things that I want, but nothing that you can give me." He then cheesily wraps up the narrative arc with the realization of the lesson he was to have learned all along:

> I realized that wishing just doesn't work. All my life I wished to be better looking, to be richer, to be successful, talented, whatever. And I always thought wouldn't it be great if someone could just wave a magic wand and make that happen. Well, I've realized it just doesn't work by magic ... I've been starting to think it really isn't that important how far we go in life anyway; it's how we get there that really matters.

This conclusion is, of course, sappy and overly sanguine (and the jokes along the way are arguably racist and homophobic). However, there is something unintentionally brilliant about it nevertheless. Going through the process of securing what is in one's interests may change one, and therefore jumping over the process itself can result in a mismatch

Discourse and Ideology

between what one wanted at the beginning and what one (differently) wants at the end. Elliot will have to become the leader of a drug cartel on his own to enjoy the extent to which that capacitates certain cultivated interests. In any case, as a result of the lessons Elliot has learned from going through this set of experiences brought to him by God and the devil, he has become a different person. By the end of the film, he has a different set of desires and interests. He drops his crush on Allison and instead pursues another young woman who, it seems, is a much better match for his personality than Allison ever was.

Ultimately, Elliot wants something different than what he wanted at the beginning. In *It's a Wonderful Life*, George Bailey discovers that what he thought was in his interests—his subjective interests—was in fact not in his *real* interests. By contrast, in *Bedazzled*, the Elliot at the beginning is quite literally different from the Elliot at the end; through the lessons he learned from God and the devil along the way, what is actually in his real interests at the end is different from what was actually in his real interests at the beginning.

Note the multiplication of complexities learned from Dyrberg's discussion and this example:

- subjects have short-term desires and long-term interests, which may in some cases be at odds with one another;
- what is ultimately in a subject's real interests, on Dyrberg's definition, depends on knowledge of counterfactual possible futures unavailable to us that must, instead, be speculated upon—which makes real interests epistemically subjective; and
- even were we to have access to some of those imaginary counterfactuals—as did George Bailey and Elliot Richards—a subject's desires and interests might shift over time—which makes real interests ontologically subjective as well.

How difficult it is, then, in any particular case, to tell what may be in a subject's interests, even if we aimed at an "objective" definition of interests along the lines of Superson's objective definition of harassment.

At several points in his discussion, Dyrberg contrasts his analysis with that of more liberal theorists who identify the goal of a social structure or political philosophy as protecting the free exercise of individual autonomy. Steven Lukes and William E. Connolly, which feature prominently as foils in his book, "want to fix the meaning of autonomy be equating it with the elimination of power" (Dyrberg 1997: 181). For them, an autonomous subject is the one who, once shown the various counterfactuals that reveal her real interests, chooses on the basis of enlightened self-interest, but without influence from any powers that would override or interfere with her autonomy. Autonomy, on their view, means freedom from outside influence. Dyrberg and I would argue, however, not only that subjectivity is a product of power but also that the realization of real interests depends crucially on the operation of power. First, and as Dyrberg hints, it would be impossible for a subject to imagine all potential counterfactuals; at most we are presented with a few paths. Options have costs—including the cost of the effort to

Domination

consider options and the cost of abandoning some options for the pursuit of others. An infinite number of options would be infinitely costly and, ultimately, debilitating. Power offers constitutive exclusions (see Dyrberg 1997: 172–173), or, to put it differently, power limits the number of options available to any particular subject at any particular moment—and without that operation of power we could not even be subjects. Second, the satisfaction of our desires and interests assumes the existence of social institutions outside our control. For petty bourgeois subjects in the twenty-first century to enjoy a restaurant dinner and a pleasing night out on the town, they must depend upon a transportation industry and related regulatory agencies, a food industry and regulatory agencies, educational systems that prepare workers to staff those industries and agencies, patent agencies that safeguard the rights to intellectual property that makes investment in these various businesses profitable, banking industries and regulative agencies that make the use of credit cards and employee payrolls possible, and so on. For any particular subject in a society with a high division of labor to pursue a career and a life of leisure outside of work, an indefinite number of institutionalized powers have to be already in place for her interests to be served.

In summary,

- what is in a subject's interests is, in the abstract, whatever will help her satisfy the long-term desires toward which she aspires;
- consideration of those interests involves imagining counterfactual possibilities, and identifying which paths will best serve what a subject desires;
- however, the consideration of such counterfactuals is substantially complicated by the fact that,
    - first, these attempts to calculate are extremely uncertain, at best and,
    - second, thinking about or exposure to counterfactuals may change who one is or what one desires—plasticity exists not only at the beginning of the processes of socialization or training, but all throughout the pursuit of life projects; and
- removing the operation of power on subjects is unlikely to help them satisfy their interests, as their satisfaction *depends on* that operation of power.

Toward an Objective Definition of Domination

In formulating an objective definition of domination based on Dyrberg's definition of interests, we would do well to avoid some of the problems identified above.

- Unlike Lincoln, we should avoid attributing unmanifested desires to subjects for which we have no epistemic access.
- Unlike Mahmood, we should avoid implying that subordinated subjects are liberated merely because they get what they are socialized to want.

- Like Zia, a definition of domination should consider the social and political effects of an ideology, set of practices, or set of social relations: do these things capacitate subjects in any appreciable way?
- Unlike both Lincoln and Mahmood, we should avoid making domination relative to individuals' desires; rather, a definition of domination should be objective in the way that Superson's definition of sexual harassment is objective: its primary point of reference is the social structure and subject positions within that structure, not individual subjects.
- Like Dyrberg, we should recognize that determining what is in someone's interests involves intersubjectively verifiable knowledge about what will actually serve a subject's interests—as opposed to any particular individual's limited knowledge or predictions—even as that knowledge is admittedly to a large extent uncertain because of the nature of imaginary counterfactuals.
- Last, we should note that not only does power operate on subjects in ways that makes their desires variable but also that any consideration of counterfactual possibilities or pursuit of them may change what any particular subject desires, consequently altering what is actually in her interests.

The most crucial point here is the next to last one. If readers will recall, for Superson, "when A sexually harasses B, the comment or behavior is really directed at the group of all women, not just a particular woman" (Superson 1993: 51), and this is true *even when* a woman does not recognize that fact—namely, she may not be cognizant of how sexism can reinforce systematic, asymmetrical power relations. Along the same lines, I propose a stipulative definition of social domination as follows:

> domination is a relationship that takes place when the capacity of a member of a particular *subject position* to act in support of her own interests—not as a result of her idiosyncratic biography but rather the *powers, privileges, and demands articulated onto her subject position* in the social organization as a whole—is either systematically thwarted or asymmetrical in relationship to the capacities of members in other subject positions.

On this definition, here are a few possible types of domination.

System Domination. One can also be dominated by a social system when the system creates subjects with tragic interests, where tragic interests are defined as ones that cannot be served by the system. North American culture, for instance, creates a large number of subjects who desire to be famous: movie stars, rock stars, etc. However, the way the social structure is set up makes it impossible for every subject who desires to be a rock star to be one. The widespread interest in being a rock star is a tragic interest—it is impossible for all of those interests produced by the system to be satisfied by the system. This is, I would argue, a mild form of domination—I don't have that much sympathy for people disappointed they were unable to become rock stars—but nevertheless this would qualify as a form of domination.

A more significant example: Judith Lorber notes, in *Paradoxes of Gender* (1994), that heterosexual males and females are socialized in contemporary Western societies in ways that are paradoxical.

> Femininity is framed by a relationship with one man that is romantic at first and sexual later, but masculinity is framed by sexual conquests of many women and only secondarily by an emotional attachment to one. To be considered feminine, a woman has to pry a man loose from his friends and cleave him to her; sex is her lure. To prove he is masculine, a man has to show his friends that he is a sexual conqueror; an emotional attachment to one woman can feel like a trap.
>
> (Lorber 1994: 69)

As far as this is correct—to some extent it is a generalization, and there are exceptions—we could say that this is an example of tragic interests: heterosexual men and women are socialized into their gendered positions in such a way as to permit neither group to satisfy their interests fully. In such a case we could say that the system of gender roles dominates subjects in that system by setting things up so that the interests the system produces are systematically thwarted by the system itself.

Relational Domination. The domination of a subject in relation to other subjects in a social system can take at least three forms, all of which require a comparative analysis of privileges awarded and demands required along a particular social axis for subjects in different social positions. First, all subjects in a social system are required to conform to social codes, many of them arbitrary. However, *subjects can be dominated when, as a result of their social position, they are required to conform to a disproportionately greater number of arbitrary social codes on a particular social axis compared to subjects in other positions.* Almost all social positions have some completely arbitrary social codes attached to them. Workplace dress codes are among the most obvious social codes attached to social hierarchies. At most colleges, students can wear whatever they want; faculty typically have to dress "more professionally" than the students; but administrators usually need to wear something much more formal. All of these social codes might serve a useful or even necessary social function of delimiting social hierarchies, but the nature of the specific codes is completely arbitrary. There is nothing about a suit that makes it intrinsically more suited to administrative work than jeans and a T-shirt. Nothing justifies the specific details of dress codes, other than the weight of tradition.

In my opinion, there is nothing inherently bad about such social codes. They make it easier for subjects to navigate social relations. Seeing someone in a uniform tells an individual that she can likely expect certain behaviors from that person; without these sorts of social markers we would be stumbling around in the dark, so to speak. Once a colleague of mine curtly brushed off and dismissed a strange visitor to his office who stopped by to say hello, only to find out later that the visitor was a board member at the college; when he found out what he had done he was mortified. This faux pas would never have happened if board members wore uniforms.

Discourse and Ideology

Nevertheless, some arbitrary social codes are much more costly or burdensome than others. For instance, consider retail work uniforms. Some retail stores make their employees mark themselves off from customers with little more than a nametag. Others require a uniform shirt, while others require uniform hats, shirts, ties, pants, and shoes. The choice of one marker over another may not be entirely arbitrary. A security guard with a head-to-toe uniform would be more visibly obvious—and therefore more able to dissuade thieves—than a security guard with nothing more than a nametag. However, in most cases of these sorts the social markers are equally functional—one marker would be just as good as another. But some businesses choose social markers that are more burdensome on their employees. It would typically be received as more burdensome to have to purchase a full uniform, as compared with a mere shirt or nametag. In those situations we can say that those employees are—as a result of the demands placed on their social position—in a relationship of domination compared with those people in the social hierarchy that are not required to purchase expensive uniforms to be eligible to work in the institution.

Of course, whether or not such requirements are received or felt as burdensome will be relative to an individual subject's desires. Whereas a retail employee might find purchasing a full uniform to be needlessly expensive, some people entering the petty bourgeois business world out of college look forward to getting a well-paying job so that they can afford to purchase expensive suits to demarcate themselves from others. Those suits are expensive, and their selection as a social marker is largely arbitrary, but such subjects might in fact *enjoy* this requirement. For this reason the multiplication of arbitrary social codes is not necessarily received as burdensome or repressive in and of itself.

However, despite the fact that some individuals might have developed a desire for the arbitrary social codes placed on them, such demands would nevertheless not serve their general interests because—and this is why it is crucial to go beyond Dyrberg's analysis in one respect—*their desires might change*. Many young women in American society desire to comply with the requirement that they shave their legs and armpits. This is an arbitrary and unnatural social requirement for conformity to the North American ideal or norm of femininity; however, many young women are so socialized into North American bodily practices that *not* to shave would make them feel extremely uncomfortable. The socialization process has directed their desires toward that social practice. Shaving perhaps makes them feel good about themselves. However, not all women feel similarly, and some who feel good about shaving might experience a change in their desires. Perhaps they once desired to shave, but no longer have such a desire. Nevertheless, our society *still places that demand for conformity* uniquely on subjects in the social position of "female." (It is not, of course, a legal requirement, but women who choose to violate this arbitrary social code may lose much of their social privilege or social capital or find themselves suffering from discrimination in a number of implicit and explicit ways—a woman who refuses to shave her legs likely has less of a chance of being hired as a server or flight attendant where skirts are part of the uniform for women who fill such positions.) While not all women chafe at the demand, some may find the demand to comply with the arbitrary social code to be considerably burdensome, and some who enjoy it today may not enjoy it tomorrow. To reiterate the main point here: this arbitrary requirement that women shave their legs may not be *repressive* for an individual woman if she desires to comply, but the requirement reflects *domination* if such demands are not placed on members of other subject positions (like men).

A second form of relational domination involves asymmetrical access to capital, privilege, and authority, as well as the means to manipulate, produce, or reproduce these, compared to other subject positions. By capital I include all of the following: material capital (such as money, property, etc.), cultural capital (knowledge or mastery of cultural elements that garner respect in a particular society), and social capital (network connections to and respect of peers or superiors with their own capital, privilege, or authority). By "privilege," I mean advantages or benefits conferred on a subject—but denied to others—simply because of his or her social position. By "authority," I mean the ability to direct the behavior of others without the use of force. Obviously these elements are not mutually exclusive and overlap to some extent (for instance, authority typically operates in ways related to cultural capital and social capital); they are not intended to be understood as discreet. I take it for granted that it is obvious how access to capital, privilege, and authority serves one's interests: persons who occupy subject positions with access to capital, privilege, and authority are much more capable of satisfying their interests than those who do not have such access. Consequently, *a subject is dominated when those in her social position have a disproportionate access to these when compared with subjects in other social positions.*

Third, it serves one's interests to be able to *alter* the social arrangements in which one is situated. This includes the ability to move subjects (either oneself or others) from one social position to another social position or to rearrange the relationship between social positions. The ability to move subjects from position to position might include, for example, the ability to promote or demote subjects in a social hierarchy. For instance, college presidents generally have the power to fire untenured professors, but that power is not reciprocal, of course. In addition, the ability to rearrange the relationship between social positions would be something like the ability to change a social hierarchy. For instance, many college presidents have the power not only to hire or fire people into or from existing positions, but to create and eliminate positions in the hierarchy altogether. The reason this ability serves a subject's interests is because when the social arrangements are not well suited to work toward the satisfaction of an individual's desires, she can change the social arrangements so that they will. Consequently, *domination takes place when subjects in particular positions have a disproportionately lower ability to alter those arrangements, compared with subjects in other social positions.*

In summary, particular social positions are dominated if the system produces tragic desires in them that it cannot fulfill, if they have an asymmetrical number of arbitrary social demands placed on them, if they have disproportionate access to capital, privilege, and authority given the existing social arrangements, or if they lack the ability to alter the social arrangements compared to subjects in other positions.

Discourse and Ideology

Most importantly, this definition of domination is objective—in Superson's sense—in that it is not relative to an individual's desires; what is crucial on this definition are the capacities available to the subject as a result of her social position, whatever her particular desires may be.

This approach avoids some of the difficulties identified above. Unlike Lincoln, this definition of domination doesn't require us to attribute hidden desires to dominated subjects. Contrary to Mahmood, this definition offers us grounds for drawing attention to asymmetrical power relations, even when those relations are fully accepted by dominated subjects. Contrary to both Lincoln and Mahmood, this definition focuses on a subject's capacities as a member of a social position, not as an individual. Along with Zia's critique of Mahmood, this definition invites us to draw attention to possible social and political consequences of domination—for example, we can ask how members of classes are capacitated to serve their potentially changing interests rather than focusing on whether they are getting what they want at this moment in time. Finally, along with Dyrberg, we can recognize that any particular subject could have limited knowledge about what is in his interests and that he could therefore be wrong about whether he is dominated, at least on this definition.

I would like to note that my proposed definition is not the only one possibly of interest for scholars studying domination. There could be other, related definitions of domination that focus on how members of subject positions can or cannot serve their theoretical interests or personal sympathies. Thus I intend this definition to be a conversation opener rather than a discussion closer—scholars with different sympathies than me may offer equally valuable definitions focused on other ways in which social structures asymmetrically capacitate members of subject positions.

A Caveat: "All Other Things Being Equal ..."

There are many variables in this approach to thinking about domination: subjects' interests change, the subjects who occupy particular subject positions change, and the actual social relations themselves, in which subjects are embedded, can be rearranged or dissolved on occasion. Each of these variables makes a calculation of the member of a subject position's interests increasingly complicated. One thing that is crucial to keep in mind is that any particular analysis likely leaves out some of these variables when considering questions of domination. As noted above, were we faced at every moment with infinite possibilities we had to review and choose from, we would be infinitely incapacitated. We may imagine a few counterfactuals, but leave others uninvestigated. There is often an unspoken "all other things being equal, subjects in position x would better be able to serve their interests with resource y." However, having access to bank credit, for instance, might not serve ones interests in the long run if one's society is on the verge of a communist revolution wherein the banks will be destroyed. Consequently, focusing on some counterfactuals while ignoring others may have the effect of naturalizing or depoliticizing certain background conditions that are, in fact, alterable. We risk reifying certain social conditions or social structures by failing to consider counterfactuals in which they are changed rather than, for instance, the resources available to a subject position within that given structure.

One example: some leftists in the United States publicly supported extending the right to marry to same-sex couples, but only hesitantly—and some opposed it altogether (see, for instance, *The Trouble with Normal* [Warner 1999])—because legalizing gay marriage could have the effect of naturalizing the state's regulation of families. Yes, heterosexuals have access to certain social resources or privileges that are unavailable to gays and lesbians in countries in which same-sex marriage is illegal. In that sense, there is a relationship of domination between heterosexuals and homosexuals. However, there is a significant lack of imagination in the proposal that we eliminate the relation of domination by making the resources that come with marriage available to all adult couples. "All other things being equal, gays and lesbians would benefit from the legalization of gay marriage." Yes, *but it is not necessary that all other things be equal*: this solution to reversing domination imagines changing one element—the privileges extended—while ignoring others—such as the fact that citizens across the board might better be able to serve their interests were we to abolish state-sanctioned marriage altogether (see the case made, for instance, by Clare Chambers in *Against Marriage: An Egalitarian Defense of a Marriage-Free State* [2017]). As such, it is crucial that we not ignore some counterfactuals at the expense of others; *ignoring a set of counterfactuals can have the effect of depoliticizing certain variables by presenting them as invariable*. Depoliticizing or naturalizing such social structures by taking them off the table forecloses a number of counterfactuals that would otherwise be available to our imagination.

Analyzing Domination

In conclusion, I want to return to the oversight Zia identified in Mahmood's work: "there is no discussion of the implications, outcomes, or effects of such agency which has been, in the experience of Pakistan, both vociferously anti-women at worst or silent and hence complicit at best." Consequently, if we are to use the objective definition of domination I have proposed, any particular analysis of domination should take into account the "implications, outcomes, or effects" of discourse, practices, social relations, etc. for both real and counterfactual, possible subjects. It will of course always be true that, on the proposed definition, most subject positions will be dominat*ed* in relationship to some positions and dominat*ing* in relationship to others. The task of analysis, then, will require the analyst to be specific.

- In this context, what social relations hold between members of this subject position and that subject position?
- What forms of capital, privileges, or duties accrue to members of these subject positions?
- Which subject positions are capacitated by the status quo and which might not be?

Discourse and Ideology

- With respect to which particular capacities is this subject position arguably dominated?
- How might members of this subject position be further capacitated if we altered the social relations between positions or shifted the number or nature of privileges or duties assigned with each?
- What social or political consequences might follow from the very diagnosis of domination?
- How might a consideration of counterfactuals change the interests of a member of a particular subject position?
- Which elements of domination or groups of dominated persons elicit the greatest sympathy—or antipathy—and from what particular ideological perspectives?
- How does socialization lead to asymmetrical sympathetic attachments? How might other forms of socialization have led to alternate sympathies?

The content of all the terms in play here—desires, interests, subjects, subject positions, capacities, privileges, demands—is relative, and our analysis must attend to their relativity.

The distance from the liberal analytic should be clear: on this definition of domination people are not free from domination when freed from all forms of social power. Without social power there would not be subjects with interests in the first place. The distance from Mahmood's analytic should be clear as well: subjects without access to privilege are not free from domination simply because—at this particular moment—they do not desire something different than what the social system allows them. On the contrary, on the proposed definition subjects would be more or less free of domination in relationship to a reconfiguration of asymmetrical power relations, particularly when such reconfigurations capacitate members of particular social positions in pursuing their interests *even when* their interests change over time.

No analytic is perfect, and all approaches have costs; consequently, it would be foolish to suggest that this analytic is cost-free. However, the analytic I have suggested—requiring us to focus on asymmetrical social relations and disproportionate allocation of social resources such as privilege and capital, as well as the extent to which these capacitate (or not) subjects who occupy particular subject positions—benefits from the fact that it does not authorize us to tell *individual subjects* that they ought to feel oppressed or dominated. Rather, it invites us to supply evidence that members of social positions may have disproportionately low access to resources as a result of their membership in those positions. This analytic is therefore never about individuals, and would not warrant overriding individuals' claims about how they feel or whether they experience their social place as dominated. In addition, insofar as this approach to domination intends to be "objective" in Superson's sense, it remains at the level of intersubjectively available evidence—individuals who do not feel dominated but who are members of an allegedly dominated class are welcome to provide contrary evidence about the resources available to members of their social position. This is the difference between, for example, telling a woman she should feel oppressed and telling a woman that, as a result of the law, she has access to fewer public resources than men do. The latter claim is falsifiable and challengeable in ways the former is not. In addition, insofar as this analytic allows that sympathies are products of socialization or training—so that different subjects might well view domination differently—it invites analysts to make their sympathies part of the object of study, as opposed to leaving them off the table, naturalized, or depoliticized. Last, insofar as the analytic encourages focus on possible consequences of changes in social relations or the distribution of capital and privilege, it encourages those analysts with normative projects to consider all of the possible results that could be produced by their proposed interventions.

Of course, whether one has sympathies for subjects of domination in the sense proposed in this chapter is another matter. In a sense I hope this definition will be morally neutral; some forms of domination (such as the domination of parents over children) are unlikely to provoke sympathies in most of us, while others (such as the expansion or contraction of abortion rights) might solicit sympathies from some but not others. As Twain notes, sympathies derive from one's training, and different training produces different sympathies. While this analytic provides a way of thinking critically about domination, it does not commit the analyst to any particular moral evaluation of domination.

***

I would like to close with an anecdote about my grandmother that, I believe, sheds light on the usefulness of this particular definition of domination. My grandmother grew up in a conservative Christian community wherein women—but not men—were prohibited from wearing pants. They interpreted the Bible as prohibiting cross-dressing of any sort, and they saw pants as a "male" clothing item. This would count as a relationship of domination on my definition because this was one of a large number of completely arbitrary social norms disproportionately required of women in her community. However, my grandmother fully internalized the social norms, and therefore most of her life actually desired to wear skirts and dresses, and she looked askance at those women who did wear pants. To my knowledge this relationship of domination was willingly entered, and therefore in no way was she repressed.

Late in life, however, she experienced a stroke that seriously debilitated one side of her body. It became much harder for her to take care of herself, get dressed, and so on. In addition, since she could not entirely control her body, when she wore skirts or dresses it became more likely that she would sit down or fall down in ways that her underwear would show, producing some shameful or embarrassing situations. Because of this her *desires* began to change. She no longer was entirely opposed to wearing pants; in fact, she actually started wearing sweat pants, both because they covered her well and because they were easier to slip on and off than other types of clothing.

Her experience and consequent change in desire did not alter the community's expectations. As far as they were concerned, a rule was a rule—there was nothing in the Bible about permitting cross-dressing in the case of a stroke. They stuck to their arbitrary

Discourse and Ideology

social norm. As a result, my grandmother was shamed by her peers into going back to wearing skirts and dresses, despite the increased difficulty these gave her.

This case reveals some crucial differences between the approach to domination I have proposed and that of others. Lincoln might suggest that my grandmother never really did enjoy wearing skirts and dresses and that she was secretly repressed all along. Mahmood might suggest that for most of her life my grandmother was liberated because she was exercising the moral code that capacitated her moral life. By contrast, on my reading, my grandmother, prior to her stroke, was not repressed by this arbitrary social norm—she actively desired to wear the clothes her community desired for her. However, she was nevertheless, as a woman in a particular social hierarchy, in a relationship of domination. The arbitrary social norm placed on her did not, for the most part, repress her desires—she was socialized from birth to accept the norm. However, subjects and their interests change, and she was in a subject position that did not capacitate her to deal well with her changing desires. Thus, on my definition, she was dominated all along—not because I have access to secret knowledge about hidden, repressed desires—but because she was in a relationship of subject positions that placed asymmetrical demands on her, independently of whether she wanted to fulfill those demands.

We are surrounded by social structures with which subjects actively desire to comply. On the one hand, we can ask if these social structures serve the immediate *desires* of subjects in the system; on the other hand, we can ask if these social structures serve the potentially changing *interests* of subjects in the system. We should not, however, confuse these two radically different questions.

CHAPTER 5
IDEOLOGY

Karl Mannheim's *Ideology and Utopia: An Introduction to the Sociology of Knowledge* ([1929] 1985) is to some extent a lost voice in the contemporary literature on the concept of ideology. Originally published in 1929 in German, and then in 1936 in English, *Ideology and Utopia* provides readers with a sophisticated set of distinctions and concepts that not only provide a stipulative definition of "ideology" that doesn't fall into the problematic territory of contrasting ideology with objective reality, but also simultaneously anticipate a number of theoretical claims that became part of the new common sense for mainstream poststructuralist philosophers and social critics in the latter third of the twentieth century. Most importantly for my purposes is the fact that Mannheim's discussion of the concept of ideology maintains the crucial distinction between constitutive and empirical discourses, which I defended in Chapter 3 of this book. As such, his contributions to the legacy of social critique not only dovetail with the preceding chapters, but add crucial elements that enrich the project outlined in this book as a whole—particularly regarding his view of empiricism.

In what follows, I will start by summarizing the key points of *Ideology and Utopia* that are most relevant to my particular project. Notably, some of what he considers important to his project I set aside without comment as either unrelated, outdated, unpersuasive, or contradictory to the argument of the book thus far. In addition, where appropriate I have translated the terms of his argument into the terms I have been using—at least where the distinctions seem sufficiently identical to warrant their substitution—to make the argument more accessible to those without prior familiarity with Mannheim's work. His appreciation of the distinction between constitutive and empirical discourses is crucial to the definition of ideology I will offer at the end of this chapter, and thus most of what follows is an attempt to defend a definition of empiricism that doesn't violate the strictures of poststructuralism but which is nevertheless adequate for engaging in ideology critique. In addition, I will go on to supplement Mannheim's approach by taking into account the work of philosopher of science Helen E. Longino, the work of philosopher James Woodward on causation, and the work of social theorists Jason Glynos and David Howarth on the use of retroduction (as opposed to deduction or induction) in social scientific theory and hypotheses. After outlining what precisely I mean by empiricism, I will offer a definition of ideology according to which ideologies are discourses that to some extent violate the rules of empiricism I will defend.

Discourse and Ideology

Contingent Knowledge Production

Mannheim accepts Hegel and Husserl's description of the phenomenal field of vision: "The world of external objects and of psychic experience appears to be in a continuous flux. Verbs are more adequate symbols for this situation than nouns. The fact that we give names to things which are in flux implies inevitably a certain stabilization oriented along the lines of collective activity" ([1929] 1985: 22). The nouns we use to "fix" or "stabilize" the objects we substruct in consciousness result in empirical claims that are perhaps best considered collective fictions useful for navigating the continuous flux. Those empirical claims "cover[] up, in the interest of collective action, the permanently fluid process underlying all things" (22). (Careful readers will note throughout this section that all of Mannheim's most insightful claims are more or less the same as Hegel's.)

In addition, although working independently of the American pragmatist tradition, Mannheim's project echoes some of the most important conclusions of pragmatism. Most notably, for Mannheim the production of human discourses and knowledge is situated, contextual, and driven by human desires or interests—or, to put it in Hegel's terms, knowledge of objects is *mediated* by subjects who produce knowledge. On the grounds that bias leads to the distortion of knowledge, earlier philosophers or social theorists took it for granted that "objective" knowledge required the elimination of all human interest or bias from the process of knowledge projection. By contrast, Mannheim insists that bias cannot be eliminated, as human interests are a necessary condition of possibility for the production of knowledge in the first place. In the particularly incisive "Preface" to the English edition of *Ideology and Utopia*, translator Louis Wirth writes,

> if the earlier discussion of objectivity laid stress upon the elimination of personal or collective bias, the more modern approach calls attention to the positive cognitive importance of this bias. Whereas the former quest for objectivity tended to posit an "object" which was distinct from the "subject," the latter sees an intimate relationship between the object and the perceiving subject. In fact, the most recent view maintains that the object emerges for the subject when, in the course of experience, the interest of the subject is focused upon that particular aspect of the world.
>
> (Mannheim [1929] 1985: xvii)

To use the terms outlined in Chapter 2 of this book, the substruction of an object requires a subject or group of subjects to attend to particular aspects of those "things" that arise in phenomenological experience. A graphic designer and a sociologist watching a contemporary political news program are likely to individuate different things of interest to them, given their different vocabularies, different interests, and different goals (e.g., to explain why a graph is visually persuasive or, by contrast, why certain political ideologies are received as more persuasive when a news anchor shares their gender or race). What each "sees" in the phenomenological field is conditioned by the discourses they use to divide up and analyze that field. To rephrase this point in other terms, the conceptual scheme we use to individuate the stuff of the world is contingent upon the interests of the person or group deploying the conceptual scheme. If viewers removed the interests that guide vision, they might see nothing—much as daily commuters drive to work with their eyes open but may "see" few of the daily objects they drive past on a regular basis but in which they are uninterested. The interests open vision; no interests, no vision. "Henceforth the world as 'world' exists only with reference to the knowing mind, and the mental activity of the subject determines the form in which the world appears" (Mannheim [1929] 1985: 66). (Of course, this quote implies that knowledge is the product of individual subjects, but Mannheim follows this claim with an insistence that we must move beyond Kant's insights to Hegel's, insofar as the latter historicized consciousness and revealed it to be a social rather than individual product [66–67].)

Some truths, Mannheim notes, are only accessible from the perspective of certain interests: "it is easily possible that there are truths ... which are accessible only to a certain personal disposition or to a definite orientation of interests of a certain group" (Mannheim [1929] 1985: 167). Indeed, "only one who loves or hates gets to see in the loved or hated object certain characteristics which are invisible to others who are merely spectators" (169).

As a result, definitions of "objectivity" that attempt to identify objective knowledge through the removal of all interests fail to make sense of how humans actually produce knowledge and depend on the fantasy that we could see without looking. For Mannheim, what makes knowledge "objective" is not the removal of human interest, but, on the contrary, necessitates controlling for interests by attending to empirical evidence or what scholars today might call "independent verification." Briefly, by "independent verification," all I mean is that subjects who use identical concepts to individuate things from the field of phenomenological experience verify finding the same objects. Referring back to the "wetlands" example in Chapter 2, subjects with competing definitions of a wetland will literally see different things when looking at the same plot of land—precisely because they apply competing constitutive discourses. However, subjects can control for those differences by making the contributions of constitutive discourses to empirical claims explicit. For instance, subjects with competing definitions of "wetlands" could *independently verify* that on one definition, it is empirically true that x percentage of the land falls under the definition, whereas on a second definition it is empirically true that y percentage of land falls under the definition. As Mannheim writes, on this "new type of objectivity," our goal is not "the exclusion of evaluations but ... the critical awareness and control of them" (Mannheim [1929] 1985: 5). (I will elaborate further on this idea below in "Contingency in Philosophy of Science.")

Wirth elaborates, "objectivity in the second sense is concerned with relevance to our interests. In the realm of the social, particularly, truth is not merely a matter of simple correspondence between thought and existence, but is tinged with the investigator's interest in his subject matter, his standpoint, his evaluations, in short the definition of his object of attention" (Mannheim [1929] 1985: xviii). From the classic perspective that defines "objectivity" in terms of the removal of all subjectivity, this is a disaster because it makes the truth of claims relative to human interests. However, from Mannheim's perspective, nothing of import is lost with this epistemological shift that refuses to ignore the constitutive role of interests in knowledge production. Specifically, shifting to define "objectivity" in terms of independent verification relative to a constitutive discourse that in some way reflects human interests, "does not imply that henceforth no distinction between truth and error is ascertainable. It does not mean that whatever people imagine to be their perceptions, attitudes, and ideas or what they want others to believe them to be corresponds to the facts" (xviii). On the contrary, whether something is empirically true depends not on some state of affairs that holds independently of human interest; rather, on this view something can be considered "true" if subjects *with competing sympathies or interests* can use the same constitutive discourse and independently verify the same empirical claims.

The realist who fears this will thrust us into a relativism whereby anything goes need not worry: arguably, noting that interests guide, mediate, or condition the collection and organization of the empirical data we gather would make our arguments *more* rather than less persuasive to critics. If my claim is contested but I can point to the fact that people with competing values can independently verify what I have found—provided that they deploy my discourse and its rules—they are more likely than less likely to take seriously what I have to say, at least if they are open-minded enough to entertain arguments and evidence contrary to their interests or sympathies. And if they are not willing to entertain empirical evidence at odds with their sympathies, then insisting that my discourse is "objective" rather than "contingent upon my interests" will not persuade them either. Consequently, nothing is lost by noting that one's knowledge is always conditional, and nothing is gained, with respect to persuasiveness to skeptics, by claiming one's knowledge is unconditioned—although it might be useful for condescending to your skeptics.

Of course, we do not always attend to the fact that humans employ competing constitutive discourses, particularly in societies with a high division of labor, which—as Émile Durkheim so deftly demonstrated in *The Division of Labor in Society* ([1893] 2014)—requires us to use specialized discourses that may be largely useless to fellow citizens with different labor tasks. The concepts that biologists or chemists use to individuate the world when attempting to find a cure for cancer are likely useless to an accountant when attempting to discern what tax bracket her client is in, and vice versa. Wirth writes,

> [a] society is possible in the last analysis because the individuals in it carry around in their heads some sort of picture of the society. Our society, however, in this period of minute division of labour, of extreme heterogeneity and profound conflict of interests, has come to a pass where these pictures are blurred and incongruous. Hence we no longer perceive the same things as real, and coincident with vanishing sense of common reality we are losing our common medium for expressing and communicating our experiences.
>
> (Mannheim [1929] 1985: xxviii)

Ideology

The sort of reality gap generated by competing substructions of the world by biologists and accountants is far greater when it comes to subjects with competing interests, particularly when their goal is to change reality in a way that conforms to their competing interests. Consequently, what one subject sees as "out of control political correctness," another subject might see as "innovative efforts to reduce the burdens society disproportionately places on disadvantaged minorities." While these subjects with competing interests could temporarily adopt one another's constitutive discourses to arrive at "independent verification" of the empirical claims each is making, they are unlikely to do so because they are unlikely to see their interests as being served by adopting another's discourse. Consequently, these subjects are unlikely to "perceive the same things as real." As Mannheim notes, "the same world can appear differently to different observers" (Mannheim [1929] 1985: 6).

For Mannheim, it follows from this that knowledge production is agonistic: subjects or groups of subjects with competing interests produce empirical claims about their world to draw attention to what is most important to their interests, whereas groups with other interests produce competing empirical claims. Wirth writes, "whereas the intellectual world in earlier periods had at least a common frame of reference which offered a measure of certainty to the participants in that world and gave them a sense of mutual respect and trust, the contemporary intellectual world … presents the spectacle of a battlefield of warring parties and conflicting doctrines" (Mannheim [1929] 1985: xxiv). Mannheim specifies that whichever reality subjects are invested in reproducing is conditioned by their social or political interests. Competing groups each reveal "contradictory meanings which correspond to their own peculiarly conceived understanding of the world. What was a king for one was a tyrant for another" (22–23).

For Mannheim, this has resulted in the following unfortunate situation: competing groups each produce knowledge claims that reflect their interests and denounce their opponents' claims as distortions or lies, while none of the parties attend to the fact that the differences between them are in part the result of the competing sympathies and interests that condition their particular knowledge; in addition, none of the parties provides a means of adjudicating between the competing claims. Everyone calls everyone else's claims mere "ideologies," thereby raising "the problem implicit in the term ideology—what is really real?" (Mannheim [1929] 1985: 72). Without a reliable means of adjudicating between competing ideologies, it was "inevitable," Mannheim writes, that under these conditions "more and more people took flight into skepticism or irrationalism" (41). This led "finally to a juncture at which it is no longer possible for one point of view and interpretation to assail all others as ideological without itself being placed in the position of having to meet that [same] challenge" (74). Parties with competing interests can easily use the term "ideology" as a weapon and mercilessly denigrate their opponents' knowledge claims, "as long as there is no analytical method for demonstrating [one's claims] and no criteria have been adduced which will provide a control over the demonstration" (50). Consequently, "nowadays groups of every standpoint use this weapon against all the rest" (75). Arguably, this is because those on either side are realists and, as such, cannot fathom that their neighbors might literally live in other worlds. Consequently, they cannot see that changing society might involve, at times, translating their concerns into a discourse that structures their opponent's lives.

Two options remain for those of us who don't want to throw up our hands in defeat when faced with the possibility that there are no satisfactory means of adjudicating knowledge claims other than asking ourselves if the claims serve our interests. The classic response is to attempt to "escape" from the dilemma of competing knowledge claims by attempting to "take flight into a supra-temporal logic and assert that truth as such is unsullied and has neither a plurality or forms nor any connection with unconscious motivations" or human interests (Mannheim [1929] 1985: 42). For this option to remain persuasive, however, we would have to hide from ourselves the nonuniversal conditions—outlined above—that both mediate knowledge as well as make knowledge possible in the first place. In addition, Mannheim notes, claiming an "absolute" status for the results of one's own forms of knowledge production is unlikely to be persuasive to subjects with competing interests. "The absoluteness of thought is not attained by [merely] warranting … that one has it or by proceeding to label some particular limited viewpoint (usually one's own) as supra-partisan and authoritative" (43). As I noted above, if one's argument or empirical demonstration is persuasive, nothing of value is added by the additional claim that one's knowledge is objective, and if one's demonstration is not persuasive, adding that one's knowledge is objective will not make it more persuasive.

The other option available to those who want to avoid the flight into universal skepticism—and the option Mannheim prefers—is to be reflectively aware of how one's interests shape the knowledge claims one makes and to seek out independent verification for one's claims:

> Man attains objectivity [in the new rather than old sense] … with reference to his conception of his world not by giving up his will to action and holding his evaluations in abeyance but in confronting and examining himself. The criterion of such self-illumination is that not only the object but we ourselves fall squarely within our field of vision.
>
> (Mannheim [1929] 1985: 47)

A full account of knowledge will therefore involve both our objects of study and ourselves. Of course, once again, this does not mean that our knowledge is strictly determined by what we want to be true—*intersubjectively verifiable evidence will also be necessary* for some set of claims to count as knowledge. Something can be considered "true" according to the rules of a particular discourse if subjects *with competing interests* can use *the same constitutive discourse* and independently verify the same empirical claims. Of course, this would require us to be rather specific about what referents are picked out by our stipulative definitions, particularly when we produce knowledge that is likely to be contested. What counts as a wetland is contested as we move from one social formation, discourse, and constellation of interests to another; consequently, if an ecologist's empirical claims about wetlands are going to be persuasive, she must make it clear how exactly she is using the term in her discourse.

Ideology

To put Mannheim's point in a slightly different way, the fact that truth is relative to discourses or conditioned by them does not mean that there is no difference between truth and falsehood, but rather that whether some claim is true is conditioned by (although not strictly determined by) the discourse and set of interests from which it arises. At this point Mannheim suggests readers make a distinction between relativism and relationalism. According to the specter of relativism, that knowledge claims are conditioned by subjectivity makes them insufficiently trustworthy, and consequently people attempt to slay relativism by appealing to a reality that is observer-independent. Relationalism, by contrast, recognizes that knowledge claims are human products and therefore necessarily conditioned by human subjectivity, but notes that this does not prevent us from attempting to adjudicate between competing knowledge claims. In a crucial passage, Mannheim elaborates:

> [a] modern theory of knowledge which takes account of the relational as distinct from the merely relative character of all historical knowledge must start with the assumption that there are spheres of thought in which it is impossible to conceive of absolute truth existing independently of the values and position of the subject and unrelated to the social context …
>
> Once we recognize that all historical knowledge is relational knowledge, and can only be formulated with reference to the position of the observer, we are faced, once more, with the task of discriminating between what is true and what is false in such knowledge. The question then arises: which social standpoint *vis-à-vis* of history offers the best chance for reaching an optimum of truth? In any case, at this stage the vain hope of discovering truth in a form which is independent of an historically and socially determined set of meanings will have to be given up.
>
> (Mannheim [1929] 1985: 79–80)

Crucial to pursuing which knowledge claims are true and which are false requires us to attend to the variability of contingent conceptual schemes. "It dawns upon us that not only does the content of thought change but also its categorical structure" (Mannheim [1929] 1985: 82). Consequently, "a system of meanings" or, arguably, a set of knowledge claims, are "possible and valid only in a given type of historical existence" (86).

> Every perception is and must be ordered and organized into categories. The extent, however, to which we can organize and express our experience in such conceptual forms is, in turn, dependent upon the frames of reference which happen to be available at a given historical moment. The concepts which we have and the universe of discourse in which we move … are dependent largely upon the historical-social situation.
>
> (Mannheim [1929] 1985: 86)

Discourse and Ideology

Again, none of this involves abandoning empirical inquiry, only acknowledging that what counts as evidence is always contingent upon historically specific conceptual schemes:

> No one denies the possibility of empirical research nor does any one maintain that facts do not exist … We, too, appeal to "facts" for our proof, but the question of the nature of facts is in itself a considerable problem. They exist for the mind always in an intellectual and social context. That they can be understood and formulated implies already the existence of a conceptual apparatus.
>
> (Mannheim [1929] 1985: 102)

What is crucial here is that, even if parties with competing interests came to an agreement about the empirical claims conditioned by a particular, invested constitutive discourse—such that those claims could be considered empirically "true" by all parties willing to suspend their competing discourses for the sake of understanding others—the "true" empirical claims would still be *conditioned by* a spatially-, temporally-, and interest-relative discourse.

The question of truth, then, is no longer "Is this true independently of any human contagion whatsoever?" but rather "Is this claim independently verifiable given the rules of the discourse from which it arises?" To use my vocabulary rather than Mannheim's, constitutive discourse makes empirical discourse possible, and constitutive discourses are relative to or conditioned by human interests—consequently, any empirical investigation must be attentive to the contingency of the constitutive discourse on which it logically depends. However, once we clarify the nature of the constitutive discourse being activated in any particular historical context, empirical claims conditioned by those discourses are, theoretically, mutually verifiable by subjects with *any* set of interests, provided that their empirical inquiry faithfully and rigorously deploys the relevant constitutive discourse, even if it does not necessarily serve everyone's interests to do so.

In this section, I have argued:

- we have a great deal of empirical evidence that knowledge production is agonistic, as are charges that one's opponent's views are ideological;
- knowledge production is contingent not only upon the interests of the subjects producing it but also on the historically contingent conceptual schemes they deploy, such that what subjects see in the world depends upon the concepts they use to divide up that world, and those concepts are also interest-dependent; but
- despite the fact that competing groups might live in different phenomenal worlds, it is nevertheless possible to warrant empirical claims if one demonstrates that such claims are supported by empirical evidence open to verification by subjects with competing interests, provided that they are willing to provisionally employ the relevant conceptual scheme and apply the same rules of discourse.

Contingency in Philosophy of Science

Mannheim's considerations of how we can check our bias to produce knowledge that is "objective" in some sense are unlikely to persuade sophisticated critics; he doesn't elaborate on the problem and its resolution with much philosophical sophistication. However, in the brilliant—and underrated—*Science as Social Knowledge* (1990), philosopher Helen E. Longino provides us with a much more sophisticated philosophical defense of the sorts of claims that Mannheim outlines *in nuce*.[1]

First, Longino provides an apodictic critique of forms of naïve empiricism that attempt to separate out empirical claims from our background assumptions. She notes, primarily, that what counts as empirical data is relative to the definitions and the theoretical background assumptions employed by the person or group performing the empirical study. Empirical claims about "atoms, neutrinos, quarks, et cetera" are based not only on empirical reports but are constructed on the basis of empirical evidence gathered from very particular kinds of scientific instruments, instruments whose test results are *interpreted* to point to atoms, quarks, etc. on the basis of nonuniversal background assumptions. Since no one has ever seen an atom or a quark with their own eyes, the—always contingent—interpretation of the data depends on putting together the test results in a particular manner; in such cases, there is literally nothing close to something like "direct" empirical evidence. Whether the numbers on the readout of a machine in a physics lab point to quarks or not depends on the physicist's theory of quarks. "The evidence for such statements [about atoms, quarks, etc.] is not described in statements about 'observation reports' of individual atoms but in statements about cloud chambers, lines observed in spectrographic analysis, et cetera" (Longino 1990: 24). Ultimately, "hypotheses forming part of the atomic theory of matter are not evidentially supported by statements about atoms ... but by statements containing quite different kinds of terms," like statements about the readings shown on various scientific instruments during the experiment; "the same is true for most, if not all, interesting scientific theories" (25). Longino writes, "if observation is theory-determined, then we can have no confidence that what appears to be a fact in the context of one theory will remain so in the next" (11).

Ultimately, attempts to ground science on direct empiricism fail because, insofar as one's nonuniversal conceptual scheme or background assumptions condition empirical statements about atoms that are never seen but whose existence and features are inferred from various instruments on the basis of a theoretically grounded interpretation of the data they produce, direct empiricism is impossible. A possibly uncomfortable consequence is the following: "to change one's theory (or paradigm) involves changing one's worldview and hence one's world; to change one's theory is to change what one sees and, apparently, *what there is to be seen*" (Longino 1990: 27, emphasis mine).

In addition, as noted in previous chapters, time always threatens to destroy the seemingly "objective" knowledge we sometimes claim to arrive at—or, as the American pragmatists put it, all knowledge is fallible because new information may someday come to light that will force us—depending on our interests—to divide up the world with different categories or to revise the empirical claims we make using the existing set of categories. At any point, the claim "that a particular hypothesis (or theory) *h* offers the best explanation of some set of data *e* is not in itself grounds for believing that *h* is true" (Longino 1990: 30). History of science provides us with "a long list of theories that were eminently successful in their day but that we now regard as untrue (not on the basis of a supra-temporal point of view but on the basis of empirical evidence that falsified claims or assumptions prior theories made). Since truth cannot be an explanation for the success of those theories, we are certainly not compelled to believe that current successful theories are true" in any universal, objective, or noncontingent way (31). The fact that a hypothesis or theory works to explain the widest range of available empirical evidence never warrants the claim that no future evidence or change in our theory will force us to abandon our existing hypotheses. To suppose so "is to ignore the fact that the history of science, even the very recent history of science, is littered with failures" (31). In sum, our present scientific knowledge about empirical matters is contingent upon our current background assumptions or theories, which are always subject to change should new evidence come to light, and therefore to pass current knowledge off as noncontingent is always unwarranted. As Thomas Kuhn once put it, while people often think of science as "a single monolithic and unified enterprise," it is "seldom or never like that"; science is "instead a rather ramshackle" affair (Kuhn 2012: 49). Or, as Hegel put it, knowledge of phenomena is inherently "wobbly" (Hegel [1830] 2010: 80).

Much like Mannheim, Longino notes that this is distressing only if one assumes a realist epistemology according to which knowledge should mirror reality, as opposed to viewing human knowledge and interests as something that conditions our empirical reality. For Longino, *a priori* the assumptions we deploy when producing knowledge make the knowledge produced contingent upon those assumptions, which are themselves contingent and variable. In addition, for Longino, *a priori* people look for evidence because they are invested—if they weren't invested they wouldn't exert the effort to look in the first place. This raises red flags for the realist: because our assumptions and interests change all the time, this depicts science as too contingent, or awards science too little authority. For them, it seems, what we call objective knowledge ought not be contingent on something so unreliable and variable as human assumptions and investments. "When we are troubled about the role of contextual values or value-laden assumptions in science, it is because we are thinking of scientific inquiry as an activity whose intended outcome is an accurate understanding of whatever structures and processes are being investigated" (Longino 1990: 36). For the realist, if our scientific knowledge "is itself conditioned by our or others' values, it cannot serve as a neutral and independent guide" to reality (36). For Longino, this is not the only way we can view reality, empiricism, and scientific knowledge.

Turning to an alternate way to think about empiricism and scientific knowledge, Longino notes—much like the American pragmatists—that human interests appear to always, in practice, direct our investigations. She notes, for instance, that in practice scientific inquiry appears to be "the search for descriptions of the natural world that *allow for the prediction and control* of an increasing number of its aspects" (Longino 1990: 32, emphasis mine). People who seek a cure for cancer do not do it for reasons completely independent of particular social goals; those goals are conditions of possibility of their research. Unlike those who suggest that scientific research should be entirely value-free, the history of actual scientific practices reveals "both how social and cultural values play a role in scientific inquiry" (37).

Second, as we have already noted in her critique of naïve empiricism, because empirical claims depend on background assumptions or theories, "anything that is the case or is imagined to be the case can be taken as evidence that something else is the case" (Longino 1990: 41). The amount of water saturating a plot of land could be evidence that it *is* a wetland, or could be evidence that it is *not* a wetland. "What determines whether or not someone will take some fact or alleged fact, x, as evidence for some hypothesis, h, is not a natural (for example, causal) relation between the state of affairs x and that described by h but are other beliefs that person has concerning the evidential connection between x and h" (41)—and those beliefs are "always susceptible to change" (45). Nevertheless—and this is the crucial point—*evidence still matters* to us.

> However we end up characterizing observational data, *they* are what serve as evidence for hypotheses (and theories). Data … do not on their own, however, indicate that for which they can serve as evidence. Hypotheses, on the other hand, are or consist of statements whose content always exceeds that of the statements describing the observational data.
>
> (Longino 1990: 58)

Although hypotheses cannot be reduced to empirical observations, empirical observations, at the end of the day, are necessary to judge whether or not a hypothesis is persuasive, even if that hypothesis in some way shapes the empirical observations. The extent to which a hypothesis is persuasive, however, appears to be relative to the interests and background assumptions of those evaluating the hypothesis. As such, a hypothesis is more likely to be taken as persuasive if the hypothesis has the "ability to accommodate the interests of the different communities that have a stake in any given scientific research program" (Longino 1990: 60). For a hypothesis to be persuasive, the scientist must attend to the questions that people with competing interests or background assumptions might ask, particularly the following: "What is the evidence? And why is this data evidence for this hypothesis? … Why should I believe (or accept) this" (60–61). Only hypotheses and evidences that can answer such questions to people with competing views and interests are likely to be persuasive.

Consequently, to be persuasive we must make two things public. First, we must make public the "theoretical assertions, hypotheses, and background assumptions" that lie behind our conclusions. Second, we must demonstrate that these are confirmed (or at least not falsified) by evidences that "are public in the sense that they are intersubjectively ascertainable" (Longino 1990: 70). Longino goes on, "this does not require a commitment to a set of theory-free, eternally acceptable observation statements but merely a commitment to the possibility that two or more persons can agree about the description of objects, events, and states of affairs that enter into evidential relationships" (70). Rather, to put it in my terms, it is only to require that the evidence we offer could be verifiable to someone with competing interests if they used our conceptual scheme or set of discursive individuations. Only on that condition can we justify that "the objects of experience which we describe and about which we reason are purported to exist independently of our seeing and thinking about them" (70). This latter formulation is too realist for my tastes, as an "object"—at least an object that is not a mid-sized object—is an object for us only on condition that it is brought into relief via a conceptual scheme and related constitutive discourse. That is why, for instance, two people with competing conceptual schemes might look at the same state of affairs and see different objects. As such, some objects are visible only for subjects using the same set of individuations. However, this is "objective" enough for most scientific claims worthy of being taken seriously. If one requires—for one's empirical claims to be persuasive—that we use a noncontingent conceptual scheme, one would have to demonstrate that humans have access to such a noncontingent conceptual scheme. To my knowledge, we have no empirical evidence for the existence of a noncontingent conceptual scheme.

To conclude my discussion of Longino's work, I will point to her discussion of what makes scientific knowledge "objective"—not in the sense of removing all interests that might guide research, but in the sense of delivering independently verifiable claims that are, of course, subject to revision because they are contingent on existing evidence and therefore fallible. She writes,

> As long as background beliefs can be articulated and subjected to criticism from the scientific community, they can be defended, modified, or abandoned in response to such criticism. As long as this kind of response is possible, the incorporation of hypotheses into the canon of scientific knowledge can be independent of any individual's subjective preferences. Their incorporation is, instead, a function in part of the assessment of evidential support. And while the evidential relevance to hypotheses of observations and experiments is a function of background assumptions, the adoption of these assumptions is not arbitrary but is (or rather can be) subject to the kinds of controls just discussed. This solution incorporates as elements both the social characteristics of the production of knowledge and the public accessibility of the material with which this knowledge is constructed.
>
> (Longino 1990: 73–74)

For careful readers, it should be clear that this is in many ways very close to Mannheim's argument outlined above: the point of knowledge is not to eliminate human interest, but to control for human interests by making claims that would be persuasive to people with competing interests, precisely because they are based on publicly available or intersubjectively verifiable empirical evidences. On this view, noncontingent knowledge is not possible, and models of scientific knowledge that present that knowledge as if it were noncontingent fail to make sense of how we, as humans, create scientific knowledge in the first place. Intersubjective verification is as noncontingent as we can get, but it should be enough for any person or group willing to entertain that available evidence (and, as noted above, if they are unwilling to entertain such evidence, claiming that one's knowledge is noncontingent—despite all evidence to the contrary—is unlikely to make one's claims any more persuasive). For Longino—as the title of her book suggests—"scientific knowledge is, therefore, social knowledge" (Longino 1990: 75). Additionally, "individual values are held in check not by a [noncontingent] methodology, but by social values" (102). If a claim is received as objective, that is not because it is noncontingent, but because it withstood scrutiny from subjects or groups with the widest range of interests. For Longino, this contingency is a source of science's strength, not a source of weakness—for how reliable would our knowledge claims be if they couldn't sustain being vetted by peers with different ideas? I differ from Longino in this conclusion only insofar as I don't think "objectivity" is the most useful term to describe scientific knowledge that attains such widely accepted status, as that word still implies that the knowledge arrived at is in some way noncontingent. On my view, *all knowledge is "subjective," in the sense that it is produced by subjects, not by objects.*

Rather than call scientific knowledge "objective," I would prefer to say that those forms of scientific knowledge that attain widely accepted status are *persuasive* rather than objective. "Persuasive" won't be objective enough for many readers, but to them I will just point out that just about everything people throughout human history have respected as "objective" knowledge has, over time, been downgraded to "formerly persuasive but no longer persuasive." Given time, we can see that "objective" is, for all practical purposes, ultimately little different than "persuasive," and "persuasive" is better because it more easily accounts for the fact that new evidence may make old claims less persuasive than does the claim that such knowledge was really "objective" in the first place.

Following Longino, in this section we have seen:

- the objectivity to which naïve empiricists aspire is thwarted, *a priori*, by the fact that their interpretations of empirical evidence are always and necessarily contingent upon background assumptions and theoretical considerations that are never entirely based upon empirical evidence, as those background assumptions condition what counts as empirical evidence and are therefore logically prior to empiricism;
- we cannot therefore "deduce" objective "laws of nature" from empirical evidence;
- instead, the best we can do is construct theories that are based on the widest available intersubjectively verifiable empirical evidence, while acknowledging that those theories are contingently produced because that evidence is conditioned by nonuniversal assumptions; and
- our theories are at their most sophisticated when we take into account the fact that not only is evidence historically contingent upon regnant scientific theories, but evidence is also contingent upon the conceptual schemes we use to bring evidence into relief in our phenomenological field in the first place.

Discourse and Ideology

Causation

To expand my definition of empiricism, I want to suggest that empirical claims depend in part on *explanatory, causal claims*. This might be perplexing to some poststructuralists, for whom causal claims involve an ontological commitment they are not willing to incur. Pointing to the skepticism of David Hume, they might say that one never empirically observes causation in the world. As I noted in Chapter 1, when watching billiard balls bounce off of one another on a table, we easily note correlations: when this ball touches that ball, it stops but the other ball starts moving. However, from Hume's perspective, no "cause" appears in the phenomenological field—only moving balls. One might argue that there is a "transfer of energy" from one ball to the next, forcing the next one to move, but such energies are inferred from the evidence, not seen. Perhaps the billiard balls are not causing one another to move; perhaps invisible spirits are pushing the balls around. In addition, while the balls might bounce off of one another consistently for years and years, we have no empirical evidence that tomorrow they will continue to do so in the same manner. In summary, healthy skepticism perhaps requires us to admit that (1) correlation is all we have phenomenal evidence for, and (2) while those correlations hold for now, they may not in the future.

However, this is not the only way to frame the discussion about causation. In *Making Things Happen: A Theory of Causal Explanation* (2003), James Woodward argues that it would be more useful to define causation in terms of what he calls "manipulability" or "intervention." Note: the claim here is that this is more useful, not more correct or adequate to the world, as definitions are logically prior to empirical claims and, as such, cannot be more or less adequate to the world, only more or less useful for particular purposes. Much like the American pragmatists who draw attention to how knowledge is always produced in relation to human interests and human interaction with the world around us, Woodward notes that "our interest in causal relationships and explanation initially grows out of a highly practical interest human beings have in manipulation and control" (10). Consequently, he argues that the most useful way of defining causation is to think of it in terms of those variables that we can reliably manipulate to bring about changes in other variables. "According to this account, causal and explanatory relationships are relationships that are potentially exploitable for purposes of manipulation and control" (v). On this definition, "any explanation that proceeds by showing how an outcome depends (when the dependence in question is not logical or conceptual) on other variables or factors counts as causal" (6). Woodward points out that, unlike abstruse definitions of causation that talk about invisible things such as transfer of energy, this definition is much closer to the way "causation" is used not only in the sciences but also in all human cultures with which we are familiar.

> Few cultures have developed the systematic procedures for investigating nature that we think of as science, but all cultures, including those in the distant past, have been curious about causal and explanatory relationships and have accumulated a

great deal of causal knowledge of the mundane sort: for example, that exposure to fire or heat causes pain and tissue damage.

(Woodward 2003: 18)

Indeed, it is difficult to understand how humans or nonhuman animals could survive without such an ability to manipulate the variables in their contexts in the world to serve their interests.

One example Woodward provides is derived from an essay by Nancy Cartwright, who describes a promotional letter she received from TIAA-CREF, which claimed the following:

> It simply wouldn't be true to say, "Nancy L. D. Cartwright … if you own a TIAA life insurance policy you'll live longer."
> But it is a fact, nonetheless, that persons insured by TIAA do enjoy longer lifetimes on average, than persons insured by commercial insurance companies that serve the general public.

(Woodward 2003: 32)

The letter thus identifies a correlation, but holds off on asserting a causal relation between the two (although not hesitating to imply one). It should be clear to readers that, on the manipulationsist or interventionist account of causation, there is no causal relation here. One cannot reliably increase one's lifetime by manipulating this particular variable (i.e., by getting insured by TIAA). There are, however, other variables that, statistically, we *can* reliably manipulate to increase our life span. Unlike Hume, we need not throw up our hands in defeat before the skepticism that correlation is not causation; by intervening in or experimenting on the world we can find variables that *reliably* allow us to manipulate our environment in ways that serve our interests. "The contrast between [causal] relationships and those that are merely correlational is real and important in both science and ordinary life" (Woodward 2003: 37).

One point that Woodward doesn't emphasize but which is nevertheless relevant here is made by Thomas Kuhn in *The Structure of Scientific Revolutions* (2012). In his discussion of the discovery of X-rays, Kuhn notes that finding this new variable threw prior research into doubt. "Previously completed work on normal projects would now have to be done again because earlier scientists had failed to recognize and control a relevant variable. X-rays, to be sure, opened up a new field and thus added to the potential domain of normal science. But they also, and this is now the more important point, changed fields that already existed" (59). It is always possible that we could discover new variables that unsettle prior knowledge. No one can control for the impact of a variable that is not yet part of their scientific vocabulary. Tomorrow we might need to rethink everything that came before.

Discourse and Ideology

Woodward's book is quite technical, and there are many other details relevant to his defense of this definition of causation. Not all are relevant for my purposes, but a few distinctions are worth reviewing. For one, he distinguishes between relationships that can be manipulated in ways that *always* bring about the result one desires, as opposed to relationships that *statistically are more likely* to bring about the desired result. He further makes relevant distinctions between necessary and sufficient causes, as well as the fact that causal relationships are always contextual, and if one changes the context the variables may function in a different manner than one expected or desired.

Woodward also introduces the concept of "invariance." We can call a causal relationship "invariant" when, *under certain conditions*, the manipulation of one variable reliably leads to identical results for another variable. This is similar to the concept of "laws of nature," something that is supposed to always hold no matter the conditions. The problem with the concept of universal laws of nature, however, is that the discourse doesn't sufficiently emphasize the extent to which the invariances "laws of nature" attempt to identify are always contingent on some conditions being controlled for. Woodward draws his example from a physics textbook that shows how the speed of "a block sliding down an inclined plane" is explained by attending to the mass of the block, gravitational pull, friction, the angle of the plane, etc. The invariant relationship at which the textbook arrives ($F=mg$) ultimately "holds only approximately, even near the surface of the earth, and fails to hold even approximately at sufficiently large distances from the earth's surface. It is obviously contingent upon the earth's having a particular mass and radius," etc. (Woodward 2003: 16). "Laws of nature" are supposed to be unconditional, always holding no matter the circumstances. However, we have no empirical evidence that this is ever the case. Even the measureable speed of light changes depending on whether it is going through air or water. By contrast, the concept of "invariance," as Woodward uses it, builds such contingencies into the definition. We may find that a relationship between two variables is invariant, but *only if* we control for a wide variety of variables potentially influencing their relationship. Once again, knowledge is necessarily contingent, but acknowledging that contingency arguably strengthens rather than weakens our knowledge.

Woodward also notes that what counts as a cause is contingent on how widely the observer draws a circle around the relevant variables and the relevant contexts. In any context, there is a potentially indefinite number of variables that could be manipulated to bring about a desired result. One example Woodward gives concerns firing a gun. In a courtroom, we might say that the defendant pulling the trigger of a gun *caused* the death of another person, and if he had not pulled the trigger—namely, if he had manipulated his environment differently—that death would not have been caused. By contrast, if one is in a chemistry lab doing research on black powder, one might note that if the percentage of a particular chemical in the bullet casing is increased or decreased by some amount, this may *cause* the gun not to fire. If one is a politician attempting to pass gun control laws, manipulating the conditions under which it is possible to buy a gun might reliably allow a community to *cause* a reduction in the number of bullets fired. All of this is to say: in any state of affairs there are, for all practical purposes, an indefinite number of manipulable conditions; which condition we consider the "cause" is relative to what we are trying to accomplish, what our particular discourse brings into relief, and what is within our bodily, technological, or political ability to manipulate. When we change the discourse, the reliably manipulable causes we see in the world may change as well.

For Woodward, the interests that guide our causal investigations make our findings somewhat contingent, insofar as the circle we draw around the variables we want to or are capable of intervening on are conditioned by what we want to accomplish, what variables we choose not to manipulate, and what our existing technologies permit us to reliably manipulate. However, it does not follow that those contingencies are destructive to the reliability of our conclusions:

> to the extent that subjectivity or interest relativity enters into causal judgments, it enters because it influences our judgments about which possibilities are to be taken seriously. However, once the set of serious possibilities is fixed, there is no further element or arbitrariness or subjectivity in our causal judgments; relative to a set of serious possibilities or alternatives, which causal claims are true or false is determined by objective patterns [that we can observe].
>
> (Woodward 2003: 90)

For example, should we choose, politically, not to interfere with the conditions under which people can procure firearms, we might turn to look at other manipulable variables that permit us to reduce deaths resulting from firearms, such as the availability of gun safes, mandatory safety training, and so on. Our choice to freeze some variables rather than others is highly contingent, in this case, contingent upon politics, but once we do freeze those variables, if we did a study finding that mandatory safety training reduced gun deaths by a particular percentage, that finding would by no means be arbitrary. Subjects with competing interests could potentially run the same study and find the same results, provided they used the same definitions of relevant terms and find the same results—and if they didn't find the same results, we might have to revise our account after considering their competing results. Either way, from the fact that interests *condition* our causal explanations it does not necessarily follow that our interests *distort* the results.

Before turning to the next section, I would like to return once more to the skeptic. Does this account overcome Hume's criticisms? Remember, Hume proposed two major objections. First, he questioned whether we could distinguish between correlations and causation, insofar as the latter is not empirical. I believe Woodward's approach overcomes this objection, insofar as his definition of causation allows us to individuate empirical evidence for causation and thereby reliably distinguish between causation and correlation within a particular discourse (at least when there is sufficient empirical evidence to do so). While a falling barometer might correlate with the arrival of a storm, on Woodward's definition this is a correlation, not a causation, since manipulating the barometer—empirically—will not reliably cause a storm to arrive (Woodward 2003: 14). However, at some point in the future, if we were to develop the technological ability to manipulate clouds, wind patterns, humidity levels, etc., we could likely identify reliably manipulable causes that are more than mere correlations, as is the case with the barometer.

Discourse and Ideology

Hume's second objection was that the future is outside our existing empirical evidence, and as such the apparent causal relations we find today may no longer hold tomorrow. I do not believe Woodward overcomes this objection. In particular, this is because changes in conditions or discourses may make formerly reliable manipulations no longer so. For instance, planning seeds in a field may reliably cause a crop to grow, *until* there is a drought; a change in the conditions in which we intervene results in a change in the effects of our manipulations. Or, as we saw with the discovery of X-rays, what was previously held as knowledge might need reconsideration given this new variable that we could not control for previously (because, before that, we didn't even have the means to see them—such as a new technical vocabulary and a particular technical apparatus). Because the objects that appear to us are indefinitely open to revision—precisely because of the changes wrought by time—in principle and *a priori* it is never possible to control for all possible conditions or contingencies, and as a result the causal relations we can reliably manipulate today may cease to be reliable tomorrow. As I noted in previous chapters, Derrida's point that time threatens to destroy any particular form of knowledge is more or less the same point that the American pragmatists are making when they argue that knowledge is always fallible because future evidence could force us to revise our accounts. In any case, by deploying Woodward's definition of causation we do not necessarily overcome this particular objection to causal claims.

Another reason Woodward's account does not fully overcome this objection: a change in the discourse we use may alter what counts as the most reliable manipulation of our environment. For example, access to water in the ancient world was without doubt a condition of possibility of reliably sustaining life. However, in a twenty-first-century chemist's laboratory, the object individuated by "water" is very different than the object individuated in the ancient world. What we call "dangerous bacteria" might be *included in* what ancients called "water," although in a chemist's lab today we would likely disambiguate the two: "water" is restricted to dihydrogen monoxide, and "bacteria" is considered something else entirely. Consequently, access to what ancients called "water" might *less reliably* sustain life than what contemporary chemists refer to as "water." That is to say, if the discourse we use divides up the stuff of the world in a different manner, a particular variable we manipulate might be disambiguated into two, or might even disappear altogether in some circumstances.

Despite these caveats about Hume's objection that causal accounts are contingent in relationship to time, we are not thrust into utter relativism, a position from which we cannot make any reliable empirical claims about causation. It is, rather, just once more to note that what counts as empirical is contingent upon discourse and open to revision. This is not damning to knowledge, but simply one of the conditions that necessarily limits the universality or objectivity of all human knowledge.

In this section we have seen:

- it might serve our interests to define causation not in terms of correlation or invisible energies that are transferred from one object to the next, but instead in terms of variables that we can manipulate to bring about desired ends;

- defining causation in this manner would make our overall approach more empirical, at least in the sense that it requires us to demonstrate empirical evidence that the interventions we make on relevant variables reliably "cause" the results we claim they do;
- we can define the discovered relations as "invariant" when they hold independently of changes in other variables;
- nevertheless, even such causal claims must remain open to revision because time potentially brings new and competing empirical evidence or even changes in the discourses we use to divide up the world.

Retroduction and Ontological Commitments

There is one more element to the way in which I am using the concept of empiricism that I must add before returning to my definition of ideology and ideology critique. Empiricism concerns the evidence we can muster in support of the claims we make, including causal claims, but when it comes to the social as opposed to the natural sciences, we need a somewhat relaxed standard of what counts as a justified causal explanation.

In the natural sciences, studies can be run in a way that controls for more variables than in the social sciences. In a chemistry lab, scientists can isolate the chemicals on which they are experimenting from a wide variety of variables that would interfere with their ability to identify possibly invariant relationships. Such stringent controls are simply not possible when it comes to the study of social formations, as a result of ethical limitations we place on ourselves. The generation of empirical data on populations is contingent upon potentially millions of relevant cultural variables for which we cannot control, without intervening greatly—and potentially harmfully—on the lives of the relevant population. Although it might be revealing, given the ethical standards of modern universities we cannot, for instance, intentionally separate two identical twins at birth and manipulate their environment throughout their lifetime to arrive at which relationships between genetics and behavior are invariant despite varying social conditions.

It is for this reason than some social scientists resort to what pragmatist Charles S. Peirce called retroduction or abduction. In *Logics of Critical Explanation in Social and Political Theory* (2007), Jason Glynos and David Howarth (writing explicitly from within the tradition of poststructuralism [see 4–8]) demonstrate the considerable significance of retroduction—as opposed to deduction or induction—for social science (the summary of retroduction that follows is based on Glynos and Howarth's description of how it is useful to distinguish between deduction, induction, and retroduction, which I find useful for my present project, although I make no claims about whether their reconstruction of Peirce's distinction is accurate in a way acceptable to Peirce scholars; however, the usefulness of the distinction for my project is not necessarily dependent upon Peirce's particular formulation).

Discourse and Ideology

Deduction involves identifying what logically follows—rationally or empirically—from existing definitions of terms or available empirical evidence. We can deduce from the rules of mathematics—provided we are working with a base 10 numbering system and not a base 2—that, as a result of how the terms are defined, 2+2=4, 4+4=8, and 8+8=16. Similarly, we can make empirical deductions such as the following based on available information:

> Premise 1: All the cats in room x have four legs.
> Premise 2: Jackson is a cat in room x.
> Conclusion: Therefore, Jackson has four legs.

If we follow the rules of mathematics precisely, or if our premises are correct, we can reliably deduce that 8+8=16 and that Jackson has four legs. Induction, by contrast, makes plausible or probable generalizations on the basis of available evidence, but the conclusions are less certain than deduced conclusions because they are dependent upon, for example, sample size. For inductive generalizations to be increasingly reliable, we would have to preform studies on greater sample sizes.

By contrast, retroduction, like induction, is not as certain as deduction, and involves hypothesizing causes that would best explain the available empirical evidence before us. Quoting Peirce, Glynos and Howarth write,

> retroduction, finally, "is the provisional adoption of a hypothesis ... For example, all the operations of chemistry fail to decompose hydrogen, lithium, [etc.] ... We provisionally supposed these bodies to be simple, for if not, similar experimentation will detect their compound nature, if it can be detected at all."
>
> (Glynos and Howarth 2007: 25)

That is to say, based on the evidence that existed at the time—Peirce lived and wrote around the turn of the twentieth century—there was no evidence that those chemicals could be broken down any further, and thus retroductive reasoning suggested that the best explanation of that fact—the fact that they couldn't be broken down any further—was because they were, ontologically, simple rather than composite bodies. Of course, since then, we have evidence that these can be broken down into composites, and now physicists retroductively hypothesize that such atoms are made up of quarks, other subatomic particles, and possibly strings. Such hypotheses are never certain, but are the best explanation that we can give based on the available empirical evidence at a given point in time. "While deductive reasoning purports to *prove* what is the case, and inductive reasoning purports to *approximate* what is the case, retroductive reasoning *conjectures* what is the case" regarding causal relations (Glynos and Howarth 2007: 26). While retroductive arguments must attend to empirical evidence, quite literally retroduction entails making claims for which we do not (yet) have sufficient empirical evidence to warrant.

Ideology

Glynos and Howarth describe the process by which retroduction proceeds:

> explanation begins with something we encounter in the present—an anomalous phenomenon that needs to be rendered intelligible for example—which calls for thought and theorization. This active process of problematization involves the constitution of a problem [for which we desire a causal explanation] ... Work is then started on furnishing an explanation that can render the recalcitrant phenomenon more intelligible. This process is understood in terms of the logic of retroductive explanation and theory construction, which involves a to-and-fro movement between the phenomena investigated and the various explanations that are proffered.
>
> (Glynos and Howarth 2007: 34)

Much like Woodward, Glynos and Howarth claim that we produce knowledge by following a kind of circle: we form a hypothesis, look at evidence, revise either the hypothesis or background assumptions to account for the evidence, form a new hypothesis, and so forth.

Glynos and Howarth note that although retroductive explanations don't carry the certainty of deduction desired by positivists, and although such explanations are contingent upon the availability of new evidence, this doesn't mean that the conclusions we arrive at are entirely arbitrary. "Though our criteria are not as hard and universal as those put forward by positivists," they still employ guidelines that encourage conclusions that are "more illuminating than rival interpretations" (Glynos and Howarth 2007: 34). In particular, on their view, "an account is accepted as valid only if it produces insights and greater illumination according to criteria which can be publicly articulated, criteria concerning evidence, consistency, exhaustiveness, and so on" (38). We can always, provided we have the resources, go on to perform additional tests that produce evidence that potentially supports or falsifies our retroductive conclusions. The conclusions at which we arrive will always be contingent; as they note, "of course, we accept that such criteria are themselves subject to interpretation and contestation" (38).

Because they are not certain, retroductive hypotheses are not "laws of nature" but useful provisos. However, that fact does not negate their fundamental usefulness. On the contrary, when it comes to the social sciences—and given the ethical restrictions that prohibit invasive human experiments—retroductive hypotheses are often the most certain conclusions we can draw.

One further contingency that Glyons and Howarth note afflicts social science is the fact that the people are shaped by the discourses they use, such that the introduction of new discourses often produces new behaviors. The philosopher Ian Hacking, as I noted in Chapter 3, calls some concepts "looping concepts" because they have a causal effect on the people who use or internalize them. Calling Pluto a planet or a dwarf planet does not appear to have a looping effect on its mass, orbit around the sun, etc. Calling a patch of land a wetland or not a wetland likely won't change its ability to absorb rainwater.

Discourse and Ideology

However, calling a child "retarded" does appear to have a looping effect on the child (and, it seems, a harmful one). We as humans respond to the words we use to construct our identities, and as those identities change so do our behaviors. As such, the invariances between variables that we find in social contexts are invariant—as noted above—*only if* other variables are controlled for, and it turns out that it is impossible to control for all of such variables, especially when we are dealing with subjects who have internalized looping concepts. Glynos and Howarth write, "as far as the social world is concerned, we argue that [a particular] invariance may be historically specific ... a structure or pattern shaped in significant ways by the (ontological) fact that we are 'meaning producing' or 'self-interpreting' animals" (Glynos and Howarth 2007: 23).

Because of these contingencies that are impossible to fully control for, social science can never attain the sort of certainty about its inductions and retroductions as in the sciences in which experimental conditions can be more thoroughly controlled. Ideally, the strongest or most persuasive forms of knowledge production would require that we follow up retroductive hypotheses with experiments designed to eliminate as many independent variables as possible to see if the manipulable variables we are focusing on have relations as invariant as our hypotheses suggest. However, when it comes to discourse analysis and ideology critique, such absolutely rigorous experiments are simply not possible given social, political, and ethical constraints on social scientific research. Consequently, at times our hypotheses must be based not only on social scientific experiments but also on the available historical evidence that cannot be subjected to testing. For instance, we cannot run an experiment on 85 million American evangelical Christians to see precisely under what particular conditions they would be willing to vote for an openly misogynist presidential candidate who has a history of publicly espousing discourses and ideologies explicitly opposed to their own reported beliefs. However, that does not mean that no valuable retroductive hypothesis can be posited that might help us isolate possibly significant discursive or ideological causes that appear to demonstrably influence subjects' behaviors.

If we rigorously define "science" as the development of hypotheses and subsequent testing using experiments with strict controls, then discourse analysis and ideology critique cannot be sciences. However, this puts discourse analysis and ideology critique on the same level as disciplines such as history. This is why I view discourse analysis and ideology critique as empirically-based methods that produce valuable and interesting causal claims, but without the level of certainty that lab-based sciences can produce, although the persuasiveness of our causal claims in history, discourse analysis, or ideology critique is enriched when we can include as much of the latest experimental evidence as is available in support of our hypotheses.

The last point I need to consider here is that Glynos and Howarth rightly acknowledge that retroductive explanations of empirical evidence entail ontological commitments. They write, "any legitimate approach to social and political analysis requires at least some ontological assumptions and commitments" (Glynos and Howarth 2007: 11). However, this is not to say that their approach incurs the kind of ontological commitments wherein we discover "a kind of 'furniture of the world' that sets out the sorts of things, and their

Ideology

respective properties, which we encounter in engaging with objects and other subjects" (11). Such a realist approach seeks to find what is really real, completely independent of human subjectivity, which would entail coming to the conclusion that some description of the world holds as true in a way that is not contingent upon any historically specific conceptual scheme. If conceptual schemes are contingent—as I contend—then no description of the "reality" is the final word but, given changes in the interests guiding scientific inquiry or the availability of new evidence, we may wish to redescribe the "really real" in another contingent conceptual scheme—in which case the former "final word" on the matter (or the "furniture of the world" we thought we had found) would in turn come to be regarded as knowledge that once seemed objective but is now regarded as historically specific and perhaps no longer useful for our present purposes.

Instead, the sort of ontological commitments they describe are "marked by an 'essential instability' that problematizes a simple listing of [objects'] necessary intrinsic properties and causal capacities. Therefore, of greater import for us is their contingency, historicity, and precariousness" (Glynos and Howarth 2007: 11). However, ontological commitments of some sort are nevertheless assumed. In Foucault's work on sexuality, though it "problematizes the existing accounts of the problem, [his] logic of problemantization always relies upon certain ontological presumptions regarding the nature of discursive practices, for instance" (46–47). Judith Butler's appropriation and use of Foucault's work is a useful case in point on this matter. In *Gender Trouble* (1990), Butler argues that gender is performed rather than expressed. Contrary to the essentialist view that sees potentially discoverable gendered essences as lying within male and female bodies and which "express" themselves by directing the behavior of men and women, Butler argues that, through a process of socialization, subjects internalize behavioral expectations and repeat them over and over until they become the gender they are performing. Note all of the ontological assumptions that must be in place for such an argument to be persuasive:

- bodies do not, in fact, harbor binary biological essences that entirely determine the gendered behavior of men and women;
- human biology is sufficiently flexible that subjects can, through socialization and habit, be turned in to humans with considerably different "natures"; and
- "performing" is a better verb for explaining the production of gendered behavior than "expressing."

All of these are ontological commitments about the nature of world, at least *as individuated in her discourse and with supporting, relevant empirical evidence.*

As I argued in Chapter 2, realism functions to naturalize historically specific conceptual schemes; that is the realist error I have attempted to avoid in this chapter, particularly by drawing attention to the extent to which truth or falsehood is conditioned by the conceptual scheme and discursive rules employed. On the other hand, I simultaneously want to avoid an error that some poststructuralists make; put simply, from the fact that there are multiple regimes of truth, it does not follow that nothing can be false or that all ontological claims are nonsense. On the contrary, once discourses are in place,

Discourse and Ideology

many things exist for subjects who use those discourses, and we can make true and false statements about those things *within* the appropriate discourse, and those statements inevitably incur or entail ontological commitments.

In this section, I have argued:

- empirically warranted research on social formations is limited by social, political, and ethical constraints that prevent us from controlling for all relevant variables which might permit us to discover those reliably "invariant" relations between variables;
- just as induction is less certain than deduction, retroduction—as the best theory that accounts for the widest available empirical evidences—also falls short of the apparent certainty of deduction, but is nevertheless the most useful approach for producing knowledge about human groups when we cannot do experimental research that would allow us to control for all the variables we might want to control for; and
- retroduction inevitably entails ontological commitments about how things work, although they are, *a priori*, always open to revision should new interests or new evidence force us to revise our ontological commitments.

Ideology and Ideology Critique

As noted at the beginning of this chapter, Mannheim defines ideology in a way designed to focus on its function: a discourse and set of related knowledge claims are ideological insofar as they function to preserve the status quo, likely protecting a dominant group that benefits from the reproduction of the status quo, and which may or may not be strictly true. By contrast, I want to return to a definition of ideology that affixes it to a concern for falsehood or untruth. Throughout this book, I have emphasized a distinction between constitutive discourse and empirical discourse, and my definition requires careful attention to the differences between the two. I propose to define ideology in the following manner:

> ideology consists of a bundle of agonistic empirical discourses or sets of knowledge claims designed—intentionally or unintentionally—to advance a group's interests, which always depend on a logically prior constitutive discourse, but in a way that (1) violates the rules of that discourse or another discourse or (2) entails the distribution of demonstrably false or inadequately supported empirical claims, empirical claims that are false on grounds accepted by that very discourse or another discourse.

I would like to add a gloss on several parts of this definition:

- *Agonistic* and *designed to advance a group's interests*. On the stipulative definition offered here, ideologies are agonistic, in the sense that they are means of waging war on groups with competing interests. Thus a mere "mistake" would not count as ideological, unless one could demonstrate the mistake was motivated or obscured by a set of interests or associated discourses in a way that serves the interests of the group that made the "mistake."

- *Empirical discourses or sets of knowledge claims.* Because discourse analysis and ideology critique are forms of *social critique*, a single false empirical claim does not rise to the level of something with social consequences for groups. On the contrary, groups produce a wide variety of agnostic discursive interventions designed to serve their purposes; mutually bolstering clusters of such discursive interventions must exist for an analysis to be about a group ideology, rather than merely an interpersonal spat or calculation error.
- *Violates the rules of that discourse or another discourse.* For ideology critique to be persuasive or effective on this definition, the critic must demonstrate not only that an ideology serves a group's interests but also that their ideology shades the truth in some way according to the rules of some discourse—for instance, when their arguments depend upon logical fallacies they would never permit their opponents to use.
- *Entails the distribution of demonstrably false or inadequately supported empirical claims on grounds accepted by that very discourse or another discourse.* For ideology critique to be persuasive or effective on this definition, the critic must demonstrate that the ideology makes empirical claims that are in some way problematic, either according to its own standards or the standards of another discourse. Crucially, however, such a demonstration must attend to a particular, historically specific standard—either that of those who deploy the ideology or that of those who critique the ideology—not a suprahuman, universal standard (for we have no empirical evidence such a standard exists).

Because I have stipulatively defined ideology in terms of falsehood, for my purposes ideology critique must be sensitive to both constitutive discourse and the potentially true or false empirical claims made possible by the rules of the constitutive discourse. At least three ways of demonstrating falsehood or distortion are possible, each of which would be differently persuasive to competing parties: (1) people who accept the critic's background assumptions and sympathies, (2) people in the larger society who accept a widely adopted, hegemonic doxa, or (3) the insiders who espouse the ideology targeted by the critic. Three steps can be taken:

1. for ideology critique to be persuasive to those *who share the critic's sympathies*, ideology critique must only demonstrate that an ideology is inconsistent with logical or empirical claims made possible by the critic's own discourse's rules of evidence;
2. for ideology critique to be persuasive to *a wider audience that may or may not accept the critic's assumptions and sympathies*, ideology critique must demonstrate that an ideology is inconsistent with logical or empirical claims widely accepted as true by all relevant parties in an agnostic ideological struggle; and

3. to be possibly persuasive to *insiders who espouse or sympathize with the ideology under consideration*, ideology critique must demonstrate, through immanent critique, that an ideology is
    a. logically inconsistent with itself;
    b. inconsistent with empirical claims it accepts as true; or
    c. inconsistent with empirical claims that it does not accept as true but which the critic can demonstrate ought to be accepted as true on the basis of other grounds accepted or entailed by other claims the ideology makes.

One problem with realist approaches to ideology critique is that they tend to assume that what counts as "ideology" is objective or universal, they fail to see that people interpellated by different discourses perceive different worlds, they fail to attend to the fact that what makes a claim persuasive for one person may not make it persuasive for others, and thus they are more likely to start and stop with step one, never making an effort to engage in steps two or three. By contrast, the form of ideology critique I am proposing notes that what counts as ideology, and what forms of ideology critique will be persuasive, are discourse-relative. If your audience has sympathies with the ideology that you are subjecting to criticism but are, nevertheless, willing in good faith to listen to one's criticism, they are most likely to be persuaded by the third approach, which emphasizes immanent critique of their ideology, or the second approach—both of these forms of critique focus on constitutive discourses or empirical evidences that are accepted as authoritative by one's opponent and with which they sympathize. The first approach is to some extent "preaching to the choir," as they say—it is a form of critique that is less likely to be persuasive because it attempts to persuade on the basis of grounds that the audience is more likely to contest than accept.

An analysis of ideology can also focus on the function of the ideology in drawing the audience's attention away from possible contradictions or empirical evidences that do not support the ideology:

- ideologies may refuse to ask particular questions if the answers to those questions contradict the ideology's overarching narrative;
- ideologies may draw attention away from potentially relevant empirical evidence by pointing to evidence that supports or can be manipulated to support the overarching narrative; and
- ideologies may offer caricatures of opposing views or the apparent motives that drive those who espouse competing discourses or ideologies—few things are more political than caricatures of one's opponent's motives.

Consequently, the form of ideology critique I am proposing proceeds, roughly speaking, through the following steps:

1. The critic must *individuate the relevant discourse* subject to ideology critique by
    a. drawing boundaries around what will be included in the analysis, along with

Ideology

   b. providing a justification for why this collection of discourse warrants being treated as a particular object.
2. The critic must go on to provide an initial *discourse analysis* of the ideology by
   a. summarizing the contents of the discourse and noting
      i. the distribution of sameness and difference within the discourse,
      ii. the systematic positive and negative valuations associated with the objects of or homologies within the discourse,
      iii. how those associations distribute sympathies and antipathies,
      iv. the empirical claims made possible within the discourse,
      v. the rights and duties or political program assigned by the discourse, and
      vi. the extent to which the discourse is actual (i.e., already interpellates subjects and their institutions) or merely aspirational (i.e., utopic rather than actual); and
   b. noting the extent to which the discourse arguably encourages, justifies, or legitimates social domination.
3. The critic then turns from discourse analysis to *ideology critique* by asking the following questions.
   a. Does the ideology arguably *caricature* opponents' motives or claims and, if so, how?
   b. Does the ideology use *emotionally charged paradigmatic cases* that are not particularly representative of a group, a practice, or an idea?
   c. Which claims in the ideology are *logically contradictory or merely rhetorical* (e.g., if they depend on rhetorical slippage or rhetorical displacement in order to be persuasive), and on whose discursive standards are they contradictory or rhetorical?
      i. If so, how would the ideology's master narrative have to be revised to remain coherent or persuasive?
   d. Which claims in the ideology are *falsifiable*, and on who's discourse?
      i. If claims are *empirically supported*—on the ideology's own discourse or another's—
         1. do they nevertheless appear to function
            a. to obscure another possibly relevant set of empirical facts?
            b. to reinforce an otherwise demonstrably false ideological narrative?
            c. to encourage manipulation of relevant variables in a way that arguably increases relations of social domination (for instance, by making minorities who suffer from social domination solely responsible for overcoming their domination)?

Discourse and Ideology

  ii. If claims are *not empirically supported or demonstrably false*—either on the ideology's own discourse or another's—do they contradict in any way other empirically supported and possibly relevant evidences?
     1. If so, how would the narrative they function to support have to be modified to remain coherent and persuasive?
     2. Do we have any existing empirical evidence for that modified narrative, or is it unlikely to be a warranted given the existing evidence?
  e. Do the possible caricatures, contradictions, gaps in evidence, or empirical falsehoods in the ideology arguably contribute to encouraging, justifying, or legitimating social domination?

In the last chapter of this book I will offer an extended example of how to apply this form of ideology critique going step by step through these stages of analysis; at present I will offer just one brief example of how available empirical evidence can usefully contribute to ideology critique, even if the forms of critique produced are not universal, objective, or noncontingent.

Consider a dominant conservative evangelical Christian view on the nature of gender difference. Most—although not all—of evangelical views on gender are essentialist, in the sense that they claim that gender difference is created by their god (insofar as he gave men and women different ontological characteristics), is always binary (in the sense that there can be either males or females but no other genders), and fixed from conception to death. There is a massive amount of literature on evangelical views on gender, and the literature shows that gender differences are often deeply contested, but for the purposes of this example it is enough to point out that the *dominant* view among evangelicals, at present, is essentialist in this manner. In *Remaking the Godly Marriage* (2001), John P. Bartkowski summarizes conservative evangelical propagandist James Dobson's writings on gender difference. "A series of best-selling family advice manuals authored by James Dobson frequently return to this claim that gender differences are largely immutable" (45). Assuming that women are intrinsically more verbally and emotionally expressive than men, Dobson writes, "many men ... find it difficult to match the emotions of their wives. They *cannot* be what their women want them to be. ... A leopard can't change his spots, and an unromantic, uncommunicative man simply cannot become a sensitive talker. The marital impasse is set in concrete" (quoted in Bartkowski 2001: 45). Dobson bases his claim on apparent scientific evidence: "nothing can be done to change the assignment of sex made by God at the instant of conception. That determination is carried in each cell, and it will read 'male' or 'female' from the earliest moment of life to the point of death" (quoted in Bartkowski 2001: 45).

Whether or not this claim is true depends, of course, on one's constitutive discourse. If one simply defines male and female in terms of, for instance, whether an individual has XX or XY genes, then perhaps it is true that people with XX genes will have XX genes from conception to death, and vice versa. Note, however, empirical evidence

Ideology

that such an account glaringly leaves out. First, empirical evidence shows that some humans' "sex-determining" genes are neither XX nor XY, but rather XXY or XYY, in which case the binarism assumed by Dobson does not reflect all the available evidence. Second, empirical evidence shows that some humans with XX genes grow penises and some with XY genes grow vaginas; of course, this need not contradict his claim, as he could still say that, on his definition, "women" with XX genes but penises are still "women" from birth until death. Third, empirical evidence shows that genetic codes for any particular human may not be fixed from birth to death, as they may be altered by cancerous mutations, or a person may be a "chimera"—someone whose body contains multiple genetic codes because, according to the best available evidence, some human babies appear to grow from two distinct zygotes with different DNA strands which fused at some point.

None of these is necessarily damning for Dobson's claim, but the following point arguably is (at least for anyone open-minded to consider the latest available genetic evidence). To return one more time to Jordan-Young's work in *Brain Storm* on how scientists have attempted to link masculine and feminine behaviors to brains, hormones, and genetics, consider the example with which she closes the book, designed to call into question the often-used distinction between nature and nurture. While some social critics would like to attribute all gendered behavior to nurture, while Dobson would like to attribute all gendered behavior to nature, we have substantial empirical evidence that organisms develop in ways contingent upon both. In particular, Jordan-Young draws off of a study in which biologists cloned plants and grew them at different climates and elevations from sea level. "These experiments dramatically disrupt any simple sense of genetics as a 'blueprint' for development, because the appearance of genetically identical clones was strikingly different in the distinct climates" (Jordan-Young 2010: 273). In sum, the results show that plants with identical genetic structures might grow taller than plants with a different genetic structure at one elevation but grow shorter than them at another. If genetics were straightforward blueprints, we would expect that plants with genetic codes that allow them to grow taller than other plants would function identically, independently of environment or context. For instance, if this were the case, plants with "tall" genetics would grow taller than other plants at low elevations, medium elevations, and high elevations. However, that is not the case. We have no evidence for genetic markers that make plants tall or short independently of the context in which they are grown—*what makes a plant comparatively tall at one elevation may make the same plant comparatively short at another*. Jordan-Young writes, "there is no way to arrange the plants by height that is 'environment-neutral'; the plant that is tallest at high elevation and low elevation is none of the shortest plants at medium elevation. And there is no single environment that is uniformly favorable for producing taller plants" (275). In addition, this is not unique to particular plants. "Instead, it is a general feature of development that is well recognized by developmental and evolutionary biologists" for all biological organisms (275).

Whereas Dobson attempts to draw upon the biological sciences in support of his claim, insisting that the potential for gendered behaviors is contained entirely within the genetic codes found in cells from the moment of conception to the moment of death, those very biological sciences offer strong *prima facie* evidence that demonstrates that the potential for an organism's behavior is conditioned not only by its genetic code but also by its environment, in which case it is simply not empirically demonstrable that genes directly and noncontingently determine that human's gendered behavior from conception to death. Of course, this argument depends on retroduction: the best available evidence—based on studies of plants—shows that an organism's growth and development is contingent on more than merely its genetics, and at present we have no reason not to think that the same would not be as true of human organisms as it is for other biological organisms. We cannot, however, given the social, political, and ethical strictures on scientific research, clone humans, place them in different environments, and see if their gendered behavior would differ as a result of empirically demonstrable invariant relations other than genetic codes. As a result of historically specific limits on experimental research on humans, the retroductive explanation—that an organism's growth and behavior is contingent on more than genetic factors, and that this appears to apply to humans as well as plants—is the best explanation that we can presently offer and, despite depending on theoretical and ontological assumptions we cannot test to confirm, is nevertheless empirically supported and far from arbitrary.

This is an example of ideology critique because I have attempted to demonstrate that the scientific evidences and authorities that *Dobson himself appeals to* do not warrant the conclusions he draws from them. Notably, this is not based on any direct comparison of his ideology with an unmediated reality or noncontingent knowledge of the world, but rather based on the sort of scientific evidence that his own discourse appeals to. Should new empirical evidence come to light, we might of course have to revise our claim that his view is ideological, insofar as what counts as ideology is always discourse-relative. However, once again, the fact that our knowledge is contingent is not damning to our knowledge but merely one of the many conditions of possibility for knowledge in the first place.

Consequently, my ideology critique of Dobson is not "objective" in the sense of "independent of particularity or a normative stance or a historically contingent conceptual scheme," but rather is based on historically contingent empirical claims that can be verified by subjects with competing interests willing to deploy the conceptual scheme of the biological sciences available at the beginning of the twenty-first century. Arguably, no more authority than that is necessary at any particular juncture in history, because historical subjects open to persuasion always demand to be persuaded by evidence persuasive *on their own discourses* rather than on the basis of noncontingent discourses to which they have no access—and because those not open to considering evidence contrary to their existing ideology will not be persuaded by our arguments even if we insist our knowledge ought to be viewed as authoritative because it is in some way truly objective or noncontingent.

CHAPTER 6
RECREMENT

Throughout this book I have made a series of claims about the effects of the production of discourse and ideology; specifically, I have argued (1) that discourse conditions the individuation of objects—individuation that is always historically contingent and tied to human interests—(2) that discourse is constitutive of social formations, and (3) that ideologies, although in some way epistemically unwarranted discourses, function to advance the interests of some groups over and against the interests of others. Insofar as discursive conditions are part of the causal field that make individuation, social formations, and the advancement or retardation of interests, these are all *causal* claims; the concepts of discourse and ideology are useful because they help bring into relief the *causal* relations between words and the worlds they constitute and affect. This is not, of course, to say that the causal effect of discourse is simple or straightforward. One important question we must ask is whether it is useful to say that people "believe" in their discourses or ideologies, and whether we as scholars can discern how their purported "beliefs" affect their behavior.

In the field of the academic study of religion—my institutional home—scholars have for the last few generations called into question the value of the concept of "belief" for understanding the behavior of religious practitioners. Although we sometimes fall back on a folk theory according to which people are taught or form beliefs that direct the behavior of individuals, there are a wide variety of possible problems with this folk theory. As Kevin Schilbrack notes in "Must Religious People Have Religious Beliefs" (see Schilbrack 2014: ch. 3), first, there is the problem of epistemological access to "beliefs"; while individuals might report holding beliefs, and may describe their behavior as caused by those beliefs, it is always possible that those reports are attempts at deception—and there are, as yet, no means of getting inside someone's head to see if they really believe what they say they believe (56). Second, it is possible that the emphasis on "belief" in discourses on religion reflects a Christian bias; not all of those cultural traditions we call religions emphasize that adherents to the tradition hold beliefs or cognitively accept doctrines. "Most religious communities do not give belief this privileged role" (56). A third problem, highlighted by current research in the fields of social psychology, cognitive science, and behavioral economics (some of which I will discuss below), is that there is often a large gap between the beliefs reported by subjects and their actual behaviors. A fourth problem is that an emphasis on belief in explaining a subjects' behaviors may mystify other causes behind their behaviors. For instance, in what is now a classic essay simply titled "Belief" (1998), Donald S. Lopez Jr. offers a useful example: according to Christian myth, Peter Martyr died at the hands of the Cathars because he remained committed to his Catholic beliefs, so much so that, when dying, he wrote "CREDO" (I believe) in the dirt with his finger. By contrast, Lopez argues, the people who killed him appear to have done so not because they objected to his acceptance of Catholic doctrines, but rather because he collaborated with the Spanish Inquisition to persecute and imprison some Cathar nobles and confiscate their property (see Lopez 1998: 25–27). Consequently, saying he died for his beliefs may function to mystify the actual causes for the actions under consideration.

Last, and most important for my purposes, is the fact that reporting belief appears, from an anthropological perspective, sometimes to serve social functions largely unrelated to the content of the reported beliefs. To go for one of the simplest and most obvious examples, "white lies" are shared not because they are believed by the person speaking—we offer white lies knowing that they are false—but because they serve a social function—usually avoiding a difficult conversation or possible social confrontation. Consider the following, fictional example. The NBC sitcom *Superstore* is about a group of employees at a "superstore" called "Cloud 9," which is, for all practical purposes, Wal-Mart by a different name. In the first season, the assistant manager Dina (played by Lauren Ash) develops a crush on a new employee, Jonah (played by Ben Feldman). She believes that he is equally interested in her, but her perception is based on the misinterpretation of social cues he sends her way. This crush on Jonah builds across several episodes, culminating in a confrontation that takes place in the episode "All Nighter" (Gernon 2016). In that episode, Dina confesses her love for him and shares the fact that company policy has recently changed, so that "relationships between supervisors and subordinates is now just strongly discouraged" rather than outright prohibited; Dina notes that their shared passion "is not forbidden anymore!" Jonah rhetorically stumbles in his initial response: "uh, right, yeah, uh, hmm." Eventually he formulates a partially intelligible response; "uh, but, you know, … alas, it, it, *it is discouraged*. Besides, the idea of dating my boss, oof, the sexual politics are just so nuanced. Otherwise, believe me"—at this point he gestures back and forth to her and him—"I, I, I am, I would love to do everything there is to do." Dina is crushed by this response and sets about to change her social location in relation to Jonah: she immediately goes to the manager and asks for a demotion, for "personal reasons," which he grants. In the next episode, when she invites him over to her place Jonah comes clean and admits that he doesn't feel the same way about her, despite what he previously claimed. Not surprisingly, she becomes angry that he was previously disingenuous with her.

How are we to make sense of his discourse? I would argue that it is fairly clear that when Jonah said he did not want to date his boss because the company policy "discouraged" relationships between supervisors and subordinates, he was—to put it frankly—bullshitting her. If it were true that the only reason he didn't want to date her was the company policy, then he would have started dating her once she was no longer his supervisor. Because he didn't want to fess up that he wasn't attracted to her, he blamed the company policy—blaming the policy was a way of avoiding a difficult social situation (one that he was only able to temporarily avoid). In addition, in future episodes he starts to date *another* supervisor. His behavior contradicts his discourse—it appears that he is fine breaking company policy when it serves his interests. Although this anecdote is fictional, it is a great example of a behavior that we engage in quite frequently: arguably, humans make claims all the time which they do not in fact believe because making such claims serves the interests of subjects in their social position.

There are, then, many reasons for us to doubt the folk anthropology according to which people have and report beliefs that have a direct causal relation to their behavior. In what follows, I will first consider the epistemic question: if we are to accept that people do have beliefs, how do we determine what their beliefs are? I will argue that in some cases we should distinguish between actual beliefs and beliefs that are merely reported but not actual. Second, according to social scientific research, what reasons are there for us to question a direct causal relation between reported beliefs and action, and how can this research provide us with a more sophisticated way of thinking about their possible relationship? Third, I argue that there are grounds for demonstrating that some reported beliefs are by-products of social functions, and I will offer a substantial example from E. E. Evans-Pritchard's research on witchcraft among the Azande to substantiate the functionalist argument I will present. "Recrement," the title of this chapter, is a term somewhat analogous to refuse, dross, unnecessary surplus, or leftover sediment. I will stipulate a precise definition that builds upon the argument established thus far in this book; in particular, I will use it as a technical term to pick out reported beliefs that are by-products of social functions, but which do not warrant being treated as actual beliefs having a causal relation to behavior. In the chapter's conclusion, I will suggest it might serve our interests as social critics to attend to how reported beliefs serve a number of social functions, rather than direct human behavior in the straightforward manner that the folk anthropology of belief and action assume.

Credorationalism, Reported Beliefs, and Actual Beliefs

"Credorationalism" is the term I stipulatively define as the practice of, when analyzing people's behaviors, *defaulting* to the explanation that they act the way they do because their reported beliefs direct their behavior. In those cases, the default assumption is to fall back on the folk theory that imagines a simple and uncomplicated relationship between belief and behavior. Malory Nye puts it well when he writes (in a discussion of how pointing to religious belief functions as explanations for behavior):

> What is happening here is, in fact, that this idea of belief is being used ... as an explanation. That is, religious belief becomes an explanation in itself: our absence of understanding what a person from another religion is doing or thinking leads us to fall back on our basic knowledge of their beliefs. Thus we assume that a Hindu is acting a certain way because s/he "believes" in reincarnation, and a

Muslim in another way because s/he believes in Allah. Such an explanation may or may not be correct—but what it does is rule out a number of other possible explanations.

(Nye 2008: 117)

While I, like Nye, want to reserve the right to say that sometimes actual beliefs *do* have a causal relation to a subject's behavior, I also want to argue that reported beliefs *do not always* function in that manner. In sum, when credorationalism guides analysis, it defaults to a simple explanation that may rely upon problematic assumptions that in many cases deserve serious reconsideration.

By "reported beliefs," all I refer to are the discourses distributed by subjects when asked questions like, "what do you believe/think about x?," "do you believe in God?," or the creeds they may recite in ritual contexts, such as the Nicene Creed, the American "Pledge of Allegiance," and so forth.

To distinguish "actual beliefs" from those "reported beliefs," I want to return to Kevin Schilbrack's essay on belief briefly mentioned above. There he tackles the epistemological conundrum: how do we gain access to people's actual beliefs if they may be deceitful, lying, or shading the truth—in ways that serve their interests—when they are delivering their reported beliefs? As yet there appear to be no means—scientific or otherwise—of getting inside an individual's head and identifying her beliefs. However, Schilbrack notes, contemporary philosophers have long since abandoned the idea that a belief is an invisible, mysterious thing in one's head.

> For philosophers … the concept of believing refers to holding that something is true … A belief is therefore a kind of commitment or attitude that a person takes on … Beliefs in this sense are … something that one must have in order to be an agent, and they are something that one must attribute to others if one is to see them as agents.
>
> (Schilbrack 2014: 61)

Having what social scientists call a "theory of mind" requires us to imagine that persons with whom we interact have a consciousness like we do, that they hold things to be true, and that their behavior—insofar as they recall those things they hold to be true (which they may not)—directs their behavior. For Schilbrack, "what we mean by belief need not refer to an invisible entity stashed away in the person's head, but refers instead to a pattern of activities" (Schilbrack 2014: 63). To give a trivial example, let's say that a professor misses an email reporting that class was canceled due to snow and, consequently, drives to work only to find the campus closed. We could attribute to this professor the "belief" that classes were not canceled in order to explain her behavior; if she had "believed" classes were canceled we would have expected different behavior. On this view, "beliefs" are not based on insiders' reports; rather, "attributions of beliefs are then counted as accurate to the extent one's predictions [about an individual's behavior] are satisfied" (64).

On this account, it is particularly important to consider counterfactuals when attributing belief. It could also be the case, using the same example, that the professor knew that classes were canceled but had some work she nevertheless had to accomplish despite the snow. In a case in which we had empirical evidence that she *had* checked her email but still drove to her office, we would not be justified in projecting onto her the "belief" that classes were not canceled. It could also be the case that she read the email but then forgot about it as she went about her morning routine, such that she drove to work "on autopilot," so to speak. In any particular case, a great number of variables potentially shape a subject's behavior, and we would be fully warranted in projecting an actual belief only after we had controlled for all of those possible variables.

Notably, if we define "actual beliefs" in this manner, they are open to independent verification by subjects with competing interests based on publicly available behavioral evidence. Additionally, from this perspective subjects may not even be conscious of their actual beliefs, or what they hold to be true. When we "say that a person believes something (e.g., that he believes that the earth is round), [we] do not mean that he is consciously believing this. Believing that the world is round does not mean that the idea is presently 'on one's mind'" (Schilbrack 2014: 65). As such, it could be theoretically possible to show a person (at least one who is open-minded enough to listen to what one has to say) who denies that they are racist that they are in fact racist in some manner, simply by pointing to public actions in which they treat people of different races differently and showing them that those actions appear to be based on holding as true something that is racially inflected. For instance, we need no access to the recesses of someone's consciousness to point out to them that they cross to the sidewalk on the other side of the street when they see Black people ahead but not white people. In addition, because such behavior is mutually verifiable, that person could point to competing data—perhaps there were other variables (such as holes in the sidewalk) relevant to explaining their behavior.

As always, knowledge of objects is always subject to reconsideration because of time: because, in the future, we may have new information about a particular object, we may have to update either our knowledge, or perhaps change our individuation so as to separate that object into two objects (as might be required, given our interests). This is true of what I am calling "actual beliefs" as well; as noted just above, given new data, such as pointing to the less hazardous sidewalk on the other side of the street, we would be required to revise the "actual beliefs" we are attributing to the person with whom we are interacting. What counts as a person or a group's actual beliefs would never be fully stable, but rather would always be open to revision.

On this view, a person's reported beliefs need not coincide with the actual beliefs we attribute to them, and, in addition, there are reasons to suspect these might often diverge considerably from one another. The actual beliefs we as scholars attribute to practitioners to best make sense of their independently verifiable public behavior may in many cases have nothing to do with the beliefs they report to, for example, ethnographers. "For a great deal of religious phenomena, ... *it will not matter whether religious speakers believe their discourse*" (Schilbrack 2014: 69, emphasis mine).

Discourse and Ideology

Overall, we should always avoid credorationalism; while defaulting to the view that people's reported beliefs directly cause their behavior would be simple and straightforward, we can explain a wider range of data by separating actual beliefs and reported beliefs.

Thus far in this chapter I have argued:

- credorationalism, or defaulting to assuming that people's behaviors are best explained by their reported beliefs, is a questionable strategy for scholarly analysis;
- because people's reported beliefs do not always align with their actions, it may be useful in some cases to distinguish between reported beliefs and actual beliefs;
- in those cases, we would have to define actual beliefs in terms of what we, as scholars, project onto subjects to explain their behavior, such that our claims about actual beliefs are empirical rather than based on invisible things inside people's heads; but that
- the actual beliefs we attribute to people are contingent upon the available behavioral evidence, and are thus always subject to revision should new empirical evidence come to light.

After this point, "actual beliefs" will largely drop out of my discussion, for two reasons. First, given all of the possible counterfactuals we would have to control for to attribute an actual belief to someone, we would rarely be fully warranted in attributing belief to subjects, apart from beliefs that inform how they go about the mechanics of everyday life (for instance, the belief that we should drive on the right side of the road in North America, or the belief that a credit card will stop working if we do not pay our bills). Second, those beliefs generally are not typically useful when going about the task I am attempting to accomplish in this book: trying to understand how discourses function to maintain relations of social domination. Discourses can function to encourage sympathies and antipathies in subjects without them necessarily having any actual beliefs about the reported beliefs they perpetually generate.

Social Scientific Evidence about Reported Beliefs

Social scientific research from the last half century has a great deal to teach us about human cognition and its relation to subjects' reported beliefs. The literature is massive and there is no way I could summarize all of it here. However, for my purposes, I only need to establish *prima facie* evidence that behavior often—even if not always—appears to be caused by variables other than reported beliefs, so I will consider just a few studies.[1]

In a classic article that reviews the early literature on belief and action, "Attitudes versus Actions: The Relationship of Verbal and Overt Behavioral Responses to Attitude Objects" (1969), Allan Wicker summarizes a wide variety of empirical studies that show people's "attitudes" are poor predictors of their behaviors (the term "attitude" is not identical to what I am calling "reported belief," but it is very close—it is usually defined in terms of statements people express or agree to on surveys—sufficiently so that the claims he makes about the studies of "attitudes" largely apply to what I have defined as "reported belief"). We have empirical evidence for all of the following:

- reported beliefs about jobs and job performance "have only a slight and often insignificant relationship with job performance and absences from work" (Wicker 1969: 52);
- studies of (negative) beliefs about racial minorities "reveal[] little correspondence between [attitude and behavior], and in several cases there are reversals of expected relationships" (59)—that is to say, the fact that a subject reports racist views is not a good predictor of how such a subject will interact with racial minorities in daily life; and
- students' reported beliefs about cheating are less reliable predictors of whether or not they will cheat than "the number of test questions students missed"— "subjects' motivations to improve their grades were more 'potent' than their motivations to behave honestly" (68).

Overall, attempts to connect reported beliefs to behavior often fail. The research is complicated in part by the fact that people often report beliefs that are, in some cases, competing or outright contradictory. In addition, people also exhibit a wide variety of behaviors to which the reported beliefs might be potentially connected; "there are many possible behaviors relevant to a given attitude, and if inconsistency [of reported belief and a particular behavior] is observed, it may be attributed to the failure [of the researcher] to consider other behaviors" with which the reported belief may be consistent (Wicker 1969: 68). Consequently, how can we connect a particular observed behavior to a particular reported belief, if that behavior could be caused by other actual beliefs unrelated to their reported belief? Matters are further complicated when we take into account competency: some subjects may lack the competency—namely, "verbal, intellectual, and social abilities"—to make their reported beliefs and actions cohere (68).

What are better predictors of behavior than reported beliefs? Wicker notes "that predictions of overt behavior can be made more accurately from knowledge of the situation than from knowledge of individual differences" in attitude or reported belief (Wicker 1969: 69). That is to say, the demands of the social context or the social role an individual is performing are better predictors than reported beliefs. In addition, "actual or considered presence of certain people" also appears to have a stronger correlation to behavior than reported beliefs, for instance when a "respondent may have to justify his actions or be influenced by group pressures" (69). This appears to be why "subjects, when asked to explain their behaviors, often mention their thoughts about other people who are important to them" (70). Wicker concludes his study by noting that "the present review provides little evidence to support the postulated existence of stable, underlying attitudes within the individual which influence both his verbal expressions and his actions" (75).

Discourse and Ideology

In "The Emotional Dog and Its Rational Tail: A Social Intuitionist Approach to Moral Judgment" (2001), Jonathan Haidt considers a body of empirical evidence that shows that humans have gut reactions to moral issues and appear to form justifications for those gut reactions after the fact. He begins by dismantling the assumption that moral behavior (and "moral" here is largely used in a colloquial rather than technical sense) is based on moral reasoning. He writes, "people undeniably engage in moral reasoning. But does the evidence really show that such reasoning is the cause, rather than the consequence, of moral judgment" (817)? He cites a study that looked at people's views on abortion and found that those who opposed abortion offered reasons suggesting possible harm to the fetus, which they viewed as a living person, while those who supported abortion tended to assume that "life begins later" (817). The study seemed to suggest that subjects' views about life directed their view on abortion, but Haidt objects:

> in making this interpretation ... [the authors] made a jump from correlation to causation. The correlation they found between judgment and supporting belief does not necessarily mean that the belief caused the judgment. [An alternative] interpretation is just as plausible: The anti-abortion judgment (a gut feeling that abortion is bad) causes the belief that life begins at conception (an ex post facto rationalization of the gut feeling).
>
> (Haidt 2001: 817)

Since correlation is not causation, the intuition about whether abortion is good or bad may not be caused by their beliefs about life; rather, their beliefs about life may be caused by their prior intuition.

On Woodward's definition of causation—discussed in Chapter 5 of this book—it might be possible to produce evidence regarding the relation of dependence across the correlating empirical evidences. And indeed, Haidt produces evidence in support of his claim that it appears that reported belief appears to be, in many cases, caused by intuition rather than vice versa. He cites a study in which people were asked about possibly offensive but seemingly materially harmless actions, "such as eating one's dead pet dog, [or] cleaning one's toilet with the national flag" (Haidt 2001: 817).

> The stories were carefully constructed so that no plausible harm could be found, and most participants directly stated that nobody was hurt by the actions in question, yet participants still usually said the actions were wrong, and universally wrong. They frequently made statements such as, "It's just wrong to have sex with a chicken." Furthermore, their affective reactions to the stories (statements that it would bother them to witness the action) were better predictors of their moral judgments than were their claims about harmful consequences.
>
> (Haidt 2001: 817)

In this case, "affective reactions were good predictors of judgment, whereas perceptions of harmfulness were not" (Haidt 2001: 817). By manipulating the questions asked—posing questions where participants *couldn't* appeal to reasons relating to harm—researchers were able to solicit negative affective reactions that correlated with negative moral judgments, but without a correlation between reasons about harm and moral judgments. Another, similar study, "found that participants were often 'morally dumbfounded' … that is, they would stutter, laugh, and express surprise at their inability to find supporting reasons, yet they would not change their initial judgments of condemnation" (817).

Not only did these studies find little correlation (and hence no causation) between moral reasoning and moral judgment, but—in addition—other studies show that moral judgments are offered instantaneously, without the opportunity for subjects to have found reasons for their judgments. "Commentators on intuition have generally stressed the fact that a judgment, solution, or other conclusion appears suddenly and effortlessly in consciousness, without any awareness by the person of the mental processes that led to the outcome" (Haidt 2001: 818). Intuition, the studies demonstrate, happens immediately, whereas reasoning developed to support, justify, or legitimate the intuition "occurs more slowly, requires some effort, and involves at least some steps that are accessible to consciousness" (818).

Further evidence against the priority of reason over intuition is the fact that, when challenged, some people bring up irrelevant evidence. People "frequently cite factors that could not have mattered and fail to recognize factors that did matter" (Haidt 2001: 822). One study, for instance,

> asked participants to take electric shocks, either with or without a placebo pill that was said to produce the same symptoms as electric shock. Participants in the pill condition apparently attributed their heart palpitations and butterflies in the stomach to the pill and were able to take four times as much shock as those who had no such misattribution available for their symptoms. However, when the placebo condition participants were asked if they had made such an attribution, only 25% of them said that they had. The remaining participants denied that they had thought about the pill and instead made up a variety of explanations for their greater shock tolerance, such as, "Well, I used to build radios and stuff when I was 13 or 14, and maybe I got used to electric shock."
>
> (Haidt 2001: 822)

That is to say: the reasons offered for their reported physical experiences, by all accounts, could not have been the reasons for those experiences. When that was pointed out to them, their explanation for their reported physical experience changed. The conclusion? "Such causal explanations [are] post hoc constructions" (Haidt 2001: 822). Humans, the empirical evidence shows, apparently suffer from what Haidt calls the "*wag-the-dog illusion*: We believe that our own moral judgment (the dog) is driven by our own moral reasoning (the tail)" (823) but the tail is the recrement, not the cause.

Moral reasoning, in many if not all cases, thus appears to be derivative in relationship to instantaneous intuition. Haidt compares moral reasons to the arguments given by

Discourse and Ideology

lawyers in defense of their clients; first they find out what conclusion their client needs them to reach, and then they come up with arguments in support of that conclusion. Empirical evidence shows that those arguments correlate with particular social demands: perhaps they need to justify a conclusion they have already committed to and are unwilling to back away from without losing face, perhaps it serves their interests to persuade others to accept their judgment, or perhaps they need to appear to be consistent and hence need to overcome a contradiction or tension between the present judgment and prior reported beliefs or claims they have made.

Of course, this does not tell us from where humans get their intuitions in the first place. Haidt mentions a couple of possible sources, biological and social. On the one hand, research done by scholars such as Frans de Waal demonstrates that even nonhuman primates show some moral intuitions about fairness that do not appear to be the result of learning or socialization, which suggests evolution may have predisposed some mammals to certain sorts of gut reactions to some types of unequal treatment (Haidt 2001: 826). Socialization may, by contrast, be more important for understanding intuitions and gut reactions. Evidence for this includes the seemingly obvious cross-cultural disparities about what counts as tasty cuisine or disgusting food. Much of what we, as humans, take to be disgusting depends on socialization, which is why one person's "escargot" is another person's "slimy snails."

While Haidt does not deny that people reason, and that sometimes they discipline themselves such that their behavior coheres with the forms of reasoning they develop, it is by no means evident that reasons have a temporal or logical priority in relationship to our moral intuitions or judgments. On the contrary, since this sort of social scientific research began, a wide variety of studies in social psychology, cognitive science, and behavioral economics have shown that humans are widely "irrational," in the sense that many of the behaviors they exhibit appear to correlate with or be caused by factors other than logical arguments, reported beliefs, or desired goals.

What does any of this have to do with the distinction between reported belief and actual belief? It appears that humans are cognitively predisposed to offer reported beliefs without reflection, based on gut reactions that follow from evolutionary predispositions or forms of socialization. However, there may be no substantial thought process or actual belief behind the reported belief. People are willing to say that it is obviously wrong to wipe one's toilet with the national flag but may have no actual beliefs regarding why that is the case. Indeed, they may not have ever actually "believed" anything at all about the matter prior to when the social scientist provoked the gut reaction or intuition. Consequently, there are reasons to suggest that humans are willing to report beliefs without any prior thought about them. The causes of behavior, and the causes that make subjects report beliefs, might often be found elsewhere than in what I am defining as actual beliefs.

In his later work, Haidt expands on this research by noting that, in general, reason appears to be a slave to the passions, and those passions are in some cases tied to accomplishing something socially. "Moral talk serves a variety of strategic purposes such as managing your reputation, building alliances, and recruiting bystanders to support your side in the disputes that are so common in daily life" (Haidt 2013: 55). In these cases, moral reasoning is tied to social influence:

> other people influence us constantly just by revealing that they like or dislike somebody ... Many of us believe that we follow an inner moral compass, but the history of social psychology richly demonstrates that other people exert a powerful force, able to make cruelty seem acceptable and altruism embarrassing, without giving us any reasons or arguments.
>
> (Haidt 2013: 56)

That is to say: our reported beliefs may be a means of manipulating our social standing, may be based on immediate intuition about how our interests are served in the immediate social context, and may have no relationship to actual belief or any substantial thought. "Intuitions come first, *strategic* reasoning second" (Haidt 2013: 59, emphasis mine). It is quite possible that in some cases, neither intuitions nor strategic reasoning—namely, reporting beliefs to strategically influence one's peers—bear a relationship to actual beliefs.

The last study directly relevant to my argument that I would like to consider is John T. Jost and Mahzarin R. Banaji's work on system justification in "The role of stereotyping in system-justification and the production of false consciousness" (Jost and Banaji 1994). My review of Haidt's studies may leave us with the impression that people's reported beliefs are always primarily strategic and self-serving; perhaps racists report "I'm not racist" because they intuitively grasp that such reports assist them in managing their reputation before a particular audience. However, this picture is complicated by Jost and Banaji, who demonstrate that people often produce justifications for exploitative or asymmetrical social relations, justifications that "explain the poverty or powerlessness of some groups and the success of others in ways that make these differences seem legitimate and even natural," *even when they are among the impoverished or powerless* (10).

Jost and Banaji begin by noting that psychologists have long argued that there is evidence that people produce self-serving stereotypes in the service of ego-justification and group-justification. That is, people produce stereotypes about themselves, their groups, and other groups to defensively justify their individual or group's agenda or behaviors. In societies marked by racialized class divisions, the stereotype that Black people are lazy may be required for whites to justify the social standing of whites over Blacks. However, in many cases *members of dominated classes* produce or reproduce negative stereotypes *about themselves* even when doing so is not obviously self-serving. In those cases, Jost and Banaji hypothesize, the stereotypes produced may be motivated by a desire to justify the social system as a whole, perhaps because to recognize the "insidiousness of the system" would produce unbearable cognitive dissonance (Jost and Banaji 1994: 16). "Somewhat paradoxically, it may be that the more painful, humiliating, or unfair a system is, the more it evokes the system-justification response, as cognitive dissonance researchers found when investigating the effects of initiation rites" (16). It appears that "people will form negative ideas about themselves in order to make sense of social reality" (13). It appears that in some cases people "would rather blame themselves for their plight than admit that the world in which they live is 'capricious and unfair'" (14). Consequently, "under some circumstances, stereotypes that serve to justify an existing state of affairs will operate *at the expense of individual or collective self-interest*" (3, emphasis mine)—hence their use of the term "false consciousness" to describe such justifications. Whereas critical theorists usually insist that ideologies are produced *because* they are self-serving, it is possible that the "belief in a just world" might be a "natural, universal motivation" (14).

The empirical evidence Jost and Banaji provide—drawing on a wide variety of studies—includes the following:

- studies have shown that "people will ascribe to themselves and others traits which are consonant with their social position, whether positive or negative, rather than question the order or legitimacy of the system which produced such an arrangement or outcome" (Jost and Banaji 1994: 11);
- this holds "even when subjects know that the arrangements or outcomes were arrived at arbitrarily and result in negative consequences for them" (11);
- in some circumstances, the false attribution of empirically unjustified stereotypes persists "even when subjects judge their *own* [group's] abilities" (13);
- in some cases, "the powerful are stereotyped, even by the powerless, in such a way that their success is explained or justified; meanwhile, the powerless are stereotyped (and self-stereotyped) in such a way that their plight is well-deserved and similarly justified" (13); although
- once internalized, through the process of socialization, such justificatory ideologies may begin to have a causal influence on an individual's or group's behavior; evidence shows that "stigmatized groups may begin to act in such a way that other people's negative expectations of them are supported, thereby ensuring their continued subordination"—for instance, one study found that "white interviewers' stereotypic expectations about black job applicants evoked nervous behaviour and poor performance on the part of the black respondents" (17).

Jost and Banaji also note that these justifications are likely intuitively and unconsciously produced; people may not be aware that they are producing justifications, or may not be aware that the justifications serve a possible psychological function for them. However, the fact that system justification possibly serves a psychological function does not mean that justifications are produced by "individual motivations"; rather, they "argue for a system-justification view of stereotyping whereby the attribution of role-specific traits arises *not* out of individual motivations *but* results from information processing in an ideological environment" (Jost and Banaji 1994: 4, emphasis mine). That is to say, if people living under conditions of poverty reproduce the stereotype that poor people are lazy, that is possible only on condition of there being objective class differences and having access to previously circulating justificatory ideologies. Jost and Banaji's point seems to be the same as the one made by Karl Marx and Friedrich Engels in *The German Ideology*: material conditions are the foundation of thought (see Marx and Engels 1978: 163–175). Stereotypes that function as system-justifications arise "from objective, material factors including divisions of labour and social practice rather than, for example, as ideas prior to or independent of material forces in society" (Jost and Banaji 1994: 17). Such an approach does not explain human "practice from [ideas] but explains the formation of ideas from material practice" (Marx and Engels 1978: 164). All of that is to say: perhaps Haidt is correct that reported beliefs are, at times, the product of self-serving intuitions about how to manage one's public image, but perhaps reported beliefs are, at other times, the result of false consciousness, or the unreflective internalization of dominant ideologies, even when those ideologies harm rather than serve one's group's interests—possibly because some humans are psychologically incapable of accepting that the world is tragically unfair. In addition, as I argued in the chapter on domination, no one is omniscient about what serves their interests; perhaps some members of disadvantaged groups accept the myth of meritocracy simply because no other frame of interpretation for understanding failure and success is culturally or cognitively accessible (no one can think with ideas they have not yet been exposed to), in which case they might assume that those who fail to succeed must be individually responsible for their own fates.

I hesitate to endorse Jost and Banaji's psychological explanation for why dominated subjects might reproduce negative stereotypes about their own group—that is, that they possibly suffer from an inability to accept that the world could be unfair. While I would not like to rule out that explanation, I suspect that, on the one hand, dominated subjects are more likely to consume and reproduce the myth of meritocracy because few other frames of interpretation are readily available, or, on the other hand, dominated subjects might report negative stereotypes about members of their own group because, in some cases, they intuit that doing so might serve their individual (rather than group) interests. For instance, some variables Jost and Banaji do not explicitly consider but that might be relevant here are raised by Paula Ioanide in "'Obama Say Blacks Should Just Work Harder; Isn't That Right?': The Myth of Meritocracy" (2018). As Ioanide notes, regarding the US context, insofar as racial minorities have been systematically "blamed and demonized" for the last several decades, "some people of color invest in notions of hard work, merit, and personal responsibility *in order to disassociate themselves* from these negative stereotypes" (66–67, emphasis mine). Racial minorities might report negative stereotypes about other racial minorities not because they cannot believe that the world is unfair, but because reporting the negative stereotype puts them, as individuals, on the right side of the stereotype. In addition,

> at times people of color who obtain middle- and upper-class status through education, entrepreneurship, or employment also adopt the rhetoric of blaming poor people of color for their class status and begin advocating the myth of

> meritocracy and hard work. They offer their experiences as "proof" of other people's unwillingness to pursue opportunities. … [S]uch views often minimize the number of systemic obstacles poor people of color would have to overcome to reach economic ascendance *as a group*.
>
> (Ioanide 2018: 67)

That is to say, they may report stereotypes about unsuccessful people of color because they fail to see that their own success may be exceptional rather than exemplary; once again, if the myth of meritocracy is the only frame of interpretation for understanding failure and success they have been socialized to accept, it would be difficult for them to interpret their own success in any other terms. Last, "middle- and upper-class people of color may also advocate notions of meritocracy and hard work in order to obtain or preserve higher positions of power. Such positions, particularly if they are situated in predominantly White institutions, often require that people of color adopt the values, rhetoric, and practices of those institutions" (Ioanide 2018: 67). If adopting white people's stereotypes helped certain minorities gain access to some of the privileges whites enjoy, they may encourage other minorities to publicly endorse those stereotypes as well. Ioanide notes that conservative Black public figures such as "former Secretary of State Condeleezza Rice or Justice Clarence Thomas" likely could not have "gained entry into such high governmental and judicial positions had they made public critiques of institutional racism in the United States" (67).

Similarly, in *Race to the Bottom: How Racial Appeals Work in American Politics* (2020), LaFleur Stephens-Dougan describes what she calls "racial distancing": a rhetorical gesture sometimes used by African American politicians to attract white voters. Racial distancing is "an effective way of communicating to [both] racially moderate [and] racially conservative whites … that they will not disrupt the status quo" (7). This is why, she hypothesizes, that Barack Obama publicly denigrated absentee Black fathers and used racially charged words such as "thug"—"a nominally polite way of using the N-word" (2). "If the nation's first black president felt compelled, or at the very least incentivized, to espouse some of the worst stereotypes about black people to get elected, then it is indicative of the constraints black candidates face when discussing race" (6). In any case, if members of dominated classes reproduce negative stereotypes about their own class, it might not result from a psychological inability to accept an unjust world or a failure to manage cognitive dissonance about unfair social systems, as Jost and Banaji hypothesize; rather, such reports might provide short-term benefits to relatively privileged minorities who want to distinguish themselves from less-privileged minorities, or who are required, for their immediate political agendas to be advanced, to reproduce negative stereotypes about their own group. Existential angst might be less useful for explaining their use of negative stereotypes than the demands of their immediate material context. (In the next chapter I will look at several examples of African Americans who produce conservative propaganda designed to blame African Americans for their subordinated status in the United States.)

In this section, I have argued the following:

- social scientific research provides us with evidence that subjects report beliefs or moral judgments without any prior conscious thought to support them;
- intuitions about such matters are formed effortlessly, and reasons or reported beliefs generated to support them appear, in many cases, to be *post facto* productions—often intuitively designed, apparently strategically, to improve one's immediate social standing; however,
- unreflective intuitions and reports may reflect negatively rather than positively on an individual or their group membership, perhaps because of an innate desire to accept that the world is ultimately just in some manner or to justify the social system as a whole; however,
- individuals may also produce negative stereotypes about groups of which they are members if such reports are in some way useful for distancing themselves from others within their groups; consequently
- the causes of a person's behavior or belief reports might in some cases be better accounted for by something other than credorationalism or the assumption that their reported beliefs and actions followed directly from their actual beliefs.

Social Scientific Explanation, Functionalism, and Recrement

What I am calling recrement is similar in many ways to the *post facto* rationalizations invented by the participants in some of these social scientific studies; as I am defining recrement, the discourses humans produce sometimes follow from something other than an already formed set of actual beliefs. Arguably, some of Haidt's conclusions about moral reasoning are functional in precisely the same way I am arguing recrement are functional; in particular, when challenged by others, people may be required by social expectations to offer reasons to justify to others the judgment they have just made—in these cases the moral reasoning may function to fulfill a social demand or reduce psychological tension produced by cognitive dissonance generated by the moral confrontation. I would like to focus, however, on a very specific kind of social function: the function of reporting beliefs to sanction identity claims or social behaviors of which a subject approves or disapproves.

Before turning to a consideration of such a function, I need to say a few words about functionalism and social scientific explanation. What does it mean for something in society serves a social function? The language of functionalism derives from early sociology, when sociologists used the metaphor of a body with organs to explain how society is sustained over time. Just as human hearts, lungs, and livers evolved to serve particular organic functions in human organisms—to pump blood, exchange oxygen and carbon dioxide, and filter toxins—perhaps different "organs" of society evolved to keep society alive, metaphorically speaking. Religion, many early sociological theorists argued, functioned to reinforce social solidarity. Why don't groups disintegrate? Perhaps because religious rituals produce a feeling of "collective effervescence" in group members, which binds them together by making them feel a part of a unified whole (see Durkheim [1912] 2001: esp. ch. 7). As Richard W. Miller notes in *Fact and Method: Explanation, Confirmation, and Reality in the Natural and Social Sciences* (1987), such "explanations of a social phenomenon appeal to its tendency to benefit a larger system in a certain way" (119).

The problem, however, is that sociologists were unable to provide a causal account of just how religion evolved to fulfill such a function. Charles Darwin, by contrast, provided a causal account of how organisms could evolve in such a manner: a theory of random mutation and natural selection permitted post-Darwinian biologists to account for how organs might evolve to provide certain organisms with a competitive advantage. Miller notes, "modern biologists, in saying that the opposing thumb evolved in humans because of its function in using tools" are able to offer at least a "sketch" of a causal account of how that could happen, including reference to "differential survival rates and natural selection," even if biologists cannot give a step-by-step historical account of every random mutation along the way (Miller 1987: 119). Unfortunately, when it came to offering a causal account of how a social "organ" such as religion evolved to serve the function of reinforcing social solidarity, sociologists were unable to provide any sort of persuasive argument. Their answers to the question about how religion could evolve in such a manner were "mysterious" (119) and, I would argue, no better than pre-Darwinian explanations that accounted for organs and organisms by appealing to a divine, intelligent designer—that is, their explanations were magical rather than explanatory. Sociologists couldn't even develop a "sketch," as Miller puts it, of such an evolutionary transition. If we want to avoid this problem, we must be precise about what we mean when employing functionalist arguments, particularly regarding the necessity for empirical evidence for our causal account of how functions operate.[2]

Here I want to turn to Mary Douglas, arguably the most important anthropologist of the twentieth century. In her brilliant treatise, *How Institutions Think*, she offers a precise definition of functionalism designed to avoid the errors of prior generations of anthropologists. Drawing on the work of the critic of functionalism, Jon Elster, she suggests that he appropriately sets the bar for what a functionalist explanation must demonstrate for it to be persuasive. To demonstrate that some form of culture (X) serves a function (Y) for a group (Z), the following conditions must be met:

1. Y is an effect of X;
2. Y is beneficial for Z;
3. Y is *unintended* by the actions producing X;
4. Y or the causal relationship between X and Y is *unrecognized* by actors in Z; and
5. Y maintains X by a causal *feedback loop* passing through Z.

(Douglas 1986: 33, emphasis mine)

There are two key parts to this definition worth drawing attention to. The first key part is that the social function is *neither intended nor recognized* by the members of the group. Putting a flag up in one's front yard in the United States serves the function of signaling to others one's national identity and perhaps pride in that identity, but when pointing that out one would not be making a functionalist argument of the sort Douglas is discussing, because those who do so are generally aware, at some level, of what they are doing. Scholars perhaps arguably add nothing substantially new with such an analysis. In those cases, scholars are perhaps merely *describing*, neither adding to *explanatory* knowledge nor advancing a deeper understanding of the action. (Below I will argue that things are not so simple: the fact that some subjects perform behaviors to *knowingly* do something that serves a social function in no way negates the fact that they are engaging in behaviors that serve a social function. I suspect that the early European anthropologists' attachment to the idea that the social functions of the "primitive cultures" they studied *must be unconscious* was tied to their desire to depict those they studied as stupid and unaware. By contrast, I think those who produce the most sophisticated ideologies are often quite well aware of what they are doing when they produce ideology.)

The second key part is the necessity to demonstrate that the form of culture under consideration is both caused by and an effect of the functional loop. It is all well and good to say, for instance, that religion functions to bind people together in a community, and that religion was therefore caused to produce that effect, *but then one must demonstrate the feedback loop or actual mechanism by which religion is caused to serve that need*. As Douglas notes, far too often, step 5 above was completed with little more than "rhetorical arm waving" (Douglas 1986: 34).

Rather, the sort of case that successfully fits the definition of functionalism she has outlined would be more like an example that Douglas draws from the work of Robert Merton. She writes,

> Merton describes a community that holds the purse strings of educational funds and believes in the mental inferiority of blacks. Their belief justifies them in withholding schooling from black families, and they are naively delighted when the scholarships won by their own children confirm their belief, justify their allocations, and maintain their control.
>
> (Douglas 1986: 42)

To spell out how this case fits the model:

1. The advantages (Y) that accrue to whites over Blacks in the community is—in part—an effect of the widespread belief in the mental inferiority of Blacks (X);
2. those advantages (Y) are beneficial for whites (Z);
3. those advantages (Y) are not consciously intended by the widespread acceptance by whites of the mental inferiority of Blacks (X);

4. those advantages (Y) or the causal relationship between the widespread belief (X) and those advantages (Y) is unrecognized by the whites (Z) in the community; and
5. those advantages (Y) maintain the belief in the inferiority of Blacks (X) by a causal feedback loop whereby whites (Z) deny Blacks the advantage of access to education, which in turn produces evidence that appears to confirm the widespread belief.

Here, the two key parts of this definition of functionalism are respected. First, if it were obvious to whites that Blacks were "mentally inferior" *as a result of* denying them access to the forms of education available to whites, then this wouldn't be a social function so much as direct, intentional oppression. The belief in Black inferiority serves this social function on this definition *only if* some whites are to some extent unconscious of what is going on. Second, the argument specifies a mechanism that closes the feedback loop that runs from (1) a form of culture that has a causal effect to (2) a demonstration of how that effect benefits some group, and then to (3) a demonstration of how that effect causes the form of culture that started the feedback loop. In this case, the widespread belief causes an advantage, that advantage benefits whites, but then that advantage causes the widespread belief that initiated the circle. Consequently, we don't have to take the anthropologist's or sociologist's word for it (or their "rhetorical arm waving"); rather, they must—if the argument is to be persuasive—provide intersubjectively verifiable empirical evidence for the mechanism and the feedback loop that causes it.

Having established that it is theoretically possible to provide empirical evidence for such a social function and its feedback loop, I want to turn to the main argument of this chapter: the production of some reported beliefs can serve a social function within particular communities and, as such, those discourses are misunderstood when interpreted by scholars as reflecting actual beliefs that have a causal relation to community members' behaviors. In these cases, those reported beliefs are better understood as recrement, by-products of the social functions they serve, rather than actual beliefs.

There is, however, one crucial difference between the classic view of functionalism and my own: on my definition, recrement need not be unintended or unrecognized. While it seems clear that many people report beliefs in a self-serving manner and without a great deal of reflection, I would argue that many people know exactly what they are doing when they produce recrement. For instance, some people produce and share political propaganda without knowing it is propaganda, while some people produce and share it knowing full well it is propaganda, but they knowingly do so precisely because it serves their interests. Whether recrement is knowingly or unknowingly produced is largely beside the point for my purposes.

Modifying Douglas and Elster's definition of functionism, on my view to successfully demonstrate that a form of discourse is recrement, one would have to demonstrate the following:

1. a form of discourse I am calling recrement (R) serves a particular social function (F);

2. the social function operates in a way that allows members of a group (G) to accomplish something that, to them, is useful to subjects in their particular social position;
3. members of the group (G) *knowingly or unknowingly* produce recrement (R) for the purpose of serving that social function (F);
4. the fact that recrement (R) serves that function (F) *may or may not be unrecognized* by members of the group (G); and
5. there are conditions under which members of the group (G) unconsciously learn how to use the relevant recrement (R) to accomplish the particular social function under consideration (F)—or, to put it otherwise, in their community they develop what Pierre Bourdieu calls a "practical sense" about how to use recrement.

To offer a quick gloss on the concept of a "practical sense," Bourdieu uses the term to refer to the everyday "know-how" that subjects develop about how to interact daily with others (see, for instance, Bourdieu 1990). When someone reaches out their right hand with fingers extended—their palm facing their left—this means that they expect you to reciprocate and "shake hands" in greeting; this is likely part of the practical sense of most of my readers. It functions largely unconsciously, because we are socialized so that it becomes second nature. This example is bodily, but it is clear that humans also develop a discursive practical sense, in that they develop an ability to intuit whether claims being made will reflect positively or negatively on them, a group they are a part of, or a group they sympathize with. After spending a decade reading and teaching about race and the myth of meritocracy in the United States, I have developed a relatively sensitive discursive practical sense that permits me to intuit an individual's apparent sympathies and antipathies: certain key words or phrases, such as "personal responsibility," talk of "absent fathers" or "Black on Black crime," appeals to "color-blindness," criticisms of "unearned handouts," or concerns about "political correctness" are often—although not always—likely to be bound up with other claims that function to discourage sympathy with impoverished African Americans. These sorts of discursive markers function as red flags that trigger my intuitions about where a conversation might be headed. It is usually not difficult for invested subjects to develop just such a discursive practical sense after even a little bit of familiarity with popular rhetoric on race in the United States (although, as should be clear, people with different investments than I may find their intuitive, discursive practical sense triggered by different phrases, such as talk about "open-mindedness," "tolerance," "white privilege," or "safe spaces").

Regarding the two crucial parts of Douglas's definition of functionalism: my approach respects the demand to offer an account of the specific mechanisms by which social effects are connected to their causes, and their causes to prior effects (here I specify that mechanism is the development of an intuitive, discursive practical sense of how to navigate common social situations in ways that serve one's interests), but I ignore her insistence that social functions must be unrecognized by those who take advantage of the function of recrement—for people often know exactly why they produce bullshit.

Discourse and Ideology

The social functions of recrement that can be explained by this sort of argument are limited to a rather narrow set of social signals (at least on my defense; others might wish to expand the argument to include other social functions). In particular, I am thinking of forms of discourse that function to permit subjects to perform the following sorts of social work:

- to encourage sympathies or antipathies toward an individual or group;
- to sanction (admonish or praise) or assign a value (positive or negative) to another form of discourse, a set of behaviors, or a particular subject (potentially including themselves);
- to signal virtue;
- to signal shared identity or opposing identity;
- to attempt to relegate a subject to the center or margins of the group; or
- to justify the status quo.

The claim that people produce recrement in response to social situations or social demands would be consistent with Wicker's finding that "predictions of overt behavior can be made more accurately from knowledge of the situation than from knowledge of individual differences" in attitude or reported belief (Wicker 1969: 69). That is to say, we may better predict a person's behavior by attending to what the immediate social situation or social role demands of them than pointing to the beliefs they previously reported.

To offer a straightforward and, I hope, relatively uncontroversial example, consider those American evangelical Christians who report believing that the Bible is literally true in all respects. For those who report such a belief, it is almost certainly not an actual belief, as is usually confirmed, when challenged, by the very people who say such things in the first place. For instance, I once had a student who told me that she (and the people from her church) believed that the Bible was not only inerrant but also *literally true in all respects*. I followed up by asking her if she interpreted literally those passages in the New Testament in which Jesus refers to himself as the "bread of life"—is Jesus a baked good? When Jesus said you should become a eunuch for the Kingdom of God, do the members of your church take this to mean men should literally castrate themselves, as opposed to—for instance—metaphorically becoming eunuchs by devoting themselves to celibacy in their dedication to the mission of the church? It did not take long for her to back away from the claim—*prima facie* evidence that she had not actually given any substantial thought to this point prior to the moment I provoked the response—and for her to admit that they took some but not all of the Bible "literally." I would argue that, for her, the initial claim that she and the members of her church interpreted the Bible literally in all respects was actually recrement that functioned in the following manner:

1. this reported belief or recrement functioned to signal, rhetorically, her church's distance from and moral superiority to more liberal forms of Christianity;

2. the social function operates in a way that allows members of her group to accomplish something that, to them, is useful (attempting to establish their superiority);
3. I do not think she would have made that claim if she did not want to signal moral social distance or moral superiority in the first place—that is, the recrement was produced, likely unknowingly, for that particular purpose, not because it reported an actual belief held;
4. the fact that recrement can serve such social ends is probably largely or wholly unrecognized by the members of the church to which she belongs (although it is quite possible that some members of the church fully understand that this is in a way a type of virtue signaling—even sociologists are evangelicals on occasion); and
5. what makes this all possible is that she is surrounded by people who have developed a practical sense whereby they reliably know how to use recrement to signal social distance or moral superiority in just such a manner, even though they literally do not actually believe the recrement or reported belief shared.

I can think of a wide variety of other possible examples. Conservative evangelicals often claim that their god is all-powerful and can heal any injury or disease, and yet I have never heard one pray to ask their god to heal an amputee—perhaps their actual belief is that "amputated limbs cannot be healed according to all available evidence," in which case "God can heal anything" might just be something people say in their community to signal group membership. Similarly, many conservative evangelicals publicly support capital punishment for first degree murder and simultaneously report that "abortion is murder," but in my experience when asked "what should happen to such women who obtain abortions," I have yet to come across an evangelical who takes those two claims to their logical conclusion—that is, that we should execute women who get abortions. In this case, perhaps "abortion is murder" is not something they actually believe, but something they say to signal their group's moral superiority.

Much like the evidence offered in Haidt's work above, subjects are capable of offering reported beliefs or judgments on the spot, without prior thought, on the basis of an intuition or gut reaction. From where do these intuitions or gut reactions come? Haidt identified two primary sources: biological and social. Since it is unlikely that humans have any biological predispositions to make claims about the literal truth of the Bible, it is much more likely that this student's response was based on socialization. And, in fact, it would likely not be difficult to empirically demonstrate that she was situated in a social context in which she regularly heard the words "inerrant" and "literal" repeated over and over again with a positive valuation attached to them, as well as hearing them used in ways directly tied to the group's very self-identity. She would not have had to think about or form any actual beliefs about what it means to say that all of the Bible is literally true for her to develop the cognitive association, one which she was able to draw upon easily and without reflection in her conversation with me, even though she immediately went on to abandon it. The fact that she immediately abandoned it is, I would argue,

Discourse and Ideology

evidence that the reported belief was based on an unreflective intuition. It appears that she didn't really believe the belief she said she believed. Credorationalism, in such cases, is an inferior explanation—given the existing empirical evidence—compared to the claim that this reported belief was merely recrement.

In this section, I have argued:

- reporting beliefs in some cases may serve a social function rather than reflect a previously existing actual belief held by the relevant subject;
- such beliefs are, in those cases, recrement or by-products of the social function rather than truthful reports of beliefs previously actually held by the subject;
- this may very well be the case when the reported beliefs distributed by a subject appear to function in a way that signals social distance, social or moral approval or approbation, etc.;
- it does not matter, on this approach, whether or not a subject is consciously aware that they are producing recrement when doing so;
- the claim that some reported belief is merely recrement is bolstered when we can offer *prima facie* evidence that subjects do not actually believe their reported beliefs;
- in those cases, the claim that some reported belief is recrement is a superior explanation of what generated the discursive claim than credorationalism.

Human animals are, arguably, *invested echo machines*; we systematically repeat what we have heard others say, but never at random: we tend to repeat what we have heard others say when we intuit that saying those things served their interests or sympathies—precisely because repeating those claims might similarly help us serve our own interests or sympathies—even in cases in which we don't actually believe the claims we echo.

Witchcraft, Moral Valuation, and Recrement among the Azande

Now I would like to turn to a more substantial example that, I will argue, supports the claim that some reported beliefs perhaps ought to be regarded as recrement. In E. E. Evans-Pritchard's magisterial *Witchcraft, Oracles, and Magic among the Azande* (1976), readers are introduced to the magical practices of a kinship tribe from the Sudan (Evans-Pritchard's fieldwork dates to the first half of the twentieth century; I am aware of no evidence that the following practices and reported beliefs are still regnant in the Sudan, so I imply no claims about contemporary Sudanese culture). During his time with the Azande, Evans-Pritchard observed a community that reported witches lived among them. According to the Azande, what made someone a witch was a material yet magical substance that existed in their belly, which gave them supernatural powers to affect the lives of their neighbors. According to Zande reports, "it is attached to the edge of the liver. When people cut open the belly they have only to pierce it and witchcraft-substance bursts through with a pop" (2). Most types of misfortune were attributed to the witches in their midst. If one's house caught on fire, it must have been caused by a witch. If one's crop did not grow, it must be because of a witch's curse.

Notably, Evans-Pritchard insists that by no means did the Azande deny the existence of immediate efficient causes that brought about the misfortune. Of course, one's barn cannot fall down without, for instance, termites having eaten away at the supports. The question for the Azande was, however, what caused the termites to eat the supports in the first place? "Zande philosophy can supply the missing link. The Zande knows that the supports were undermined by termites ... But he knows besides why [this event] occurred at precisely ... [this] moment in time and space. It was due to the action of witchcraft" (Evans-Pritchard 1976: 23).

When misfortune falls, a Zande has at his disposal an elaborate social system for figuring out which witch cursed him, and how to rectify the situation so that he is no longer cursed. The details are not central to my account, so I will gloss over them here, but in sum they involve attending to a witch doctor, participating in an oracle to determine which witch cursed the Zande, and approaching the witch via an intermediary with a ritual designed to appease tension so as to invite future peaceful relations. Evans-Pritchard offers an incomplete functional explanation for the practice, suggesting that the whole system appears to function to reduce tension in the community.

> It is ... to the interest of both parties that they should not become estranged through the incident. They have to live together as neighbors afterwards and to cooperate in the life of the community. It is also to their mutual advantage to avoid all appearance of anger or resentment for a more direct and immediate reason. The whole point of the procedure is to put the witch in a good temper by being polite to him. The witch on his part ought to feel grateful to the people who have warned him so politely of the danger in which he stands.
>
> (Evans-Pritchard 1976: 43)

Overall, the resulting effect seems to "eliminate[e] friction" within the community (Evans-Pritchard 1976: 43). I say this is an *incomplete* functionalist analysis, because Evans-Pritchard never supplies an account of any feedback loop or mechanism whereby the function causes the belief in witchcraft in the first place (that is not to say such an account could not be given—only that he does not provide one). In any case, what is particularly important for my purposes is not this social function, but another.

When Evans-Pritchard turns to discussing who is most likely to be called a witch, he notes that it is almost always (1) someone socially proximate to the man who considers himself bewitched and (2) someone toward whom an enmity already exists. Evans-Pritchard writes:

> since accusations of witchcraft arise from personal enmities it will at once be seen why certain people are left out of consideration ... People do not accuse nobles and seldom accuse influential commoners of witchcraft, not merely because it

Discourse and Ideology

> would be inadvisable to insult them but also because their social contact with these people is limited to situations in which their behavior is determined by notions of status. A man quarrels with and is jealous of his social equals. A noble is socially so separated from commoners that were a commoner to quarrel with him it would be treason.
>
> (Evans-Pritchard 1976: 46)

Not only that, but "offense is more easily taken at the words or actions of an equal than of a superior or inferior" (Evans-Pritchard 1976: 47).

Accusations of witchcraft also appear to be tied to moral judgments of others. "Zande morality is so closely related to their notions of witchcraft that it may be said to embrace them. The Zande phrase 'It is witchcraft' may often be translated simply as 'it is bad'" (Evans-Pritchard 1976: 48). After social exchanges involving "hatred, jealousy, envy, backbiting, slander, and so forth," accusations of witchcraft are soon to follow (48).

> Behaviour which conflicts with Zande ideas of what is right and proper, though not in itself witchcraft, nevertheless is the drive behind it, and persons who offend against rules of conduct are the most frequently exposed as witches ... Moral condemnation is predetermined, because when a man suffers a misfortune he meditates upon his grievance and ponders in his mind who among his neighbours has shown him unmerited hostility or who bears unjustly a grudge against him. These people have wronged him and wish him evil, and he therefore considers that they have bewitched him, for a man would not bewitch him if he did not hate him.
>
> (Evans-Pritchard 1976: 50)

In sum, the Azande report widespread belief in witchcraft, accept that anyone could be a witch, but in practice reserve the charge of witchcraft to those immediate peers with whom the Zande man already has experienced some social conflict. As such, the charge of witchcraft might function as a means of displaying public moral disapprobation. Indeed, Evans-Pritchard notes, "belief in witchcraft is a valuable corrective to uncharitable impulses, because a show of spleen or meanness or hostility may bring serious consequences" (Evans-Pritchard 1976: 55).

Given these reported beliefs and their apparent function within the community, I would like to formalize Evans-Pritchard's argument in the manner outlined above:

1. accusing someone of being a witch functions to display public social disapprobation of those behaviors viewed as immoral or unkind within the community, perhaps relegating the immoral witch to the margins of the community;
2. it benefits individual Zande to do so, as the practice distributes subjects across the moral high ground and the moral low ground, awarding the person who

alleges witchcraft to claim the moral high ground before the community as whole;
3. evidence shows that any particular Zande is motivated not strictly by belief in witchcraft to make the accusation of witchcraft, but rather appear to be motivated only in cases where enmities between individuals already exist;
4. there is no widespread empirical evidence that most Zande are consciously aware that his allegation of witchcraft functions as a form of social disapprobation, although it is quite possible some are conscious of this; and
5. because the practice is widely modeled within the community, all Zande men develop a practical sense such that they intuitively "know" ("know" is in scare quotes here because I am arguing that this "knowledge" is unconscious) that they stand to gain social standing and reduce the social standing of their enemies by calling them witches.

I argued above that such a functionalist argument is greatly enriched when we have *prima facie* evidence that people might not believe the things they report believing. We do, in fact, have a small bit of evidence. First, despite the fact that the Azande report believing that *any* man can be a witch, the fact that only immediate peers rather than superiors are ever accused of being witches would be consistent with the assumption that reported belief in witchcraft and the experience of misfortune are not in themselves sufficient to generate a public accusation of witchcraft; the possibility of gaining standing over peers through the accusation of witchcraft seems to be a further necessary causal condition of the accusation. In addition, Evans-Pritchard notes that he directly observed a witch doctor fabricating evidence of witchcraft when performing a "surgery" on someone afflicted by a material witchcraft substance. The witch doctor's assistant made an incision on the subject apparently afflicted, while the witch doctor handed over a poultice in which—Evan-Pritchard claims to have directly seen—the doctor had inserted a piece of charcoal that the assistant could "find" when holding the poultice over the incision. Evans-Pritchard removed the piece of charcoal as he passed it to the assistant, and watched as the assistant registered surprise at finding nothing in the cut while the doctor searched for another piece of charcoal (Evans-Pritchard 1976: 103). Evans-Pritchard adds,

> in the future he, like his colleagues, excused to me their sleight-of-hand on the grounds that it is not the pretended extraction of bones, pieces of charcoal [etc.] … and other supposed objects of witchcraft from the bodies of their patients which cures them of their diseases, but the *mbiro* medicine [i.e., the poultice] which they administer internally and externally at the same time.
>
> (Evans-Pritchard 1976: 104)

According to the witch doctors, even "if their surgery is fake, their physic is sound" (Evans-Pritchard 1976: 104). Of course, this is not conclusive evidence, but it is at the very least

Discourse and Ideology

prima facie evidence that the behavior of some Azande seemed to have been directed not by actual beliefs that directly lined up with their reported beliefs—if so, the witch doctors would not have needed to manufacture evidence for the missing witchcraft substance—but, rather, their behavior and reported beliefs about the practice of witchcraft appear in some cases to be conditioned by social necessities. Credorationalism that took at face value the claims about witchcraft generated among the Azande would fail to explain these anomalies as well as would the argument that accusations of witchcraft might in some cases be best understood as recrement.

In addition, note that this particular witch doctor likely makes public claims—recrement—to the effect that he believes he will find a witch substance in certain persons should he perform a surgery, but nevertheless brings along a substance to secretly "plant" during the surgery. It would be difficult to square these facts with the idea that his recrement was produced unconsciously—if he consciously makes an effort to bring along something to plant, he likely consciously knows he produces recrement when he claims to have found what he planted. Once again, Douglas's definition of functionalism—confined to completely unconscious social mechanisms—would not help us make sense of those cases wherein social actors appear to be conscious of the function of their recrement. I do not see that we as theorists lose anything of value if we define a social function as something that is performed *either knowingly or unknowingly*.

To take my argument one step further, it is particularly interesting that in the book Evans-Pritchard reports both disbelieving and believing in witchcraft. On the one hand, he writes from a position of methodological atheism, according to which rejecting supernatural causal claims at the start is the condition of possibility for looking for other causal—and, in his case, functional—explanations for the talk of witchcraft. He explicitly writes, "witches, as the Azande conceive them, *clearly cannot exist*" (Evans-Pritchard 1976: 18). However, in an appendix titled "Some Reminiscences and Reflections on Fieldwork," he also claims, quite remarkably,

> I have often been asked whether, when I was among the Azande, I got to accept their ideas about witchcraft. This is a difficult question to answer. I suppose you can say I accepted them; I had no choice. In my own culture, in the climate of thought I was born into and brought up in and have been conditioned by, I rejected, and reject Zande notions of witchcraft. In their culture, in the set of ideas I then lived in, I accepted them; in a kind of way I believed them. Azande were talking about witchcraft daily, both among themselves and to me; any communication was well-nigh impossible unless one took witchcraft for granted.
>
> (Evans-Pritchard 1976: 244)

If we take him to mean that "I believed them" in the sense of "I held *actual beliefs* according to which witchcraft was real," this passage is a bundle of nonsense and contradiction. If, however, he means that he consciously had to utilize the regnant discourse to communicate with those around him, it makes perfect sense. Even if he held no actual belief that witchcraft was real, he may have had to knowingly produce recrement—that is, he may have been required to talk as if witchcraft were real—to negotiate his social standing among the Azande. He goes on:

> you cannot have a remunerative, even intelligent, conversation with people about something they take as self-evident if you give them the impression that you regard their belief as an illusion or a delusion … I had to act as though I trusted the Zande oracles and therefore give assent to their dogma of witchcraft, whatever reservations I might have. If I wanted to go hunting or on a journey, for instance, no one would willingly accompany me unless I was able to produce a verdict of the poison oracle that all would be well.
>
> (Evans-Pritchard 1976: 244)

That is to say, as a condition of possibility of having any social interaction, social standing, or influence—in other words, to prevent himself from being relegated completely to the margins of the social formation—he had to produce discourse that assumed facts for which he has no actual beliefs whatsoever. The production of recrement was a condition of possibility of functioning at all in the society for Evans-Pritchard.

In this section, I have built upon the previous sections by arguing the following:

- the reported belief that someone is a witch among the Azande tribe may not reflect actual beliefs but may in fact be recrement generated by the social need to display moral disapprobation and to gain social standing over the person identified as a witch;
- Evans-Pritchard himself had to knowingly produce recrement that made sense on the regnant discourse to function in the community, despite the fact that he had no actual beliefs that witchcraft was real in the supernatural sense; and
- the claim that some forms of discourse are recrement helps us to explain a wider range of empirical evidence than does credorationalism.

Which cases are better explained by credorationalism or the appeal to recrement would be highly contingent on the available evidence. Since the Azande no longer exist in the same way that they did during Evans-Pritchard's life, we can no longer gather empirical evidence to bolster either argument. However, future social scientific studies sensitive to the possibility that some forms of discourse may be recrement might be more sophisticated in their conclusions as a result.

Of course, by no means do I think all forms of discourse are recrement, but I would argue we have sufficient evidence to accept that some forms of discourse are. In those cases, treating recrement as if it were equivalent to actual belief would be a serious analytical mistake.

Conclusion

I have produced definitions for the terms offered in this chapter—reported belief, actual belief, credorationalism, and recrement—not for the purpose of having a more accurate view of the world. As I have argued, definitions can be neither empirically accurate nor inaccurate, as they serve as the condition of possibility of empirical evidence in the first place. The purpose of the use of these terms is not accuracy but rather analytic usefulness for achieving particular social ends. To use the approach deployed by Woodward, as discussed in Chapter 5, if we want to intervene on variables in the world that allow use to reliably produce results that serve our interests, we have to pick the right variables.

It seems clear to me that we have evidence that some forms of discourse are recrement, but of course not all. My theory of recrement shares with vulgar Marxism the view that people often say things that directly reflect the interests of their social and political position. My theory and vulgar Marxism both insist that it seems we have evidence that people sometimes say things only because those things appear to serve the immediate interests of the people who occupy their own particular social position. However, unlike vulgar Marxists, I accept that this only takes place some of the time. It also appears that we have evidence that people struggle with cognitive dissonance; these troubled individuals may say things that do not serve the immediate interests of people in their social position. If they are attempting to reconcile something they hold to be true with the things typically said by people in their social position, they might very well abandon what is typically said, even if it does not serve their immediate interests to do so.

Ideology critique, particularly forms of ideology critique similar to the one I have offered in this book, often appears to focus on false claims or beliefs, with the apparent goal of attempting to persuade people to abandon those beliefs. However, if those reported beliefs are recrement rather than actual beliefs, intervening on the false beliefs will not necessarily bring about a change in their behavior. Wicker, in his review of the studies on attitudes and behaviors, quotes S. M. Corey: "it would avail a teacher very little, for example, so to teach as to cause a change in scores on a questionnaire measuring attitudes toward Communism if these scores are in no way indicative of the behavior of his pupils" (Wicker 1969: 66). It is widely known that the infamous D.A.R.E. curriculum designed to discourage youth from using illegal drugs in the United States in the 1980s and 1990s did not produce the desired effects—drug use rates increased rather than decreased among some of the communities that implemented the curriculum. Similarly, using "character education" programs to teach children to publicly report that, for example, "racism is bad" are unlikely to produce the desired behavioral effects if that report bears no relation to children's behavior. In some cases, having a person change their belief—either reported or actual—may have no effect on their behavior.

People's behavior may be deeply shaped by the sympathies and antipathies encouraged by the discourses they habitually consume and produce, but in ways disconnected from many of their actual or reported beliefs. If a white person in the United States is systematically exposed to discourses—like the one I will examine in the next chapter— that only speaks about African Americans in the context of narratives about poverty being linked to laziness, narratives that portray African Americans as somehow inherently violent or inherently bad at parenting, narratives that talk about "Black on Black crime," narratives that depict Blacks as racist because they keep playing "the race card," etc., it is unlikely that such a person would have a great deal of sympathy for, for example, the Black Lives Matter movement. Such a person, however, quite likely understands precisely what sort of recrement about Black people must be publicly produced to resist being labeled a "racist" among their peers—at the very least, if challenged for publicly making a possibly offensive claim or exhibiting a concerning behavior, they will insist that they are "not racist," that they are "colorblind," that they "treat all people the same," and so forth. Nothing less than that is acceptable in the mainstream US discourse for managing one's public reputation—one would likely be excoriated rather than praised in public if one right out claimed that Blacks are somehow fundamentally inferior than whites. However, recrement or reported beliefs such as "I'm not racist" may in fact have no causal relation to a person's actions; such a person might thus continue to feel comfortable sharing memes on social media that systematically distribute antipathies toward African Americans, even if those memes might discourage whites from exhibiting any sympathy or solidarity with African American political platforms (thereby arguably harming the material interests of some Blacks in the United States). Persuading such a person to publicly report more sophisticated recrement—"OK, I get why 'colorblindness' is problematic and I now accept that systemic racism is real"—is unlikely, in itself, to change their behavior, particularly if the peers they most immediately want to impress share their antipathies for African American political platforms. The sympathies and antipathies produced by the discourses in which they are embedded are likely much more important for predicting their behavior than their reported belief that "I'm not racist."

To summarize, I began this chapter by noting that throughout this book I have been arguing that discourses and ideologies have causal effects within the world. However, this is not to say that discourses are beliefs that people hold in their heads and which direct their behavior in any simple and straightforward manner. In fact, there is a great deal of empirical evidence that demonstrates that reported beliefs may not reflect actual beliefs, and that belief reports may be generated because they serve particular, useful social functions for those who offer such reports. In particular, the field of social psychology has produced a massive body of empirical evidence that this is often the case. Consequently, a theory of recrement likely better explains a greater amount of empirical data in some instances than does credorationalism. As a result, analyses of the effects of discourse must be attentive to whether a form of discourse is a reported belief or an actual belief, and if merely the former, is it perhaps recrement? If so, demonstrating the falseness of recrement may not have the desired effect that intellectuals often hope it might. For better or worse, it is demonstrable that stereotypes are more likely to be changed when the social structure changes, and intellectual persuasion alone may not be a very effective way of bringing about those desired structural changes.

Julie Ingersoll, in her book *Evangelical Christian Women* (2003), offers a cautionary tale for those of us on the left who might make efforts to produce discourse to change society. One of the central claims of her book is that the construction and maintenance

Discourse and Ideology

of gender roles is central to contemporary evangelicalism. That is why, according to Ingersoll, debates over whether women can be ministers, leaders, or teachers, as well as the debate over gay rights, generate so much heat within the evangelical subculture. In the chapter "The Power of Subtle Arrangements and Little Things," Ingersoll notes that practically everything in evangelical communities is gendered in some way or another. Her examples include the following:

- small groups or prayer groups are often segregated by gender
- groups such as Promise Keepers are for men only
- father-and-son and mother-and-daughter events are segregated by gender
- kitsch sold at Christian bookstores is gendered more often than not, as are books, memorabilia, Bibles, toys, and so forth

Ingersoll notes that although there are a wide variety of feminist evangelical voices in the evangelical subculture, they remain counter-hegemonic and have been unable to gain a hegemonic status. Why? Her explanation, in part, is that evangelical feminist cultural production has been primarily literary—namely, through the production of feminist theology. Evangelicals are surrounded by patriarchal material culture almost all the time, but they are exposed to feminist culture rarely and intermittently—or perhaps never—and that feminist culture is primarily intellectual rather than material. Ingersoll writes,

> Within the evangelical subculture, the opponents of hierarchical gender roles have largely abandoned the power of material culture to the proponents of gender ideology ... Evangelical feminists spend most of their time fighting institutional and theological battles, but dualistic constructions of gender are more readily represented materially than are fluid constructions that emphasize equality ... [T]he fact remains that gendered dualism is perpetuated on a popular level by virtue of the fact that the material culture that gives shape to everyday life reproduces it.
>
> (Ingersoll 2003: 107)

Similarly, as long as leftist intellectuals attempt to change society primarily by operating on discourses and ideologies rather than material conditions—especially when the relevant ideologies are recrement—they may be as unsuccessful at producing social change as the evangelical feminists in Ingersoll's narrative.

The discourses that people produce and consume entail all sorts of claims about which those who use the discourse never seriously consider the logical coherence of, the empirical evidence for, or the logical or social consequences of, or who never systematically investigate their discourse's "truth," in the widest sense, so as to thereby learn its contours, subtleties, and possible tensions or contradictions. Consequently, the fact that those same discourses *condition group members' affective sympathies and antipathies* (that is, toward other, discursively constructed groups)—in ways we can empirically demonstrate—may assist us in accounting for far more human behavior than the assumption that people really "believe" the words that come out of their mouths.

CHAPTER 7
CASE STUDY: RACIST IDEOLOGY IN THE UNITED STATES

In this chapter, I want to demonstrate how the theory and method outlined in this book can be applied as a means of analyzing racist ideology in the United States. Notably, much of the empirical evidence that informs the following critique is widely accepted as common sense among scholars who study race in the United States. I claim to add nothing original, other than to demonstrate that to do a rigorous, empirically-based ideology critique, particularly if it is on a subject matter where there is a great deal of available, reliable studies, all you have to do is your homework. Of course, in many cases what counts as "rigorous" and "reliable" depends on one's interests or sympathies; *I* specifically mean "rigorous" and "reliable" in the sense that the studies involved abide by the empiricist standards outlined in the chapter on ideology. I believe—perhaps wrongly—that my sympathies will be served if we widely entertain evidences that meet those standards, as I am persuaded that, provided we were motivated to do so, we could reorder or reorganize our society in a manner so as to reduce asymmetrical power relations, but only if we are attentive to precisely such evidences. (Of course, if there is evidence to the contrary I am open to entertaining it.)

To recall, for my purposes I have defined ideology such that it consists of a bundle of agonistic empirical discourses or sets of knowledge claims designed to advance a group's interests or reinforce domination, which always depend on a logically prior constitutive discourse, but in a way that (1) violates the rules of that discourse or another discourse or (2) entails the distribution of demonstrably false or inadequately supported empirical claims, empirical claims that are false on grounds accepted by that very discourse or another discourse. In addition, I have outlined the steps of ideology critique in the following manner:

1. The critic must *individuate the relevant discourse* subject to ideology critique by
    a. drawing boundaries around what will be included in the analysis, along with
    b. providing a justification for why this collection of discourse warrants being treated as a particular object.
2. The critic must go on to provide an initial *discourse analysis* of the ideology by
    a. summarizing the contents of the discourse and noting
        i. the distribution of sameness and difference within the discourse,
        ii. the systematic positive and negative valuations associated with the objects of or homologies within the discourse,

iii. how those associations distribute sympathies and antipathies,
iv. the empirical claims made possible within the discourse,
v. the rights and duties or political program assigned by the discourse, and
vi. the extent to which the discourse is actual (i.e., already interpellates subjects and their institutions) or merely aspirational (i.e., utopic rather than actual); and

b. noting the extent to which the discourse arguably encourages, justifies, or legitimates social domination.

3. The critic then turns from discourse analysis to *ideology critique* by asking the following questions.
   a. Does the ideology arguably *caricature* opponents' motives or claims and, if so, how?
   b. Does the ideology use *emotionally charged paradigmatic cases* that are not particularly representative of a group, a practice, or an idea?
   c. Which claims in the ideology are *logically contradictory or merely rhetorical* (e.g., if they depend on rhetorical slippage or rhetorical displacement to be persuasive), and on whose discursive standards are they contradictory or rhetorical?
      i. If so, how would the ideology's master narrative have to be revised to remain coherent or persuasive?
   d. Which claims in the ideology are *falsifiable*, and on who's discourse?
      i. If claims are *empirically supported*—on the ideology's own discourse or another's—
         1. do they nevertheless appear to function
            a. to obscure another possibly relevant set of empirical facts?
            b. to reinforce an otherwise demonstrably false ideological narrative?
            c. to encourage manipulation of relevant variables in a way that arguably increases relations of social domination? (for instance, by making minorities who suffer from social domination solely responsible for overcoming their domination)?
      ii. If claims are *not empirically supported or demonstrably false*—either on the ideology's own discourse or another's—do they contradict in any way other empirically supported and possibly relevant evidences?
         1. If so, how would the narrative they function to support have to be modified to remain coherent and persuasive?
         2. Do we have any existing empirical evidence for that modified narrative, or is it unlikely to be a warranted given the existing evidence?

e. Do the possible caricatures, contradictions, gaps in evidence, or empirical falsehoods in the ideology arguably contribute to encouraging, justifying, or legitimating social domination?

In this chapter I will apply, step by step, this method of analysis to a particular ideology that, I will argue, entails empirically false claims and legitimates a racialized economic hierarchy in the United States.

Discourse Analysis: PragerU, Conservatism, and Leftism

To illustrate the application of the method of discourse analysis and ideology critique I have defended in this book, I would like to consider the propaganda distributed by a well-funded, conservative American organization called PragerU. According to their website, "PragerU is not a university, nor do we claim to be. We do not offer degrees. However, we are the most influential online resource for explaining the concepts that have made America great" (PragerU 2021a). In sum, PragerU is a privately-funded nonprofit propaganda machine (based in Los Angeles, California) that distributes five-minute information videos on their own website, YouTube, Facebook, Twitter, Instagram, as well as via their Apple and Android apps, about political topics of interest to Americans on both the left and the right. According to their website, "Thousands of educators and university professors utilize PragerU videos as teaching supplements in their classrooms" (PragerU 2021b). On their online FAQ, they claim to have a worldview or "value system" and a set of interests that organize the presentation of the information they share:

> Every person and every organization has a value system and a set of beliefs. PragerU is no different. We believe in the principles that have made America great. We believe in economic and religious freedom, a strong military that protects our allies, and in the religious values that inform western civilization, also known as Judeo-Christian values.
>
> (PragerU 2021a)

Overall, their videos advance a type of meritocratic libertarianism, according to which America's citizens are most free when government is small and when it avoids interfering with the individual freedoms, aspirations, and hard work of its citizens; consequently, they typically deride leftist projects as violating freedom or generating unfairness or inequality. PragerU's discourse is Manichaean, imagining a battle between the conservative forces for liberty and the leftist forces for social control; this Manichaean frame inflects their discourse with the sense that they are fighting a battle of good against evil.

Why does my selection warrant being considered at all in the first place, and why does it warrant being treated as a distinct object, an object that I will argue is a racist ideology? First, this ideology is not only PragerU's ideology; their claims reflect long-standing

Discourse and Ideology

discursive interventions that have long shaped public discourse on race in the United States. As such, their iteration of that ideology is not particularly unique, but just well-funded, well-produced, polished, and carefully designed to appeal to conservatives who view themselves as thoughtful and well-informed. For all practical purposes, I am treating PragerU's ideology as a metonym for a much more widely distributed ideology. As that ideology has had substantial influence on US race relations, it warrants consideration for its possible material effects. Object individuation is always relative to human interests; I am interested in social domination, so this object is of interest to me precisely because it produces material effects that offend my sympathies. For those uninterested in social domination, therefore, my selection will perhaps not be seen as justified or relevant. Second, the selection of web content I have chosen to focus on reflects central rather than marginal claims made by PragerU. That is, it should be clear to anyone willing to spend a few hours browsing their site that I have pulled out content that is part of an overarching narrative that runs throughout the website's discourse as a whole. Consequently, avid fans hopefully would find my summary of PragerU's discourse to be fair, even if they object to the critique launched against that discourse.

Note: PragerU's content is rather wide-ranging in its scope, and in the following analysis I will introduce a great number of claims that trigger my antipathies; however, as I cannot respond in this chapter to all of their claims which I might wish to contest, I have decided to focus narrowly on the ones about race. This is not to say that their other claims are not worth contesting. As always, whichever claims warrant addressing depends not on intrinsic features of the claims themselves but rather the immediate investments of the critic.

I would like to begin with their general assertions about America that are assumed by or which dovetail with their normative and empirical claims about race and race relations in the United States that I will consider in the next section. In a video titled "How Do You Judge America? Left vs. Right" (PragerU 2015b), their discourse separates Americans into two types: conservatives who think America is great and leftists who think America is horrible. Arguably, their presentation of leftism is central to understanding their portrayal of conservatism, as the former serves as a foil for the latter; in their discourse, leftism is a mirror that inversely reflects the values of conservatism. According to the narrator,

> The left … sees America as having been and continuing to be a very flawed country, morally no better than many, and morally inferior to many. The left's view is that America was founded by rich white males who are intent on protecting their race, wealth, and, in many cases, their slaves. America was and remains sexist, intolerant, xenophobic, and bigoted, a country of unacceptable inequality, where the super rich and big corporations have far too much power and influence.

They quote historian Howard Zinn as a leftist who holds this view; according to Zinn: "If people knew history, they would scoff at the idea that the United States is a force for the betterment of humanity." In addition, the narrator notes that leftists often cite slavery as proof that America is "evil."

Case Study: Racist Ideology in the United States

By contrast, conservatives rightly understand that the United States is a great nation and always has been despite its missteps, most of which it has corrected for. "While acknowledging America's flaws, conservatives regard America as the best society ever created, giving more people of more backgrounds more freedom, more opportunity, and more affluence than any other society." Contradicting Zinn, the narrator insists that "America has done more good for humanity than any other country." Of course slavery was wrong, but, the narrator asks, "which societies were the first to abolish slavery? Since all societies had slavery [in the past], that is a far more important question to ask than who had slaves … [A]ll of the societies that first abolished slavery were rooted in the Jewish and Christian Bibles"—and, as the United States is similarly based on the "Judeo-Christian tradition," it follows a trustworthy moral compass despite the fact that it may not have been the *actual* first to abolish slavery. In summary,

> was America morally better than other societies in just about every other regard? … Yes. America gradually became the least racist, least xenophobic country in the world. In no country do people of every race and ethnicity become accepted as full members of the society as do immigrants to America.

Further, the narrator goes on to assert that America has committed itself to the liberty of other nations more than any other, citing the war against communism in Korea as an example; "37,000 Americans died in Korea … [to] protect Koreans from communist tyranny. Today, South Korea … is one of the wealthiest and freest countries in Asia. Meanwhile, North Korea … is the least free and poorest country on earth." In addition, the video adds that nations in which American troops are still stationed—including German, Japan, and South Korea—are better "economically and morally" than before, whereas those nations American troops have abandoned—for instance, Vietnam and Iraq—"have experienced mass murder and other horrors." This allows them to imply, although they do not literally state it, that the fate of these apparently successful countries was tied to the United States' benevolence. In sum, here are all of the associations built up in the video's binary or Manichaean discourse:

(-) / (+)

leftists/conservatives

tyranny/liberty

mass murder/liberation from mass murder

communism/liberation from communism

devaluing America's greatness/recognizing America's greatness

deny equal opportunity exists/accept equal opportunity exists

unable to see the value in abolishing slavery/able to see the value of abolishing slavery

[atheism? Islam?]/Jewish and Christian values

Discourse and Ideology

The central objects created by this discourse include an idealized block of conservatives, and a negatively-idealized block of leftists. Without doubt, either idealization is likely to differ from the actual stated views of many who identify as conservative or leftist; that is to say: not all who identify as conservative share the views attributed to the object titled "conservatives" in these videos. As far as the distribution of sameness and difference, this discourse identifies leftists as the same as, similar to, or on the side of those who support mass murder, tyrannical communism, or who opposed abolition, and identifies conservatives as the same as those who hold Jewish and Christian values. The ranking or normalization of objects individuated, or the distribution of normative associations is clear: those on the left are devalued in relationship to those on the right. As such, the discourse functions to distribute sympathies and antipathies; persuaded viewers are invited to extend their sympathies to conservatives and their antipathies to leftists.

Of course, the chain of associations on the left and right are potentially problematic, even from a conservative position. For instance, it is clear that some who identify as conservative in America are atheist or Muslim, and some leftists identify as Christian or Jewish. In addition, no leftist I know would support mass murder or tyrannical forms of communism, even though those terms are associated with leftists in this discursive block. Last, it seems clear that, even if they devalue America's moral status compared to those on the right, leftists generally do value the abolition of slavery, despite the fact that this video depicts them as on the wrong side of history there. This discourse therefore provides a wide variety of emotionally charged paradigmatic exemplars that may not very well represent such groups.

A number of potentially falsifiable empirical claims are made in this narrative, depending on what counts as evidence for their falsification and how the terms of each are defined. For instance, how is "freedom" defined, such that we could demonstrate whether Americans experience more freedom than citizens in other countries? How is "affluence" defined? If we defined affluence in terms of total wealth amassed per capita, it might be true that America is the most affluent nation; if we defined affluence in terms of median household income, America is not apparently the most affluent, at least given the statistical evidence currently available. How do we define action for the "good of humanity"? If we define it in terms of "least number of civilians of other countries killed," America will be nowhere near the top. How do we define "racism" and "xenophobia," for such definitions will be crucial in determining whether it is true that America is the least racist and least xenophobic nation. Arguably, since the concept of race was not invented, it would be *a priori* true that premodern nations were the least racist, but that would require more attention to the details than PragerU can provide in a five-minute video.

In addition, note what is not said in the video, but merely implied: that there are causal connections between the correlations noted. For instance, even if it is true that all nations that abandoned slavery first were in some ways based on "Judeo-Christian" values, does it follow that those values were the *cause* of the abolition of slavery? Similarly, was the economic and "moral" prosperity in Germany, Japan, and South Korea *caused* by

American military support, or in spite of it? If Vietnam and Iraq have "experienced mass murder and other horrors," is that *because* America withdrew its military from those countries? In these cases, causal claims are implied but not explicit, perhaps because the causal claims are not falsifiable due to lack of evidence or, conversely, because existing empirical evidence possibly contradicts a causal claim in these cases.

Turning to another of the "Right vs. Left" videos on PragerU's website, consider "How Do We Make Society Better?" (PragerU 2015c). According to the narrator, conservatives believe that the improvement of a nation necessitates starting with the individual. "Each person … [must do] battle with his or her own weaknesses and flaws," or his or her "moral failings." By contrast, the left alleges that to improve society we must begin with "society's moral failings"—hence the left's obsession with "sexism, racism, intolerance, xenophobia, homophobia, islamophobia [*sic*], and … many other evils the left believes permeate American society." This is why, the narrator suggests, that leftists are more concerned with politics than the right. Consequences of these differences include the fact that leftists desire sweeping social change, while conservatives favor individual, incremental change. The so-called "founding fathers," the video insists, were on the conservative side: "the founders of the United States recognized that the transformation that every generation must work on is the moral transformation of each citizen. Thus character development was at the core of both child rearing and of young people's education from elementary school through college." Quoting John Adams, the narrator notes, "our constitution was made for a moral and religious people. It is wholly inadequate to the government of any other." Quoting Benjamin Franklin: "Only a virtuous people are capable of freedom." "Why is that? Because freedom requires self-control." Leftism, however, has destroyed the character education so important in America from its creation until the 1960s: now, "children are taught not to focus on their flaws, but on America's. Social issues have replaced character education." Examples provided are curricular emphases on global warming, economic inequality, white privilege, and "the alleged rape culture on [college] campuses." The narrator questions the latter allegation and concludes the video with the following words:

> ironically, if there really is a rape culture on college campuses, the only reason would have to be that there is so little character education in our schools or, for that matter, at home. Fathers and religion, historically the two primary conveyers of self-control, are nonexistent in the lives of millions of American children. We are now producing mass numbers of Americans who are passionate about fixing America, while doing next to nothing about fixing their own character. The problem, however, is that you can't make society better without making its people better.

Notably, when "religion" is mentioned, a cross and a star of David are depicted on the screen. Consequently, here are all of the oppositional associations—either strictly discursive or visually signified—built up in this five-minute video:

Discourse and Ideology

(-) / (+)

leftists/conservatives

more political/less political

too critical of America/appropriately critical of America

lack of self-control/encourage self-control

interested in controlling others/interested in self-control

oppose mythical (i.e., social) moral failings/oppose actual (i.e., individual) moral failings

lack of character/virtuous character

against the Founding Fathers and the Constitution/faithful to the Founding Fathers and the Constitution

[atheism? nonreligious? Islam?]/Judaism and Christianity

ignore importance of fatherhood/value fatherhood

The central objects individuated by the discourse employed here are, as above, conservatives and leftists. Sameness and difference are distributed in the following manner: the object "conservatives" is lined up alongside and treated as equivalent with people who control themselves, people who care about virtue and character, as well as people who are Jews or Christians; the object "leftists" are treated as equivalent with people who are overly political and controlling of others, unfairly critical of the United States, lack self-control, and who are perhaps nonreligious, or at least not members of the religions from which the nation's central values are derived. Clearly, the discourse functions to encourage persuaded audiences to extend positive valuations and sympathies to the objects that fall on the right side of the homologies above, as well as to distribute antipathies toward the objects that fall on the left side. Last, the political program encouraged by the discourse demands that persuaded members of the audience expend more effort on improving their or others' moral character and less effort on criticizing systemic problems, which are either minor, few, or now corrected by the appropriate moral progress America has made.

As before, it is clear that the discursive equivalences set up here are contestable according to commonsense ideas accepted by those on the left and the right. They employ emotionally charged exemplars that are in many cases not particularly representative of leftists and conservatives. For instance, many leftists value fatherhood and character education, and many conservatives have bastard children, to say nothing of the fact that some conservatives are atheists and some leftists are Christians or Jews. In addition, arguably there is nothing more political than distributing propaganda, so it is odd that this conservative video depicts conservatives as apolitical in contrast with leftists.

Just as with the previous video, a number of possibly falsifiable empirical and causal claims are made that potentially deserve investigation. In particular, the video presents concerns over sexism, rape culture, racism, white privilege, homophobia, Islamophobia, global warming, and economic inequality as potentially inflated or, even if legitimate, best solved through character education or the development of individual virtue rather than political activism. However, given the empirical evidence discussed in Chapter 6 of this book, it is not clear that character education would produce the desired social effects, as character education may simply produce people who can regurgitate the right recrement required by the immediate social context, but in a way that bears little or no relationship to their behaviors. We can produce subjects who denounce racism more easily than we can produce subjects who suffer from no unconscious biases or who are capable of contesting rather than fully participating in or further contributing to the conditions that make racialized social relations possible.

Before moving on to the PragerU content focused directly on race, I want to consider one more "Right vs. Left" video, titled "So, You Think You're Tolerant" (PragerU 2018b). According to the narrator, tolerance has always been defined in the following manner: "tolerance is the ability to live with people whose opinions and behavior you don't agree with." The narrator raises debates over the death penalty, minimum wages, or whether individuals voted for a Democrat or a Republican in the last election. "Whatever differences we have, tolerating others' opinions is a prerequisite to a functioning and a free society. America itself was built on a foundation of tolerance. The Declaration of Independence guarantees us life, liberty, and the pursuit of happiness." This means, of course, that individuals have to be tolerant of the lives, liberties, and pursuit of happiness of other citizens. However, according to "mainstream media"—another rhetorical opponent—only leftists are tolerant.

> The right, according to the media, is intolerant of everyone, except those darn white, heterosexual, Christian males. There's only one problem: it's just not true. Incredibly, the left isn't even tolerant of the very people they say they're tolerant of. If you're gay, or black, or an immigrant, and you're not in lock-step with current leftist orthodoxy, you know exactly what I'm talking about. If you believe we should judge people on the content of their character and not the color of their skin, the left calls you racist … If you believe men and women are equal but fundamentally different, the left calls you sexist. Here's the thing: those who only tolerate those they agree with or like aren't actually tolerant.

By contrast, the narrator insists, who is really tolerant? "It's actually those scary right wingers that the media and universities demonize every day." The left, unfortunately, "has become utterly intolerant of anyone with whom they disagree. Why? Because they believe that they know how you should live and how you should think." Unlike the left, however, "the right welcomes diversity of thought … The right, much more than the left, believes in 'live and let live.'"

Discourse and Ideology

Here are the discursive associations set up in this five-minute video:

(-) / (+)

leftists/conservatives

intolerance/tolerance

controlling/live and let live

hypocritical/consistent

racist/colorblind

ignores obvious gender differences/acknowledges obvious gender differences

supports narrow orthodoxy/supports diversity

critical of minorities who don't conform to leftist orthodoxy/tolerant of minorities who don't conform to conservative orthodoxy

---

The central objects are, once more, conservatives and leftists. The distribution of equivalences makes conservatives the same as those who are truly tolerant and leftists as those who are truly intolerant. The discourse encourages sympathies for conservatives and antipathies for leftists, particularly ones who object to or raise concerns about racism or sexism. The political program recommended encourages conservatives to emphasize colorblindness and to stand up for the truth that women and men are different, despite the fact that leftist discourses wrongly present them as the same.

As before, some of these associations are objectionable if considered as equivalences, and the exemplars they choose are again emotionally charged. For instance, some leftists believe in intrinsic gender differences, and some conservatives do not. In addition, the entire purpose of the PragerU website appears to be to influence public opinion, with the goal of effecting change in society—in which case the creators of this content are not as uninterested in the beliefs and behaviors of other Americans as "live and let live" implies. Last, and most importantly for my purposes, are the claims about race. There are people on both the left and the right who are "racist" in the sense of "not colorblind," which is how this discourse defines "racism." Throughout this book I have suggested that constitutive discourse is a condition of possibility of empirical discourse, and that is particularly relevant here. For PragerU or those who adopt its ideology, whether something is racist depends not on, for instance, whether a policy disproportionately impacts people of color or whether stereotype threat functions to disadvantage minorities; instead, what makes something racist is apparently—and only—explicitly discriminating on the basis of skin color. On this view, affirmative action is racist because it depends on discrimination on the basis of race, even though affirmative action programs are designed to improve the social or economic standing of people of color. In sum, what empirically counts as racism depends on a logically prior, constitutive definition of racism; people with competing definitions—for instance, the leftist theorists of race relations I will discuss

Case Study: Racist Ideology in the United States

below—will literally see a different world than devoted viewers of PragerU because they define racism differently.

Thus far I have shown,

- PragerU presents conservatives as tolerant of difference, thoughtful, respectful of America's greatest strengths, "not racist" in the sense of "colorblind," and interested in promoting personal responsibility for themselves and others; in addition,
- PragerU presents leftists as intolerant of everyone except lazy minorities, overly and unfairly critical of America's past (which we are past), "racist" in the sense that they keep making more of an issue of race than anyone else, and largely interested in controlling others and forcing them to conform to their own political agenda.

If I have attended at length to the discourses distributed on their website, it is because discourses are not just slogans but collections of slogans, statements, principles, associations, empirical claims, and so on, which are all connected, interlaced, and mutually reinforcing. To understand the discourse as a whole, we have to consider sizeable chunks of the discourse, as homologies and rhetorical equivalences span across and mutually invoke various sub-discourses that are a part of the whole. (To be clear, strictly speaking there never is a "whole," as what we individuate as PragerU's discourse is neither synchronically bound—insofar as the meanings of PragerU's claims depend upon other, outside discourses it draws from, such as American history, American libertarian discourses, second-wave feminist discourses, civil rights-era discourses on racial equality, etc.—nor diachronically bound—for in the future, new evidence could come to light that would force us to reconsider the interpretation or meaning we attributed to old evidence, etc.) In the next section, I want to focus on PragerU's claims that more directly address race.

Discourse Analysis: PragerU and White Privilege

Turning, then, to the content that more centrally addresses race in America, consider PragerU's video short, "Do White Americans Have White Privilege?" (PragerU 2020). The video format is somewhat different from the previously discussed videos. First, rather than have a narrator expound on what is right about conservative views and what is wrong or hypocritical about leftist views, this video begins with a series of video snapshots of American politicians discussing race; the introductory clips are followed up with a man presenting himself as a reporter interviewing whites and Blacks about whether or not white privilege exists or concerns them. The opening shot is of Hillary Clinton—apparently from 2016, the time period during which she was running against Donald Trump for the position of President of the United States of America—saying that whites must recognize their privilege. The narrator's voice then takes over after the short

Discourse and Ideology

clip, suggesting that the concept of white privilege has become part of the "bulwark of democratic party's ideology." What is white privilege? "I don't know, let's find out."

The video shifts to street interviews outside of a "white privilege conference" in Kansas City, with "over a thousand attendees." The racial makeup of the conference's audience is unclear (we are not shown the whole group), but all of those who are interviewed in the video are white. The interviewer asks the white conference attendees some questions like the following: "Do all white people have white privilege?" Do the conference attendees believe that "white people in this country generally are prejudiced?" Because the attendees likely attended the conference as a result of their sympathies for concerns about race and white privilege, it is not surprising to find that they do think white privilege exists and that white Americans are racist. Are "white people in this country generally prejudiced?" One interviewee replies, "I'd go further and say we're all racist."

At one point, the interviewer and narrator shifts to questions designed to get the interviewees to contradict themselves. "Is it fair to say that all white people are racist? Throughout the country?" "Yes, absolutely." "Not just the South?" "Correct, yeah, absolutely." After one flustered, young female interviewee says, "sometimes it's okay to say that all white people do this, or white people are x, especially in a negative light," he follows up (given the editing it is unclear if this follow-up was immediate or after a change to a new part of the conversation) by asking if it is "wrong to judge people collectively?" "Yes." Another interviewee gives a similar answer: "It's *wrong* to judge everyone collectively." Another interviewee: "yeah, absolutely, no one's a monolith." The editing together of these responses, juxtaposed with the conference attendees' answers to the previous questions, leaves the viewer with the following message: people who believe in white privilege say it is not okay to judge an entire racial group on the basis of the actions of a few, and yet they are willing to judge all white people as racist on the basis of the actions of a few white racists. The fact that the conference-goers' constitutive discourse might define "racism" as something other than "colorblind" is neither raised as a possibility nor addressed.

The interviewer shifts to asking the white conference attendees for examples of white privilege that they have experienced thus far on this particular day of the conference. "Tell me about some of the white privileges that you have, uh, encountered over the past, let's say today." All of the interviewees included in the final edit struggled with this question. The young woman who was previously flustered cannot come up with an answer while thinking on her feet and apologizes for it: "Uh, not really today, but, maybe, sorry, I'm not good at thinking." One interviewee, a much more confident white woman who later identifies as a college professor confirms that she experiences white privilege but declines to offer specifics: "Today? I mean, just being in the world."

Shifting away from asking for examples, the interviewer turns to asking about how pervasive white privilege is. "Is it fair to say that on a daily basis, black people around this country face obstacles because of white privilege?" "Absolutely." The interviewer asking another conference attendee about "how black people are consumed with this day to day," or whether "they deal with this issue day to day?" "Oh, 100%." The edits cut back to the confident, female college professor: "I mean, I think that's just so obvious, if you're not admitting that you're blinding yourself to reality." The interviewer follows up: "Are you a professor?" Laughing, she replies, "yeah." He quips, "that makes sense now." (Why include that last comment, which doesn't have anything to do with white privilege, in the edit? In PragerU's narrative, college professors are deluded leftists who want to brainwash young, impressionable minds, and here we have *prima facie* evidence that college professors are among those self-contradictory leftists; that is, this last quip by the interviewer reinforces PragerU's other narratives about higher education.)

The video then moves on to a different location, where the same interviewer meets and interacts with a rather different crowd. "Now I'm here in Harlem, in front of the Jackie Robinson housing projects, to ask residents what they think of white privilege." While not all occupants of the apartment building are necessarily Black, all of those included in the video edit appear to be Black. Some interviewees seem confused by the questions about white privilege, noting that it is not something they think about. One Black man suggests, "I've heard about it, but I don't think about it." To a Black woman, the interviewer asks, "when you wake up in the morning, do you immediately think about, and are consumed with the idea of white privilege?" Rolling her eyes in apparent annoyance, she simply says "no." "You don't think about that all day long?" "No." "No?" "No." Another Black woman says, without looking up from her phone as she's answering the questions, "no I'm not consumed with it. At all." Another Black woman: "I teach students; I'm not consumed with anything except for runny noses and pencils." One Black woman falls back on the discourse of colorblindness that PragerU defends elsewhere: "My mom didn't raise me to view color as the object of anything."

The interviewer shifts from questions about whether they are consumed with white privilege to the possible effects of white privilege on the opportunities they experience and whether it is useful for them to dwell on the concept. "Do you wake up every day thinking, um, I am not gonna succeed today because of white privilege?" One Black man standing behind a food cart responds, while gesturing at the food cart, "no, obviously not. You see I'm my own businessman." To one woman the interviewer asks, "would you ever think it's damaging to tell your kids or teach your kids, if you're a black kid, that you're not gonna succeed in life because of white privilege?" She replies, "of course, of course, it makes them think, okay, well I'm gonna be nothing. If I wanna be a doctor, I can't even do that anymore. It gives them no hope." One Black man claims that it is a myth that race matters for opportunity: "color ain't stopped nothing, I mean, it's a myth." Later, gesturing to the apartment building, the same man says: "I got kids in here, man, [that are] lawyers, doctors, that grew up out of this building." Other Black interviewees make claims that appear close to the pull-yourself-up-by-your-own-bootstraps discourse that PragerU uses elsewhere. "It's America. If you're willing to put forth an effort, you'll do what you gotta do." Another: "I know it sounds clichéd, but I can accomplish anything." Another: "if you let something stop you, then that's you. Me, I ain't had nothin' stop me." One woman insists that Black people can succeed in America: "my daughter is graduating at the top of her class."

Near the end, the edits return to the Clinton speech that framed the video, with Clinton stating that "we white Americans need to do a better job of listening when

Discourse and Ideology

African Americans talk." The import, it seems clear, is that only self-contradictory or confused whites (one of whom literally said, "I'm not good at thinking") are concerned with white privilege; by contrast, if whites really listened to African Americans like Clinton suggested, we would learn—as we do from the Black folks who live in a "housing project" in Harlem—that white privilege either does not exist or, if it does, it is not sufficient to warrant thoughtful consideration. Indeed, if Blacks can graduate at the top of their class or become lawyers or doctors, then opportunity in America must be sufficiently meritocratic such that white privilege is, at best, a silly concern.

The discursive associations set up in this discourse appear to include the following:

(-) / (+)

white leftists who believe in white privilege/Black people who doubt white privilege

hypocritical thinkers/clear thinkers

people who judge on the basis of race/people who are colorblind

people who condescend to Blacks/people who identify and respect the hard work of Blacks

people who ignore what Blacks say/people who listen to other Blacks

unjustified doubts about equal opportunity/belief in equal opportunity

---

The resulting discourse—deftly and carefully pieced together by the video editors from potentially competing discourses—functions to encourage persuaded viewers to shift sympathies toward hard-working Blacks who apparently don't acknowledge white privilege and to shift their antipathies toward self-contradictory leftists who bemoan white privilege.

The empirical claims made, of course, depend on the discursive frame that makes them possible. Note what the interviewer did not ask the Black interviewees: he did not ask them if they believed that white privilege or equal opportunity exists in America. On the contrary, he asked them if they were daily consumed with white privilege from the moment they wake up in the morning. In addition, rather than ask them if equal opportunity exists in America, he asked them whether white privilege functions entirely to prevent Blacks from succeeding in America's competitive marketplace. It is quite possible that some of these interviewees believe both that white privilege exists and disadvantages them *and* that, although equal opportunity does not exist in America, Black people can sometimes succeed *in spite of* the existence of white privilege. Only one of the Black interviewees—the one who seemed to say that it is a complete falsehood that race affects opportunity—explicitly said or implied a claim at odds with that possibility. In any case, the overall effect of the video is designed to persuade viewers that white privilege, if it exists, is beneath serious consideration.

I would like to suggest that it is possible that some of the responses to the questions asked were recrement. It is possible that the white conference-goers were intuitively regurgitating stock claims they were exposed to at the conference, but without having given conscious thought to the details or possible tensions in their claims. For instance, in the constitutive discourses on white privilege, generally "racism" is defined as a social system in which people—all people—are situated. Studies—some of which I will introduce below—demonstrate that people suffer from racially inflected implicit biases that direct the formation of judgment in ways unconnected to their conscious views on race. Consequently, someone who quite explicitly and intentionally thinks that whites are no better than Blacks might nevertheless behave in ways that reflect an unconscious racial bias. In addition, that could be true even of Black people in their interactions with other Black people. For instance, if a Black police officer shot an unarmed Black man, conservatives might say racism could not have been a factor because the police officer himself was Black ("are we to believe the officer was racist against himself?," they might ask). By contrast, in the constitutive discourse on white privilege, that Black officer might hold the same implicit biases as do white officers whose behavior reflect a racial bias. As such, that Black man would be considered—in the discourse of white privilege—a part of a racist system. Consequently, when asked if all whites are "racist," those conference-goers might have heard the following question: do all whites in the United States live and participate in a racist system? If their answer is yes, then not only are all whites part of a racist system, but so are Blacks. "We're all racist" likely means something very different in this leftist discourse than it does in PragerU's discourse, something that may not have been well captured in the confrontational, on-the-spot interviews wherein conference goers arguably fell back on their intuitions about what recrement should be produced in response to questions about race—particularly if the interviewees didn't realize the person asking them questions was trying to trap them in possible contradictions.

I would like also to suggest that it is quite possible that the Black interviewees similarly may have been regurgitating recrement in response to the questions asked them. Remember: recrement serves an immediate social function in relationship to social standing—perhaps signaling an identity, expressing disapprobation of particular behaviors or discourses, etc. The fact that many, if not most, of the Black respondents answered questions with a look of annoyance on their faces is *prima facie* evidence that they may have interpreted the questions about white privilege as if they were questions about the lack of African American ability. "Do you think about white privilege all day?" may have been interpreted as "Do you have a victim mentality and think that Blacks can't overcome the possible barriers they face in society?" If they interpreted the question in that way, their responses arguably make more sense. One response went something like this: "I'm not consumed with white privilege—I'm a teacher and thus I'm consumed with things like runny noses." Arguably, this sort of response comes across as a defensive gesture. Why else bring up her career? What does the existence of white privilege have to do with her students' runny noses? However, if she interpreted the question as asking "are you incapable of succeeding because of white privilege," then raising her career and the things to which she successfully attends as a teacher would be evidence that she is, in fact, a successful person. If so, then the apparent denial of the relevance of white privilege might actually have been little more than a defensive form of recrement designed to mark herself as successful rather than unsuccessful. Similarly, the claims of the business owner who gestured to his food cart as evidence of his success or the man who said "I ain't had nothin' stop me" would not make sense as responses to a question about whether white privilege exists, unless the question was interpreted as implying that African Americans are *incapable of holding a career* because of the existence of white privilege. They may have interpreted the question as derogating Blacks to the bottom of society without exception, and their responses appear not to have been about whether white privilege exists but, instead, about the fact that they are not so lazy they cannot hold a job. If their statements were not reports of actual beliefs about white privilege but rather recrement designed to defend against not-so-subtle implications in the questions, then we can draw no conclusion as to whether they actually believe white privilege exists or not. This claim is supported by the fact that none of the interviewees explicitly denied the existence of white privilege; they appeared to deny only that white privilege consumed them or that it prevented them from holding a job. If so, the conclusion that the video's editors want the viewer to draw—that white privilege must not exist if even Black people deny it exists—doesn't follow from the evidence shown. And, of course, there may have been many African American interviewees who did report that white privilege exists and disadvantages them, even if it doesn't prevent them from succeeding altogether, but their responses may not have been included in the edit.

Notably, the video seems to take it for granted that it is possible that racism exists in America and, if so, that fact would rightly be disconcerting. In addition, the video's discourse also seems to take it for granted that barriers to equal opportunity would be concerning; the video suggests not that it is wrong to be concerned about equal opportunity, but merely that the fear that white privilege affects equal opportunity is empirically misguided. If there were other empirical evidences demonstrating that advantages accrue to whites as a result of something other than their hard work, personal merit, or luck, and if those advantages negatively affected equal opportunity in the United States, that evidence should be of interest *even on grounds accepted by those sympathetic to PragerU's ideology*. The video searches, however, for that evidence in only two limited contexts: in the discourses produced on the fly by attendees of a white privilege conference (some of whom appear flustered when put on the spot, and some of whom appear not to notice the tension between their condemnation of whites and their agreement that we should judge people individually rather than on the basis of group membership) and in the discourses of Black people who were not even asked if white privilege or equal opportunity exists. As one of the functions of ideology is to discourage attention to possibly relevant empirical evidence that contradicts the ideology or posits challenges to the ideology's internal consistency, this video seems deeply ideological in that it seeks evidence for white privilege or unequal opportunity by (1) asking conference attendees on the spot to provide anecdotal rather than systematic evidence for white privilege and (2) explicitly *not asking* some Black people whether white privilege exists or if opportunity in America is equal. These are not particularly good ways to gather empirical evidence for the existence of white privilege or equal opportunity, and later in

Case Study: Racist Ideology in the United States

this chapter I will turn to more substantial empirical evidences that potentially warrant us to give more credence to the existence of white privilege than PragerU allows.

Collectively, the overarching narrative presented in the PragerU content I have surveyed thus far appears to want to persuade viewers of the following:

- leftists who express concerns about race, racism, and the lack of equal opportunity are not to by sympathized with because they distort matters of fact by attending to what they—unjustifiably—see as a racist legacy that, although a significant stain on America's ancient past, conservatives rightly understand we have moved beyond or overcome;

- conservatives deserve sympathy because they understand and fight for what truly makes America great: individual virtue, merit, and hard work; leftists who complain about racism are incorrect about their complaints because racism is largely a thing of the past, and, as a result, continued concern over racism is tantamount to making excuses for minorities who are lazy;

- whereas leftists complain that conservatives are racist and intolerant, it is actually those on the left who are racist and intolerant, precisely because they refuse to adopt colorblindness and because they are intolerant of or oppressive toward heterosexual white males—men who actually support racial equality precisely because they are colorblind and evaluate minorities on the basis of individual merit rather than offering them benefits that accrue on the basis of race alone; and

- white leftists who complain about white privilege apparently have no empirical evidence to support their claims, while the empirical evidence gathered in the video interviews demonstrates that Blacks deny that white privilege or racism prevents them from succeeding in America today; if only we listened to those minority voices—like Hillary Clinton suggested—we would understand that equal opportunity now exists in the United States.

Next, I will turn to PragerU videos that offer further, more explicit empirical claims about race and equal opportunity in the United States.

Discourse Analysis: PragerU, Race, Merit, and Equal Opportunity in the United States

It should be increasingly clear that central to these overlapping discursive sites is a series of unstated or barely stated empirical claims about the relation between merit and opportunity in America. These claims are, however, made explicit in other videos. One video on diversity in university science departments—titled "What Does Diversity Have to Do with Science?"—claims that the goal of increasing the representation of women in the sciences entails breaking the meritocratic standards we have had in place all along (PragerU 2019a). Ultimately, the attempt to increase minority representation asks the following question: "How can we promote more women and minorities by changing,

Discourse and Ideology

i.e., lowering, the requirements we had previously set for graduate level study?" The narrator—a professional white woman—draws attention to the fact that the National Science Foundation (NSF) has made it an explicit objective to increase the diversity of minority representation in academia. "Somehow, NSF-backed scientists managed to rack up more than 200 Nobel prizes before the agency realized that scientific progress depends on diversity." The implication? Merit was appropriately rewarded prior to this point in history; why should we lower the standards for merit now? Unfortunately, the narrator claims, "identity politics is altering the standards for scientific competence." "Solving the mystery of dark energy now apparently takes a back seat to social justice." After noting that lowering the standards for entry to medical school might be disconcerting as we make our way to surgery, she says, "the promoters of identity politics are literally playing with our lives. Medical schools' admissions committees' are now told to overlook the low test scores of black and Hispanic applicants." She goes on to note that "racial preferences in med school programs are sometimes justified on the basis that minorities want doctors who look like them. Really?! Seems much more likely than minority patients with serious illnesses want the same thing we all do: a well-trained, skilled doctor." She notes that increasing the representation of women in STEM fields "is also based on the idea that, absent discrimination, women and men would be equally represented in the sciences. This is highly unlikely, however. Differences in math proficiency between boys and girls show up as early as kindergarten" and grow from there, so that if women are not in STEM fields, it must not be because they are discriminated against but because they lack the merit men hold. In addition, the narrator is a woman herself: if we are to listen to minority voices, we should trust her judgment. Note what is not said: if these cases are parallel, then apparently Black and Hispanic applicants to medical school succeed at lower rates than whites because of innate ability rather than discrimination; of course the narrator could not explicitly say so, as it would constitute an explicitly racist claim on PragerU's own definition of racism. The narrator ends with a strong empirical claim: "the unique accomplishments of western science were achieved without regard to sex or skin color of its creators." The implication seems to be that if science has succeeded thus far, it must be because scientific discoveries go to those scientists with merit, and to change the standards of merit at this point would be to give up on the methods that seem to have worked up until this point in history.

Similarly, one video—titled "Who Are the Racists?" (PragerU 2019b), narrated by a professional Black man—notes that Black Americans can live up to the same standards as whites—that is why we see examples of Black success at every level of American society. "The policy [of affirmative action] is no longer necessary," because equal opportunity already exists.

> By lowering admission standards for blacks and some other minority students, colleges set many of these students up for failure. They get placed in schools for which they are not prepared … How could it be otherwise? If academically unprepared white students were admitted to Ivy League schools, they too would

be set up to fail. Conservatives believe blacks and other minorities are every bit as capable as whites at succeeding ... and therefore lowering standards for blacks is unnecessary as well as insulting. Yet for this belief, conservatives are called racist. The irony, of course, is that those who accuse conservatives of being racist believe blacks and other minorities are not as capable of whites of succeeding and therefore still need affirmative action.

Consequently, it is the leftists who are racists, not the conservatives, and the policies advocated by the left are the ones that hurt minorities, not the policies advocated by conservatives. In addition, if we are to listen to minority voices, we should trust this Black man.

Dennis Prager himself, in one video on the values that make America unique—titled "The American Trinity: The Three Values that Make America Great" (PragerU 2018a)—*explicitly* makes the empirical claim that equal opportunity exists in America. "America gives people the liberty to end up wherever their abilities, work ethic, and luck take them." Because America offers liberty and equal opportunity to all, he claims, the nation ended up as "the world's freest and most prosperous country." America will cease to be free, he suggests, if we displace meritocratic values with the celebration of "racial and ethnic identity."

Collectively, these videos on race, white privilege, and equal opportunity form the following discursive oppositions and associations:

(-) / (+)

leftists who believe people of color are inferior in merit compared to whites/ conservatives who believe people of color are equal in merit compared to whites

leftists who think standards must be lowered to accommodate minorities' inferior abilities/colorblind conservatives who think minorities should be held to the same standards as everyone else

leftists who prioritize equal representation in job openings above rewarding merit/ conservatives who prioritize qualified and deserving applicants meriting job placements over racist standards for distributing available jobs

leftists who value appearance over substance/conservatives who value substance over appearance

leftists setting up minorities to fail by promoting them past what merit deserves/ conservatives who don't want to unfairly set minorities up to fail

leftists who are racist/conservatives who are colorblind

leftists who want to perpetuate racialization/conservatives who rightly understand racialization is behind us since we now have equal opportunity in the United States

---

Discourse and Ideology

This set of discursive oppositions entails a considerable caricature of leftists concerned with race and racialization in the United States, and once again the writers have chosen emotionally charged exemplars to depict leftists and conservatives. As I will note in the next section, it is not that leftists think that minorities don't hold merit, but rather than standards of merit may be racist or, alternatively, gerrymandered in their operationalization so as to primarily include forms of merit most likely to be exhibited by whites. Consequently, the goal of most leftists is not to lower standards of merit but rather to change them so that they don't function to reproduce asymmetrical power relations. As such, contrary to the narrative proposed by PragerU, leftists concerned about race don't wish to perpetuate racialization but to disrupt the social conditions—including the distribution of PragerU's very ideology—that sustain it. Note: my claim that these videos caricature leftists is not based on empirical data only available to me or to dominated subjects, but rather publicly available evidence—even brief exposure to leftists propaganda will reveal that the perpetuation of racialization is the problem rather than the goal in the discourses of leftist agitators.

PragerU's overarching narrative about race, merit, and opportunity is reinforced or supported by other videos on their site, including the following:

- one in which a young Black woman encourages colorblindness by arguing that Blacks shouldn't be judged by the color of their skin but by their merit and hard work, arguing along the way that "condescending" white leftists concerned about race are worse than white supremacists because, unlike the supremacists, they judge people on the basis of race while pretending not to, making excuses for "bad behavior" done by Blacks rather than holding them to the "same standards as everyone else" (PragerU 2015a);

- one in which a professional Black man claims that if Blacks cannot succeed in America, it is not because of a lack of equal opportunity but rather because African American parents don't have the requisite family values that make their children's success possible (PragerU 2016b);

- one in which a professional Black man argues that white conservative leaders such as Richard Nixon and Ronald Reagan were not racist because they encouraged colorblindness, whereas leftists—in promoting affirmative action—are the ones who are racist because they continue to judge or evaluate people on the basis of race (PragerU 2019b);

- one in which a professional Black man says that the reason Blacks often don't succeed in America is not because of lack of equal opportunity but rather because many Blacks hold a "victim mentality," because of "Black on Black crime," or because Black fathers abandon their families (PragerU 2016d); and

- one in which a professional Black man claims that police violence against Blacks doesn't contribute to holding back the Black community so much as the "Black crime" that results from the lack of values in Black communities (PragerU 2016a).

Case Study: Racist Ideology in the United States

In each case, if racial disparities exist, they are perpetuated not in any way by social structures, laws that exhibit a disproportionate impact on minorities, or the beliefs, biases, or actions of whites in America. Rather, racial disparities exist, we are to understand, apparently because of lazy Blacks without virtue or values and leftist whites who make excuses for unemployed or criminal African Americans rather than encouraging minorities to behave in ways that earn the merit that members of other groups, such as whites, already have.

Last, I would like to point out that PragerU weaponizes standpoint epistemology against the very leftists who insist that we must always defer to the voices of the oppressed. In their videos, they carefully choose women to deny that sexism matters and choose Blacks to deny that racism matters. Naïve leftist uses of standpoint epistemology are here cleverly turned against the leftist project.

Ideology Critique: Implicit Bias

To recall, the five steps of ideology critique involve attention to the following:

1. caricatures of opponents;
2. emotionally charged exemplars;
3. claims made that are empirically supported but that might nevertheless
    a) serve to draw attention away from other, potentially relevant empirical claims,
    b) support a demonstrably false narrative, or that
    c) encourage manipulation of relevant social variables in a way that might contribute to rather than attenuate social domination;
4. claims that are not empirically supported or demonstrably false; and
5. the extent to which the former four things encourage or legitimate domination.

Although we have already to some extent moved past discourse analysis, insofar as I have already begun to point to easily demonstrable falsehoods or caricatures ("easily demonstrable," of course, on grounds that are relatively uncontested in our society), in this section I will turn to focus more extensively on the empirical claims ignored or invoked in PragerU's discourse.

Let's begin with a claim that is largely uncontested by those PragerU considers conservative or leftist: the claim that racialized economic disparities exist in the United States. For instance, in *The Color of Wealth: The Story Behind the US Racial Wealth Divide* (2006), Lui et al. show that at the turn of the twenty-first century, not only was the per capita income gap between whites and Blacks growing rather than shrinking, but so was the wealth gap. Notably, at both the median and the mean, white wealth comes out to about five times Black wealth. Again, these claims are largely uncontested. Both those on the left and on the right accept that a racialized economic gap exists. In addition, it is largely uncontested that that gap had its origin in historical conditions that began with the widely practiced institution of slavery in the early United States, a gap that was perpetuated by Jim Crow laws and institutionalized segregation even after slavery had ended. What is contested, rather, are accounts of the causes that have sustained that gap since the civil rights era.

According to mainstream leftist discourses, those economic gaps continue to exist because of three main factors: (1) discrimination based on explicit or conscious racial prejudice; (2) discrimination that result from unconscious prejudice, implicit bias, or stereotype threat and which obviate equal opportunity; and (3) structural racism—specifically, laws or institutional policies that, independently of the purported intentions of their creators and despite being colorblind on the surface, in effect have a disproportionate impact on racial minorities.

According to mainstream conservative discourses, namely, the type for which PragerU's propaganda serves as a metonym in my analysis, the causes or conditions of the racialized economic gaps individuated within the discourse include the following: (1) explicit or conscious racial prejudice, (2) individual minorities' merit and effort, and (3) minority culture, values, or family practices.

Insofar as what counts as empirical evidence varies depending on the discourse employed, the same empirical evidence might count—depending on the sympathies, interests, or background assumptions of the interpreter—as evidence that supports competing, retroductive causal accounts. In their brilliant sociological study of discourses on race in American evangelical communities, *Divided by Faith: Evangelical Religion and the Problem of Race in America* (2000), Michael O. Emerson and Christian Smith note that when they confronted conservative evangelicals with evidence for the racialized wealth gap in the United States, the evangelicals were neither concerned nor troubled. Although leftists might take the racialized wealth gap as evidence for the fact that equal opportunity does not yet exist in the United States, the conservatives they studied largely tended to take the wealth gap as evidence for the fact that African Americans are either lazy or held back by a Black culture that discouraged the formation of two-parent families—neither was disconcerting to these evangelicals because they did not view themselves as responsible for causing those problems, and therefore felt they had no responsibility for fixing them. In sum, these conservative evangelicals appeared to employ an unstated retroductive explanation that accounted for the racial gap in a manner completely different from how leftists tend to account for the gap.

I want to argue, however, that the leftist retroductive accounts make better sense of the widest array of empirical evidences than do conservative discourses like those distributed by PragerU. That is to say, we have empirical evidence for anomalies that the leftist discourse better accounts for than the conservative discourse, even on grounds that the conservative discourse explicitly states or implies are relevant. In this section and the next two, then, I want to focus on empirical evidence in support of the leftist account, before returning to the conservative discourse and considering what it potentially obscures with its own retroductive causal account of the racialized economic gap.

To begin with, leftists acknowledge that one apparent cause of the racialized economic gap is explicit or conscious prejudice. That claim is uncontested by the conservative discourse. On the contrary, they explicitly allow that such prejudices result in discrimination. If they differ from leftists on this account, it is likely only regarding the extent to which such explicit prejudices shape the behavior of people in the United States, as well as who is most likely to demonstrate such prejudices (for instance, conservatives are probably more likely to point out when a minority makes a claim about race that implies they're not colorblind than they are to report instances in which explicit anti-Black prejudice is reported by whites). The second and third causes or conditions of the racialized wealth gap for leftists include unconscious biases (such as unreported, implicit biases or stereotype threat) and institutional racism. I will consider each in turn.

Implicit bias has been an object of social scientific study for decades now. Not only have there been a variety of sophisticated university studies performed, but the literature is so well established that its results have been accessibly summarized in widely available trade books written for popular audiences. In *Blindspot: Hidden Biases of Good People*, Mahzarin R. Banaji and Anthony G. Greenwald (2016) review the literature and outline its consequences for our knowledge about race and equal opportunity in the United States, among other things. Much like Jonathan Haidt's work outlined in Chapter 6 of this book, Banaji and Greenwald's work shows that humans appear to have unreflective, unconscious responses to features of our social world—both discursive and material—that are in many cases largely unconnected with our conscious thought or reported beliefs. "For the purpose of building theories and conducting research, psychologists speak about two systems that characterize the mind: reflective and automatic" (54). The example they offer is a man named Jerry[1] who reports believing in equal rights for gays and lesbians, but who might nevertheless harbor negative responses to LGBTQ persons or discourses, practices, and policies that reflect sympathies for LGBTQ persons:

> the reflective or conscious side of Jerry's mind is indeed gay-friendly, and he can honestly say that he believes there's nothing wrong with being gay. But Jerry is also the product of a culture that has for centuries treated homosexuality to be at best an unfortunate psychological disorder, and more likely an abomination, a sin guaranteeing a quick passage to hell. If Jerry's automatic, less conscious mind makes this simple yet culturally potent association (*gay = sinful*), surely this will influence his own thoughts, feelings, and behavior. This other side of Jerry, the side to which he has less conscious access, experiences uneasiness, perhaps even shame at the thought that others might view him as gay.
>
> (Banaji and Greenwald 2016: 54)

Anecdotally, this is precisely the experience I had as I transitioned from being a conservative evangelical Christian (which is how I was raised) opposed to "the gay agenda" to someone who no longer cognitively assented to the view that there is anything intrinsically immoral or sinful about non-monogamous non-heteronormative romantic or sexual relations. For years after my conscious views changed, I remained squeamish around LGBTQ persons or any public displays of affection they demonstrated. It takes a great deal of time and effort to bring one's unconscious, unreflective affective responses into alignment with one's conscious, cognitive commitments.

To test gaps between reported beliefs and implicit attitudes, scholars developed what they call the Implicit Attitude Test or Implicit Association Test (IAT). The test, usually administered online, invites test-takers to respond to two discourses or set of cognitive associations at the same time. To describe the test on my own terms, what the IAT does is throw two competing sets of things at the test-taker—discursive or visual—that might provoke positive or negative affective responses. For instance, they might present a series of discursive markers that are likely to be associated with positive and negative valuations, such as "pleasant" or "unpleasant" words like "disaster," "agony," "hatred," "smile," "honest," or "sincere" (Banaji and Greenwald 2016: 43). At the same time, they might follow those words with pictures of white or Black children. The test asks the test-taker to record whether each serially presented word or picture is either a positive or negative term, or whether each is a Black or white child. The trick is that they switch up the means of reporting—namely, clicking "left" to signal one answer and clicking "right" to signal another; on one run-through of the test, signaling "Black child" and signaling "pleasant word" may require a left click, whereas on the next run-through signaling "Black child" and "unpleasant word" may require a right click. It appears that people who have intuitive negative associations about Black faces take longer to accurately respond to the prompt if clicking "Black child" is on the same side as "pleasant words," and will respond more quickly if clicking "Black child" is on the same side as "unpleasant words." The retroductive explanation for this is that it takes more mental energy for the test-taker to consciously overcome the unreflective, intuitive reactions they have to register the correct answer when they have to click the same side (i.e., left or right) for a series of things for which they have both positive and negative affective responses. For instance, for a test-taker with negative intuitions about African Americans, responses are quicker when clicking "left" for "pleasant" words and "white" faces, but slower when clicking "left" for "pleasant" words and "Black" faces, because they have to intermittently make an effort to turn off the automatic, intuitive negative response to those things on the left. Ultimately, the research shows that "automatic white preference is pervasive in American society—almost 75 percent of those who take the Race IAT on the Internet or in laboratory studies reveal automatic white preference" (47).

We additionally have evidence that implicit attitudes appear to affect behavior. Banaji and Greenwald's subtitle to *Blindspot* is: *Hidden Biases of Good People*. By "good people," Banaji and Greenwald mean people who report egalitarian beliefs or attitudes. They write,

> the "GOOD PEOPLE" of this book's title are people who, along with their other good traits, have no conscious race preferences. But even though they regard themselves as egalitarian, they nevertheless obtain an "automatic white preference" result on the Race IAT. This, as we know, is no small group. Among the more than 1.5 million white Americans who have taken the Race IAT on the internet, about

40 percent show this pattern of having *explicit egalitarian beliefs accompanied by automatic white preference* results of the Race IAT.

(Banaji and Greenwald 2016: 158, emphasis mine)

They call such people "aversive racists," by which they mean white people who report egalitarian values but demonstrate implicit positive associations with whites and negative associations with Blacks (see Banaji and Greenwald 2016: 158–163). This racism is "aversive" because although these subjects don't report conscious prejudices, they exhibit some form of aversion, dislike, or distrust of Blacks in their behavior. Among such individuals, "the automatic white preference expressed on the Race IAT is now established as signaling discriminatory behavior even among research participants who earnestly (and, we believe, honestly) espouse egalitarian beliefs" (47). I cannot review all of the studies here, but they write, "by early 2007, thirty-two studies had been done in which the Race IAT was administered together with one or more instances of discriminatory behavior" (49). Collectively, these studies showed that "the Race IAT predicted racially discriminatory behavior" on measures related to voting behavior, "laughing at anti-Black racial humor," and differential medical treatments offered by doctors to Black and white patients (49–52). In summary, while the "Race IAT has little in common with measures of race prejudice that involve open expressions of hostility, dislike and disrespect," it is nevertheless clear that it "is a moderate predictor of racially discriminatory behavior" (52).[2]

The findings of implicit bias research might help us explain other social scientific evidence that shows African Americans are treated differently than whites on the job market. Consider the following, from *The Hidden Rules of Race: Barriers to an Inclusive Economy* (Flynn et al. 2017).

- Studies have demonstrated that light-skinned and dark-skinned Blacks are treated differently on the job market. If we control for "level of schooling, high school performance, work experience, health status, self-esteem, age, marital status, number of dependents, workplace characteristics, and parental socioeconomic status and neighborhood characteristics at age sixteen, [scholars] found lighter-complexioned black males experienced treatment in U.S. labor markets little different from white males. On the other hand, using the same controls, black males with medium and dark skin tones incurred significant discriminatory penalties relative to white males" (42). Consequently, "greater proximity to white-identified norms of appearance and attractiveness carries benefits" (42).

- Studies show that employers sometimes evaluate applicants on the basis of shifting criteria, depending on the race of the applicant. "Employers willingly overlook[] missing qualifications in white job applicants and weigh[] qualifications differently depending on the applicants' race" (87). In particular, one study showed that "deficiencies of skill or experience appear to be more disqualifying for minority job seekers" (87).

Discourse and Ideology

- One study showed that white men with a felony record were more likely to be called back for job interviews than Black men without a criminal record but holding the same skills; that is to say, it appears that we have statistical evidence that felony records are more likely to be overlooked if one is white, so much so that whites with felonies are apparently seen as more qualified than Blacks without, despite all other qualifications being equal (87).

- Another study showed that, in large and racially diverse cities such as Boston or Chicago, applicants who submitted resumes with white sounding names (e.g., Emily or Greg) were 50 percent more likely to be called for an interview than applicants with identical resumes but with Black sounding names (e.g., Lakisha or Jamal). How about when the resumes are different? For instance, what are the effects when the study was done with resumes that showed a greater or lesser number of skills or years of work experience? "In summary, employers simply seem to pay less attention or discount more the characteristics listed on the resumes with African-American sounding names. Taken at face value, these results suggest that African-Americans may face relatively lower individual incentives to invest in higher skills" (Bertrand and Mullainathan 2004: 1003–1004).

PragerU's propaganda claims that equal opportunity already exists in America, but these findings suggest otherwise. It is difficult to see how PragerU could account for these anomalies within their own narrative. For the leftist narrative, however, according to which people suffer from implicit biases that correlated with discriminatory behavior, these findings are not particularly difficult to account for.

The findings of research on implicit bias also likely help us explain why African Americans and whites are treated differently in the US criminal justice system. Consider the following evidence, also from *The Hidden Rules of Race*.

- The darkness of African Americans' skin also correlates with "greater odds of harsher sentences if convicted of comparable crimes, including greater odds of receiving the death penalty for similar capital crimes" (Flynn et al. 2017: 42).

- In addition, "research has shown that more than 80 percent of defendants sentenced for crack offenses are African American, despite the fact that more than 66 percent of users are white or Hispanic" (119). That is to say, while Blacks make up 44 percent or less of crack users, they are 80 percent of those sentenced for its use. This statistic is likely to be conditioned by a number of possible causes, such as implicit bias or racial profiling on the part of the officers investigating and arresting Black users, or the fact that whites or Hispanics (more likely whites) have access to wealth that permits them to hire those more expensive lawyers more capable of preventing conviction or reducing sentencing for those who are convicted. Whatever the reason, the application of crack cocaine sentencing laws disproportionately impact African Americans.

Case Study: Racist Ideology in the United States

- In general, studies show that "African Americans comprise only 15 percent of the country's drug users, yet they make up 37 percent of those arrested for drug violations, 59 percent of those who are convicted, and 74 percent of those sentence to prison for a drug offense" (119). That is to say, they make up a minority of drug users but a majority of those convicted and sentenced for drug offenses. Another considerable disproportionate impact of an apparently colorblind set of laws.

Michelle Alexander provides further evidence in *The New Jim Crow* (2012).

- Studies show rates of marijuana use are relatively uniform across race, but studies also show that "white students use cocaine at seven times the rate of black students, use crack cocaine at eight times the rate of black students, and use heroin at seven times the rate of black students" (99). In addition, "white youth have about three times the number of drug-related emergency room visits as their African American counterparts" (99). However, despite the fact that we have little empirical evidence that Blacks use drugs at rates higher than whites, "in seven states, African Americans constitute 80 to 90 percent of all drug offenders sent to prison" (98). In addition, "in at least fifteen states, blacks are admitted to prison on drug charges at a rate from twenty to fifty-seven times greater than that of white men" (98).

- As a result of the fact that police engaged in the so-called "war on drugs" tended to target Black neighborhoods, "1 in every 14 black men was behind bars in 2006, compared with 1 in 106 white men. For young black men, the statistics are even worse. One in 9 black men between the ages of twenty and thirty-five was behind bars in 2006" (100). Again, however, based on the statistics cited above, "these gross racial disparities simply cannot be explained by rates of illegal drug use activity among African Americans" (100). Nor can these incarceration rates be explained by an increase in violent crimes, as "today violent crime rates are at historically low levels, yet incarceration rates continue to climb" (101).

- Racial profiling in policing has consistently been ruled acceptable by the Supreme Court and, as a result, racial profiling persists across the United States, despite studies that have demonstrated, for instance, "in New Jersey, whites were almost twice as likely to be found with illegal drugs or contraband as African Americans, and five times as likely to be found with contraband as Latinos" (133). However, because of racial profiling, "in New Jersey, the data showed that only 15 percent of all drivers on the New Jersey Turnpike were racial minorities, yet 42 percent of all stops and 73 percent of all arrests were of black motorists—despite the fact that blacks and whites violated traffic laws at almost exactly the same rate" (133). We have similar evidence for racial profiling in other states as well, including Maryland (133), Florida (134), Illinois (134), California (134), and New York (135).

Discourse and Ideology

In summary, "racial disparities exist at every level of the U.S. criminal justice system" (Alexander 2012: 109). While those sympathetic to PragerU's discourse might like to attribute those disparities to higher crime rates among African Americans, the studies cited above show that, at least when it comes to drug use, Black people are convicted and sentenced at rates *much higher* than their rate of drug use. Just as implicit bias might help us explain the racialized discrepancies of opportunity in the United States, it likely also helps us explain why Blacks are treated so differently in the criminal justice system. In addition, it is difficult to see how PragerU could account for this sort of differential treatment, given their denial that any significant barriers to minorities' success persist.[3]

Ultimately, the importance of *explicit* prejudice in retroductive explanations accounting for the causes of racialized economic discrepancies may be overestimated; the forms of discrimination that contribute to the wealth gap may be just as much unconscious as conscious. While both leftists and conservatives note the possible impact of explicit prejudice on equal opportunities for minorities, conservative discourses like those generated by PragerU do not emphasize or explicitly take into account the possible effects of unconscious bias.

In summary, according to academic research,

- the wealth and income gap between whites and Blacks in the United States has largely stayed the same since the civil rights era, despite the common narrative that presumes all race issues were solved by the end of the 1960s;
- we also have a great deal of evidence for the claim that people tend to hold unconscious, implicit biases that shape how they interact with people different from them—people who consciously view themselves as not racist may nevertheless exhibit behavior that is shaped by the introduction of racially related variables in particular social situations;
- arguably, this evidence for implicit bias helps us explain those studies that demonstrate that there is still a great deal of discrimination both on the job market and in the criminal justice system in the United States; and
- PragerU's discourse fails to explain such findings—indeed, they fail even to draw attention to the findings in the first place.

Ideology Critique: Stereotype Threat

Much like the research on implicit bias, social scientific research on stereotype threat has been going on for decades, and its results are accessibly summarized in literature widely available to the public. The most valuable introductory source on stereotype threat is Claude M. Steele's *Whistling Vivaldi: How Stereotypes Affect Us and What We Can Do* (2010). According to Steele's work and his survey of the work of others, people who have been "primed" to think about a possible stereotype about a group of which they are a member apparently suffer from an additional "cognitive load" (122) the stereotype puts on them, and in a way that negatively affects their performance. "The problem is that the pressure to disprove a stereotype changes what you are about in a situation. It gives you an additional task" (110). In a college classroom, for instance, you are not only attempting to learn the course content, "you are also trying to slay a ghost in the room, the negative stereotype and its allegation about you and your group" (111).

Some of the most interesting studies have been on the stereotype that women are not good at math. Not only is there a widespread stereotype that suggests women are not as good at math as men, some studies show that women perform worse than men on math tests. The question arises: "perhaps women's lower performance reflected a *lesser biological capacity* for math" (Steele 2010: 34, emphasis mine)? Or, by contrast, is their lower performance caused by the stereotype threat the women must think about but which the men can blissfully ignore? Steele writes, this puts researchers in a position "where two plausible, but very different ideas could explain our simple finding that, after we had carefully selected women and men who had strong and equal math skills, the women did worse on a difficult math test we gave them than the men" (37). "We needed an experiment that could tell us which of the two was the better account of our findings" (37). That is, to describe this in my terms, they needed an experiment to see if the women test-takers' performance was invariant in relationship to biological variables or cultural ones. They therefore constructed an experiment where they "primed" the test-takers in a way so as to make "the cultural stereotype about women's math ability irrelevant to their performance" (38). They did this by priming the test-takers with the following sort of claim: "You may have heard that women don't do as well as men on difficult standardized math tests, but that's not true for the *particular* standardized math test; on this *particular* test, women always do as well as men" (38). As a result, when it came to their cognitive load "they were now in the same boat as men taking this test" (39).

How did the women do?

> The results were dramatic. They have us a clear answer. Among participants who were told the test did show gender differences, where the women could still feel the threat of stigma confirmation, women did worse than equally skilled men, just as in the earlier experiment. But among participants who were told the test *did not* show gender differences, where the women were free of confirming anything about being a woman, *women performed at the same high level as equally skilled men. Their underperformance was gone.*
>
> (Steele 2010: 40)

What does this demonstrate? At the very least it shows that scientists can manipulate test-takers' performance by adjusting cultural variables, in which case performance is not wholly conditioned by biological variables, such as genetics. In addition, it demonstrates that no one need deploy a stereotype for the effect to take place. When it came to the poorer performance of women who were not told that women do well on this test, it turns out that "this could happen without bad intentions, without the agency of prejudiced people … Our test takers were alone in a room. They had no reason to believe that the experiment was run by people biased against women. What they did know, of course, was the culture of society" (Steele 2010: 42). Consequently, much like implicit bias, unconscious cognitive processes may function to disadvantage minorities in a way completely independent from conscious prejudice.

The results of these experiments have been further supported by studies that have replicated their finding and by new studies that seek ever-more-precise invariances between cultural variables and individual performance. It turns out that it is pretty easy for researchers to manipulate conditions to reliably produce the effects they predict with the retroductive theory of stereotype threat. Early studies focused on math performance and gender difference, but later studies focused more on race. For instance, in one experiment,

> Black students performed dramatically worse than equally skilled white student when the test was presented as an ability test, when they were at the risk of confirming the negative ability stereotype about their group; but they performed just as well as equally skilled whites when the test was presented as nondiagnostic of intellectual abilities, when they were at no risk of confirming the ability stereotype.
>
> (Steele 2010: 56)

Whites were equally easy to manipulate in other tests (Steele 2010: 8). Even people in the dominant group, it appears, are vulnerable to stereotype threat in the right conditions.

One major consequence of this research is that ability or merit is not contingent entirely upon any particular individual's abilities or hard work; on the contrary,

> places like classrooms, university campuses, standardized testing rooms, or competitive-running tracks, though seemingly the same for everybody, are, in fact, different places for different people. Depending on their group identity, different people would simply have different things to contend with in these places—different stereotype threats, different ambiguities about how to interpret their experiences, [etc.].
>
> (Steele 2010: 40)

That is to say, two people apparently taking the same test may in fact be operating under very different conditions if they each experience different stereotype threats. Performances on tests of ability and merit quite literally are shaped by more than biological ability.

As Steele moves through the literature on stereotype threat, he unfolds what researchers have increasingly learned. Their theories were never static; they constantly offered new retroductive hypotheses to explain the data they produced, and then invented new tests that would help them identify, more precisely, which cultural variables affected performance. Along the way, Steele starts to develop a theory that identity "cues" with which a subject can connect appear to reduce cognitive load or performance anxiety. One study involved showing study participants literature about what it might be like to work at a particular Silicon Valley tech company. The literature was varied in terms of how many minorities were depicted as working at the company. "The results were strong for virtually every sample we studied" (Steele 2010: 146). The representation of minorities did not appear to affect the interest of whites who might like to work at the company. Whites apparently "felt they would belong in the company and trusted the company no matter what cues the newsletter contained" (146). By contrast, for Black respondents, "when the company was depicted as having a moderate number of minorities, they trusted it and felt they would belong in it as much as white respondents did" (146). However, "when the company was depicted as having a low number of minorities, blacks' trust and sense of belonging were more conditional" (146). It appear that cues matter—if there are no cues signaling the presence of people whose identities intersect with one's own, one may not feel welcome in that social context.

In one of the PragerU videos discussed above, a young African American woman suggests that patients at the hospital want to see a competent doctor, not a doctor who looks like them. She argued, "racial preferences in med school programs are sometimes justified on the basis that minorities want doctors who look like them. Really?! Seems much more likely than minority patients with serious illnesses want the same thing we all do: a well-trained, skilled doctor." By contrast, Steele's research on cues reveals that patients may, in fact, want a doctor who looks like them—they may not feel comfortable or at ease when surrounded by no one who looks like themselves. She ended her video by noting that "the unique accomplishments of western science were achieved without regard to sex or skin color of its creators"; by contrast, the empirical evidence produced by Steele and others shows that such accomplishments likely depended on particular social conditions in which gender difference and skin color shaped, improved, or attenuated the performance of "western scientists." We can empirically demonstrate that minorities afflicted by stereotype threat or a lack of cues that make them feel welcome are negatively affected in their performance.

Notably, *PragerU attends to "cues" of exactly the same sort* that Steele discusses and complains that leftists use discourses on diversity to distribute cues that are hostile to conservatives. This is most evident in their video, "Just Say 'Merry Christmas,'" narrated by Dennis Prager himself (PragerU 2016c), in which he attacks leftists who not-so-subtly replace "Merry Christmas" with "Happy Holidays."

> The change from wishing fellow Americans "Merry Christmas" to wishing them "Happy Holidays" is a very significant development. Proponents of "Happy Holidays" argue, "it's no big deal. Proponents of 'Merry Christmas' are making a mountain out of a molehill." But the "Happy Holidays" advocates want it both ways: they dismiss opponents as hysterical, but at the same time, in addition to replacing Merry Christmas with Happy Holidays, they have relentlessly pushed to replace "Christmas Vacation" with "Winter Vacation" and "Christmas Party" with

Discourse and Ideology

"Holiday Party." So, then, which is it? Is all this elimination of the word "Christmas" important, or not? The answer is obvious: it's very important. That's why so much effort is devoted to substituting other words for Christmas, and these efforts have been extraordinarily successful.

Prager reports that, although Jewish, he happily tells others "Merry Christmas" at holiday times. "Many of those I wish 'Merry Christmas' are probably relieved to hear someone who feels free to utter the 'c-word.'" He goes on:

> the opponents of Merry Christmas and other uses of the word Christmas know exactly what they're doing. They're disingenuous when they dismiss defenders of "Merry Christmas" as fabricating some "war on Christmas." Of course it's a war on Christmas! Or, more precisely, a war on the religious nature of America.

What PragerU is discussing is, empirically, the same phenomenon that Steele defines as "cues." Cues matter, because *the group that gets to determine which cues are hegemonic gets to determine what identities are received as normal in society.*

By replacing "Merry Christmas" with "Happy Holidays," leftists are tinkering with public cues, and ones that matter for many people. Prager suggest that leftists can't have it both ways: they can't insist that these words or cues matter and don't matter at the same time. The same, then, is true of PragerU's discourse: either cues like "Merry Christmas" and television commercials with minorities have material effects, or they don't. Consequently, I would argue that not only do leftists have grounds on the basis of which they can accept Steele's theory of stereotype threat and cues, but conservatives who accept PragerU's discourse also have grounds on the basis of which to accept his theory.

Note that, if we accept Steele's research on the negative effects of stereotype threat, ignoring that research has the effect of potentially reinforcing social domination. For instance, if minorities are disadvantaged by stereotype threat and members of the dominant group ignore that fact, then the dominant group permits that disadvantage to work to the ongoing benefit of the dominant group and ongoing detriment to minority groups.

In addition, if we accept this research as persuasive, it is clear—once again—that full, equal opportunity does not exist in the United States. Despite PragerU's insistence that we do, in fact, have equal opportunity, these studies demonstrate that minorities face barriers or hurdles that members of dominant groups don't face. Steele's research militates against the conclusion that we live in a society where merit alone is sufficient for success—and, if we ignore such evidence, it is likely that unequal conditions will persist, for we cannot alter conditions that we ignore in the first place.

In this section, I have argued:

- we have a great deal of evidence that social factors—for instance, stereotype threat—shape individual performance in ways that cannot be reduced to individual ability;

- the public cues a group presents send signals to individuals about whether they will be comfortable in a particular social context, and thus individuals may perform poorly under conditions where few social cues reflect their own culture or personal experiences; and
- PragerU accepts that such cues matter—for they complain when people eliminate Christian cues from public spaces in the United States—but fail to take into account how cues might affect racial minorities.

Ideology Critique: Structural Racism

The three alleged causes on leftist discourses for the racialized wealth gap in the United States included explicit racism, unconscious cognitive biases such as implicit bias and stereotype threat, and structural racism. I would now like to turn to the last. Much like implicit bias and stereotype threat, we have a great deal of empirical evidence for the existence of structural racism, defined as laws or institutional policies that are colorblind on the surface but which have a disproportionate impact on minorities. As I am using the term, the disproportionate impact could be the result of two conditions. On the one hand, sometimes disproportionate impact is the result of the fact that laws or policies bear on matters statistically more relevant for minorities; for instance, it is clear that voter ID laws in the United States, intentionally or not, are statistically more likely to bar racial minorities from voting than whites. On the other hand, sometimes disproportionate impact results from the implicit or explicit biases of the people who apply the apparently colorblind laws or policies; for instance, while a particular workplace may purportedly abide by equal opportunity hiring practices, according to which race, gender, ethnicity, religious identity, and so on are irrelevant with respect to an individual's qualifications for the job, nevertheless the person or persons making hiring decisions may suffer from implicit bias in a way that negatively affects the chances of minority applicants. As I have already discussed how implicit bias likely affects the *application* of apparently racially neutral rules or laws, in this section I will review evidence we have that prior or current laws or policies have had and continue to have a disproportionate impact on minorities.

To begin with, studies show that access to wealth (in addition to income) is a crucial condition of possibility of upward mobility. As Thomas M. Shapiro demonstrates in *The Hidden Cost of Being African American: How Wealth Perpetuates Inequality* (2004),[4] studies show that "working-class and poor families use wealth for life support, to cushion bad times, and to meet emergencies"—in sum, they use wealth as a buffer against homelessness (35). "Middle class families, in contrast, use their assets to provide better opportunities that advantage" their children, such as moving to a home in a better school district, paying for private schooling, or paying for college (35). Wealth inequality is highly racialized, as noted above. At the median, white families hold five or six times the wealth compared to Black families. According to one study, in 1999 "26 percent of all white children grew up in asset-poor households, compared to 52 percent of black American children and 54 percent of Hispanic children" (40). In addition, parents often help their children economically well into adulthood, and "the capacity of white parents to help, or to have helped already, their adult children financially is at least four times greater than that of black parents" (97). It is clear, based on this evidence, that whites have an easier time, at the median, of leveraging that wealth to secure conditions that make their children's economic mobility more likely. Notably, these wealth gaps hold independently of income. That is to say, when comparing whites with high salaries and Blacks with high salaries, the wealth gap holds; "even when incomes are equal and high, a cavernous [wealth] gap remains" (50). While some might attribute the gap to differential savings rates, that is not supported by the empirical evidence, which shows that Blacks and whites save at similar rates (96). If whites are able to save more money, it appears to be because on average they make more money, not because they save a greater percentage of their money than do African Americans.

The wealth gap is also explained, in part, by the fact that the accrued value of homes is greater in predominantly white communities compared to Black ones. "The higher the segregation, the wider the black-white home value gap; [by contrast,] lower levels of residential segregation produce narrower gaps" (Shapiro 2004: 121). As a result, it appears that "residential segregation costs African American homeowners enormous amounts of money by suppressing their home equity in comparison to that of white homeowners" (121). In addition, the ability of Blacks to move out of predominantly Black neighborhoods and into predominantly white neighborhoods is limited compared to that of whites, because of the systematic lack of material wealth necessary to acquire the sort of homes in neighborhoods where house values are less depressed. Quite simply, access to wealth makes the accrual of wealth easier, and Blacks systematically have less wealth to begin with. In summary,

> the major implication is that whites' upward residential mobility typically places them into better-off communities with more educational resources and thereby improves their educational advantage. The fact that most whites live in homogeneous and financially viable communities during the years they have school-age children ensures white children greater access to higher quality education.
>
> (Shapiro 2004: 140)

It is clear that whites systematically move to segregated communities that permit their house values to accrue more quickly and their children to attend better schools; as a result, "white flight" is a demonstrable phenomenon. Note: none of this assumes that these whites are racist in the sense of "prejudiced." On the contrary, the "issue is not that some innate, unalterable racism drives neighborhood and school segregation but that better-off white families reap benefits from segregated schools and communities whether they acknowledge it or not, and people of color, especially children, pay the steepest price" (Shapiro 2004: 153). Consequently, white flight is perhaps better explained by the fact that whites make decisions designed to facilitate their children's upward mobility—that is, white flight serves white families' long-term interests—than by racism, although the practice disproportionately impacts Blacks negatively in a way that is intersubjectively verifiable.[5]

Why do these wealth gaps exist in the first place? What prior, historical circumstances contributed to the disparities in handed-down wealth? First, during the times of slavery and Jim Crow, explicitly racist laws existed to disenfranchise Blacks and prevent them from accruing either income or wealth which they could pass on to their descendants. Once those explicitly racist laws were abolished, they were in many instances replaced with laws that were colorblind on the surface, but nevertheless had a disproportionate impact on the accrual of wealth among Black families. For instance, consider the following evidence gathered by historian Ira Katznelson in his book, *When Affirmative Action Was White: An Untold History of Racial Inequality in Twentieth-Century America* (2005).

- When Social Security was signed into law by Franklin Delano Roosevelt in 1935, the available benefits were contingent upon "prior wages, which, for blacks, often had been derisory" (42). In addition, farmworkers and domestic workers—specifically, the sorts of jobs African Americans were more likely to hold—were excluded from the program altogether. "Across the nation, fully 65 percent of African Americans fell outside the reach of the new program; between 80 and 80 percent in different parts of the South" (43).

- These exclusions were remedied by legislation passed in 1954, but "even then, African Americans were not able to catch up since the program required at least five years of contributions before benefits could be received" (43). Consequently, "for the first quarter century of its existence, Social Security was characterized by a form of policy apartheid" (43).

- New Deal legislation under Roosevelt was also racially disproportionate in the protections offered to laborers. The new laws were designed to improve the "health, efficiency, and well-being of workers," in part through the establishment, for instance, of a minimum wage and a forty-hour work week (55). However, once again, predominantly Black farmworkers and domestics were excluded from these protections. The decision to exclude farmworkers and domestics appears to have been motivated by explicitly racist concerns. One southern lawmaker noted, for instance, that an equal minimum wage for whites and Blacks "might work in some sections of the United States, but those of us who know the true situation know that it just will not work in the South. You cannot put the Negro and the white man on the same basis and get away with it" (60). Of course, at the end of the day, for my purposes the intention is largely irrelevant; what matters, rather, is not what motivated the law but the fact that the law had a disproportionate impact that systematically disadvantaged farmworkers and domestics, which were more likely to be Black, as well as the fact that the contemporary wealth gap is in part a result of such laws and their legacies.

Discourse and Ideology

One other particularly relevant past practice with still-lingering consequences was the practice of "redlining." One part of Roosevelt's New Deal involved the creation of the Federal Housing Administration (FHA) in 1934. Once formed, the FHA developed policies according to which home loans could be offered to possible home buyers. They favored offering loans for homes in predominantly segregated, homogenous, and white parts of town surrounded by a "green line" on FHA maps and avoided offering loans for houses in those homes in predominantly Black or desegregated parts of towns surrounded by a "red line," insofar as homes within the red line were of lower quality and value, as well as less likely to accrue in value. "Because of the way the administrative rules were set up, the growth in housing was channeled into [predominantly white] suburbs at the expense of central cities" (Flynn et al. 2017: 69).

What evidence do we have that *current* laws, policies, or their implementation contribute—in the present—to the racialized wealth gap in the United States? As noted above, it appears that implicit bias dramatically shapes minorities' job opportunities and their treatment within the criminal justice system. Consider the following findings, which introduce further evidence about how Blacks and whites moving through our social institutions have different experiences. First, although PragerU would prefer to attribute the wealth gap to minorities' laziness or their "victim mentality," it is clear that the racial gap persists *even among people who hold the same educational level.* "At every level of education, earnings for black men and women lag behind those of their similarly skilled white counterparts" (Flynn et al. 2017: 78). That is to say, median income for hard-working Blacks with college degrees, master's degrees, or further, advanced degrees (such as doctorates) is lower than the median income for hard-working whites who have accomplished the same level of education and hold the same skills (79). Second, segregation in the workplace appears to economically benefit whites. One study revealed "a $10,000 increase in the average annual wage of an occupation is associated with a seven percentage-decrease in the proportion of black men in the occupation" (86). That is to say, when there are fewer Black men in an occupation more money is made for the remaining members of the occupation. Crucially, once again, this holds independently of education and skill level, and thus cannot be attributed to laziness or "victim mentality." "The relationship between wages and racial makeup of an occupation is true across all skill levels, which tells us that wage disparities cannot be explained away by education or training differentials" (86).

We therefore have studies that collectively demonstrate that African Americans systematically inherit and hold less wealth (wealth that is, statistically, a condition of possibility for upward mobility), face significant discrimination in hiring, are convicted and sentenced at disproportionate rates, are less well paid than whites even when holding the same credentials, and tend to be grouped together in lower-income occupations. If these studies are to be believed—and the fact that PragerU cites similar social scientific studies themselves is a sign that they ought to be accepted as authoritative under the rules their its own discourse—then African Americans are systematically disadvantaged by the legacy of prior practices and continuing discrimination that persists under ostensibly colorblind laws. PragerU's discourse, however, completely ignores this empirical evidence at odds with their overarching narrative about equal opportunity. These inconvenient facts are nowhere found in their narrative, presumably because they cannot account for them without undermining their narrative.

In addition, if discriminatory treatment persists, the domination of whites over Blacks is reinforced by PragerU's overarching narrative, insofar as a discourse cannot address and attempt to correct for what it does not allow to exist in the discourse. One metaphor I often find useful is that of a medical diagnosis: if the causes of a symptom are misidentified, the proposed treatment is more likely to cause a subject more sickness, and for two reasons—first, because of the side effects of the new treatment and, second, because the actual cause(s) of the sickness remain unidentified and unaddressed. PragerU's discourse blames inequality on Blacks themselves and ignores the intersubjectively verifiable evidence we have for barriers to equal opportunity. As such, those barriers are undiagnosed and unaddressed and, as such, likely will persist. In any case, we have no empirical evidence that the barriers will magically disappear on their own, particularly if discourses like those of PragerU *systematically discourage whites from taking racial disparities seriously*. Their discourse's systematic production of antipathy toward poor Blacks assumed to be lazy or to hold a victim mentality is more likely *to contribute to* racial discrimination than attenuate it. Since PragerU encourages its viewers to believe equal opportunity exists, a white viewer sympathetic to its ideology who is interviewing a poor Black applicant knows all he needs to know about the person: they must be poor for a reason, and that reason apparently has nothing to do with barriers to equality, and consequently they probably don't deserve to be hired—in addition to the fact that any cues on the body or their practical sense that reflect African American culture will likely make the white interviewer unconsciously uncomfortable with the Black interviewee. In sum, ignoring discrimination likely functions to sustain or even increase discrimination.

Ideology Critique: Ideological Explanations for the Racialized Wealth Gap

In the previous three sections (on implicit bias, stereotype threat, and structural racism), I have focused on retroductive explanations for the racialized economic gap in the United States preferred by and used in leftist discourses. Now I want to turn to PragerU's explanation for that gap. Like leftists, they acknowledge some explicit prejudice may negatively affect minorities. However, at the same time, they explicitly claim that equal opportunity exists in America. These claims are logically contradictory with one another. Defenders of PragerU's discourse would likely resolve such a contradiction by claiming that yes, explicit prejudice exists and attenuates equal opportunity, but at a level so slight as to be negligible (as should be clear form the preceding section, the evidence against equal opportunity is far from negligible).

Their second and third explanations for the economic gap are that those minorities who don't succeed must individually lack merit or hard work, or they are held back by African American culture, values, or family practices, such as single-parent rather than dual-parent families. If a Black woman, for instance, is poor, it must be because she lacks intelligence, a work ethic, or has too many children with absent fathers such that she cannot hold a good job and care for her children at the same time. As I noted above, in one video the narrator claims that if we find fewer women in STEM fields, it must be because women lack the ability that men do. I drew attention to the fact that she brings up another example at the same time, suggesting that "Medical schools' admissions committees' are now told to overlook the low test scores of black and Hispanic applicants." The unstated parallel is that Black and Hispanic applicants to medical school lack the merit that whites have, just as women lack the merit men hold when it comes to mathematic ability. Notably, the claim about women is explicitly sexist and the implication about Blacks and Hispanics is racist. Here PragerU's propaganda is literally suggesting that the reason women and racial minorities fail is perhaps because women and racial minorities inherently have inferior capacities for work in scientific fields. So, in addition to the fact that they say individual racists might disadvantage minorities, and that might help us account for the racialized economic gap in the United States, here they seem to *contribute* to the discourse by implying racist claims that, if used when taking into account college admissions or hiring in STEM fields, would likely further contribute to that racialized economic gap. In sum, how does PragerU account for the fact that racial minorities make less money and hold less wealth? Either because they are lazy, because they have bad values, or because they are just inherently inferior.

What empirical evidences does PragerU provide for their claim that individual Blacks don't succeed because of lack of merit or hard work? Crucially, *none is provided*; rather, the claim seems to be *deduced from the assumption that equal opportunity exists in the United States*. If equal opportunity exists, and minorities don't succeed, it must be because of some variable other than opportunity, such as their merit or work ethic. Since they deduce this from the (demonstrably false) assumption that equal opportunity exists, the deduction is also false. However, they have a ready-made narrative designed to discourage investigation into other potentially relevant variables—like the ones discussed in the previous section—that affect minority achievement: we live in a society where lazy people make excuses for themselves. In fact, it is unlikely that any subject in a modern workplace has failed to experience interactions with lazy and incompetent coworkers—of whatever race—for whom their lack of success is purportedly always someone else's fault. Consequently, anecdotes that confirm the stereotype that lazy people make excuses for themselves are instantly cognitively accessible. If we are predisposed to accept that equal opportunity exists and that people who fail do so because they are lazy, and if we all have had lazy coworkers, it is easy to reach for and find anecdotal evidence that confirms the stereotype; for those sympathetic to PragerU's claims, confirmation bias rushes in to confirm them. As such, no systematic empirical evidence that laziness correlates with lack of minority success is required, and the sort of research into the effects of implicit bias and stereotype threat are never taken into account, as they have nothing to account for. On the contrary, on this discourse, all that needs accounted for is why the racialized economic gap exists, and anecdotal evidence provides all the confirmation necessary for someone whose discourse discourages sympathies for minorities in the first place.

So PragerU acknowledges that explicit prejudice attenuates minority success (and they make implicitly prejudiced claims about racial minorities) but fail to offer any evidence for the fact that racial minorities lack merit or a work ethic, apparently because they simply deduce it from their assumption that equal opportunity exists (excluding those few, explicitly prejudiced racists). However, they do offer empirical evidence for their third explanation for the racialized wealth gap: the claim that the lack of Black fathers' involvement in their children's lives negatively affects their children's success. In "Black Fathers Matter" (PragerU 2016b), a professional Black man notes that "children who grow up without a father are five times more likely to live in poverty and commit crime, nine times more likely to drop out of school, and twenty times more likely to end up in prison." Citing a social scientific journal, they note that "even after controlling for varying levels of household income, kids in father-absent homes are more likely to end up in jail. And kids who never had a father in the house are the most likely to wind up behind bars." Supplementing this, he goes on to add that "out-of-wedlock births" among African American has risen from 25 percent in 1965 to 73 percent in 2015. By contrast, for whites the numbers were 5 percent in 1965 to 25 percent in 2015. (The same statistics are also brought up in another video, "The Top 5 Issues Facing Black Americans" [PragerU 2016d]). The implication appears to be the following: if there is a racialized economic gap in the United State, and Blacks end up disadvantaged according to the numbers, absentee fatherhood appears to be a variable demonstrably relevant for explaining that gap. The Black narrator notes that he learned an important lesson from his father on this point: "Hard work wins. You get out of life what you put into it. You can't control the outcome, but you are 100% in control of the effort. And before blaming other people, go to the nearest mirror and ask yourself, 'what could I have done to change the outcome?'" "Fathers matter," he concludes.

Collectively, then, we have empirical evidence that several manipulable variables arguably contribute to the racialized economic gap in the United States, and those variables include (1) explicit prejudice, (2) implicit biases, (3) stereotype threat, (4) cues, (5) structural racism, and (6) family structures that don't include a father (I don't include the other PragerU causal explanations here because they offer zero empirical evidence for them). As noted in Chapter 5, in any particular social context there are an indefinite number of manipulable variables we might adjust to bring about particular results. The leftist narrative sensitizes its users to the fact that things outside the control of minorities negatively affect minority success, while the conservative narrative sensitizes its users to the fact that things apparently within the control of minorities negatively affect minority success. As such, the leftist narrative emphasizes that privileged members of the dominant group ought to be responsible for controlling for their prejudices, biases, and so on, whereas the conservative narrative emphasizes that minorities ought to be responsible for building two-parent families. That is, not only do their discourses offer competing causal accounts, but their discourses also make different parties responsible for efforts that might attenuate the economic gap.

Discourse and Ideology

One of the central issues for ideology critique was that, when it comes to empirical claims that appear to be intersubjectively verifiable, it is nevertheless useful to ask if those empirical claims (1) obscure another possibly relevant set of verifiable empirical claims, (2) reinforce a larger narrative that has demonstrably false elements, or (3) encourages manipulation of variables in a way that arguably increases rather than decreases social domination. Consequently, consider the following. (1) Even if it is intersubjectively verifiable that absentee fatherhood contributes to the racialized economic gap, emphasizing that fact exclusively involves drawing attention away from a wide variety of other potentially relevant variables (such as implicit bias, stereotype threat, evidence for employment discrimination, etc.). (2) Even if it is intersubjectively verifiable that absentee fatherhood contributes to the racialized economic gap, in PragerU's discourse this point functions to prop up the claim that equal opportunity exists in the United States, despite the fact that we have empirical evidence that that is simply not the case. Those who consume PragerU's discourse are encouraged to accept that equal opportunity exists, and they have a ready-made narrative to account for the fact that despite the existence of equal opportunity: of course Blacks don't succeed at the same rate as whites, but that is the fault of absentee Black fathers. So, this causal explanation, even if true—in that absentee fatherhood probably is a variable that, if we manipulated it, would have an effect on the racialized economic gap in ways that are intersubjectively verifiable to people with different sympathies—is expliclty used to prop up an overall narrative about equal opportunity that is demonstrably false. (3) Even if it is intersubjectively verifiable that absentee fatherhood contributes to the racialized economic gap, encouraging that we make minorities responsible for acting on that variable arguably contributes to displacing responsibility for the lack of equal opportunity on the minorities that suffer from the lack of equal opportunity—that is to say, it appears to increase domination by *encouraging us to shift all social responsibility for the economic gap from the dominant group that benefits from that gap to the minority group that suffers from that gap.* In sum, PragerU's discourse appears to make Blacks solely responsible for removing the hurdles that disadvantage them and which benefit whites—whites apparently have no responsibility for doing anything whatsoever about the economic gap.

At the end of the day, do we have any means of determining which causes for the racialized economic gap are the *real* causes? In the sense that we can offer intersubjectively verifiable empirical evidence that certain variables have an invariant relationship with other variables, they are *all* real causes. The question, ultimately, is not what is *the* cause for the economic gap, because there is no *one* cause—there are likely millions of possibly relevant causes or variables. Rather, from the perspective of the social critic interested in relations of domination, the question is this: which variables do we want to intervene on, and who are we going to make responsible for those interventions? Those who have internalized the leftist discourse appear to hold sympathies for minorities who are not solely responsible for their social standing, while those who have internalized PragerU's conservative discourse appear to hold antipathies toward such minorities, insofar as they view them as responsible for their own fate. Consequently, it is clear that the

Case Study: Racist Ideology in the United States

interventions recommended by each are in line with the sympathies and antipathies generated by the discourse itself.

In this section, I have argued,

- PragerU offers no evidence for their claim that there are no significant barriers to equal opportunity in the United States—rather, they seem to deduce it from their other ideological commitments;
- PragerU attempts to account for economic disparities between whites and Blacks on the undemonstrated hypothesis that Blacks must be lazier than whites, or on the grounds that Black men make poor fathers (based in part on some statistical evidence about the rate of absentee fatherhood among African American families) and, as such, their children grow up incapable of competing with whites on the US job market; consequently,
- their narrative ignores variables related to the wealth and income gap that might be within the control of whites and focus entirely on the one variable that might to some extent be within the control of African American fathers—that is, their narrative arguably reinforces domination because it makes Blacks entirely responsible for overcoming their own domination and relinquishes individual whites of seriously considering their possible role in structurally reinforcing that domination.

On balance, it does seem to me that the leftist discourse has more empirical evidence in support of its overarching narrative. Leftist discourses, for instance, could include and account for why rates of absentee fatherhood vary by race and how and why that might affect the economic gap, while the conservative discourses don't even attempt to account for the empirical evidence we have for implicit bias, stereotype threat, structural racism, and so on. The leftist account, consequently, appears to be able to include and account for a wider range of empirical data than does the conservative discourse, which has to ignore a great deal of evidence for the narrative to be entirely persuasive. If I prefer the leftist discourse, it is in part because my sympathies have been generated by discourses that discourage producing or contributing to asymmetrical power relations, but also because the leftist discourse has a greater amount of intersubjectively verifiable empirical data in support of its overall claims, data that even people with competing sympathies can accept as true on their own discursive grounds.[6]

Conclusion

My goal in this book has been to demonstrate that we can do discourse analysis *and* ideology critique from a poststructuralist perspective. In fact, I think that attending to the conditions of possibility of knowledge makes our knowledge stronger rather than weaker. In this chapter, I have attempted to demonstrate how we as scholars can analyze a discourse, analyze the empirical claims the discourse makes, weigh those

Discourse and Ideology

empirical claims against other claims within the same discourse or claims found in other discourses—and all with the goal of showing how discourses and ideologies may contribute to reproducing social domination.

While I would never claim that my analysis of PragerU's discourse is "objective" or based on "reality-as-it-is-in-itself," I hope the benefits of such an approach is clear to those who, like me, are similarly interested in how rhetoric and social domination are related to one another. As always, I am open to considering new vocabularies, new discourses, or new empirical findings. In fact, as I was completing this book I was informed by a colleague in social psychology that Claude Steele's research has been difficult in some cases to replicate—it appears that the effects of stereotype threat, while real, may be overstated in his account. In the spirit of Hegel—who prods his readers to dialectically take into account and attempt to incorporate new ideas and new evidences—I have let my account of Steele's research stand, even as I eagerly look forward to learning more about how social psychologists are emending his findings. All forms of knowledge reflect their conditions of possibility; if we waited until all evidence was in before taking a stand on a subject matter, we would have to wait until the death of the universe. Until then, contingent knowledge is the only knowledge available to us, but recognizing that fact arguably encourages us to be open-minded to future evidence that could disrupt what we hold to be certain knowledge. I look forward to dialectically improving my account as new knowledge about stereotype threat is produced.

CODA

In this book I have attempted dialectical thinking: I have reviewed the history of the concepts often used for thinking about the connection between the way people talk and the relations of social domination they inhabit, shown where they might be more or less useful for particular projects, and have arrived at the conclusion that the most useful concepts for doing discourse analysis and ideology critique—at least given my particular sympathies—include the following:

- *a priori* and *a posteriori*;
- categories and the phenomenal field;
- things-for-us and object individuation, idealization, or substruction;
- constitutive vs empirical discourse;
- empirical and nonempirical;
- critique and conditions of (im)possibility of knowledge production, including:
  - phenomenal evidence,
  - time,
  - language,
  - education,
  - capital and power,
  - invested researchers,
  - etc.;
- discourse analysis and ideology critique;
- sympathies and antipathies;
- interpellation and the capacitation of subjectivity;
- desires and interests;
- social domination (on an objective rather than subjective definition);
- intersubjectively verifiable evidence;
- causation, deduction, induction, and retroduction; and
- reported belief, functionalism, and recrement.

I am persuaded—at this point in time—that these are the most useful concepts for understanding the functions of discourse and ideology, for example, the discourse and ideology produced by PragerU.

Notably, dialectical thinking is complicated by the fact that we can never consider all of these concepts at the same time, and thus could always consider the usefulness of these concepts in a different order. Consequently, at any particular point in the book I may (tentatively) use a concept that I later discard. Suspicious readers might go back and read through the book and point out: "Martin talked about x in Chapter 1 but in Chapter 3 he says that x is a useless idea." Yes, of course, but this is how dialectical thinking progresses—there is no way around it for temporal subjects; the fact that thinking takes place in time makes thinking difficult.

In Chapter 1, I noted that Hegel dialectically considered the vocabulary and empirical findings of phrenology and rightly concluded they were not worth saving for his particular philosophical project. Similarly, I have considered and discarded the following terms as not useful for my project:

- realism—in particular, realism defined as the view that what makes a claim true has nothing to do with the conditions of possibility of knowledge, such as consciousness, language, historically situated subjectivity, and so on;
- things-in-themselves or reality-as-it-is-in-itself;
- God, souls, and free will;
- unconditioned, unmediated, or objective knowledge;
- internalized oppression;
- social domination (on a subjective definition); and
- autonomy and liberal theories of subjectivity, according to which power is only restrictive rather than constitutive of subjectivity.

Other scholars may continue to wish to use these concepts in their work; I don't have the authority to enforce my vision of the study of culture on others. However, I hope readers sympathetic to my goals will at least consider the potential weaknesses of these concepts that I have attempted to identify along the way.

***

The approach I have defended in this book is, to no one's surprise, the approach I use as an instructor in the college classroom. Much of what I do as a teacher involves showing students how, in particular contexts, people have to say x—namely, to utilize locally authoritative discourses—to serve their interests, whether x is "the Bible says," "it's the law," "you're bullying me," or "this assessment demonstrates I met the outcomes I set for myself." In many cases, it doesn't matter if x is true, or if x is something they actually believe—it is just what we have to say to influence the behavior of other persons in this context. While some may view this as overly cynical, it seems to me to be one of the most useful lessons one can learn in college: what counts as persuasive is always context-dependent.

For those in institutional settings like mine, examples are easy to identify. When I served as Chair of the Faculty Senate at my college, I was charged with acting in ways that served the interests of the faculty. However, to serve the interests of the faculty, I had to learn what sorts of discourses are persuasive to those who occupy subject positions in other parts of the institution. What is persuasive to a member of the board of trustees may not be persuasive to the president, and what is persuasive to the president may not be persuasive to the provost, and what is persuasive to the provost may not be persuasive to the registrar, the office for student services, or the athletics director, etc.—despite the fact that we all work in the same institution and, in principle but not in fact, are theoretically working toward the same social ends. What serves the interests of occupants of some positions in the social structure is often different from what serves the interests of those in other positions, and sensitivity to that fact is a condition of possibility of speaking persuasively to people in other social positions.

In addition, what counts as relevant empirical evidence sufficient to move them varies: while pointing out that some rule in the dorms appears to unfairly punish students who are already disadvantaged might move the provost to initiate a revision process for the rule, that evidence is unlikely to move members of the security staff, who, if confronted by that information, might very well say "that might be true, but this is the rule and I'm obligated to do my job and write up this student for their infraction." The fact that a student is often rude to her professors might be something of interest to a student's advisor attempting to help that student improve her academic performance, but if a student complains to the dean that I graded her unfairly, the fact that she was rude to me will be entirely beside the point to the dean if there is actual evidence for the assignment of an unfair grade. Navigating any complex social institution requires attending to which discourses, ideologies, or empirical evidences are relevant in which context, and those who fail to understand this fact will likely be unable to serve their own interests or the interests of those they represent.

With the rising costs of a college education, and increasing concerns over whether a college education is a worthwhile investment, the question of domination often presses itself upon me—especially as many of my students are not economically privileged (this is why US News and World Report lists us as a "Top Performer of Social Mobility" [U.S. News 2021]). As I regularly point out to my students, when I am acting as a professor and they are acting as students, we are in a relationship of domination; by all accounts, I gain more privilege and material capital as a result of our relationship than they do. If they are successful in completing their degree (this is to leave aside those students who pay a great deal in college tuition but are set up to fail because they were admitted without the requisite qualifications or were not sufficiently served by the available academic resources for weak students), they gain a credential that will likely—although not always—bear a significant value across their lifetime; the costs they incur in gaining that credential, however, are enormous. By contrast, for privileged, tenure-track professors the benefits of participating in this relationship are greater—and more directly assured, insofar as we command a salary whose value is not as contingent as the value of the credential students are earning—and the costs fewer.

For that reason, by helping students identify what is in their interests and how to manipulate discourses so as to serve their interests, I hope to reduce the asymmetry of

Discourse and Ideology

costs and benefits built into our institutional relationship of domination. I never feel justified in telling them what discourse they ought to adopt, or what sympathies they ought to feel. However, I do think their interests are served when I show them how to switch from one register to another and produce varying empirical evidences as needed. Which discourses will be useful to them will always of course be contingent on their particular interests and sympathies. If they are attempting to cure cancer, biological discourses will be more useful for identifying which variables in the world they can manipulate to serve their interests than the discourses they learn in a sociology class. By contrast, if they are attempting to reduce the racial economic gap in the United States, sociological discourses will likely be more useful for intervening in relevant variables than biological discourses. Ideally, each part of the curriculum teaches them forms of knowledge that assist them in achieving their interests; in English classes they learn how to use clear writing to persuade, in graphic design classes they learn how to use the visual arrangement of words and shapes to persuade, and in statistics classes they learn how to use math to persuade.

This seems to me to be the best justification—at least on discourses I accept as authoritative—for the ongoing relevance of the liberal arts: we train students how to use varying discourses, show them how those discourses are more or less useful depending on their immediate needs or interests, and show them how to switch from one discourse to another as their needs, interests, or contexts shift. When we are successful, we equip our students with the skills they need to serve their interests for the remainder of their lifetime. This does not eliminate my relationship of domination with them, but attenuates it.

In addition, some of my more privileged students have sympathies for disadvantaged subjects. By equipping such students with discourses that allow them to bring into relief relations of social domination, as well as means of manipulating the social order so as to reduce those relations, I am helping them sharpen their sympathies.

In many ways, this distinguishes me from faculty who openly make normative claims about what is just or what is unjust, insofar as I am less prepared than they are to insist that students ought to share my sympathies. While I wish more students did share my sympathies, I also maintain that Hume was right when insisting that no "ought" ever follows from any "is." The claim that racism saturates American culture might be empirically warranted, but whether or not one is moved by this is contingent upon one's sympathies, which are never universal. Were I to naturalize my sympathies, or were I to present them as if they were universal, I would be mystifying part of the world rather than showing students how to understand it. We cannot independently verify—by appealing to empirical evidence—claims like "privileged people ought to care about racial minorities" in the way that we can with claims such as "*if* you have sympathies for minorities, you can serve the interests of those minorities by acting on the social order in these particular ways." (With all due respect to Kant, hypothetical imperatives are the only ones that can be empirically warranted.)

This is as objective as I think we can be if we accept the claims of poststructuralism, for instance, that knowledge is always conditioned by human investments and power relations, as well as historically contingent upon regnant discourses. But this is objective enough for me, and, I hope, helps to authorize what I see as uniquely valuable in the modern liberal arts university—namely that, unlike most other public spaces, what we teach is in some way empirically warranted or intersubjectively verifiable by students *no matter their interests or sympathies*, and the method of inquiry we model will be useful for them throughout their lifetime, even if their interests diverge from our own.

***

Despite the fact that I am situated within the academic study of religion and hold a post as a professor of religious studies, many readers will have noted that at no point does "religion" serve as a term with any sort of load-bearing capacity in this project. Yes, the word religion appears on occasion, but usually when quoting a primary source that uses it. In my experience, most (but not all) uses of the word religion in our field reflect one of two impulses: the impulse to lift up and *revere* or *romanticize* religion as a special form of culture—one that teaches people to be moral, for instance, or which functions to ensure social solidarity—or to *demean* religion as a special form of culture—one that systematically employs false empirical claims or reinforces social domination.

For instance, in *Soul Searching: The Religious and Spiritual Lives of American Teenagers* (2005), Christian Smith and Melinda Lundquist Denton frame their analysis of teenagers' religion in frankly normative terms: "How are our teenagers doing in life? ... How will they turn out? Happy and responsible? Troubled and depressed? Or worse?" (3). Adults, they insist, fear the "dark side" of youth: "Dangerous peer pressure. Parties. Foolish choices. Drugs. Drunk driving. Crime. Pregnancy. Abortions. AIDS. Suspensions. School dropouts. School shootings. Suicide" (3). Perhaps there is "something profoundly wrong about the lives of American teenagers" (3). Ultimately, Smith and Denton discover that the millennials they studied are, for all practical purposes, deists—in which case these millennials have perhaps lost or forgotten the authentic moral substance of the religious traditions they claim to participate in. How can religion be a moralizing force if people are making it up as they go along? Consequently, in their postscript—explicitly written for "Religious Communities and Youth Workers" (Smith and Denton 2005: 265)—Smith and Denton claim that "youth need to be challenged" and that if congregations spent more time encouraging youth to reflect on the moral resources of their traditions, the youth would have a better understanding of

> the potential not only for human goodness but also for potential human failings and evils, [and] the arguably relative long-term vulnerabilities of broadly humanistic moral and social systems ... [Y]outh may then better appreciate the strengths and weaknesses of the moral grounding and teaching of their own religious traditions and take more seriously in their own lives the particularities of their own faith communities and commitments.
>
> (Smith and Denton 2005: 269)

If youth are going to avoid drugs, drinking, abortion, and AIDS, they will apparently need a bit more Jesus and a little less secular humanism.

Discourse and Ideology

On the other hand, some scholars in the academic study of religion tend to define or portray religions as cultural traditions that systematically make empirically false claims about imaginary beings such as gods and angels. According to D. Jason Sloan in *Theological Incorrectness: Why Religious People Believe What They Shouldn't*, religious people are "prone to reasoning errors" (Sloan 2004: viii). "Religion involves the attribution of agents in the world (often none are actually seen to exist)" (58). Sloan arguably mocks the sorts of claims he imagines such believers make: "the gods caused me to win the lottery; demons made me do it; ghosts haunt the house; angels saved my life; there's a devil in that blue dress; the goddess killed the dinosaurs" (58). While I, like Kant, would agree that we tend to lack empirical evidence for gods, it appears to me that defining religion in this way functions to present religions as uniquely, fundamentally irrational. By contrast, I tend to take it for granted that humans *in general*—including myself and those who share my own culture—are fundamentally irrational in a wide variety of ways (depending on how we define "rationality," of course), in which case those cultural traditions we colloquially call "religions" are not all that unique on this score.

I desire neither to revere nor demean those groups often called "religious." In addition, from my perspective, "religion" doesn't seem to be all that special. Many institutions—not just those ones colloquially referred to as religious—arguably teach people to be "moral" in some way, capacitate social solidarity, systematically employ unwarranted or false empirical claims, or reinforce asymmetrical social relations. In addition, the idea that Christians, Jews, Muslims, Hindus, Buddhists, and the Azande systematically employ nonempirical or insufficiently warranted empirical claims more than institutions such as PragerU or the Trump administration just is not a persuasive one to me. Such a claim is nevertheless useful for permitting atheist scholars to enjoy a sense of intellectual superiority over their rhetorical opponents—to sneer at them—or useful for encouraging antipathies toward those groups sometimes called religions.

Husserl argued that all empirical knowledge must be warranted by phenomenal evidence, but then goes on to say that European geometry is objectively true, in the sense that it can never be revised—*a claim for which he* a priori *lacked empirical evidence*. He also claimed that Europe was united by an invisible spiritual entelechy or telos that unfolded in a way that made European philosophy objectively superior to that of other cultures—*a claim for which he* a priori *lacked empirical evidence*. Lincoln argued that the academic study of religion must focus on temporal and material rather than transcendent matters (see, for instance, his well-known "Theses on Method" [Lincoln 2012: 1–3]). However, as I pointed out in Chapter 4, even he at times seems to employ a theory of internalized oppression, wherein subjects have desires that are suppressed or mystified by the ideologies they inhabit—that is, *desires for which we do not have empirical evidence or which, if they exist, are transcendent to the phenomenological field from which we derive empirical evidence*. Who among us doesn't on occasion appeal to things for which we do not have evidence? Who among us doesn't have blind spots or unwarranted assumptions in our theories? The idea that religious practitioners are somehow systematically less rational than other human subjects seems to be a part of an

Coda

othering technique more than anything else (for more on the idea that one's method of study may involve techniques designed to "other" the subjects one studies, see Driscoll and Miller 2019).

As far as I can tell, those discourses and ideologies we might call religious appear to function similarly to those discourses and ideologies we don't normally call religious. PragerU's discourse, it seems to me, functions very similarly to nineteenth-century Protestant discourses in the United States on "Ham's curse," which were derived from the book of Genesis and functioned to reinforce the social standing of whites over Blacks. As Frederick Douglass notes in *Narrative of the Life of Frederick Douglass, an American Slave*,

> my master attended a Methodist camp-meeting ... and there experienced religion. I indulged a faint hope that this conversion would lead him to emancipate his slaves, and that, if he did not do this, it would, at any rate, make him more kind and humane. I was disappointed in both these respects. It neither made him to be humane to his slaves, nor to emancipate them. If it had any effect on his character, it made him more cruel and hateful in all his ways ... Prior to his conversion, he relied upon his own depravity to shield and sustain him in his savage barbarity; but after his conversion, he found religious sanction and support for his slaveholding cruelty.
>
> (Douglass 2016: 15)

In my opinion, we don't need a special theory of religion to understand the phenomenon Douglass describes. While some scholars might refer to nineteenth-century Protestant discourses as "religious" and PragerU's discourse as "not religious," what do we gain by making that distinction? In my opinion, we don't gain anything: *what I want to know about these matters I have already learned by doing a discourse analysis and ideology critique*—adding the claim that some are religious and some are not doesn't tell me anything additionally of use. Consequently, as should be clear, this was a book not about religions but rather about discourses and ideologies. The method and theory outlined here could be used to understand any discourse or ideology, religious or not.

***

To close, I invite readers to consider memes posted to social media in 2020 by one of my family members with conservative sympathies—a family member who also enjoys and shares PragerU videos. One meme features an image that apparently shows several African American Black Lives Matter protesters—some with raised fists and some holding protest signs—sitting on a car on which they have scrawled "No Justice No Peace" and other slogans; the air around them is densely clouded with smoke, as they seem to be participating in a protest in which buildings or cars have been set on fire. The caption reads: "CLAIMS TRUMP WILL DESTROY AMERICA ... AS THEY GO OUT AND ACTUALLY DESTROY AMERICA." A second meme has fourteen images of

Discourse and Ideology

buildings on fire with protesters or rioters cheering, with a caption that says: "If you want this for your neighborhood, vote Democrat." A third meme features a picture of Jordan Peterson—a famous conservative public intellectual whose academic credentials lend credibility to his conservative views—and the following (grammatically incorrect) text:

> Just like the terrorists in the Middle East surround their hideout with women and children, so if you bomb the hideout, you kill these innocent people.
>
> The "Social Justice Warrior" types do the same thing. They find a hypothetically vulnerable group, and they use them as a protective shield while they move incrementally forward. If you object, suddenly you're picking on the poor, vulnerable people. – Jordan Peterson

A fourth meme offers a quotation, apparently from conservative journalist Matt Walsh, laid over a statue of a man on a horse:

> Leftism is a religion of self-loathing. It teaches white people to hate their race, boys to hate their sex, women to hate their femininity, Americans to hate their country, westerners to hate their history. What a contemptable, toxic thing it is.
>
> It also teaches wives to hate their husbands, mothers to hate their children, children to hate their parents. That's all it does. Turns groups against each other and individuals against themselves. I hate everything about it. It's poison.

One final meme has a still from a classic Warner Brothers Looney Tunes cartoon, with Elmer Fudd standing in the forest—except instead of the shotgun he is famous for carrying, he holds what appears to be an AR15 assault rifle with a scope and a silencer. Above Fudd's head is a speech bubble, according to which Fudd is saying "Be very very quiet. I'm offending liberals."

Someone systematically exposed to leftist discourses on institutional or systemic racism are unlikely to find these memes funny or incisive, as their sympathies and antipathies will have been produced by a competing discourse. However, those family members of mine who consume and enjoy PragerU videos, the memes make perfect sense—the memes repeat back to them claims that reinforce their existing sympathies. As Hegel said (see Chapter 1), "those writers, preachers, speakers, etc., are regarded as the most intelligible who tell their readers or listeners things which they knew already by heart: things which are familiar to them and self-evident." These memes reinforce what my conservative family members already take to be self-evident—the last even uses visual cues (i.e., Elmer Fudd) they have likely been familiar with since childhood—and the memes permit them to enjoy a laugh at the expense of those who consume and reproduce competing discourses. For those who internalize PragerU's discourse, leftists are fools—apparently fools who want to watch their neighborhoods burn to the ground.

Notably, all the same things are true of leftist memes, which generally reflect sentiments produced by leftist discourses and which allow leftists who consume them to laugh at conservative fools and enjoy a sense of intellectual superiority over them—like the many memes I shared over the last four years that were insulting toward or humorous at the expense of the Republican Party or Donald Trump. Tell me what you laugh at, what enrages you, what you find emotionally moving, and I can probably tell you what you have been reading or watching.

Discourses matter, then, particularly because they *produce affective responses*, responses that, in turn, shape behavior—even when discourses are not "believed." For those family members who consume, enjoy, and share PragerU videos and conservative memes like the ones above, the Black Lives Matter protest across town is something that they can ignore or, if they cannot ignore it—for instance, if it blocks traffic as they are driving to work—they might be annoyed or even angry. These family members take for granted that Black Lives Matter concerns are entirely baseless, or, if not baseless, beneath serious consideration. None of my conservative family members are police officers, they haven't killed Black men in custody, so in their opinion there is nothing more they as individuals need to do about the matter. The production and consumption of conservative discourses fundamentally conditions their affective response to the world. And, once more, the same is true of leftists, their discourses, and their affective responses.

Readers who are interpellated by leftist discourses might be affectively moved (as am I) by the statistics on race in the United States reported in Chapter 7; however, those statistics might not be much of interest to someone interpellated by PragerU's discourse. Pointing out those statistics to fans of PragerU videos may have no effect on them, for PragerU's discourse provides them with a way to feel intellectually superior *because* they ignore those foolish leftist claims. Given their sympathies, those statistics might be seen as little more than desperate attempts by liberals to try to remain relevant. As Hume famously put it in his *A Treatise of Human Nature*, passion rather than reason appears to direct human behavior: "'Tis not contrary to reason to prefer the destruction of the whole world to the scratching of my finger" (Hume [1739–1740] 1985). At the end of the day, showing partisans empirically warranted knowledge may have less of an effect on their behaviors than the sympathies or antipathies produced by the discourses they are systematically exposed to. "Facts" alone do not move people—sympathies and antipathies are necessary as well.

NOTES

Introduction

1. To be clear, for Kant "out there" is literally false, as "there" implies space, and noumena are outside space for Kant, by definition.
2. One further note: another objection Foucault has to Marxist forms of ideology critique is that they depend upon a view of subjectivity and repression that Foucault does not accept (see Foucault 2000: 118–119 and 1980b: 58–59). I've chosen to leave discussion of this out of my introduction for two reasons. First, I wanted to focus on the epistemological issues raised by taking up Foucault's approach rather than issues related to subjectivity. Second, as should be clear in my chapter on "Domination," I too reject a view of subjectivity that sees power as only or primarily repressive of subjectivity; following Foucault, I allow that power also has a constitutive role in producing subjects and their desires.

Chapter 1

1. This line is adopted from Foucault's comments on Nietzsche: "At this point I would like to reply to a possible objection: 'All that is very fine, but that isn't in Nietzsche. Your own ravings, your obsession with finding power relations everywhere … made you believe that Nietzsche said that'" (Foucault 2000: 13). Foucault responds to the anticipated objection: "I chose this passage from Nietzsche in terms of my own interests, not with the purpose of showing that this was *the* Nietzschean conception of knowledge … but only to show that there are in Nietzsche a certain number of elements that afford us a model for historical analysis of what I would call the politics of truth" (13).
2. The secondary sources I've found most useful for interpreting Kant's work are Paul Guyer's *Kant and the Claims of Knowledge* (1987) and Frederick C. Beiser, *German Idealism: The Struggle against Subjectivism, 1781–1801* (2002). Also particularly useful is Paul Guyer and Allen W. Wood's introduction to their translation of the *Critique of Pure Reason* (Kant [1781] 1998).
3. See Guyer and Wood's introduction to the *Critique of Pure Reason* (Kant [1781] 1998: 18).
4. For Aristotle's comments on an eternal, unmoved mover, see chapter XII of *Metaphysics* (2001: 872–888); for explication and commentary, see also Mary Louise Gill and James G. Lennox's edited volume, *Self-Motion: From Aristotle to Newton* (1994).
5. "One can only wonder, then, why one sees it repeated so often that one does not know what the *thing-in-itself* is, when there is nothing easier to know than this" (Hegel [1830] 2010: 89).
6. For instance, when Hegel was an aspiring young scholar, J. G. Fichte—an important influence on Hegel's own thought—"was forced to leave Jena after having trumped-up charges of atheism leveled against him" (see Terry Pinkard's "Introduction" to his translation of Hegel's *Phenomenology of Spirit* [Hegel [1807] 2018: x]).

7. One important exception: according to the latest research in cognitive science, it appears that we can individuate mid-sized objects (which I will define in the next chapter) without using vocabulary.
8. Kant accepted the following twelve: unity, plurality, totality, reality, negation, limitation, inherence and subsistence, cause and effect, community (i.e., reciprocity), possibility and impossibility, existence and nonexistence, and necessity and contingency (see Kant [1781] 1998: 212).
9. One might defend Kant by arguing that all of these categories can be derived from Kant's basic twelve categories, but I am unpersuaded (for reasons beyond the scope of this chapter).
10. There is clearly a contradiction here, and it is one that I have left in because I'm still pondering on whether there might be a limited use to make of the concept of "spirit"—although, clearly, a use very different from Hegel's.
11. Careful readers will note that although I value the tradition of phenomenology, I don't include phenomenologists of religion in my genealogy; this is because it appears to me that phenomenologists of religion—for instance, Rudolf Otto, Gerardus van der Leeuw, Joachim Wach, and Mircea Eliade—focus too much on things-in-themselves that *do not appear*—such as "the Sacred"—than on what does. For more on this, see Tim Murphy's systematic analysis of phenomenology of religion, *The Politics of Spirit: Phenomenology, Genealogy, Religion* (2010).
12. Hyppolite's other works include *Studies on Marx and Hegel* (1969) and *Figures de la pensée philosophique* (1971).
13. My interpretation here is deeply indebted to Rudolphe Gasché's *The Tain of the Mirror: Derrida and the Philosophy of Reflection* (1986), but I have chosen not to quote Gasché—his prose is often obscure—but rather to simplify or reduce his argument into terms that I think most readers will be able to understand.
14. Note: "time" is only one such example of something that makes objective knowledge impossible; Derrida develops a number of neologisms to point to other conditions of impossibility of knowledge, including differance, trace, spacing, writing, and many more.
15. See, for instance, Fausto-Sterling (2000: 7–8, 22–23, and 75–76).

Chapter 2

1. Richard Rorty notes that, from a realist perspective, anti-realists are often accused of being "some newfangled kind of transcendental idealist[s]" (Rorty 1991: 101); Rorty notes that the point for the anti-realist is, instead, that "she can find no use for the notion" of things-in-themselves (101).
2. There is a great deal of excellent secondary literature on Derrida's early work on Husserl. In particular, my reading of Derrida has been shaped by the following resources: Vernon W. Cisney's *Derrida's Voice and Phenomenon* (2014), Edward Baring's *The Young Derrida and French Philosophy, 1945–1968* (2011), Martin Hägglund's *Radical Atheism: Derrida and the time of Life* (2008), Leonard Lawlor's *Derrida and Husserl: The Basic Problem of Phenomenology* (2002), and Paola Marrati's *Genesis and Trace: Derrida Reading Husserl and Heidegger* (2005).
3. I have used this example in print before; see Martin (2017).

Notes

4. Hoffman notes other experiments that upset our commonsense view of temporality and perception; see, for instance, Hoffman (2000: 180–181).

Chapter 3

1. Lincoln's other key works, which indirectly inform what follows, include *Death, War, and Sacrifice: Studies in Ideology and Practice* (1991a), *Emerging from the Chrysalis: Rituals of Women's Initiation* (1991b), *Authority: Construction and Corrosion* (1994), and *Religion, Empire, and Torture: The Case of Achaemenian Persia, with a Postscript on Abu Ghraib* (2007).
2. Hacking may not be correct; the famous double-slit experiment provides evidence that quarks might, in fact, respond to their observation or how they are identified.
3. In what follows, I will still refer to the objects of discourse as "objects," whether discussing "subjects" or "objects."

Chapter 4

1. Reasons for this slip through time are never provided in the narrative; the fight, Hank's apparent concussion, and the resulting time travel are, arguably, simple and clumsy plot devices designed to set up the remainder of the story.
2. While Twain, since *Huckleberry Finn*, was sensitive to the plight of African American minorities and increasingly depicted them in a sympathetic light, slurs against Native Americans continued to appear in his work.
3. I would like to make special mention of Joel A. Johnson's provocative essay, "A Connecticut Yankee in Saddam's Court: Mark Twain on Benevolent Imperialism" (2007), for suggesting this line of interpretation of *A Connecticut Yankee* and for pointing out the connections to Twain's anti-imperialist writings about the US invasion of the Philippines.
4. Notably, after the battle American troops took photographs of themselves standing over trenches filled with corpses of men, women, and children as if they were hunting trophies.
5. For an overview of this debate and a review of the philosophical tradition from which it arises, see Michael Rosen, *On Voluntary Servitude: False Consciousness and the Theory of Ideology* (1996). Anthropologist James C. Scott offers what are some of the most valuable criticisms of the theory of false consciousness; in particular, see *Weapons of the Weak* (1985) and *Domination and the Arts of Resistance* (1990).
6. I would argue that the goal of Foucault's work on "the repressive hypothesis" is not that repression *never* takes place, but rather that repression is not the only or primary operation of power on subjectivity. As such, the rhetorical diatribe against that hypothesis is not best read as an outright rejection but an overstatement in the direction of a more sophisticated analytic.

Chapter 5

1. See also Helen E. Longino's excellent work, *The Fate of Knowledge* (2002).

Notes

Chapter 6

1. *The Enigma of Reason: A New Theory of Human Understanding*, by Hugo Mercier and Dan Sperber (2018) is probably the single-most-useful book on these matters I have read, but sadly I found the book after having completed this chapter, so I was not able to use its findings here. I highly recommend it as the best source for the latest summary of how cognitive science and social psychology show human speech is systematically invested in ways that are agonistic and context-dependent.
2. Andrew Dole's *Reframing the Masters of Suspicion: Marx, Nietzsche, and Freud* (2019) provides a particularly useful overview of some of the central problems with making functionalist claims about culture, especially as relates to the so-called "hermeneutics of suspicion."

Chapter 7

1. Some readers might recognize that "Jerry" is in fact the fictional "Jerry Seinfeld" from the show *Seinfeld*. This particular anecdote is taken from the episode in which Jerry and George Costanza keep insisting that they're not gay, but defensively add "not that there's anything wrong with that!" each time.
2. Jonathan Kahn's *Race on the Brain: What Implicit Bias Gets Wrong about the Struggle for Racial Justice* (2018) offers a valuable account of the limits of the usefulness of implicit bias research for political purposes—specifically insofar as it appears to have colorblindness as its ultimate end goal and tends to assume that accounts of merit are potentially theoretically neutral. I found chapter 3, on "Accepting Conservative Frames: Time, Color Blindness, Diversity, and Intent" to be especially valuable.
3. For more on policing and the history of the "war on drugs," see Radley Balko, *The Rise of the Warrior Cop: The Militarization of America's Police Forces* (2014).
4. See also Melvin L. Oliver and Thomas M. Shapiro, *Black Wealth/White Wealth: A New Perspective on Racial Inequality* (2006) and Thomas M. Shapiro, *Toxic Inequality: How America's Wealth Gap Destroys Mobility, Deepens the Racial Divide, and Threatens Our Future* (2017).
5. On the subject of housing, see also Richard Rothstein, *The Color of Law: A Forgotten History of How Our Government Segregated America* (2017) and Keeanga-Yamahtta Taylor, *Race for Profit: How Banks and the Real Estate Industry Undermined Black Homeownership* (2019). Also relevant is Mehrsa Baradaran's book on banking and segregation, *The Color of Money: Black Banks and the Racial Wealth Gap* (2017).
6. Other useful resources on racist ideologies—which I did not have space to discuss in this chapter—include Karen E. Fields and Barbara J. Fields, *Racework: The Soul of Inequality in American Life* (2014), Eduardo Bonilla-Silva, *Racism without Racists: Colorblind Racism and the Persistence of Racial Inequality in America* (2014), Carol Anderson, *White Rage: The Unspoken Truth of Our Racial Divide* (2017), and Ashley Jardina, *White Identity Politics* (2019).

BIBLIOGRAPHY

Ahmed, Sara. 2006. *Queer Phenomenology: Orientations, Objects, Others*. Durham, NC: Duke University Press.
Alexander, Michelle. 2012. *The New Jim Crow: Mass Incarceration in the Age of Colorblindness*. New York: The New Press.
Althusser, Louis. 2008. "Ideology and Ideological State Apparatuses (Notes toward an Investigation)." In Louis Althusser, *On Ideology*, 1–60. London: Verso.
Althusser, Louis. 2014. *On the Reproduction of Capitalism: Ideology and Ideological State Apparatuses*. Trans. G. M. Goshgarian. London: Verso.
Anderson, Carol. 2017. *White Rage: The Unspoken Truth of Our Racial Divide*. New York: Bloomsbury USA.
Aristotle. 2001. *The Basic Works of Aristotle*. Ed. Richard McKeon. New York: The Modern Library.
Balko, Radley. 2014. *The Rise of the Warrior Cop: The Militarization of America's Police Forces*. New York: PublicAffairs.
Banaji, Mahzarin R. and Anthony G. Greenwald. 2016. *Blindspot: Hidden Biases of Good People*. New York: Bantam Books.
Baradaran, Mehrsa. 2017. *The Color of Money: Black Banks and the Racial Wealth Gap*. Cambridge, MA: Belknap Press.
Baring, Edward. 2011. *The Young Derrida and French Philosophy, 1945–1968*. Cambridge: Cambridge University Press.
Barnett, Stuart (ed.). 1998. *Hegel After Derrida*. London: Routledge.
Bartkowski, John P. 2001. *Remaking the Godly Marriage: Gender Negotiation in Evangelical Families*. New Brunswick, NJ: Rutgers University Press.
Bedazzled. 2000. [Film] Dir. Harold Ramis. USA: Regency Enterprises.
Beiser, Frederick C. 2002. *German Idealism: The Struggle against Subjectivism, 1781–1801*. Cambridge, MA: Harvard University Press.
Bell, Catherine. 1992. *Ritual Theory, Ritual Practice*. Oxford: Oxford University Press.
Berger, Peter L. and Thomas Luckmann. 1967. *The Social Construction of Reality: A Treatise in the Sociology of Knowledge*. New York: Anchor Books.
Berkeley, George. 1996. *Principles of Human Knowledge and Three Dialogues*. Ed. Howard Robinson. Oxford: Oxford University Press.
Bertrand, Marianne and Sendhil Mullainathan. 2004. "Are Emily and Greg More Employable than Lakisha and Jamal? A Field Experiment on Labor Market Discrimination." *American Economic Review* 94/4: 991–1013.
Bonilla-Silva, Eduardo. 2014. *Racism Without Racists: Color-Blind Racism and the Persistence of Racial Inequality in America*, 4th Edition. Lanham, MD: Rowman & Littlefield Publishers.
Bottici, Chiara. 2007. *A Philosophy of Political Myth*. Cambridge: Cambridge University Press.
Bourdieu, Pierre. 1977. *Outline of a Theory of Practice*. Trans. Richard Nice. Cambridge: Cambridge University Press.
Bourdieu, Pierre. 1984. *Distinction: A Social Critique of the Judgment of Taste*. Trans. Richard Nice. Cambridge, MA: Harvard University Press.
Bourdieu, Pierre. 1990. *The Logic of Practice*. Trans. Richard Nice. Stanford, CA: Stanford University Press.

Bourdieu, Pierre. 1999. *Language and Symbolic Power*. Ed. John B. Thompson. Cambridge, MA: Harvard University Press.

Bourdieu, Pierre. 2000. *Pascalian Meditations*. Trans. Richard Nice. Stanford, CA: Stanford University Press.

Braver, Lee. 2007. *A Thing of This World: A History of Continental Anti-Realism*. Evanston, IL: Northwestern University Press.

Butler, Judith. 1990. *Gender Trouble: Feminism and the Subversion of Identity*. London: Routledge.

Butler, Judith. 1993. *Bodies that Matter: On the Discursive Limits of Sex*. London: Routledge.

Butler, Judith. 1995. "Contingent Formations." In Seyla Benhabib, Judith Butler, Drucilla Cornell, and Nancy Fraser (eds.), *Feminist Contentions: A Philosophical Exchange*, 35–57. London: Routledge.

Butler, Judith. [1987] 1999. *Subjects of Desire: Hegelian Reflections in Twentieth-Century France*. New York: Columbia University Press.

Butler, Judith. 1997. *The Psychic Life of Power: Theories in Subjection*. Stanford, CA: Stanford University Press.

Butler, Judith. 2000. *Antigone's Claim: Kinship Between Life and Death*. New York: Columbia University Press.

Butler, Judith. 2004. *Undoing Gender*. London: Routledge.

Butler, Judith, Ernesto Laclau, and Slavoj Žižek. 2000. *Contingency, Hegemony, Universality: Contemporary Dialogues on the Left*. London: Verso.

Calcutt, Andrew. 2016. "The Surprising Origins of 'post-truth'—and How It Was Spawned by the Liberal Left." *The Coversation*, 18 November. Available online: https://theconversation.com/the-surprising-origins-of-post-truth-and-how-it-was-spawned-by-the-liberal-left-68929 (accessed March 24, 2021).

Carey, Susan. 2009. *The Origin of Concepts*. Oxford: Oxford University Press.

Caputo, John. D. 1993. "On Not Circumventing the Quasi-Transcendental: The Case of Rorty and Derrida." In Gary B. Madison (ed.), *Working through Derrida*, 147–169. Evanston, IL. Northwestern University Press.

Caputo, John D. 1997. *The Prayers and Tears of Jacques Derrida: Religion Without Religion*. Bloomington: Indiana University Press.

Chambers, Clare. 2017. *Against Marriage: An Egalitarian Defense of the Marriage-Free State*. Oxford: Oxford University Press.

Cisney, Vernon W. 2014. *Derrida's Voice and Phenomenon*. Edinburgh: Edinburgh University Press.

Derrida, Jacques. [1962] 1989. *Edmund Husserl's Origin of Geometry: An Introduction*. Trans. John P. Leavey Jr. Lincoln: University of Nebraska Press.

Derrida, Jacques. [1967] 1976. *Of Grammatology*. Trans. Gayatri Chakravorty Spivak. Baltimore: Johns Hopkins University Press.

Derrida, Jacques. [1967] 1978. *Writing and Difference*. Trans. Alan Bass. Chicago: University of Chicago Press.

Derrida, Jacques. [1967] 2011. *Voice and Phenomenon: Introduction to the Problem of the Sign in Husserl's Phenomenology*. Trans. Leonard Lawlor. Evanston, IL: Northwestern University Press.

Derrida, Jacques. [1972] 1981. *Dissemination*. Trans. Barbara Johnson. Chicago: University of Chicago Press.

Derrida, Jacques. [1972] 1982. *Margins of Philosophy*. Trans. Alan Bass. Chicago: University of Chicago Press.

Derrida, Jacques. [1974] 1986. *Glas*. Trans. John P. Leavey Jr. and Richard Rand. Lincoln: University of Nebraska Press.

Derrida, Jacques. 1981. *Positions*. Trans. Alan Bass. Chicago: University of Chicago Press.

Bibliography

Derrida, Jacques. 1995. *Points ... : Interviews, 1974–1994*. Ed. Elisabeth Weber. Stanford, CA: Stanford University Press.
Derrida, Jacques. 2003. *The Problem of Genesis in Husserl's Philosophy*. Trans. Marian Hobson. Chicago: University of Chicago Press.
Dorrough Smith, Leslie (ed.). 2019. *Constructing 'Data' in Religious Studies: Examining the Architecture of the Academy*. Sheffield, UK: Equinox Publishing.
Douglas, Mary. 1986. *How Institutions Think*. Syracuse, NY: Syracuse University Press.
Douglass, Frederick. 2016. *The Portable Frederick Douglass*. Ed. John Stauffer and Henry Louis Gates Jr. New York: Penguin Books.
Dole, Andrew. 2019. *Reframing the Masters of Suspicion: Marx, Nietzsche, and Freud*. London: Bloomsbury Academic.
Driscoll, Christopher M. and Monica R. Miller. 2019. *Method as Identity: Manufacturing Distance in the Academic Study of Religion*. Lanham, MD: Lexington Books.
Durkheim, Émile. [1893] 2014. *The Division of Labor in Society*. Trans. W. D. Halls. New York: Free Press.
Durkheim, Émile. [1912] 2001. *The Elementary Forms of Religious Life*. Trans. Carol Cosman. Oxford: Oxford University Press.
Dyrberg, Torben Bech. 1997. *The Circular Structure of Power: Politics, Identity, Community*. London: Verso.
Eagleton, Terry. 2007. *Ideology: An Introduction, New and Updated Edition*. London: Verso.
Emerson, Michael O. and Christian Smith. 2000. *Divided by Faith: Evangelical Religion and the Problem of Race in America*. Oxford: Oxford University Press.
Evans-Pritchard, E. E. 1976. *Witchcraft, Oracles, and Magic among the Azande*. Oxford: Oxford University Press.
Fairclough, Norman. 1992. *Discourse and Social Change*. Cambridge, UK: Polity Press.
Fausto-Sterling, Anne. 2000. *Sexing the Body: Gender Politics and the Construction of Sexuality*. New York: Basic Books.
Fields, Karen E. and Barbara J. Fields. 2014. *Racecraft: The Soul of Inequality in American Life*. London: Verso.
Flynn, Andrea, Susan R. Holmberg, Dorian T. Warren, and Felicia J. Wong. 2017. *The Hidden Rules of Race: Barriers to an Inclusive Economy*. Cambridge: Cambridge University Press.
Foucault, Michel. 1972. *The Archaeology of Knowledge and The Discourse on Language*. Trans. A. M. Seridan Smith. New York: Pantheon Books.
Foucault, Michel. 1978. *The History of Sexuality, Volume 1*. Trans. Robert Hurley. New York: Vintage.
Foucault, Michel (ed.). 1980a. *Herculine Barbin: Being the Recently Discovered Memoirs of a Nineteenth-Century French Hermaphrodite*. Trans. Richard McDougal. New York: Vintage.
Foucault, Michel. 1980b. *Power/Knowledge: Selected Interviews & Other Writings, 1972–1977*. Ed. Colin Gordon. New York: Pantheon Books.
Foucault, Michel. 1994. *The Birth of the Clinic: An Archaeology of Medical Perception*. Trans. A. M. Sheridan. New York: Vintage.
Foucault, Michel. 2000. *Power: Essential Works of Foucault 1954–1984, Volume 3*. Ed. James D. Faubion. Trans. Robert Hurley and others. New York: The New Press.
Foucault, Michel. 2003. *"Society Must Be Defended": Lectures at the Collège de France, 1975–1976*. Ed. Mauro Bertani and Alessandro Fontana. Trans. David Macey. New York: Picador.
Foucault, Michel. 2007. *Security, Territory, Population: Lectures at the Collège de France, 1977–1978*. Ed. Michel Senellart. Trans. Graham Burchell. New York: Palgrave Macmillan.
Gasché, Rodolphe. 1986. *The Tain of the Mirror: Derrida and the Philosophy of Reflection*. Cambridge, MA: Harvard University Press.
Gasché, Rodolphe. 1994. *Inventions of Difference: On Jacques Derrida*. Cambridge, MA: Harvard University Press.

Bibliography

Gernon, Christine, dir. 2016. *Superstore*. Season 1, episode 9, "All-Nighter." Written by Eric Ledgin. Aired 8 February 2016, on National Broadcasting Company.

Gill, Mary Louise and James G. Lennox (eds.). 1994. *Self-Motion: From Aristotle to Newton*. Princeton, NJ: Princeton University Press.

Glynos, Jason and David Howarth. 2007. *Logics of Critical Explanation in Social and Political Theory*. London: Routledge.

Goodall, Dominic (ed.). 1996. *Hindu Scriptures*. Berkeley: University of California Press.

Goodman, Nelson. 1978. *Ways of Worldmaking*. Indianapolis, IN: Hackett Publishing.

Gopnik, Alison and Andrew N. Meltzoff. 1997. *Words, Thoughts, and Theories*. Cambridge, MA: The MIT Press.

Gramsci, Antonio. 1971. *Selections from the Prison Notebooks*. Ed. Geoffrey Nowell-Smith and Quintin Hoare. New York: International Publishers.

Guyer, Paul. 1987. *Kant and the Claims of Knowledge*. Cambridge: Cambridge University Press.

Hacking, Ian. 1991. "The Making and Molding of Child Abuse." *Critical Inquiry* 17/2: 253–288.

Hacking, Ian. 1999. *The Social Construction of What?*. Cambridge, MA: Harvard University Press.

Hacking, Ian. 2002. *Historical Ontology*. Cambridge, MA: Harvard University Press.

Hägglund, Martin. 2008. *Radical Atheism: Derrida and the Time of Life*. Stanford, CA: Stanford University Press.

Haidt, Jonathan. 2001. "The Emotional Dog and Its Rational Tail: A Social Intuitionist Approach to Moral Judgment." *Psychological Review* 108/4: 814–834.

Haidt, Jonathan. 2013. *The Righteous Mind: Why Good People Are Divided by Politics and Religion*. New York: Vintage Books.

Hegel, G. W. F. [1807] 2018. *The Phenomenology of Spirit*. Trans. Terry Pinkard. Cambridge: Cambridge University Press.

Hegel, G. W. F. [1830] 2010. *Encyclopedia of the Philosophical Sciences in Basic Outline, Part 1: Science of Logic*. Trans. Klaus Brinkmann and Daniel O. Dahlstrom. Cambridge: Cambridge University Press.

Hegel, G. W. F. [1832] 2010. *The Science of Logic*. Trans. George di Giovanni. Cambridge: Cambridge University Press.

Heidegger, Martin. [1953] 1996. *Being and Time: A Translation of Sein und Zeit*. Trans. Joan Stambaugh. Albany: State University of New York Press.

Hjelm, Titus. 2014. *Social Constructionisms: Approaches to the Study of the Human World*. New York: Palgrave Macmillan.

Hoffman, Donald D. 2000. *Visual Intelligence: How We Create What We See*. New York: W. W. Norton & Company.

Hume, David. [1739–1740] 1985. *A Treatise of Human Nature*. Ed. Ernest Campbell Mossner. New York: Penguin.

Hume, David. [1748] 1993. *An Inquiry Concerning Human Understanding*, 2nd Edition. Ed. Eric Steinberg. Indianapolis, IN: Hackett Publishing Company.

Hume, David. [1779] 1990. *Dialogues Concerning Natural Religion*. New York: Penguin Books.

Husserl, Edmund. [1935] 1970. "Philosophy and the Crisis of European Humanity." In Edmund Husserl, *The Crisis of European Sciences and Transcendental Phenomenology*. Ed. and trans. David Carr. Evanston, IL: Northwestern University Press.

Husserl, Edmund. [1962] 1989. "Origins of Geometry." In Jacques Derrida, *Edmund Husserl's Origins of Geometry: An Introduction*, 157–180. Lincoln: University of Nebraska Press.

Husserl, Edmund. 2014. *Ideas for a Pure Phenomenology and Phenomenological Philosophy: First Book: General Introduction to Pure Phenomenology*. Trans. Daniel O. Dahlstrom. Indianapolis, IN: Hackett Publishing.

Hyppolite, Jean. 1969. *Studies on Marx and Hegel*. Ed. and trans. John O'Neill. New York: Harper & Row.

Bibliography

Hyppolite, Jean. [1946] 1974. *Genesis and Structure of Hegel's Phenomenology of Spirit*. Trans. Samuel Cherniak and John Heckman. Evanston, IL: Northwestern University Press.

Hyppolite, Jean. [1953] 1997. *Logic and Existence*. Trans. Leonard Lawlor and Amit Sen. Albany: State University of New York Press.

Hyppolite, Jean. 1971. *Figures de la pensée philosophique*. Paris: Presses Universitaires de France.

Jardina, Ashley. 2019. *White Identity Politics*. Cambridge: Cambridge University Press.

Ingersoll, Julie J. 2003. *Evangelical Christian Women: War Stories in the Gender Battles*. New York: New York University Press.

Ingersoll, Julie J. 2015. *Building God's Kingdom: Inside the World of Christian Reconstructionism*. Oxford: Oxford University Press.

Ioanide, Paula. 2018. "'Obama Say Blacks Should Just Work Harder; Isn't That Right?': The Myth of Meritocracy." In *Getting Real About Race*, 2nd Edition. London: Sage Publications.

It's a Wonderful Life. 1946. [Film] Dir. Frank Capra. USA: RKO Radio Pictures.

James, William. 1996. *A Pluralistic Universe*. Lincoln: University of Nebraska Press.

Johnson, Joel A. 2007. "A Connecticut Yankee in Saddam's Court: Mark Twain on Benevolent Imperialism." *Perspectives on Politics* 5/1: 49–61.

Jordan-Young, Rebecca M. 2010. *Brain Storm: The Flaws in the Science of Sex Differences*. Cambridge, MA: Harvard University Press.

Joseph, Jonathan. 2002. *Hegemony: A Realist Analysis*. London: Routledge.

Jost, John T. and Mahzarin R. Banaji. 1994. "The Role of Stereotyping in System-Justification and the Production of False Consciousness." *British Journal of Social Psychology* 33/1: 1–27.

Kahn, Jonathan. 2018. *Race on the Brain: What Implicit Bias Gets Wrong about the Struggle for Racial Justice*. New York: Columbia University Press.

Kakutani, Michiko. 2018. "The Death of Truth: How We Gave Up on Facts and Ended Up with Trump." *The Guardian*. 14 July. Available online: https://www.theguardian.com/books/2018/jul/14/the-death-of-truth-how-we-gave-up-on-facts-and-ended-up-with-trump#maincontent (accessed March 24, 2021).

Kant, Immanuel. [1781] 1998. *Critique of Pure Reason*. Trans. Paul Guyer and Allen W. Wood. Cambridge: Cambridge University Press.

Kant, Immanuel. [1783] 2004. *Prolegomena to Any Future Metaphysics*. Ed. Gary Hatfield. Cambridge: Cambridge University Press.

Katznelson, Ira. 2005. *When Affirmative Action Was White: An Untold History of Racial Inequality in Twentieth-Century America*. New York: W.W. Norton.

King, Richard. 1999. *Orientalism and Religion: Postcolonial Theory, India, and the "Mystic East."* London: Routledge.

Kuhn, Thomas S. 2012. *The Structure of Scientific Revolutions*, 4th Edition. Chicago: University of Chicago Press.

Laclau, Ernesto and Chantal Mouffe. 1985. *Hegemony and Socialist Strategy: Towards a Radical Democratic Politics*. London: Verso.

Lawlor, Leonard. 2002. *Derrida and Husserl: The Basic Problem of Phenomenology*. Bloomington: Indiana University Press.

Lincoln, Bruce. 1989. *Discourse and the Construction of Society: Comparative Studies of Myth, Ritual, and Classification*. Chicago: University of Chicago Press.

Lincoln, Bruce. 1991a. *Death, War, and Sacrifice: Studies in Ideology and Practice*. Chicago: University of Chicago Press.

Lincoln, Bruce. 1991b. *Emerging from the Chrysalis: Rituals of Women's Initiation*. Oxford: Oxford University Press.

Lincoln, Bruce. 1994. *Authority: Construction and Corrosion*. Chicago: University of Chicago Press.

Lincoln, Bruce. 1999. *Theorizing Myth: Narrative, Ideology, and Scholarship*. Chicago: University of Chicago Press.

Lincoln, Bruce. 2006. "How to Read a Religious Text: Reflections on Some Passages of the Chāndogya Upaniṣad." *History of Religions* 46/2: 127–139.

Lincoln, Bruce. 2007. *Religion, Empire, and Torture: The Case of Achaemenian Persia, with a Postscript on Abu Graib*. Chicago: University of Chicago Press.

Lincoln, Bruce. 2012. *Gods and Demons, Priests and Scholars: Critical Explorations in the History of Religions*. Chicago: University of Chicago Press.

"Living Ohio Man Donald Miller Ruled 'legally dead.'" 2013. *BBC News*, October 11. Available online: https://www.bbc.com/news/world-us-canada-24486718 (accessed March 24, 2021).

Longino, Helen E. 1990. *Science as Social Knowledge*. Princeton, NJ: Princeton University Press.

Longino, Helen E. 2002. *The Fate of Knowledge*. Princeton, NJ: Princeton University Press.

Lopez, Donald S., Jr. 1998. "Belief." In Mark C. Taylor (ed.), *Critical Terms for Religious Studies*, 21–35. Chicago: University of Chicago Press.

Lorber, Judith. 1994. *Paradoxes of Gender*. New Haven, CT: Yale University Press.

Lui, Meizhu, Bárbara Robles, Betsy Leondar-Wright, Rose Brewer, and Rebecca Adamson. 2006. *The Color of Wealth: The Story Behind the U.S. Racial Divide*. New York: The New Press.

Lukes, Steven. 2005. *Power: A Radical View*, 2nd Edition. New York: Palgrave Macmillan.

Mahmood, Saba. 2005. *Politics of Piety: The Islamic Revival and the Feminist Subject*. Princeton, NJ: Princeton University Press.

Mannheim, Karl. [1929] 1985. *Ideology and Utopia: An Introduction to the Sociology of Knowledge*. Trans. Louis Wirth and Edward Shils. Orlando, FL: Harcourt Brace Jovanovich.

Marrati, Paola. 2005. *Genesis and Trace: Derrida Reading Husserl and Heidegger*. Trans. Simon Sparks. Stanford, CA: Stanford University Press.

Martin, Craig. 2017. *A Critical Introduction to the Study of Religion*, 2nd Edition. London: Routledge.

Marx, Karl and Friedrich Engels. 1978. *The Marx-Engels Reader*, 2nd Edition. Ed. Robert C. Tucker. New York: W. W. Norton & Company.

Masuzawa, Tomoko. 2005. *The Invention of World Religions: Or, How European Universalism Was Preserved in the Language of Pluralism*. Chicago: University of Chicago Press.

McCumber, John. 2014. *Understanding Hegel's Mature Critique of Kant*. Stanford, CA: Stanford University Press.

McCutcheon, Russell T. 2003. *The Discipline of Religion: Structure, Meaning, Rhetoric*. London: Routledge.

Mercier, Hugo and Dan Sperber. 2018. *The Enigma of Reason: A New Theory of Human Understanding*. New York: Penguin Books.

Merleau-Ponty, Maurice. [1945] 2012. *Phenomenology of Perception*. Trans. Donald A. Landes. London: Routledge.

Miller, Richard W. 1987. *Fact and Method: Explanation, Confirmation, and Reality in the Natural and Social Sciences*. Princeton, NJ: Princeton University Press.

Mills, Sara. 2004. *Discourse*, 2nd Edition. London: Routledge.

Murphy, Tim. 2010. *The Politics of Spirit: Phenomenology, Genealogy, Religion*. Albany: State University of New York Press.

Nanda, Serena. 2000. *Gender Diversity: Crosscultural Variations*. Long Grove, IL: Waveland Press.

Nietzsche, Friedrich. 1998. *Beyond Good and Evil*. Trans. Marion Fabor. Oxford: Oxford University Press.

Nye, Malory. 2008. *Religion: The Basics*, 2nd Edition. London: Routledge.

Oliver, Melvin L. and Thomas M. Shapiro. 2006. *Black Wealth/White Wealth: A New Perspective on Racial Inequality, Twenty-Fifth Anniversary Edition*. London: Routldge.

Peeters, Benoît. 2013. *Derrida: A Biography*. Trans. Andrew Brown. Cambridge, UK: Polity Press.

Powers, John. 2004. *History as Propaganda: Tibetan Exiles versus the People's Republic of China*. Oxford: Oxford University Press.

Bibliography

PragerU. 2015a. "Don't Judge Blacks Differently," April 27. Available online: https://www.prageru.com/video/dont-judge-Blacks-differently (accessed March 28, 2021).
PragerU. 2015b. "How Do You Judge America? Left vs. Right #3," December 14. Available online: https://www.prageru.com/video/how-do-you-judge-america-left-vs-right-3/ (accessed March 28, 2021).
PragerU. 2015c. "How Do We Make Society Better? Left vs. Right #5," December 14. Available online: https://www.prageru.com/video/how-do-we-make-society-better-left-vs-right-5/ (accessed March 28, 2021).
PragerU. 2016a. "Are the Police Racist?," August 22. Available online: https://www.prageru.com/video/are-the-police-racist/ (accessed March 28, 2021).
PragerU. 2016b. "Black Fathers Matter," June 13. Available online: https://www.prageru.com/video/Black-fathers-matter/ (accessed March 28, 2021).
PragerU. 2016c. "'Just Say "Merry Christmas,'" November 28. Available online: https://www.prageru.com/video/just-say-merry-christmas/ (accessed March 28, 2021).
PragerU. 2016d. "The Top 5 Issues Facing Black Americans," September 19. Available online: https://www.prageru.com/video/the-top-5-issues-facing-Black-americans/ (accessed March 28, 2021).
PragerU. 2018a. "The American Trinity: The Three Values that Make America Great," October 21. Available online: https://www.prageru.com/video/the-american-trinity-the-three-values-that-make-america-great (accessed March 28, 2021).
PragerU. 2018b. "So, You Think You're Tolerant?," July 8. Available online: https://www.prageru.com/video/so-you-think-youre-tolerant/ (accessed March 28, 2021).
PragerU. (2019a), "What Does Diversity Have to Do with Science?," January 7. Available online: https://www.prageru.com/video/what-does-diversity-have-to-do-with-science (accessed March 28, 2021).
PragerU. 2019b. "Who Are the Racists?," April 29. Available online: https://www.prageru.com/video/who-are-the-racists (accessed March 28, 2021).
PragerU. 2020. "Do White Americans Have White Privilege?," June 12. Available online: https://www.prageru.com/video/do-white-americans-have-white-privilege (accessed March 28, 2021).
PragerU. 2021a. "Frequently Asked Questions." Available online: https://www.prageru.com/faq/ (accessed March 28, 2021).
PragerU. 2021b. "What Is PragerU." Available online: https://www.prageru.com/about/ (accessed March 28, 2021).
Putnam, Hilary. 2004. *Ethics Without Ontology*. Cambridge, MA: Harvard University Press.
Rehmann, Jan. 2014. *Theories of Ideology: The Powers of Alienation and Subjection*. Chicago: Haymarket Books.
Ricoeur, Paul. 1970. *Freud and Philosophy: An Essay on Interpretation*. Trans. Denis Savage. New Haven, CT: Yale University Press.
Roberts, David. 2011. "Is Climate Denial Postmodern?." *Grist*, March 4. Available online: https://grist.org/climate-skeptics/2011-03-03-is-climate-denialism-postmodern/ (accessed March 24, 2021).
Rorty, Richard. 1991. *Objectivity, Relativism, and Truth: Philosophical Papers*, Volume 1. Cambridge: Cambridge University Press.
Rosen, Michael. 1996. *On Voluntary Servitude: False Consciousness and the Theory of Ideology*. Cambridge, MA: Harvard University Press.
Rothstein, Richard. 2017. *The Color of Law: A Forgotten History of How Our Government Segregated America*. New York: Liveright Publishing Corporation.
Sahlins, Marshall. 1976. *Culture and Practical Reason*. Chicago: University of Chicago Press.
Sahlins, Marshall. 1985. *Islands of History*. Chicago: University of Chicago Press.
Schiappa, Edward. 2003. *Defining Reality: Definitions and the Politics of Meaning*. Carbondale: Southern Illinois University Press.

Bibliography

Schilbrack, Kevin. 2014. *Philosophy and the Study of Religions: A Manifesto.* Chichester, UK: Wiley-Blackwell.
Scott, James C. 1985. *Weapons of the Weak: Everyday Forms of Peasant Resistance.* New Haven, CT: Yale University Press.
Scott, James C. 1990. *Domination and the Arts of Resistance: Hidden Transcripts.* New Haven, CT: Yale University Press.
Searle, John R. 1995. *The Construction of Social Reality.* New York: The Free Press.
Shapiro, Thomas M. 2004. *The Hidden Cost of Being African American: How Wealth Perpetuates Inequality.* Oxford: Oxford University Press.
Shapiro, Thomas M. 2017. *Toxic Inequality: How America's Wealth Gap Destroys Mobility, Deepens the Racial Divide, and Threatens Our Future.* New York: Basic Books.
Slingerland, Edward. 2008. *What Science Offers the Humanities: Integrating Body and Culture.* Cambridge: Cambridge University Press.
Sloan, D. Jason. 2004. *Theological Incorrectness: Why Religious People Believe What They Shouldn't.* Oxford: Oxford University Press.
Smith, Christian. 2010. *What Is a Person?: Rethinking Humanity, Social Life, and the Moral Good from the Person Up.* Chicago: University of Chicago Press.
Smith, Christian and Melinda Lundquist Denton. 2005. *Soul Searching: The Religious and Spiritual Lives of American Teenagers.* Oxford: Oxford University Press.
Smith, Jonathan Z. 2007. "The Necessary Lie: Duplicity in the Disciplines." In Russell T. McCutcheon (ed.), *Studying Religion: An Introduction,* 74–80. London: Equinox Publishing.
Spinoza, Baruch. 1994. *A Spinoza Reader: The Ethics and Other Works.* Ed. and trans. Edwin Curley. Princeton, NJ: Princeton University Press.
Steele, Claude M. 2010. *Whistling Vivaldi: How Stereotypes Affect Us and What We Can Do.* New York: W. W. Norton & Company.
Stephens-Dougan, LaFleur. 2020. *Race to the Bottom: How Racial Appeals Work in American Politics.* Chicago: University of Chicago Press.
Stoler Miller, Barbara (trans.). 1986. *The Bhagavad-Gita: Krishna's Council in Time of War.* New York: Bantam Dell.
Stowers, Stanley K. 2020. "Religion as a Social Kind." Paper presented at the Redescribing Christian Origins seminar, *Annual Meeting of the Society of Biblical Literature,* December 3.
Superson, Anita. 1993. "A Feminist Definition of Sexual Harassment." *Journal of Social Philosophy* 24/1: 46–64.
Taylor, Keeanga-Yamahtta. 2019. *Race for Profit: How Banks and the Real Estate Industry Undermined Black Homeownership.* Chapel Hill: University of North Carolina Press.
Taylor, Mark C. 1982. *Deconstructing Theology.* New York: The Crossroads Publishing Company.
Taylor, Mark C. 1984. *Erring: A Postmodern A/theology.* Chicago: University of Chicago Press.
Taylor, Mark C. (ed.). 1986. *Deconstruction in Context: Literature and Philosophy.* Chicago: University of Chicago Press.
Taylor, Mark C. 1987a. *Altarity.* Chicago: University of Chicago Press.
Taylor, Mark C. 1987b. "Shades of Difference." *Semeia* 40: 21–38
Taylor, Mark C. 1993. *Nots.* Chicago: University of Chicago Press.
The Ten Commandments. 1956. [film] Dir. Cecil B. DeMille. USA: Motion Picture Associates.
Therborn, Göran. 1980. *The Ideology of Power and the Power of Ideology.* London: Verso.
Thompson, John B. 1990. *Ideology and Modern Culture: Critical Social Theory in the Era of Mass Communication.* Stanford, CA: Stanford University Press.
Twain, Mark. [1889] 1981. *A Connecticut Yankee in King Arthur's Court.* New York: Bantam Dell.
Twain, Mark. [1901] 1963. *The Complete Essays of Mark Twain.* Ed. Charles Neider. Garden City, NY: Doubleday & Company.
Twain, Mark. 1925. *Mark Twain's Autobiography,* Volume 2. Ed. Albert Biegelow Paine. New York: Gabriel Wells.

Bibliography

U.S. News. 2021. "St. Thomas Aquinas College." Available online: https://www.usnews.com/best-colleges/st-thomas-aquinas-2832 (accessed April 6, 2021).
Vásquez, Manuel A. 2011. *More than Belief: A Materialist Theory of Religion*. Oxford: Oxford University Press.
Viglione, Giuliana. 2020. "Are Women Publishing Less during the Pandemic? Here's What the Data Say." *Nature* 581: 365–366. Available online: https://www.nature.com/articles/d41586-020-01294-9 (accessed March 24, 2021).
Visker, Rudi. 1995. *Michel Foucault: Genealogy as Critique*. Trans. Chris Turner. London: Verso.
Warner, Michael. 1999. *The Trouble with Normal: Sex, Politics, and the Ethics of Queer Life*. Cambridge, MA: Harvard University Press.
Westerhoff, Jan. 2009. *Nagarjuna's Madhyamaka: A Philosophical Introduction*. Oxford: Oxford University Press.
Westerhoff, Jan. 2010a. *The Dispeller of Disputes: Nagarjuna's* Vigrahavyāvartanī. Oxford: Oxford University Press.
Westerhoff, Jan. 2010b. *Twelve Examples of Illusion*. Oxford: Oxford University Press.
Westerhoff, Jan. 2011. *Reality: A Very Short Introduction*. Oxford: Oxford University Press.
Westerhoff, Jan. 2018. *Crushing the Categories*. Somerville, MA. Wisdom Publications.
Westerhoff, Jan. 2020. *The Non-existence of the Real World*. Oxford: Oxford University Press.
White, Bouck. 1913. *The Call of the Carpenter*. Garden City, New York: Doubleday, Page & Company.
Wicker, A. W. 1969. "Attitudes versus Actions: The Relationship of Verbal and Overt Behavioral Responses to Attitude Objects." *Journal of Social Issues* 25/4: 41–78.
Williams, Raymond. 1977. *Marxism and Literature*. Oxford: Oxford University Press.
"Women Now Empowered by Everything a Woman Does." 2003. *The Onion*, February 19. Available online: http://www.theonion.com/article/women-now-empowered-by-everything-a-woman-does-1398 (accessed March 24, 2021).
Woodward, James. 2003. *Making Things Happen: A Theory of Causal Explanation*. Oxford: Oxford University Press.
Zia, Afiya Shehrbano. 2009. "Faith-based Politics, Enlightened Moderation and the Pakistani Women's Movement." *Journal of International Women's Studies* 11/1: 225–245.

INDEX

affect *see* sympathies and antipathies
Ahmed, Sara 54–6
Alexander, Michelle 231–2
Althusser, Louis 81, 108, 119–20
American pragmatism *see* pragmatism
Anderson, Carol 259
antipathies *see* sympathies and antipathies
anti-realism
    and Hegel 21
    and Mannheim 146–52
    and philosophy of science 153–7
    and poststructuralism 1–12, 31–9, 42–4, 46, 64–75, 80, 87, 166–8, 170, 257
    see also realism
a priori and *a posteriori* knowledge
    and categories 23–8
    for Hegel 20–8
    for Kant 16–20
    and poststructuralism 28–31, 38–9
Aristotle 17, 256
Azande 177, 196–201, 252

Balko, Radley 259
Banaji, Mahzarin R. 185–8, 227–9
Baradaran, Mehrsa 259
Barbin, Herculine 121
Baring, Edward 257
Bartkowski, John P. 172
Bedazzled 132–4
Beiser, Frederick C. 256
belief 175–89, 192–201
Berger, Peter L. 80
Berkeley, George 42–3, 48, 50–1, 75–6
Bhagavad-Gita 15
bias *see* objectivity
biology 32–7, 43–4, 48–51, 68–9, 167, 172–4
Bonilla-Silva, Eduardo 259
Bottici, Chiara 90
Bourdieu, Pierre 193
Braver, Lee 43
bullshit *see* recrement
Bush, George H. W. 65–6, 70, 90
Butler, Judith
    and biology 32–6, 167
    and desire 119, 121
    and Foucault 119, 121, 167
    and Hegel 29–30

    and materiality 32–6, 43–4, 68, 78
    misinterpretations of 42–4
    and poststructuralism 1–3, 6, 11–13, 31–6, 38, 70
    and subjectivity 119, 121

Call of the Carpenter see White, Bouck
Carey, Susan 72–3
Cartwright, Nancy 159
causation
    and belief 182–5
    definition of 158–63
    and explanation 189–96
    and God 15–18
    in racist accounts 241–5
    see also explanation; functionalism
Chambers, Claire 141
Cisney, Vernon W. 257
Clinton, Hilary 215, 217–18, 241
cognitive science 70–5
colorblindness 203, 213–18, 221, 223–4, 226–7, 237–40, 259
A Connecticut Yankee in King Arthur's Court see Twain, Mark
Connolly, William E. 134
credorationalism 177–80, 189, 196, 200–3
critique
    for Hegel 20–8
    for Kant 13–20
    and poststructuralism 6, 28–39

Darwin, Charles 190
DeMille, Cecil B. 94–5
Denton, Melinda Lundquist 251
desires and interests 115–24, 128–35, 146–52
Derrida, Jacques
    and conditions of impossibility of knowledge 29–31
    and deconstruction 30
    and Hegel 29–31, 42, 44–8, 51, 53, 55–6, 58, 62, 76
    and Husserl 51–64, 257
    and language 47–51, 57–64
    and materiality 43–51
    and object individuation 44–64
    and poststructuralism 1–3, 6, 11–13, 31–2, 38, 70

Index

and power 31–2
and Rousseau 42–3, 49–51, 84
and substruction 55–66
and "there is nothing outside of the text" 41–4, 47–51
and things 43–64
de Waal, Frans 184
dialectical thinking 23–5, 28, 58, 246–8
discourse
    constitutive 65–9, 78–87, 147–8, 150
    and definitions 87–91
    empirical 87–90, 147–8
    functions of 100–1
    and ideology 168–74
    and interpellation 35, 81, 119, 124, 247
    and looping effects 80–1, 165–7
    and normative associations 90–100
    and overdetermination 36–7, 81, 95–7
    and subjectivity 80–2, 165–6
    and sympathies and antipathies 6, 77–8, 87, 91–101, 180, 193–4, 196, 202–4
Dobson, James 172–4
Dole, Andrew 259
domination
    definition of 135–40
    and ideology critique 10–11, 171–2
    internalized 104–10, 115–18, 185–9
    and interpellation 108–10, 115–24
    and liberal approaches 103, 117–18, 128–9, 142
    and paternalism 115–18
    and poststructuralist approaches 117–24
    and repression 104, 115–24
    subjective vs objective 124–8, 135–44
    and subjectivity 104–11, 115–24, 128–39, 141–4
Douglas, Mary 190–3, 200
Douglass, Frederick 253
Driscoll, Christopher M. 253
Durkheim, Émile 148, 190
Dworkin, Ronald 128
Dyrberg, Torben Bech 104, 129–36, 138, 140

Eliade, Mircea 257
Elster, Jon 190, 192
Emerson, Michael O. 226
empiricism
    and discourse 87–90, 147–8
    and Derrida 51–64
    and Hegel 22–8
    and Husserl 52–64
    and Kant 16–20
    and Mannheim 146–52
    and perception 70–5
    and philosophy of science 153–7
    and poststructuralism 11, 64–70
    and power 31–7

Engels, Friedrich 187
Evans-Pritchard, E. E. 177, 196–201
explanation, causal 158–68, 177–96, *see also* causation; functionalism

Fairclough, Norman 77, 97
false consciousness 8, 116, 185–7, 258, *see also* domination
Fausto-Sterling, Anne 13, 32, 34–8, 257
Fichte, J. G. 256
Fields, Barbara J. 259
Fields, Karen E 259
Foucault, Michel
    criticisms of 120–1
    and desire 118–24
    and discourse 25, 77–80, 87, 118–9, 121, 167
    and Hegel 29–30
    on ideology 7–12, 256
    and poststructuralism 1–12, 34, 42–3, 70
    and power 31–2, 38, 68, 97, 118–22, 258
    and subjectivity 118–22, 256
    on truth 9–10, 87
Freud, Sigmund 14
functionalism 189–201, 247, *see also* explanation

Gasché, Rodolphe 257
gender 32–8, 68, 121–6, 137, 143–4, 167, 172–4, 203–4, 213–4, 234–5 *see also* sexual harassment
Glynos, Jason 145, 163–8
Goodman, Nelson 56, 69
Gopnik, Alison 71–3
Greenwald, Anthony G. 227–9
Grosz, Elizabeth 35–6
Guyer, Paul 256

Hacking, Ian 41, 43, 80–1, 165, 258
Hägglund, Martin 66–7, 257
Haidt, Jonathan 182–5, 187, 189, 195, 227
Hegel, G. W. F.
    and anti-realism 21
    and atheism 256
    and Butler 29–31
    and categories 22–8, 34, 37
    and criticisms of Kant 3, 15, 20–3, 25–6, 37
    and Derrida 29–31, 42, 44–8, 51, 53, 55–6, 58, 62, 76
    and dialectical thinking 23–7, 154, 246, 248
    and Foucault 29–31
    and Mannheim 146–7
    and poststructuralism 3, 6, 28–31, 34, 37–9, 44–8, 51, 55–6, 62–3, 76
    and things-for-us 22–4, 26–8
Heidegger, Martin 6, 28, 30–31, 42, 48, 129
Heraclitus 45, 53

Index

hermeneutics of suspicion 14, 259
Hjelm, Titus 44
Hoffman, Donald D. 70–1, 258
Howarth, David 145, 163–8
Hume, David 14–18, 20, 24, 158–9, 161–2, 250, 255
Husserl, Edmund
   and Derrida 51–64, 257
   and Eurocentrism 57, 62–4, 252
   and geometry 57–64
   and language 58–62
   and perception 51–64, 70–2, 74–5, 146
   and poststructuralism 6, 28, 41–2
   and protention and retention 53–5, 61, 63, 69
Hyppolite, Jean 21, 29–30, 257

ideology
   definition of 168–74
   and domination 10–11
   and Mannheim 146–52
   in Marxist theory 8–9
   and poststructuralism 7–12
implicit association test 228–9
implicit bias 225–32, 259
independent verification 147–50, 152, 155–7, 179, 192, 251
individuation
   and cognitive science 70–5
   and Derrida 44–64
   and discourse 78–87
   and Mannheim 146–52
   and power 68–9
   and realism 64–70
   see also substruction
Ingersoll, Julie J. 126–8, 203–4
interests *see* desires and interests
internalized domination *see* domination
interpellation 35, 81, 104, 115–25, 165–6, 247,
   see also subjectivity
Ioanide, Paula 187–8
It's a Wonderful Life 131–2, 134

Jardina, Ashley 259
Johnson, Joel A. 112, 258
Jordan-Young, Rebecca M. 13, 32, 36–8, 173–4
Joseph, Jonathan 8
Jost, John T. 185–8

Kahn, Jonathan 259
Kant, Immanuel
   and the categories 25–6, 34, 257
   and critique 13–20, 28
   and *Critique of Pure Reason* 14–20, 256
   and dogmatism 19, 27
   Hegel's criticisms of 20–3, 62–3, 147

   and hypothetical imperatives 250
   and poststructuralism 1–3, 5–6, 38–9, 42–4, 46, 48, 50–1, 62–3
Katznelson, Ira 239–40
Kipling, Rudyard 116–17
Kuhn, Thomas 154, 159

Lawlor, Leonard 257
Levi-Strauss, Claude 31–2
Lincoln, Bruce
   and discourse 78
   and domination 104, 115–17, 120–1, 124–6, 135–6, 140, 144, 258
   and empiricism 252
Longino, Helen E. 145, 153–7, 258
Lopez, Donald S. Jr. 175–6
Lorber, Judith 137
Luckmann, Thomas 80
Lukes, Steven 128–9, 134

Madhyamika 14, 30, 44–5
Mahmood, Saba 104, 117–18, 122–4, 126, 135–6, 140–2, 144
Mannheim, Karl 145–54, 156, 168
Maslow, Abraham 128–9
Marrati, Paola 60, 257
Martyr, Peter 176
Marx, Karl 14, 187
Marxism 8–9, 202, 256
materiality 34–7, 42–51, 68–9
McCumber, John 21
Meltzoff, Andrew N. 71–3
Mercier, Hugo 259
meritocracy, myth of 107–8, 187–8, 193, 207, 217–18, 220–6, 236, 241–5, 259
Merleau-Ponty, Maurice 28
Merton, Robert 191
Miller, Monica R. 253
Miller, Richard W. 190
Mills, Sara 8

Nanda, Serena 35
Nietzsche, Friedrich 8–9, 14, 256
noumena *see* things-in-themselves
Nye, Malory 177–8

Obama, Barack 187–8
object individuation *see* individuation
object permanence 72–4
objectivity
   and Hegel 27
   and Husserl 57–64, 252
   and ideology critique 7–8, 174, 246
   and Mannheim 146–52
   and philosophy of science 153–7

Index

and poststructuralism 30–2, 39, 41 57–64, 167, 246, 250–1, 257
Oliver, Melvin I. 259
oppression *see* domination
Ortner, Sherry 36
Otto, Rudolf 257

Peirce, Charles S. 163–4
phenomena
    and cognitive science 70–5
    and Hegel 20–8, 34, 38, 46, 154
    and Husserl 51–64
    and Kant 2–3, 19–23, 34, 38–9
    and Mannheim 146–52
    and phenomenology 28
    and philosophy of science 153–57
    and retroduction 165
phrenology 24
Pinkard, Terry 256
Plato 42, 47, 53, 59
poststructuralism
    and anti-realism 1–12, 31–9, 42–4, 46, 64–75, 80, 87, 166–8, 170, 257
    and biology 32–7, 48–51, 68–9
    and causal explanation 163–68
    and cognitive science 70–5
    and critique 13, 28–39
    and deconstruction 30
    definition of 6, 28–31, 37–9
    and discourse 6, 9–10, 32–9, 65–9, 77–82, 87–97
    and domination 103–4, 117–24, 129–35
    and empiricism 1–5, 11, 32–9, 51–70, 87–9, 163–8
    and Hegel 3, 6, 28–31, 34, 37–9, 44–8, 51, 55–6, 62–3, 76
    and ideology critique 7–12
    and Kant 1–3, 6, 30, 34, 37–9, 43–4, 46, 48, 50–1, 62–3
    and materiality 34–7, 42–51, 68–9
    and natural kinds 46
    and ontology 42–51, 163–8
    and power 4–5, 7–9, 11, 31–39, 68–9, 117–24, 129–41
    and subjectivity 117–24, 129–35, 165–6, 256
post-truth culture 4
power 4–5, 7–9, 11, 31–9, 68–9, 117–24, 129–41
Powers, John 91–3
PragerU
    and affirmative action 214, 222–4
    and colorblindness 213–18, 221, 223–4
    and cues 235–7
    and explanations for inequality 241–45
    and leftism 207–25
    and equal opportunity 217–25, 230
    and white privilege 215–21

pragmatism 29–30, 44, 146, 153–4, 158, 162–5
Putnam, Hilary 69

race
    and colorblindness 203, 213–18, 221, 223–4, 226–7, 237–40, 259
    and discrimination 229–32, 239–41
    and economic inequality 225–6, 232, 237–41
    and implicit bias 225–32, 259
    and the myth of meritocracy 187–8, 217–18, 220–6, 241–5
    and stereotype threat 226–7, 232–7, 242–6
    and structural racism 26, 237–41, 243, 245
    and white privilege 211, 213, 215–21, 223
racial distancing 188
racism *see* PragerU
Rawls, John 128
realism
    and caricatures of poststructuralism 2–5, 7–8, 257
    criticisms of 10, 21, 46, 64–75, 166–7, 170
    and Husserl 59–61
    and fear of relativism 2, 4–5, 148–9, 154
    and truth 1–2
recrement 6, 175–7, 189–201, 213, 218–220
Rehmann, Jan 7–8, 33
religion 175–9, 189–91, 251–3
retroduction 163–8, 174
Ricoeur, Paul 14
Roosevelt, Franklin Delano 239–40
Rorty, Richard 257
Rosen, Michael 258
Rothstein, Richard 259
Rousseau, Jean-Jacques 42–3, 49–51, 84

Schiappa, Edward 65–67
Schilbrack, Kevin 175, 178–9
Scott, James C. 258
Searle, John R. 67, 70, 90
sexual harassment 124–6, 128, 136
Shapiro, Thomas M. 237–9, 259
skepticism 2, 4, 31, 30, 33, 149–50, 158–9
Slingerland, Edward 43–4
Sloan, D. Jason 252
Smith, Christian 43, 226, 251
Smith, Jonathan Z. 12
Sperber, Dan 259
Spinoza, Baruch 15, 21
Steele, Claude M. 232–6, 246
Stephens-Dougan, La Fleur 188
stereotype threat 226–7, 232–7, 242–6
structural racism 226, 237–41, 243, 245
subjectivity
    and desires and interests 128–35
    and discourse 80–2, 165–6

and domination 104–11, 115–24, 128–39, 141–4
see also interpellation
substruction 55–66, 68–71, 76, 78, 85, 101, 146, 149, *see also* individuation
Superson, Anita 104, 124–30, 134, 136, 140, 142
Superstore 176–7
sympathies and antipathies
    and conservative ideology 207–21, 241–5, 254–5
    and discourse 6, 77–8, 87, 91–101, 180, 193–4, 196, 202–4
    and domination 142–3
    and ideology critique 169–71
    and knowledge 148–9, 250–1
    and Mark Twain 105, 107–11, 114–15

Taylor, Keeanga-Yamahtta 259
Tibet 91–3
The Onion 123–4
things-in-themselves
    and Hegel 20–3, 256
    and Husserl 51–2, 54–5, 62–4
    and Kant 13, 19–23, 26–7
    and poststructuralism 2–5, 34–5, 39, 43–4, 48, 75–6, 256
Thompson, John B. 8, 10–11
Twain, Mark
    and *A Connecticut Yankee in King Arthur's Court* 104–12
    and discourse 105–7, 114–15
    and domination 105–15
    and the Philippines 112–15
    and sympathies and antipathies 106–12
    and training 107–12

Upanishads 14–15

van der Leeuw, Gerardus 257
Vásquez, Manuel 43
Visker, Rudi 120–1

Wach, Joachim 257
Warner, Michael 141
wetlands 65–70, 78, 87, 90–1, 147, 150, 155, 165
White, Bouck 77, 82–7, 89–90, 98–100
white man's burden 105, 112, 116
white privilege 211, 213, 215–21, 223
Wicker, Allan 180–1, 194, 202
Wirth, Louis 146–9
witchcraft 196–201
Wood, Allen W. 256
Woodward, James 145, 158–63, 165, 182, 202

Zia, Afiya S. 122–4, 136, 140–1
Zinn, Howard 208–9